Virtualization Security

Virtualization Security
Protecting Virtualized Environments

Dave Shackleford

WILEY

John Wiley & Sons, Inc.

Acquisitions Editor: Mariann Barsolo
Development Editor: Stef Jones
Technical Editor: Steve Pate
Production Editor: Rebecca Anderson
Copy Editor: Judy Flynn
Editorial Manager: Pete Gaughan
Production Manager: Tim Tate
Vice President and Executive Group Publisher: Richard Swadley
Vice President and Publisher: Neil Edde
Book Designer: Maureen Forys, Happenstance Type-O-Rama; Judy Fung
Proofreader: James Saturnio, Word One New York
Indexer: Robert Swanson
Project Coordinator, Cover: Katherine Crocker
Cover Designer: Ryan Sneed
Cover Image: © alengo / iStockPhoto

Dear Reader,

Thank you for choosing *Virtualization Security: Protecting Virtualized Environments*. This book is part of a family of premium-quality Sybex books, all of which are written by outstanding authors who combine practical experience with a gift for teaching.

Sybex was founded in 1976. More than 30 years later, we're still committed to producing consistently exceptional books. With each of our titles, we're working hard to set a new standard for the industry. From the paper we print on, to the authors we work with, our goal is to bring you the best books available.

I hope you see all that reflected in these pages. I'd be very interested to hear your comments and get your feedback on how we're doing. Feel free to let me know what you think about this or any other Sybex book by sending me an email at nedde@wiley.com. If you think you've found a technical error in this book, please visit http://sybex.custhelp.com. Customer feedback is critical to our efforts at Sybex.

Best regards,

Neil Edde
Vice President and Publisher
Sybex, an Imprint of Wiley

To Karrie and Mia, who continue to put up with me.

Acknowledgments

There are lots of folks I'd like to thank, for many more things than just this book. For lots of technical professionals, or probably anyone publishing their first real book, there's this temptation to list everyone who got you to where you are. For me, that would be a pretty long list, so I'll list only a few folks along the way who made a pretty big difference in my life and career until now.

First, I have a few teachers that really steered me in my youth — Rose Bridgeman, who thought I just *might* be a good public speaker; Carol Lofgren (when I knew her), who somehow made learning Latin the coolest thing in school; and Janet Weeks, who fostered in me a deep passion for both learning and reading amazing literature and actually got me through a rough patch when I needed a friend.

I'd like to thank Paul Janus, who had some faith in me a long time ago and helped me transition from a nontechnical career to a technical one. He probably hasn't thought about me in a long time, but he made a big difference early on. Thanks to Herb Mattord, who hired me and gave me that first major exposure to corporate infosec. Thanks to my friend John Lampe, who was the first serious hacker I got to know and respect and taught me that there's *always* more than one way to do things. Thanks to my friend Lara Dawson, who got me started down the road with SysAdmin, Audit, Networking, and Security (SANS) a long time ago, and to Stephen Northcutt, who mentored me a lot in the early days and connected me with one of my more interesting gigs. Thanks also to all my fellow SANS instructors and the whole team over there — all of you are really extended family to me.

My friend Chris Farrow had a lot to do with my career at a vital point — in fact, I took over his old job, and what a wild ride that turned out to be. Chris, if you're reading this, you've turned out to be a great friend over all these years, and I'm thankful for all you've done for me. Thanks to all my friends and colleagues at IANS, especially Phil Gardner, who is a great guy to work for and with. I'd be remiss not to thank all of my awesome clients at Voodoo Security too — you'll always get my best efforts, every single time. One other shout-out must go to Robert Kiyosaki, whose book *Rich Dad*, *Poor Dad* convinced me to start buying real estate a long time ago, and that's worked out brilliantly.

Huge thanks to the team at Sybex — Pete Gaughan, Mariann Barsolo, Rebecca Anderson, Connor O'Brien, and Stef Jones, who did an amazing job editing my scribbles. My technical editor, Steve Pate, gets my everlasting gratitude as well — you're a great friend and colleague, and this book is better for your efforts.

My final thanks, of course, goes to my family. My wife, Karrie, and daughter, Mia, suffered through my last year of insanity like troopers and make everything I do worth it. I couldn't do any of this without you guys, and I love you both with all my heart.

About the Author

Dave Shackleford is the owner and principal consultant at Voodoo Security, senior vice president of research and CTO at IANS, and a SANS senior instructor and course author. He has consulted with hundreds of organizations in the areas of security, regulatory compliance, and network architecture and engineering. He is a VMware vExpert and has extensive experience designing and configuring secure virtualized infrastructures. He has previously worked as CSO for Configuresoft; as CTO for the Center for Internet Security; and as a security architect, analyst, and manager for several Fortune 500 companies. Dave coauthored the first published course on virtualization security for the SANS Institute and currently serves on the board of directors at the SANS Technology Institute. In his spare time, he helps lead the Atlanta chapter of the Cloud Security Alliance. He is an avid fitness nut, loves anything to do with the water, and enjoys traveling the world.

Contents at a Glance

Introduction . . . .*xix*

Chapter 1 • Fundamentals of Virtualization Security. 1

Chapter 2 • Securing Hypervisors 15

Chapter 3 • Designing Virtual Networks for Security 93

Chapter 4 • Advanced Virtual Network Operations. 131

Chapter 5 • Virtualization Management and Client Security 151

Chapter 6 • Securing the Virtual Machine 177

Chapter 7 • Logging and Auditing 201

Chapter 8 • Change and Configuration Management. 229

Chapter 9 • Disaster Recovery and Business Continuity 253

Chapter 10 • Scripting Tips and Tricks for Automation 281

Chapter 11 • Additional Security Considerations
for Virtual Infrastructure 303

Index. 317

Contents

Introduction . . . . *xix*

Chapter 1 • Fundamentals of Virtualization Security 1
Virtualization Architecture 1
Threats to a Virtualized Environment 4
    Operational Threats 4
    Malware-Based Threats 5
    VM Escape 6
    Vulnerabilities in Virtualization Platforms 9
How Security Must Adapt to Virtualization 9
    Challenges for Securing Virtualized Environments. 10
    Challenges of Vulnerability Testing in a Virtualized Environment. 10

Chapter 2 • Securing Hypervisors 15
Hypervisor Configuration and Security 15
Configuring VMware ESXi. 17
    Patching VMware ESXi 17
    Securing Communications in VMware ESXi 27
    Change and Remove Default Settings on VMware ESXi 33
    Enable Operational Security on VMware ESXi 34
    Secure and Monitor Critical Configuration Files in VMware ESXi 38
    Secure Local Users and Groups on VMware ESXi 40
    Lock Down Access to Hypervisor Console 47
Configuring Microsoft Hyper-V on Windows Server 2008. 52
    Patching Hyper-V 53
    Securing Communications with Hyper-V 53
    Changing Hyper-V Default Settings 56
    Enabling Operational Security for Hyper-V. 59
    Securing and Monitoring Critical Configuration Files for Hyper-V 60
    Secure Local Hyper-V Users and Groups 63
    Lock Down Access to the Hyper-V Hypervisor Platform 68
Configuring Citrix XenServer 72
    Patching XenServer 72
    Secure Communications with XenServer. 75
    Change XenServer Default Settings. 76
    Enabling XenServer Operational Security 80
    Secure and Monitor Critical XenServer Configuration Files. 81
    Secure Local Users and Groups 81
    Lock Down Access to the XenServer Platform. 88

Chapter 3 • Designing Virtual Networks for Security **93**

Comparing Virtual and Physical Networks 93
  Virtual Network Design Elements. 95
  Physical vs. Virtual Networks 98
Virtual Network Security Considerations 99
  Important Security Elements 99
  Architecture Considerations. 100
Configuring Virtual Switches for Security 102
  Defining Separate vSwitches and Port Groups 103
  Configuring VLANs and Private VLANs for Network Segmentation 112
  Limiting Virtual Network Ports in Use. 117
  Implementing Native Virtual Networking Security Policies 122
  Securing iSCSI Storage Network Connections. 125
Integrating with Physical Networking. 129

Chapter 4 • Advanced Virtual Network Operations **131**

Network Operational Challenges 131
Network Operations in VMware vSphere 133
  Load Balancing in vSphere Virtual Environments. 133
  Traffic Shaping and Network Performance in VMware vSphere 135
  Creating a Sound Network Monitoring Strategy in VMware vSphere 136
Network Operations in Microsoft Hyper-V. 141
  Load Balancing in Hyper-V Virtual Environments 141
  Traffic Shaping and Network Performance in Hyper-V. 142
  Creating a Sound Network Monitoring Strategy in Hyper-V 144
Network Operations in Citrix XenServer. 145
  Load Balancing in XenServer Virtual Environments. 145
  Traffic Shaping and Network Performance in XenServer 148
  Creating a Sound Network Monitoring Strategy in XenServer 148

Chapter 5 • Virtualization Management and Client Security **151**

General Security Recommendations for Management Platforms 151
Network Architecture for Virtualization Management Servers 152
VMware vCenter 155
  vCenter Service Account 157
  Secure Communications in vCenter 158
  vCenter Logging. 160
  Users, Groups, and Roles in vCenter. 163
  Role Creation Scenarios. 167
  vSphere Client. 168
Microsoft System Center Virtual Machine Manager 168
  SCVMM Service Account 169
  Secure Communications with SCVMM 170
  SCVMM Logging 171
  Users, Groups, and Roles in SCVMM 172
  Client Security. 175

Citrix XenCenter. 175
Secure Communication with XenCenter. 175
Logging with XenCenter 176
Users, Groups, and Roles in XenCenter. 176

Chapter 6 • Securing the Virtual Machine **177**
Virtual Machine Threats and Vulnerabilities 177
Virtual Machine Security Research 178
Stealing Guests 179
Cloud VM Reconnaissance 179
Virtual Disk Manipulation 180
Virtual Machine Encryption. 180
Locking Down VMware VMs 185
VMware Tools 188
Copy/Paste Operations and HGFS. 188
Virtual Machine Disk Security. 189
VM Logging. 189
Device Connectivity 190
Guest and Host Communications 191
Controlling API Access to VMs 192
Unexposed Features. 193
Locking Down Microsoft VMs 195
Locking Down XenServer VMs 197

Chapter 7 • Logging and Auditing **201**
Why Logging and Auditing Is Critical. 201
Virtualization Logs and Auditing Options 202
Syslog 203
Windows Event Log 204
VMware vSphere ESX Logging 205
VMware vSphere ESXi Logging. 207
Microsoft Hyper-V and SCVMM Logging. 211
Citrix XenServer and XenCenter Logging 218
Integrating with Existing Logging Platforms 221
Enabling Remote Logging on VMware vSphere 221
Enabling Remote Logging on Microsoft Hyper-V. 223
Enabling Remote Logging for XenServer 225
Effective Log Management. 226

Chapter 8 • Change and Configuration Management. **229**
Change and Configuration Management Overview 229
Change Management for Security 230
The Change Ecosystem 231
How Virtualization Impacts Change and Configuration Management 234
Best Practices for Virtualization Configuration Management 235

Cloning and Templates for Improved Configuration Management 237
  Creating and Managing VMware vSphere VM Templates and Snapshots 238
  Creating and Managing Microsoft Hyper-V VM Templates and Snapshots 242
  Creating and Managing Citrix XenServer VM Templates and Snapshots 247
Integrating Virtualization into Change and Management 249
Additional Solutions and Tools 250

Chapter 9 • Disaster Recovery and Business Continuity **253**
Disaster Recovery and Business Continuity Today 253
Shared Storage and Replication 254
Virtualization Redundancy and Fault Tolerance for DR/BCP 256
  Clustering 256
  Resource Pools 262
High Availability and Fault Tolerance 270
  Setting Up High Availability and Fault Tolerance in VMware vSphere 270
  Setting Up High Availability and Fault Tolerance in Microsoft Hyper-V 274
  Setting Up High Availability and Fault Tolerance in Citrix XenServer 277

Chapter 10 • Scripting Tips and Tricks for Automation **281**
Why Scripting Is Essential for Admins 281
VMware Scripting: Power CLI and vCLI 282
  Scripting with PowerCLI 282
  Configuring VMs with PowerCLI 283
  Configuring VMs with vCLI 285
  Configuring VMware ESXi with PowerCLI 286
  Configuring VMware ESXi with the vCLI 289
  Configuring VMware Virtual Networks with PowerCLI 290
  Configuring VMware Virtual Networks with the vCLI 293
  Configuring VMware vCenter with PowerCLI 294
Microsoft Scripting for Hyper-V: PowerShell 297
  Getting Information about VMs 298
  Getting Information about the Virtual Network 299
  Assessing Other Aspects of the Virtual Environment 299
Citrix Scripting: Shell Scripts 300

Chapter 11 • Additional Security Considerations
for Virtual Infrastructure **303**
VDI Overview 303
  VDI Benefits and Drawbacks: Operations and Security 304
  Security Advantages and Challenges 304
  VDI Architecture Overview 307
Leveraging VDI for Security 310
  Storage Virtualization 310
  Application Virtualization 313

Index *317*

Introduction

So, what exactly is *virtualization security* anyway? There are a lot of varied definitions that could fit here, but the simplest is this: the systematic lockdown and application of security-related technical and procedural controls for all components of a virtualization infrastructure. Why do we need virtualization security, or virtsec for short? Well, the world is quickly changing, my friends. The look and feel of today's modern datacenter is rapidly morphing from what it once was, and many organizations' network boundaries are blurrier than ever. We're starting to leverage both internal and external clouds, which tend to make heavy use of virtualization technology. We have entire networks "in a box." All the components are abstracted from their physical counterparts — network devices, storage, application components, entire servers, and desktops. Finally, and maybe most important, we have lots more layers in our computing stacks than ever before, and more layers equals worse security, a lesson learned over many years in IT.

For all these reasons and more, we need a solid grasp on how to lock this technology down appropriately. As with any security efforts, the amount and severity of what you do and how you do it will, and should, vary depending on your business and risk tolerance. Some of the security we need to consider is more focused on policy and process than technology. For example, change control and configuration management are two disciplines that really need some attention as part of a sound virtualization security strategy, but they don't really deal with hands-on technical topics as much as some others. On the flip side, there are lots of knobs to turn and buttons to push in the realm of virtualization, and knowing what they are and when to twist or push them is a critical skill that more operations and security teams need today. When you're building your infrastructure on a technology, you'd better know how to secure it properly.

My sincere hope is that this book proves to be a practical and useful source of guidance for you, and I welcome any feedback or improvements I can make.

Who Should Read This Book

I'd like to think that this book has a little something for everyone, but "everyone" is a pretty broad group, so I'll narrow it a bit. In particular, this book was written for IT operations teams that manage any aspect of the virtual environment (including virtual networks and storage). This book is very short on theory and "blah blah blah" and much more to the point so you can quickly apply concepts and get your jobs done. IT administrators, network engineers, technical architects, and many other operations-focused roles will likely find this book to have value.

I also wrote this book for information security teams. While they may not be performing much of the hands-on configuration of the virtualization environment, they'll likely be involved in auditing and setting policy, and the more technical know-how they have the better.

Finally, there's a good bit of material here that should be of interest to technical managers and auditors too. While not all of the material will be of interest, more than likely there's enough background material to get managers up to speed and technical controls and commands that auditors can leverage for assessing the state of the environment.

What You Will Learn

In this book, readers will learn about best practices and specific technical controls for securing virtual infrastructure. I'll cover the gamut of components ranging from virtual networks to hypervisor platforms and virtual machines. One of the book's focal points is coverage of the three major hypervisor platform vendors, namely VMware, Microsoft, and Citrix. While there are plenty of other virtualization technologies (like KVM, for example), these three tend to be the most popular, and I touch on most aspects of how they're configured and managed. You'll learn some basics for scripting and setting up disaster recovery tools and technologies, a variety of configuration options, some auditing and assessment techniques, and in most cases, how to secure the technology from both a GUI and command-line perspective.

How This Book Is Organized

Here's a glance at what is in each chapter.

Chapter 1: Fundamentals of Virtualization Security   This chapter explains how virtualization has fundamentally changed the world of IT operations and why it's important to ensure that operations teams are implementing security during normal day-to-day activities.

Chapter 2: Securing Hypervisors   The most common hypervisor platforms — VMware ESXi, Microsoft Hyper-V, and Citrix XenServer — all have a number of configuration controls that should be implemented and maintained by system administrators. This chapter will describe those controls, with pros and cons to operations teams in terms of performance, ease of maintenance, and impact on other aspects of virtualization operations. Specific areas covered include configuring VMware vSphere and ESXi, configuring Microsoft Hyper-V on Windows Server 2008 and Windows Server 2012, and configuring Citrix XenServer.

Chapter 3: Designing Virtual Networks for Security   When designing or updating virtual networks, there are many considerations for securely implementing network policies and integrating virtual networks into the existing physical infrastructure. This chapter will outline specific design elements for network and virtualization operations teams, with configuration recommendations for vSphere and Hyper-V native virtual switches and some discussion of other types of switches as well. Specific areas covered include virtual vs. physical networks, virtual network security considerations, configuring virtual switches, and integrating with physical networking.

Chapter 4: Advanced Virtual Network Operations   This chapter will build on Chapter 3 to include more detailed network operational concerns, such as load balancing, traffic shaping, and network monitoring. Integration of existing network tools will be covered, as will new types of tools and techniques (including scripting) that can benefit administrators. Specific areas covered include network operational challenges and solutions, load balancing in virtual environments, traffic shaping and network performance, and creating a sound network monitoring strategy.

Chapter 5: Virtualization Management and Client Security   The management servers and clients used to connect to them can also be points of potential exposure. This chapter describes the types of issues that may be present in the various vendors' components and outlines both configuration options and architecture considerations that can be effectively used to create a more secure implementation. In addition, roles and privileges for several specific enterprise use cases will be outlined for VMware, Microsoft, and Citrix. Specific areas covered include management platform security concerns; securing VMware vCenter, Microsoft SCVMM, and Citrix XenCenter; and role and privilege use cases.

Chapter 6: Securing the Virtual Machine   Without impacting the production environment, what can administrators do to make their virtual machines more secure? Some of the biggest security vulnerabilities stem from the inherent functionality of virtualization products themselves, so this chapter will go into some detail on how Microsoft, Citrix, and VMware virtual machines can be more effectively secured without creating additional operational overhead for administrators. Specific areas covered include security concerns, threats, and vulnerabilities for VMs and locking down VMware, Microsoft, and Citrix VMs.

Chapter 7: Logging and Auditing   Virtualization administrators will need to ensure that logs are being generated by both virtual machines and the virtualization infrastructure components. This chapter will outline some best practices they can follow to make sure that they're getting the right log information for troubleshooting and security, that the logs are managed as effectively as possible, and that logs are available for audit and security purposes when needed. Specific areas covered include why logging and auditing is critical, virtualization logs and auditing options, integrating with existing logging platforms, and effective log management.

Chapter 8: Change and Configuration Management   Virtualization can significantly enhance change and configuration management practices, but this usually requires some changes to existing processes as well as new methods of doing things. This chapter will describe some different ways to integrate virtualization into existing workflows, ways to create new (and likely more effective) policies and processes for change and configuration management, and ways that virtualization can help make these critical operations processes more effective. Specific areas covered include change and configuration management overview, how virtualization impacts change and configuration management, integrating virtualization into change management, best practices for virtualization configuration management, and improving operations with virtualization.

Chapter 9: Disaster Recovery and Business Continuity   Virtualization can play a big role in disaster recovery (DR) and business continuity planning (BCP) operations. This chapter will delve into some ways that virtualization administrators can streamline DR and BCP processes, create simpler and more effective DR and BCP workflows, and reduce costs at the same time. Specific areas covered include leveraging virtualization and private clouds for DR/BCP and tips for improving DR/BCP.

Chapter 10: Scripting Tips and Tricks for Automation   There are many ways scripts can make virtualization administrators lives much simpler in general. This chapter will outline scripting tools that can be used with VMware, Microsoft, and Citrix platforms to accomplish specific operations and security-focused goals. Specific areas covered include why scripting is essential for admins; scripting types for virtualization admins; the use of PowerShell;

scripting with VMware, Microsoft, and Citrix platforms; and additional virtualization scripting ideas.

Chapter 11: Additional Security Considerations for Virtual Infrastructure   This chapter will explore several key security considerations for Virtual Desktop Infrastructure (VDI), virtual storage, and application virtualization. Specific areas covered include VDI benefits and drawbacks, VDI architecture and leveraging VDI for security, securing storage virtualization, and securing application virtualization.

Hardware and Software Requirements

To get the most out of this book, you should have a virtualization infrastructure based on VMware vSphere, Microsoft Hyper-V, or Citrix XenServer.

Certain features and capabilities discussed within most chapters of the book may be reliant on a certain license version from the vendors discussed. You should check which features you have with your current licensing before attempting to configure your infrastructure! Links to licensing information for VMware, Microsoft, and Citrix are listed here.

◆   VMware vSphere licensing:

`www.vmware.com/products/datacenter-virtualization/vsphere/compare-editions.html`

◆   Microsoft Hyper-V licensing:

`www.microsoft.com/en-us/server-cloud/buy/pricing-licensing.aspx`

◆   Citrix XenServer licensing:

`www.citrix.com/English/ps2/products/subfeature.asp?contentID=2313292`

How to Use This Book

This book has been organized so that it does not have to be read in order from front to back. Each chapter contains specific information that can be put to good use right away.

How to Contact the Author

I welcome feedback and ways to improve the book for everyone. Please contact me at dshackleford@voodoosec.com with any feedback.

Sybex strives to keep you supplied with the latest tools and information you need for your work. Please check `www.sybex.com/go/virtualizationsecurity`, where we'll post additional content and updates that supplement this book should the need arise.

Virtualization Security

Fundamentals of Virtualization Security

Virtualization technology has been around for many years, in a variety of formats. Ranging from logical partitioning on mainframes to the highly diversified technologies of today like desktop, server, and application virtualization, the concept of virtualization is firmly embedded in today's datacenters and here to stay. However, with the rapid advances in virtualization technology comes a dark side, namely in the form of security risks. In this chapter, we'll examine the underpinnings of today's virtual technology; I'll explain what it means and how the various moving parts work together.

Then, we'll explore a variety of threats to your virtual environments, some of which are much more pressing, and some that are more theoretical but nonetheless warrant mention. Finally, we'll delve into the changing landscape of security in light of virtual infrastructure and how it's changing the way we do things.

This chapter is really intended to lay the groundwork for the rest of the book and is the most theoretical material you'll encounter. It's important to understand the theory and concepts associated with virtualization security in order to grasp why we're concerned about it in the first place. If you're a security professional, many of these concepts will be somewhat familiar to you. If you're an administrator or engineer, you'll likely be familiar with some of this, but my guess is you're more focused on just getting things done. After this chapter, the book's emphasis decidedly shifts toward "getting things done" versus "security theory."

In this chapter, you will learn about the following topics:

◆ Virtualization architecture

◆ Threats to a virtualized environment

◆ Challenges for securing virtualized environments

◆ Challenges of vulnerability testing in virtualized environments

Virtualization Architecture

At its heart, all *virtualization* represents the abstraction of computing resources from the physical hardware layer. In the realm of server virtualization, the *host* is the underlying server virtualization platform that will be used to provide virtual hardware layers to the virtual servers. The virtual *guest* (usually referred to as a virtual machine, or VM) comprises a set of files that represent the virtual server or system itself. Each of these files serves a specific purpose in interacting with the host software and the underlying hardware that the host is installed on. The virtual machines can be located directly on the host's local storage device or on a network storage device (or devices).

DEFINING SOME TERMS

The following terms are used in this book:

Host   A host is a virtualization platform running hypervisor software. Common host platforms include VMware ESXi, Microsoft Hyper-V, Citrix XenServer, Red Hat KVM, and others. All virtualized systems run on top of this host hypervisor platform.

Virtual guest, virtual machine, VM, guest system   A virtual guest, commonly called a virtual machine (VM), is any system running the environment that has been abstracted into a virtual model. In essence, a VM is a group of files that represents a hardware-based computing platform, complete with storage, memory, and configuration components.

Virtual server   Many virtualization projects start by virtualizing hardware-based servers. The term *virtual server* is commonly used to refer to these. A virtual server is really nothing more than a specific type of VM.

The hypervisor is the primary component of a server virtualization platform. Often referred to as the virtual machine monitor (VMM), the hypervisor is the central nervous system within a virtual infrastructure. It manages the host's underlying hardware resources and handles all guest-initiated operating system (OS) and application requests for CPU, memory, I/O, and disk resources. Two types of hypervisors are commonly found today:

Type I hypervisors are fundamentally their own self-contained operating platforms and are installed directly on the host hardware. For this reason, these hypervisors are often called bare metal hypervisors. VMs run at a level "above" the hardware, allowing for more complete isolation through the hypervisor software. An example of this type of hypervisor would be VMware's ESXi. An example of this hypervisor type is shown in Figure 1.1.

FIGURE 1.1
Type I hypervisor

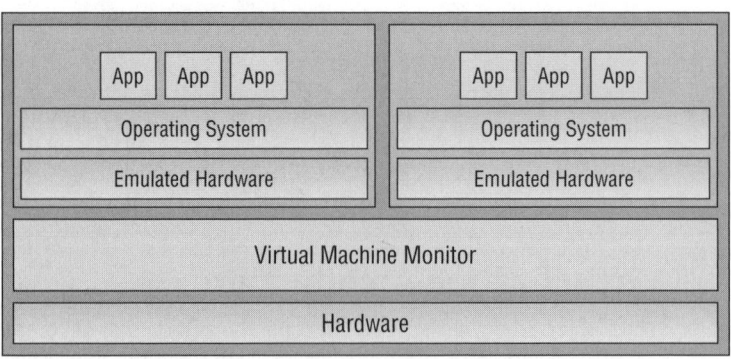

Type II hypervisors are applications installed on an existing operating system platform, as shown in Figure 1.2. An example of a Type II hypervisor would be VMware Workstation.

FIGURE 1.2
Type II hypervisor

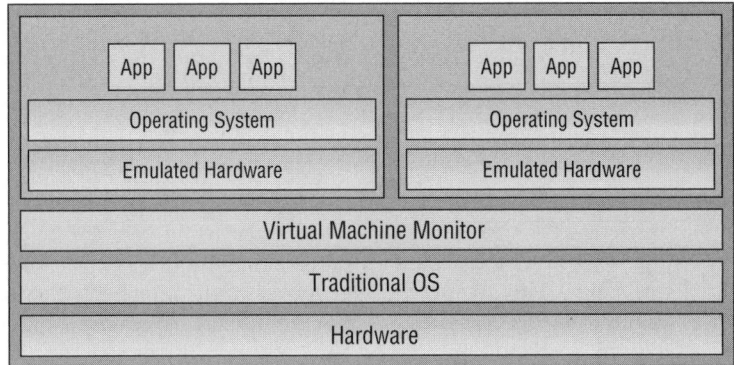

The key to understanding hypervisors and the security issues they are susceptible to is to understand the concepts of operating modes and privilege levels (or rings) for the x86 CPU architecture.

Operating modes   There are two operating modes to consider—real mode and protected mode. All modern x86 processors boot into real mode for backward compatibility, but the actual processor capabilities are within protected mode, and that's where the notion of privilege levels comes in.

Privilege levels   To visualize privilege levels, imagine a set of concentric circles, where the middle is closest to the hardware and the outer rings are further out. (See Figure 1.3.) The middle ring, known as Ring 0, is the most privileged; software running at this level has total control over the underlying hardware of the host. The other rings are labeled Ring 1 through Ring 3 (the outermost ring). In many modern operating systems, Ring 0 is known as Supervisor mode and is where all integral OS functions take place. All application functions typically occur in Ring 3, commonly called User mode.

FIGURE 1.3
x86 Processor
privilege levels
(rings)

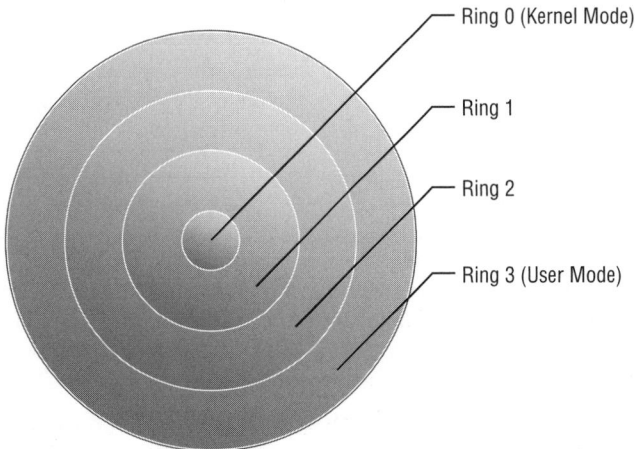

How do privilege levels (rings) relate to hypervisors?

◆ A Type I hypervisor is integrated with the operating platform, and so it runs as Ring 0, Ring 1, and/or Ring 2, while guest operating systems run at Ring 3.

◆ With a Type II hypervisor, both the hypervisor and the guests operate within Ring 3 as distinct applications.

The goal with either hypervisor model is to safely allow guests to run without ever impacting the "real" Ring 0, which could affect the underlying host platform and all the other guests. To accomplish this, virtualization platforms create a layer between the guests and the real Ring 0. This layer is the hypervisor, or virtual machine monitor (VMM), and it presents a virtual Ring 0 to the guest VMs so that they can perform standard calls to hardware when they require memory, disk, network, and other resources. Compromising the hypervisor could mean that the underlying host OS (if applicable) and all guests are vulnerable to exposure or attacks.

Threats to a Virtualized Environment

To properly evaluate the risks to an infrastructure created using any kind of information technology (IT), including virtualization technology, security and operations teams must evaluate and assess the vulnerabilities that may exist in the technology, threats to the environment that could exploit those vulnerabilities, and the potential impact of security events. The results of this risk assessment process tend to involve such actions as patching and configuring systems, restricting access to network resources, and limiting the users that can access management platforms and VMs, among many other controls and processes. To solidly grasp the risk to virtualized environments, and understand why security and compliance professionals have focused so much on virtualization since 2006, there are a number of threats to understand.

Operational Threats

All IT environments face a variety of threats, from threats that are accidental in nature, like employee mistakes, to more malicious threats like insiders looking to steal data or external attackers trying to break in. Virtualized environments face the same types of threats as physical infrastructures, but in virtualized environments the threats can manifest in different ways. In this section, we'll cover some of the major threats you should consider when evaluating the risk to your virtual environment.

VM sprawl   Virtual machines can be deployed in seconds, making it easy to create unapproved VMs (for example, short-term testing systems). VMs created on-the-fly might not be patched, updated, or configured properly. A single unpatched VM that is exposed could be compromised and thus becomes a point of vulnerability in the environment. VM sprawl is common, especially in large organizations with loose governance processes. It is a major, pervasive problem in any environment that has deployed virtualization technology without putting processes in place for managing it appropriately, including change and configuration management and provisioning practices.

Lack of visibility into virtual environments   Many virtual network environments are not monitored adequately. The use of virtual switches for porting traffic to a separate promiscuous (sniffing) security or network monitoring sensor is still the exception in most environments, and many virtual networks have quite a bit of internal traffic that is not being monitored adequately by external security and network tools. Also, the traffic between guest VMs and the underlying hypervisor platform often goes unexamined, leading to a number of potential security risks. Not monitoring your virtual network environment can be very dangerous. You might miss sensitive data leaving the environment, attacks taking place within the virtual network, or valuable performance data that could help shape your traffic management policies.

Separation of duties not maintained   Separation of duties for people managing systems, networks, and applications in a virtual environment is often lacking. A number of different groups may need to manage VMs; a group or groups will need to manage the actual virtualization infrastructure, and others may need access to database and storage components, third-party add-ons, and other "moving parts." Who manages all this, and how should it be broken down? This often ends up being a political battle, and different teams often don't understand how they should manage "their" parts of the virtual infrastructure. Do network administrators manage virtual switches and other networking systems, or should the virtualization team handle this? Who should manage the administration console systems like VMware's vCenter—the Windows administrators or a dedicated virtualization team?

Granting unilateral access to any one group could be a big security risk. Granting too many rights and privileges to certain admins—or to VMs themselves and their applications—is another big issue in virtualized environments. Defining granular roles for specific groups' use cases can be challenging from a governance perspective, and the technical controls available within the various virtualization vendors' products may not accommodate security needs adequately.

Change and configuration management is a key area to focus on for virtualized organizations, and we'll cover a wide range of configuration specifics in this book for the major virtualization products and platforms.

Configuration details for the hypervisors can encompass a vast array of settings and options, including those that pertain to VM management and monitoring, security hardening and lockdown, and user and group interaction with the platform.

Network settings can also be complex, especially as they relate to external physical networking devices like switches and routers.

Security-specific settings and systems related to firewalls and intrusion detection and auditing controls such as logging require careful attention too.

One of the most important goals for any virtualized datacenter is consistency, with well-defined templates for hypervisors, VMs, and everything in between. As organizations look to move from virtualization to a private cloud, this will become even more important. Developing and maintaining this level of uniformity and consistency is integral to a successful private cloud deployment.

Malware-Based Threats

In addition to purely operational threats, there are a number of others that have surfaced regarding virtualization technology, some more realistic and others somewhat hypothetical.

VM-Aware Malware

One of the more disturbing trends to occur since 2006 is the onset of VM-aware malware, which has been seen on many occasions in the wild. Various strains and versions of bots, worms, rootkits, and other malicious code formats are capable of determining whether they're running on a physical or virtual host by looking at memory and hardware attributes, memory locations, and process and function behavior. When these malware variants detect that they're running within a virtual environment, they will often refuse to run or behave differently than they would on a physical host. Since many security professionals use VMs to analyze malware, this malware is certainly making it more difficult!

Websense Labs described a very customized piece of malware in 2007 that wouldn't run in a VM, and this was definitely just the beginning of a longer trend. You can get more information at the following location:

```
http://securitylabs.websense.com/content/Blogs/2688.aspx
```

Packer Applications

Another trend seen in the last several years is the use of commercially available packer (compression) applications that malware authors use to compress and obfuscate their code. Some of these have anti-VM features built right in! One example is Themida, which includes a number of protection capabilities for the code being packed. Information on Themida can be found at the following location:

```
http://www.oreans.com/themida.php
```

Bots

Well-known bots such as Agobot and Phatbot are starting to include anti-VM technology. A good introduction to some of these bots can be found at the Honeynet Project website (www.honeynet.org/node/53). Another example is the Storm worm, a particularly nasty piece of malware that has circulated in a number of forms since early 2007. It leverages social engineering tactics (e-mail subject lines that reflect current news), peer-to-peer botnet capabilities, and many other advanced features. Another aspect of the Storm worm is its ability to detect whether it's running in a VM. An excellent write-up by Bojan Zdrnja on the Storm worm's VM detection capabilities can be found at the SANS Internet Storm Center site:

```
http://isc.sans.org/diary.html?storyid=3190
```

VM Escape

One of the most commonly discussed security issues related to virtualization platforms is VM escape, a security breach in which malicious code runs within a VM and is able to "break out" onto the underlying host. This is a security professional's worst nightmare! In a VM escape, trust zones are violated, access controls are circumvented, and the confidentiality and integrity of ESX hosts is suspect as soon as it happens. At one time, it was believed that VM escape was impossible, but today, most security professionals believe it can happen. Why? The main reason is that very close calls have been noted!

At conferences in 2007 and 2008, several tools were released and discussed that allow data transfer between virtual machines as well as between virtual machines and the underlying host. The reason that none of these has been classified as a true VM escape is that code must be running on both the VM and the host for the tools to function properly. A true VM escape would be independent of code running on the host, allowing a purely guest-focused attack to break out of the VM and start running on the host. Several vulnerabilities have been found that permit similar actions, where hosts can be affected by exploiting guest applications and services.

The following sections discuss several types of VM escape–type attacks that security experts have been working on in the last few years.

DIRECTORY TRAVERSAL ATTACK

Most of the VM escape flaws reported to date have been related to some sort of directory traversal attack.

The first of these was reported by iDefense in April 2007 and described an issue with the Shared Folders functionality in VMware Workstation. Due to a problem with the way Workstation interpreted filenames, a malicious user could write files from inside a guest to the underlying host with the privileges of the user running VMware Workstation on the host. IntelGuardians (now InGuardians) built on this research in its cutting-edge presentation on VM security issues during the SANSFIRE 2007 conference in Washington, DC. At this conference, Tom Liston and Ed Skoudis gave a presentation that brought the notion of VM escape much closer to reality. They wrote several tools that demonstrated that VM escape might very well be possible:

VMchat This simple "chat" program used the VMware hypervisor communication channel to pass messages back and forth between guest VMs or between a guest VM and the host. This program did not require any special code to be installed, nor did it leverage any networking capabilities.

VMcat This tool sent simple output of Standard In (stdin) and Standard Out (stdout) between the communication channel created with VMchat, which can be used to tunnel a command shell between hosts and guests.

VM Drag-n-Sploit By modifying a VMware component on the guest called VMwareService.exe, the researchers were able to monitor and change all data traversing the communication channel. This allowed them to alter data being dragged from the guest to the host via the "drag-n-drop" functionality built in to VMware Workstation. Their demonstration used this functionality to create a drag-n-drop exploit that would send a command shell from the host to the guest.

VMftp This tool was a working exploit for the iDefense Shared Folders flaw discovered earlier that year. A user on *any* guest, with any level of privilege, could read and write to the host as long as Shared Folders was enabled and at least one folder was shared with a guest VM.

In February 2008, researchers at Core Security (the company that makes the Core IMPACT penetration testing tools) discovered a flaw in certain versions of VMware Workstation, ACE, and Player that allows an attacker to locally or remotely exploit the VMware Shared Folders functionality (shared resources between guest and host) and read or write to any area of the underlying host OS. For more on this, see the following location:

```
www.coresecurity.com/?action=item&id=2129
```

BLUE PILL

Joanna Rutkowska, a researcher in Poland, created quite a stir in June 2006 by unveiling a proof-of-concept tool and exploit called the Blue Pill. The Blue Pill was essentially a rootkit that targeted the Windows Vista OS by taking advantage of the SVM/Pacifica virtualization capabilities built into AMD processors. This allowed the rootkit to create a rogue hypervisor that would actually encapsulate the running Vista OS and virtualize it! In essence, this means that the trusted OS would no longer be running on the bare metal of the system—it would be running on top of a processor-based hypervisor that had full control of everything within the OS and anywhere else on the system.

More on the Blue Pill is available at Rutkowska's website:

```
http://theinvisiblethings.blogspot.com/2006/06/introducing-blue-pill.html
```

Rutkowska's claim that this exploit was "100% undetectable" created a lot of controversy—could completely undetectable malware be created? Overall, most of the information security community disagreed. Many top-notch security researchers rose to the challenge, including Anthony Liguori, a software engineer at IBM who is heavily involved in development of the Xen hypervisor. He disputed Rutkowska's claims by explaining that encapsulating an OS undetected would take more than just "virtualizing it" because you would have to prevent it from "knowing" that it had been virtualized. This is extremely difficult to do, as he explained, due to the timing differences for executing instructions on normal computing hardware versus software-based VMM emulation. An excellent interview with Liguori can be found here:

```
www.virtualization.info/2006/08/debunking-blue-pill-myth.html
```

Another group of well-known security researchers at Matasano Security challenged Rutkowska to test her Blue Pill against their Samsara rootkit detection technology at the Black Hat conference in 2007. Rutkowska declined, and many others in the security community pointed out numerous ways by which Blue Pill could be detected using memory inspection and instruction timing techniques.

TXT HACK

At the Black Hat DC conference in 2009, Rutkowska and her colleague Rafal Wojtczuk at Invisible Things Labs discussed how they hacked the Trusted Execution Technology (TXT) built into Intel vPro chips. According to their presentation, they first exploit a bug in the Intel system software, followed by an attack against a TXT software flaw. This allows an attacker to insert code into a highly protected memory area, the System Management Mode (SMM) memory, or SMRAM. This is even more privileged than Ring 0, or hardware hypervisor code below the OS kernel. TXT mechanisms have not checked this memory for integrity or changes, and this code inserted there can bypass all boot-time security. Rutkowska and team discovered another TXT-based attack in December 2009. More information is available at the following location:

```
http://theinvisiblethings.blogspot.com/2009/12/another-txt-attack.html
```

HYPERSAFE: A SOLUTION TO VM ESCAPE?

In May 2010, researchers at North Carolina State University released a paper discussing a proof-of-concept hypervisor security tool and monitoring technique called HyperSafe. By leveraging hardware capabilities that monitor the hypervisor software's integrity, HyperSafe ensures that no malware or other nefarious escape attacks can modify the running hypervisor platform from a VM guest or any other vector. Essentially, HyperSafe monitors critical memory structures and buffer behavior associated with the hypervisor, thus preventing any modifications caused by buffer overflows and other common exploitation methods. The NC State paper can be found here:

```
www.csc.ncsu.edu/faculty/jiang/pubs/OAKLAND10.pdf
```

Vulnerabilities in Virtualization Platforms

There have also been quite a few vulnerabilities found in virtualization platforms, some considered quite severe.

In May and early June 2009, the security world was abuzz about a tool released by Immunity, Inc., called Cloudburst. Kostya Kortchinsky, one of the lead Vulnerability Research Team members at Immunity, incorporated proof-of-concept code in Cloudburst that leveraged a VMware flaw from April 2009. This flaw, which revolved around a virtual machine display driver buffer overflow, allowed code to be executed on the underlying host from within a guest. This is likely the closest thing to a VM escape scenario seen to date in the wild.

In March 2010, VMware announced a series of major vulnerabilities that affected its ESX and ESXi hypervisors, ranging from Service Console kernel flaws to numerous issues with open-source packages installed within the Service Console OS. These issues could lead to remote denial of service (DoS) attacks, code execution, privilege escalation, and other major security problems. In total, more than 40 Common Vulnerabilities and Exposures (CVE) entries were generated for this series of vulnerabilities, and all VMware enterprise users were urged to patch as quickly as possible.

Numerous vulnerabilities have also been found in Xen and Hyper-V platforms, although they've been less sensational, perhaps due to the larger market share VMware holds in this space. For more, see the following location:

```
http://lists.vmware.com/pipermail/security-announce/2010/000093.html
```

How Security Must Adapt to Virtualization

Attacks seldom occur in a vacuum. If any effort is made to protect a system, a successful system compromise almost always involves several attacks mounted in combination. Adding virtualization into the infrastructure introduces an entirely new class of attacks into the mix of possibilities

Compromising a system administrator's workstation is a traditional "holy grail" for attackers. System administrator workstations often contain network and system information such as IP addresses, passwords, and network diagrams. By installing bot software or key loggers, attackers can access sensitive credentials and other passwords as well. These workstations may be located in sensitive parts of the network, with access to management segments or other management interfaces that could provide an attacker much more leverage than they would otherwise have. A compromised system administrator workstation could be used with any and all virtualization attack types to wreak untold havoc in just about any environment.

Challenges for Securing Virtualized Environments

Overall, the risk profile for virtualized environments is somewhat different from that of hardware-based environments. There are more layers in the computing stack: hardware, OS, network, hypervisor, applications, and virtualized components. In general, there's more "surface area" for vulnerabilities and attacks to affect, and this can lead to complications in accurately assessing and defending the environment.

Virtualization technology also changes the realm of information security dramatically—for example, with regard to network access controls and firewalls. Most of us are familiar with screened subnets or demilitarized zones (DMZs) as the principal architectures employed by firewalls and other network access control devices (routers, etc.). With all of the traditional network architecture models, sensitive systems and network subnets are segmented from other parts of the network, allowing granular control of traffic entering and exiting the specific zones that are defined. Although these general concepts can still work in virtualized environments, such environments may require new tools and technologies to accomplish the same segmentation and access control goals.

One thing you need to consider when securing your virtual environment is whether to use physical or virtual firewalls (or both) within your virtual infrastructure. Physical firewalls would connect to physical network interface cards (NICs) on a virtualization host and apply access controls to the virtual switches that use these interfaces. Virtual firewalls, on the other hand, act as virtual machines or integrated components within the virtual infrastructure itself. There are security and operational concerns with these technologies, including ease of management, trust zone segregation, single point of failure concerns, and resource consumption associated with the virtual firewall VM and components.

As mentioned in the section "Operational Threats" earlier in this chapter, management of virtualization security devices and VMs and setting up systems to monitor traffic on virtual switches are important. A number of commercial solutions can enable robust monitoring, including Reflex Security and Catbird. There are also techniques you can employ without purchasing any commercial solutions. Some of these are covered in Chapter 3, "Designing Virtual Networks for Security," and Chapter 4, "Advanced Virtual Network Operations."

Challenges of Vulnerability Testing in a Virtualized Environment

Execution of vulnerability assessments and penetration tests may differ somewhat in virtualized environments. The simplest vulnerability assessment and pen testing cycle usually consists of reconnaissance, scanning, exploitation, pivoting, and then repeating the cycle, as shown in Figure 1.4.

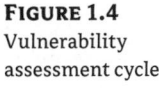

FIGURE 1.4
Vulnerability
assessment cycle

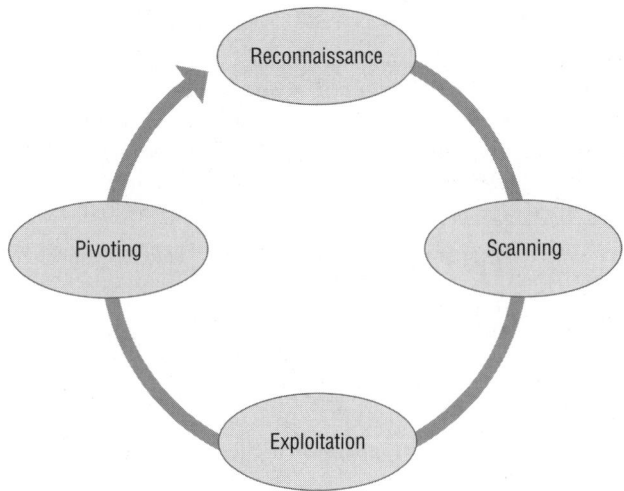

The phases can be defined as follows:

Reconnaissance   In this phase, an attacker would search for information about a target using publicly available sources like websites, search engine queries, or social media. In addition, infrastructure queries using services like Domain Name System (DNS) and Simple Mail Transfer Protocol (SMTP) are often performed in this phase. The goal of this stage is to learn about the target's people, systems, and applications.

Scanning   Network, vulnerability, and application scanning are all variations of the scanning phase that use automated or semiautomated tools to look for open network ports and vulnerable aspects of systems or applications. This information is then used to determine the best attack methods.

Exploitation   In this phase, attackers leverage the information they've gathered in the preceding phases to actively attempt exploitation of vulnerabilities on systems and in applications.

Pivoting   Pivoting is simply the act of gaining access to systems and applications and then establishing a "beachhead" to begin the cycle again from that vantage point. Good attackers can pivot through numerous systems to get to the data they're seeking.

RECONNAISSANCE CHALLENGES

For reconnaissance, which usually is done from afar and doesn't actually require interacting with target systems, virtualization really doesn't factor in. DNS queries, WHOIS records, and so on are all likely to be the same whether target systems are virtual or physical machines. Looking for administrators and other IT operations personnel posting sensitive data on VMware forums and other online sites may be interesting in this phase however.

SCANNING CHALLENGES

Scanning will almost certainly be performed a bit differently. Tools like Network Mapper (NMAP) and others can perform port scans and remote OS fingerprinting. Can they identify whether a system is physical or virtual? There may be some clues, including open ports and running services, Media Access Control (MAC) addresses (on the local subnet), and even packet fields and their values. Chris Brenton, a well-known SANS instructor, discusses some of these in a blog post titled "Passively Fingerprinting VMware Virtual Systems":

```
http://www.chrisbrenton.org/2009/09/passively-fingerprinting-vmware-virtual-
systems/
```

In addition, we need to factor in the impact these scans will have on the VMs and underlying hosts. New ways to perform scans might include scanning from within the virtual infrastructure using a VM with scanning tools installed. Some scanners are also capable of logging in to local systems and performing additional assessments. Some of these tools could be extended or scripted to also check for virtualization artifacts or other identifiers. As for actual exploitation capabilities, there are a number of new tools that can facilitate exploitation during pen tests on virtualized infrastructure. The Virtualization Assessment Toolkit (VASTO) is a set of Metasploit modules released by Claudio Criscione and contributors in 2010. This set of modules allows Metasploit users performing pen tests to scan and identify virtualization resources as well as attempt a number of attacks against them. Several well-known exploits have been included in this toolkit, including attacks against VMware Update Manager and Tomcat components, the VILurker attack that tricks a VI client user into downloading a fake "update" that runs under their credentials, and many others.

ADAPTING ANTI-MALWARE TOOLS FOR HOSTS AND GUESTS

Anti-malware tools also need to be adapted for virtualized infrastructure. Two primary concerns for anti-malware protection include host scanning and guest scanning. For the underlying host (such as VMware ESXi and Microsoft Hyper-V), the main issues are performance impacts and integrity problems that result from scanning particular virtualization-specific file structures such as virtual machine disk (VMDK) files in VMware environments. Performance impacts are a serious concern—impacting the host could easily lead to multiple VM guests performing poorly, which would not be acceptable in most operational environments. Scheduling scans becomes very important here. Additionally, file and directory exclusions from scanning need to be planned carefully to ensure that the virtualization-specific files are not affected in any way from the scans. Adverse effects have been noted from scanning VMDK files, for example.

Guests can have antivirus software directly installed much as with any normal platform (Windows, Linux, etc.), but resource consumption and availability are even more important than ever, especially if resource sharing is enabled with tools like Dynamic Resource Scheduler (DRS), which is a VMware technology for migrating VMs between cluster hosts based on resource availability. The VM file structures may also behave differently when scanned, leading to more false positives and negatives, the bane of any security administrator. Finally, offline guests need to be scanned as well, especially if they're brought back into production after any length of time (they may be missing patches or other security updates). New products like VMware vShield Endpoint and McAfee MOVE Antivirus are engineered to minimize these performance impacts by delegating the majority of antivirus scanning to dedicated virtual machines running on the hypervisor.

There are a number of other specific virtualization security risks and controls, all of which will be covered in more depth throughout the book's later chapters.

Chapter 2

Securing Hypervisors

This chapter is about locking down virtualization platforms, specifically Type I hypervisors. Hardening the hypervisor should really be viewed as a standard practice, much as it should be for enterprise servers of any importance. There are an incredible number of configuration options for the major platforms (ESXi, Hyper-V, and XenServer). In this chapter, I'll cover the most fundamental, getting you to a sound security state that conforms to industry best practices. Where appropriate, I'll refer to outside sources for more in-depth information that's somewhat outside the scope of this book. Overall, these settings will help you secure your hypervisors to a reasonable level for most organizations.

In this chapter, you will learn about the following topics:

◆ Principles of hypervisor configuration and security

◆ Configuring VMware ESXi, Microsoft Hyper-V, and Citrix XenServer

Hypervisor Configuration and Security

A virtualization hypervisor platform, as described in Chapter 1, "Fundamentals of Virtualization Security," is software that emulates physical hardware to numerous guest operating systems and applications, allowing them to run concurrently on one physical machine. Every hypervisor platform has its own architectural nuances, but most hypervisors (also called virtual machine monitors, or VMMs) have a design somewhat similar to that shown in Figure 2.1.

FIGURE 2.1
Hypervisor architecture

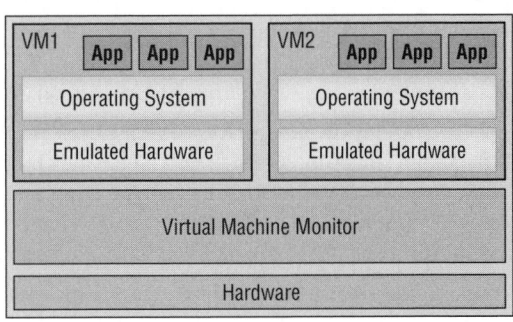

As you can see in the diagram, the VMM is a low-level component that functions in many ways as the OS of the virtual hosting platform. To ensure that the entire virtual environment is protected from attacks, bugs, or operational mishaps, it's paramount to keep it as up-to-date as possible and to configure some fundamental controls.

There are a number of distinct aspects of securing a hypervisor system of any sort, and the most common hypervisor platforms — VMware ESXi, Microsoft Hyper-V, and Citrix XenServer — all have multiple configuration controls that should be implemented and maintained by system administrators.

There are two fundamental principles to keep in mind when evaluating VMM security:

◆ The VMM is in many cases almost an operating system unto itself and has many characteristics similar to an OS.

◆ The VMM is interconnected with all hardware on the physical platform and acts as a conduit to any and all resources, such as storage, network, CPU, and memory, when virtual machines (VMs) ask for them.

Additionally, the VMM itself must be managed by administrators using a client or central console, a topic that we'll cover in more depth later in the book in Chapter 5, "Virtualization Management and Client Security".

The primary areas of concern for any VMM security configuration efforts are as follows:

Patching   In most cases, especially with Type I hypervisors, the VMM is decoupled from other OS components, and therefore the VMM must be patched separately. Patching the hypervisor should be considered a core operational practice in IT and should align with current high-priority patching cycles. Additional detail on patching processes and best practices will be covered in Chapter 8, "Change and Configuration Management."

Establishing secure communications   Many hypervisors use Secure Sockets Layer (SSL) or the newer Transport Layer Security (TLS) along with digital certificates to establish a means of securely communicating with remote clients and management platforms. In many cases, the digital certificates that are installed initially are not secure and should be configured or replaced prior to production operation. Another common control available for securing communication with the hypervisor or VMs is IPSec encryption.

Changing default settings   Many hypervisor configuration settings are not secure by default, and some hypervisors ship with default content that can be removed. For example, the older VMware ESX hypervisor had a number of Linux Web service components, binaries, and even user accounts that weren't necessary. Changing settings and removing generic default content makes up a large percentage of VMM hardening activities.

Enabling operational security   Common tools and protocols like Simple Network Management Protocol (SNMP) and Network Time Protocol (NTP) are used to provide consistency and accuracy in log files, monitoring, and numerous other operational activities. Configuring these services and protocols to function properly within the IT environment is an important step to ensuring long-term continuity for the virtual systems and applications.

Securing and monitoring critical configuration files   Every hypervisor platform has a number of files that are critical for configuration and control of the VMM system and services. These files should be carefully protected with permissions and monitoring controls.

Securing users and groups   Hypervisor platforms have a set of local users and groups that can be used to access the system and control services. In most cases, the default sets of users and groups are not as secure as they could be, with too much access and users that don't need to be active at all. Restricting these and controlling what they can access is another key step in protecting the system overall.

Locking down access to the hypervisor platform   Most hypervisor platforms have a native console interface that can be accessed both locally and remotely. This needs to be carefully controlled to ensure that unauthorized access doesn't occur. Another major element of hypervisor access control is configuring the local firewall, if one exists.

Configuring VMware ESXi

VMware has two primary hypervisor platforms in widespread use today. The older platform, ESX, has largely been supplanted by the newer ESXi (which stands for *ESX embedded/installable*). ESX has a much larger footprint than ESXi and needs a significant amount of configuration before it can be considered properly hardened. Most enterprise organizations have migrated to ESXi, or are in the process of migration, so we'll focus on the newer platform here. Most of the configuration controls for locking down ESXi will apply to both ESXi versions 4 and 5, but I'll endeavor to point out the differences where appropriate.

Patching VMware ESXi

Keeping your hypervisor platform patched should be considered one of your most critical security operations. There have been a number of fairly significant vulnerabilities found on VMware platforms, and patching your systems regularly is the best way to keep them out of harm's way.

There are a few common ways to patch systems, but administrators should be aware that VMware really offers true patch distribution only for its own platforms. In other words, if you already have a patch management infrastructure in place, it's not likely to work for patching ESXi. VMware offers a number of products for managing patching, however. If you're working in a very small environment, you can patch at the command line and with scripting tools, which I'll cover in the "Patching via the Command Line" later in this chapter. Most organizations, however, will desire a more scalable solution.

VMWARE GO

In 2011, VMware acquired patch management vendor Shavlik and has since adapted its technology to offer the vCenter Protect and VMware GO products. Both are considered stand-alone offerings that primarily serve the Small and Medium Business (SMB) market.

VMware GO is a cloud-based service that allows small organizations to reduce their operational overhead by setting up a central management system (an administrator's workstation, for example) that communicates with the VMware cloud to scan and patch hosts and VMs. Once logged in, an administrator can scan their local environment via IP range, hostnames, domains, or groups and push out patches to those systems. From there, a simple built-in help desk ticketing system can be used to assign patching and upgrade tasks to various teams or people. A fully patched hypervisor in the GO inventory looks like this.

continued

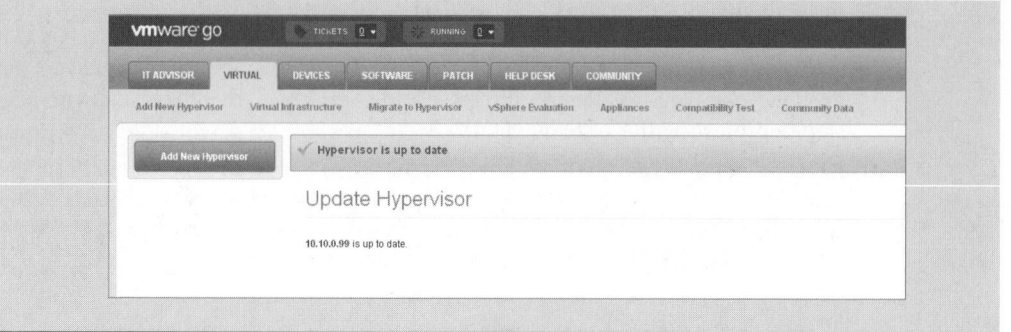

Most enterprises will use VMware Update Manager (VUM) for patching ESXi systems. VUM can automate and streamline the patching and upgrade process. With VUM, you can control just about every aspect of the patching cycle.

For example, VUM has support for clusters; all cluster members can be evaluated for resource availability to move hosts into maintenance mode for patching (which means all VMs will need to migrate to other cluster members). Once the resources have been evaluated, the cluster member you want to patch will be placed into maintenance mode, VMs will be migrated to other members, and you can start patching. You can patch all cluster members or only specific hypervisors with VUM as well. Certain services can be turned off or left alone on cluster hosts, and retries can be scheduled if the first attempt at patching fails for some reason.

In ESXi version 5, VUM can also download patches from multiple sources, and specific updates can be filtered so that only relevant patches for your environment are downloaded. VUM can perform host upgrades from ESX/ESXi 4.x to 5.x, virtual appliance (VA) upgrades for VMware and some third-party products, and VMware Tools upgrades for VMs that can be scheduled.

NOTE Installing VUM and its vCenter plug-ins is outside the scope for this book. An excellent resource is Scott Lowe's *Mastering VMware vSphere 5* (Sybex, 2011).

CONFIGURING VUM

Configuring VUM is fairly straightforward, and there are a number of clear patching best practices to follow. The first step is to define how patches will be downloaded and applied. You have two options here:

◆ Downloading via a direct connection to the Internet.

◆ Adding local (internal) storage repositories for patches. From storage repositories, you can feed patches and upgrade images to hosts. These patch and image repositories should be distributed in such a way as to easily communicate with hosts without crossing WAN or slower network links because large quantities of data will be sent out.

The shared repository option is best for larger, more distributed environments. Once you have developed a reasonably mature patching process for VMware platforms, using a shared repository is the most secure option because it gives you a lot more control over how patches get stored and distributed. Another key advantage is that your vCenter systems won't be constantly querying VMware patch repositories on the Internet, which is especially helpful when you have a lot of systems or some that are not exposed to the Internet at all.

To set up shared repositories, you'll first need to install Update Manager Download Services (UMDS) by running the `VMware-UMDS.exe` file from the vSphere install media. You can then use this simple command-line tool to download all patches and updates to a central location that any vCenter system can access.

To set up patch downloads or define storage repositories and define a schedule for downloading and applying patches, follow these steps:

1. Access the vCenter console. Select Solutions And Applications, select Update Manager, and select your vCenter location.

2. Select the Configuration tab (at the top of the right-hand pane). Click Download Settings in the column on the left. The result is shown in Figure 2.2.

FIGURE 2.2
VMware Update Manager download settings

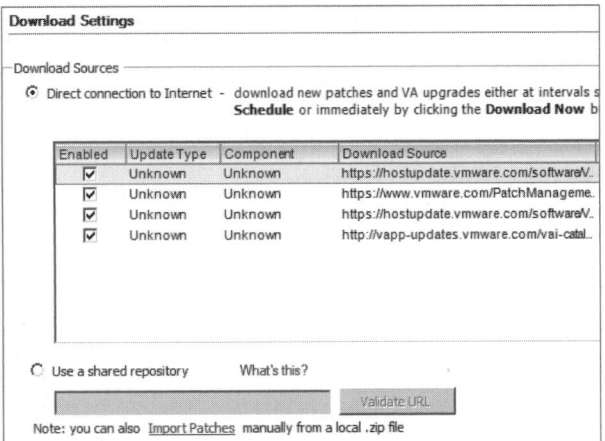

3. Specify where the downloads are. You have two options here:

    ◆ Click the radio button labeled Direct Connection To Internet, and then click Add Download Source at the right to add any new external download sources you want (make sure it is a source you trust).

    ◆ For a larger, more distributed option, click the radio button labeled Use A Shared Repository, which allows you to specify an internal storage repository. Specify and validate the location of your shared repository.

4. Click Apply, or click Download Now to get patches right away.

5. The next step is to schedule downloads on a regular basis. Click Download Schedule in the column on the left. In the Schedule Update Download window (Figure 2.3), you can specify a task name and description, the frequency and time of update, and any email notification settings.

FIGURE 2.3
VUM download
scheduling

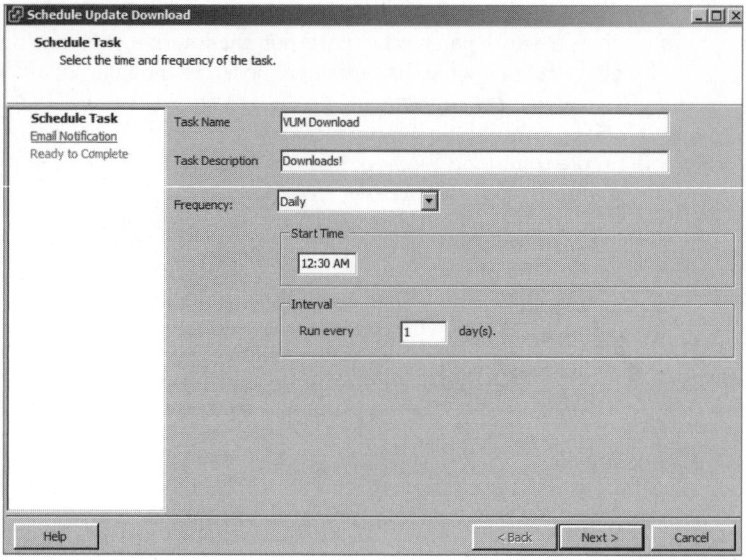

DEFINING BASELINE PROFILES

The next step to configuring updates is defining granular baseline profiles that include both critical and noncritical host patches (these are predefined) as well as specific profiles for commonly used virtual appliances. It's also wise to maintain a set of ESXi images to perform upgrades. Each of these also should have a baseline profile defined.

To get a feel for what baseline options you've got, let's walk through one of the predefined baselines:

1. Select the Baselines And Groups tab along the top of the screen in the Update Manager Administration area. You'll see two panes in this window. The left-hand pane is a list of baselines, and the right-hand pane is a list of baseline groups. In the left-hand pane, you'll also notice two buttons along the top, one for hosts and another for VMs/VAs. By default, you should have two default host baselines defined: Critical Host Patches and Non-Critical Host Patches.

2. Double-click the Critical Host Patches Baseline. The Edit Baseline window will open, and the first screen gives you a few options for what you can define:

   ◆ Baseline name and description are already populated because this one's predefined.

   ◆ Baseline type also can't be modified here because it's predefined, but you can create your own if needed. There are a few types of host baselines to choose from:

   Host Patch: This baseline applies patches to hypervisor hosts.

   Host Extension: This baseline will install or upgrade additional software components on hosts.

   Host Upgrade: These baselines contain an image file that is applied to hosts you want to upgrade from one version of ESX or ESXi to another.

- In addition, you have another category called VA Baselines with a single option, VA Upgrade. This category will apply updates to virtual appliances, from both VMware and certain third-party vendors approved by VMware.

3. In this example, the Host Patch baseline type is selected already. Click Next.

4. The next screen allows you to choose patch options. You've got two to choose from:

Fixed: This is a rigidly defined category that specifies a certain set of patches that will change only when an administrator adds or deletes patches from the list. This option requires more admin involvement but guarantees that you never push a patch you don't want. I recommend this for almost all environments because you won't take any unnecessary risks.

Dynamic: Dynamic patching allows you to specify certain patch criteria that VUM follows, and new patches that meet the criteria are automatically added to the list. This can speed up patching in certain environments, but you'll need to be careful to test first. I recommend this setting only in environments where speed is more important and the hypervisor configuration is extremely well understood. In addition, a slightly higher risk tolerance is needed because things can most definitely go wrong with dynamic patching.

The default for critical patches is Dynamic. With this type of patching, you'll need to specify criteria for inclusion, so click Next.

5. The Dynamic Baseline Criteria screen (Figure 2.4) allows you to specify criteria for patches, including vendors, products, patch severity and category, and release date information. Click Next.

6. The next screen allows you to specifically exclude certain patches, providing another level of granularity for administrators to control what patches get pushed out. Click Next.

7. The final configuration screen allows you to include additional patches in the baseline, perhaps one or several that don't meet the criteria specified earlier. Again, this is simply to allow for more granularity in dynamic patching. Click Next to reach a Summary page, and then click Finish.

Pretty straightforward, right? Creating your own baselines is simple. Right-click anywhere in the left-hand pane and select New Baseline. You'll then be looking at the same wizard we just walked through. But you'll note some differences for each different type of baseline:

- For the Fixed Host Patches baselines, you'll just select a static list of patches from a repository.

- For the Host Extensions baselines, you'll choose a list of extensions to update.

- For Host Upgrade baselines, you'll select the ESX or ESXi image file you want to apply for the upgrade.

The same thing applies for VA upgrades, only you'll create vendor- and product-specific rules to apply. There are three predefined baselines for VMs/VAs (these can't be edited):

- VMware Tools Upgrade To Match Host

- VM Hardware Upgrade To Match Host

- VA Upgrade To Latest

FIGURE 2.4
Dynamic VUM
baseline criteria

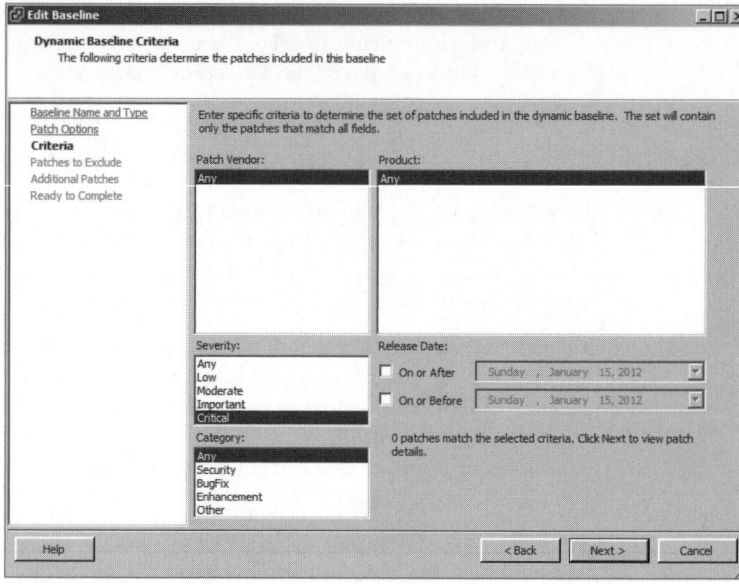

So how do you decide which options to apply? Here are some recommendations:

◆ For the most critical hosts that need to have very controlled configuration consistency, it's best to define Fixed Host Patches baselines, where each patch has to be added manually.

◆ Dynamic profiles are useful for automatically adding new patches meeting criteria to the baseline, but they can wreak havoc if deployed without adequate testing. The new filtering criteria for dynamic baselines makes it easy to control which patches are included, however, which can greatly simplify automated patching for less-critical hosts.

◆ Another sound practice is to define multiple patch repositories, both external (such as VMware's sites) and local for specific images and patch bundles.

DEFINING BASELINE GROUPS

The next important practice is to define baseline groups. What are baseline groups, exactly? Simple! They're just groups of baselines you've defined that can be applied simultaneously. For example, you may have a regularly scheduled dynamic patching baseline that you routinely apply, but once a month you apply specific patches from a fixed group. These two procedures could be combined into a baseline group that gives you more flexibility. Another option would be to combine host upgrades with patches or define a mixed group of VM or VA upgrades. You'll just need to determine what makes sense for various groups of hosts and VMs in your own environment.

To define a baseline group, follow these steps:

1. Log into vCenter and navigate to the Update Manager Administration screen. Click the Baselines And Groups tab along the top.

2. In the right-hand pane, either right-click anywhere and select New Baseline Group or click the Create button in the top-right corner.

3. The New Baseline Group Wizard opens, and you'll need to select the type of group you want — Host Baseline Group or a Virtual Machines And Virtual Appliances Baseline Group. Provide a name for the group and click Next.

4. For host groups, the next step will be to select any upgrade baselines followed by patch baselines and finally extension baselines. For VM/VA groups, you'll simply choose the option labeled Upgrade Baselines That Are Defined.

5. When you've selected these (by checking the boxes or selecting the radio buttons next to any baselines you want to include), you'll end up at the Ready To Complete screen, where you can click Finish. An example of this final screen is shown in Figure 2.5, and you can see that it includes a simple host baseline group with critical and noncritical patches as well as a default install baseline for upgrades.

FIGURE 2.5

Finalizing a host baseline group

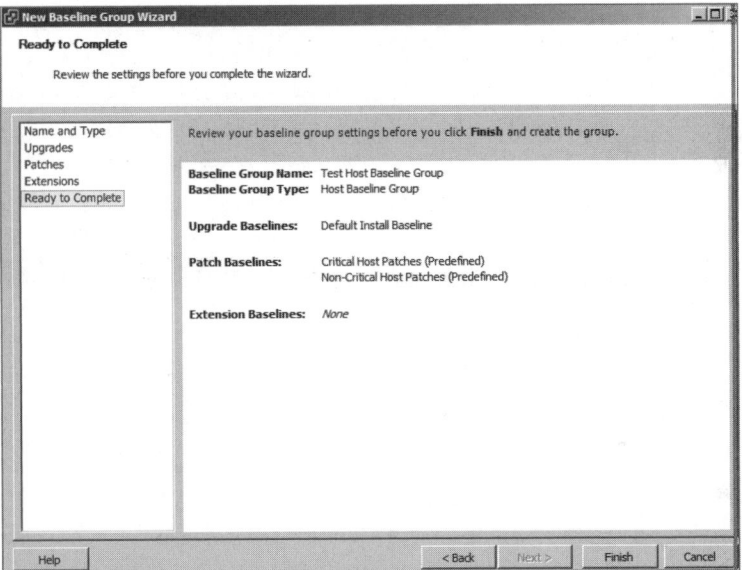

ADDITIONAL VUM SETTINGS

On the Configuration tab in VUM, there are a handful of settings that you should pay close attention to:

Network Connectivity   Here, you can set the ports used by VUM for clients to connect to as well as the patch store connectivity for ESX and ESXi hosts. You can also set the IP address or hostname of the patch store.

Download Settings   Covered earlier in the chapter in the section "Configuring VUM," this is where you specify VMware URLs from which to download patches and also where you choose internal patch stores. You can also configure proxy settings with or without authentication to access URLs.

Download Schedule   This is where you'll set up regular downloads on a schedule.

Notification Check Schedule VUM will check for patch updates and alerts on a regular basis, and this is where you can define the schedule for this as well as any email notifications you'd like to receive.

Virtual Machine Settings To be on the safe side, you can take a snapshot of any VMs before patching in case you need to roll them back. You can also specify how long the snapshots will be maintained.

ESX Host/Cluster Settings There are a number of options to consider in this area.

◆ First, you can choose whether to power off or suspend VMs before placing the host into Maintenance mode for updates. You also have the option to do nothing, which means VMs will need to be migrated to other hosts in the cluster during maintenance.

◆ You can disable removable media devices that may prevent hosts from entering Maintenance mode in the first place.

◆ For cluster settings, you can choose to temporarily disable certain features like Distributed Power Management (DPM) and Fault Tolerance and update all cluster hosts at the same time (advisable if you can do this).

The options available for hosts and clusters are shown in Figure 2.6.

FIGURE 2.6
VUM host/cluster settings

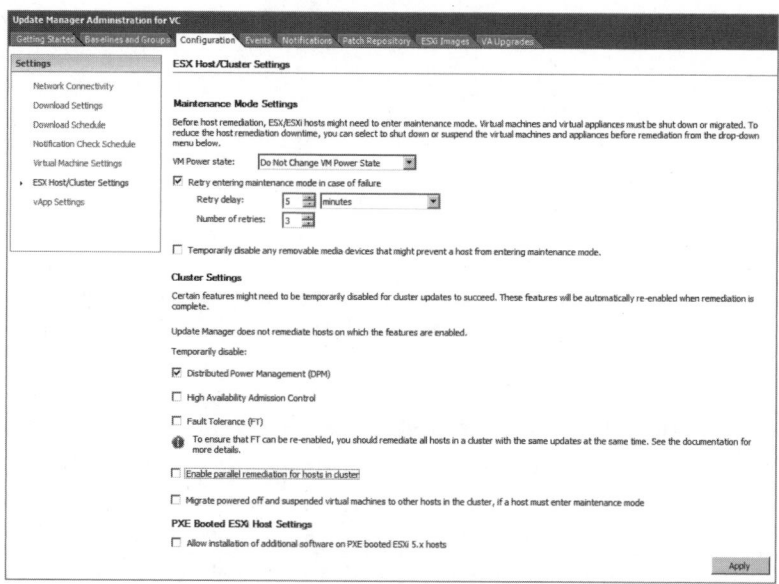

vApp Settings vApps are groups of VMs that are linked together for specific purposes. Some vApp groups may need to be rebooted to keep in synchronization with the hosts or each other, and VMware's smart reboot capability allows you to selectively reboot vApp VMs when needed.

ATTACHING BASELINES AND GROUPS

Once you have configured VUM and set up baselines and baseline groups, you need to apply the baselines and groups to hosts and VMs. This is done by *attaching* them to specific objects within vCenter. There are two locations that you'll visit to apply VUM baselines:

◆ The Hosts And Clusters view is for attaching baselines to hosts. You can attach a baseline to a datacenter, cluster, or individual host.

◆ The VMs And Templates view is for attaching baselines to VMs. You can attach a baseline to a datacenter, folder, or individual VM.

For either view, the simplest way to attach baselines and get the patching and upgrading started is by using the Upgrade Manager. Follow these steps:

1. Select the Update Manager tab along the top.

2. Once you've entered the Update Manager management tab, you'll be presented with several panes that include attached baselines, baseline groups, and simple views of the compliance status any objects have with these baselines. To attach a baseline or baseline group, right-click anywhere and choose Attach or click the Attach link in the upper-right corner.

3. The Attach Baseline Or Group Wizard appears (Figure 2.7). From here it's simple to select any defined baselines or groups or even create new ones.

FIGURE 2.7
VUM Attach
Baseline Or Group
Wizard

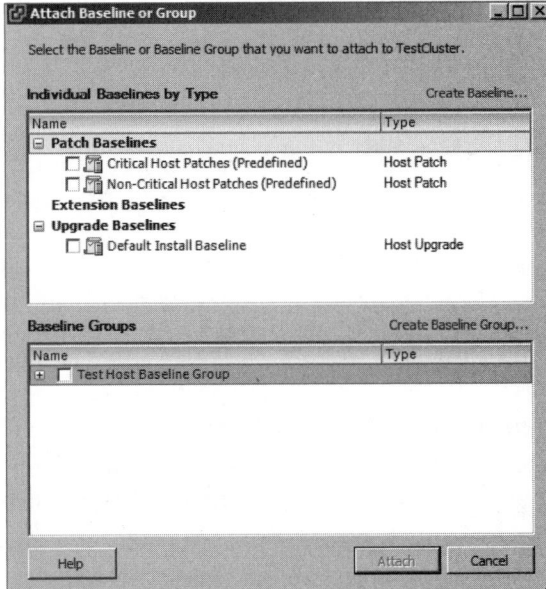

Select the baselines and/or groups and click Attach. You should see the Update Manager screen reflect these changes, as shown in Figure 2.8.

FIGURE 2.8

Host compliance status

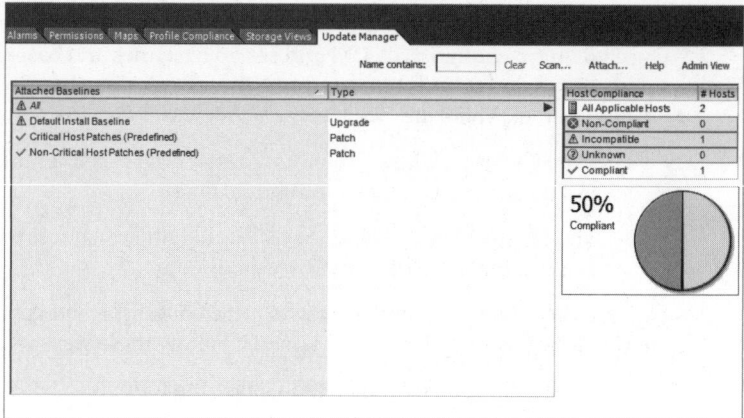

4. To manually initiate a compliance assessment, you can return to this main screen for any vCenter object and click the Scan link in the upper-right corner.

STAGING AND REMEDIATION

You've now got two more options available for patching hosts and other systems. The first, known as staging, allows you to push patches to a hypervisor host before patching occurs, which may save time when it's time to actually install the patches. This is handy when you have hosts in remote offices or locations with slow network links because you can plan appropriately before your actual change window arrives.

To set up staging, follow these steps:

1. Click the Stage button in the lower-right part of the window.

2. When the Stage Wizard opens, select Baselines And Hosts, select any exclusions for extensions and patches, and then click Finish.

The second option is to actually remediate, or immediately apply patches. Much like staging, this can be accomplished by clicking the Remediate button in the lower-right part of the window and then choosing the baselines and/or baseline groups, hosts, exclusions, and schedule you want to follow. Really, the process couldn't be much simpler!

PATCHING VIA THE COMMAND LINE

For those with a small environment who may want to push patches manually via the command line, you've got options too. Here's the process you'll follow:

1. Before performing any sort of updates, you would be wise to back up the ESXi configuration! Use the `vicfg-cfgbackup` command at the ESXi direct console or via SSH or use the vSphere CLI command of the same name. The following shows the vSphere CLI version:

```
vicfg-cfgbackup --server <Host> --save
--username root <Backup File Name>
```

2. Now, list the image profiles associated with the VMware-supplied updates:

   ```
   esxcli -s <host> --username root software sources
   profile list --depot=<path-to-zip>
   ```

3. Place the host into maintenance mode:

   ```
   vicfg-hostops --server <host> --username root --operation enter
   ```

4. Now you can run the update with the `dry-run` option, which will tell you about any potential errors or issues you may encounter:

   ```
   esxcli -s <host> --username root software profile update
   --depot=<path-to-zip> --dry-run --profile=<profile name>
   ```

5. Assuming there are no issues, go ahead and run the update:

   ```
   esxcli -s <host>--username root  software profile update
   --depot=<path-to-zip> --profile=<profile name>
   ```

6. You'll likely need to reboot the host:

   ```
   vicfg-hostops --server <host> --operation reboot
   ```

7. Finally, take the host out of Maintenance mode:

   ```
   vicfg-hostops --server <host> --operation exit
   ```

That's it! There are variations on this operation; for example, older versions of ESX and ESXi may use the `esxupdate` and `vihostupdate` tools.

Securing Communications in VMware ESXi

In general, all communications with ESXi servers uses Secure Sockets Layer (SSL) or Transport Layer Security (TLS) encryption with digital certificates. During installation, ESXi generates its own VMware certificates that are "self-signed"; in other words, these are not signed by a trusted third-party certificate authority (CA) or your own internal CA but are simply issued by VMware to provide the necessary mechanism for SSL-based encryption to take place. After installation, the default certificate and private key are located as follows:

Default SSL certificate: `/etc/vmware/ssl/rui.crt`

Default SSL private key: `/etc/vmware/ssl/rui.key`

Ideally, these should be replaced with a certificate and private key that are more trusted. Creating trusted certificates is beyond the scope of this book, but the following link describes how to create these using OpenSSL:

`www.akadia.com/services/ssh_test_certificate.html`

Replacing the default key and certificate is actually very simple on ESXi using the vSphere CLI though:

1. Remember to migrate all running VMs to another ESXi host before placing the hypervisor into maintenance mode. Place the system into maintenance mode by right-clicking the ESXi server in the vCenter console or vSphere Client interface and choosing Enter Maintenance Mode (Figure 2.9).

FIGURE 2.9
Choose Enter
Maintenance Mode.

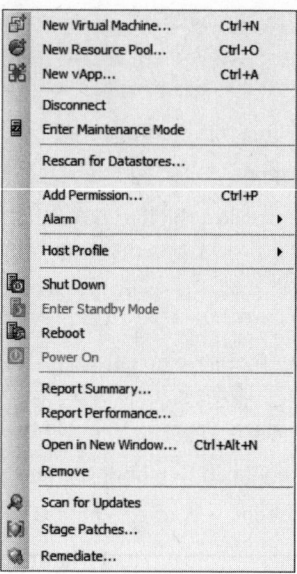

New Virtual Machine...	Ctrl+N
New Resource Pool...	Ctrl+O
New vApp...	Ctrl+A
Disconnect	
Enter Maintenance Mode	
Rescan for Datastores...	
Add Permission...	Ctrl+P
Alarm	▶
Host Profile	▶
Shut Down	
Enter Standby Mode	
Reboot	
Power On	
Report Summary...	
Report Performance...	
Open in New Window...	Ctrl+Alt+N
Remove	
Scan for Updates	
Stage Patches...	
Remediate...	

2. Next, open a vSphere CLI console.

3. At the command prompt, type the following two commands to replace the key and certificate on an individual ESXi host:

```
vifs --server <hostname> --username <user> -p rui.crt /host/ssl_cert
vifs --server <hostname> --username <user> -p rui.key /host/ssl_key
```

NOTE ssl_cert and ssl_key are actually "pointers" where those files will go, so you need to
use that exact syntax, oddly enough.

Another way to do this is even easier, in many cases. Simply replace the rui.crt and
rui.key files in the /etc/vmware/ssl directory with the new ones you've generated. To
do this, execute the following commands:

```
mv /etc/vmware/ssl/rui.crt / etc/vmware/ssl/rui.crt.old
mv etc/vmware/ssl/rui.key / etc/vmware/ssl/rui.key.old
cp <CERT FILE> /etc/vmware/ssl/rui.crt
cp <KEY FILE> / etc/vmware/ssl/rui.key
```

4. Take the host out of maintenance mode when you're finished.

That's it! There are other ways to do this, including the use of HTTP PUT commands, but this
is by far the simplest and most reasonable.

BACKING UP YOUR SETTINGS

Keep in mind that ESXi is essentially an ephemeral OS, meaning it runs only in memory. When the system reboots suddenly (from a power failure or other issue), you could lose this configuration if you're not careful. In the first minute of every hour, ESXi runs the `/sbin/auto-backup.sh` script that then writes the current configuration to `/bootbank/state.tgz`, which is the file used by ESXi when it boots to reconfigure the system. To be absolutely sure you're saving these settings, run this script manually by logging in via SSH or using the console and executing this command:

`/sbin/autobackup.sh`

Ensuring that trusted certificates are in place is a simple way to help prevent against man-in-the-middle (MITM) attacks. This can be enabled in the vCenter management console. Once you have certificates in place, log into vCenter and do the following:

1. Click the Administration menu item at the top of the window, and then select vCenter Settings.

2. In the left-hand menu, click SSL Settings. Ensure that the check box on the right side labeled vCenter Requires Verified Host SSL Certificates is checked. The SSL Settings screen is shown in Figure 2.10.

FIGURE 2.10
Verifying host certificates in vCenter

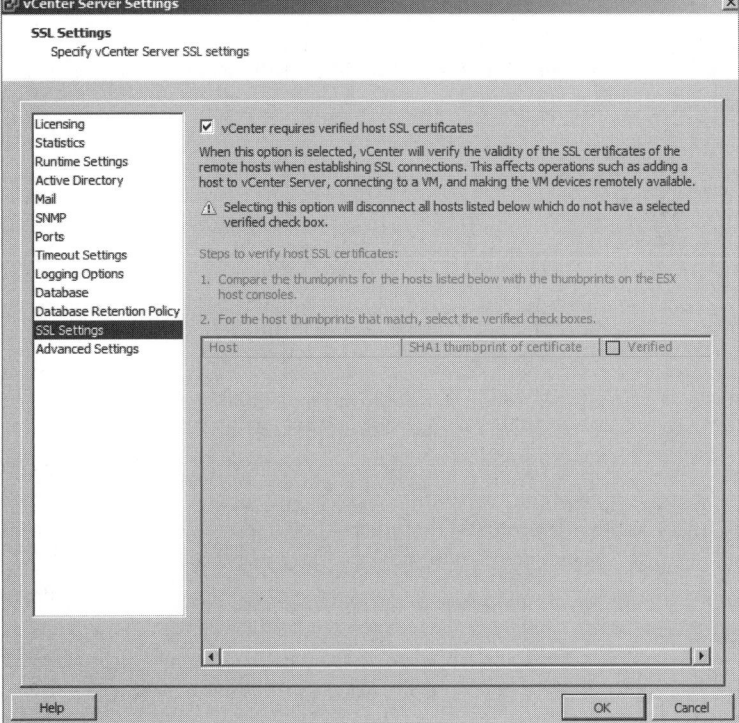

3. To verify a host certificate fingerprint for ESXi (VMware calls them *thumbprints*), log into the host's direct console. Press F2 to access the System Customization menu.

4. Select View Support Information and look for the unique fingerprint on the right-hand side, as shown in Figure 2.11.

FIGURE 2.11
Verifying ESXi SSL certificates

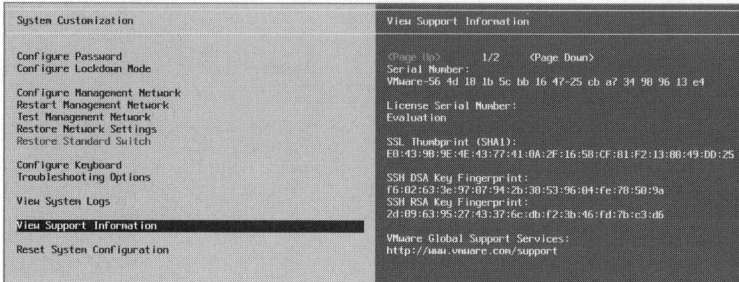

5. Ensure that these host fingerprints match for your hosts, and then select the Verify check box next to hosts in vCenter.

For more security around SSL, you should consider adding time-out values. There are two types of time-outs for SSL on ESXi:

◆ The Read time-out applies to connections that have already completed the SSL handshake process with the server on TCP port 443.

◆ The Handshake time-out applies to systems that haven't yet completed the SSL handshake.

Both time-outs should be set. To change these settings, perform the following steps:

1. Log in to the direct console or use SSH to access the ESXi Shell. Change into the `/etc/vmware/hostd` directory. Use the Vi text editor to open the `config.xml` file.

2. Look for the section header labeled `<vmacore>`. A few lines down you'll see the section header `<ssl>` with various configuration parameters. Enter the following two new lines under `<ssl>`:

```
<readTimeoutMs>15000</readTimeoutMs>
<handshakeTimeoutMs>15000</handshakeTimeoutMs>
```

Your file should look similar to Figure 2.12. These settings are in milliseconds, so the preceding lines would set both time-outs to 15 seconds, which is a reasonable value in most environments. If you have network latency or other issues that may cause longer handshake times, you may want to extend these.

3. Save the file (press Escape, then enter `:wq`).

4. Restart the hostd services by running the following command:

```
/etc/init.d/hostd restart
```

FIGURE 2.12

SSL time-out settings

```
<vmacore>
    <pluginBaseDir>/lib/</pluginBaseDir>
    <!-- default thread pool configuration for Posix impl -->
    <threadPool>
        <IoMin>2</IoMin>
        <IoMax>44</IoMax>
        <TaskMin>2</TaskMin>
        <TaskMax>18</TaskMax>
        <!-- Do not set MaxFdsPerThread if hostdMinFds is set above -->
        <!-- MaxFdsPerThread> 2048 </MaxFdsPerThread -->
        <NumKeepAlive>8</NumKeepAlive>
        <ThreadCheckTimeSecs>600</ThreadCheckTimeSecs>
        <ThreadStackSizeKb>256</ThreadStackSizeKb>
        <threadNamePrefix>hostd</threadNamePrefix>
    </threadPool>

    <rootPasswdExpiration>false</rootPasswdExpiration>

    <ssl>
        <readTimeoutMs>15000</readTimeoutMs>
        <handshakeTimeoutMs>15000</handshakeTimeoutMs>
        <doVersionCheck> false </doVersionCheck>
        <useCompression>true</useCompression>
        <libraryPath>/lib/</libraryPath>
    </ssl>
```

Another way to secure communications to and from ESX/ESXi hosts is by using IPSec. This only works on hosts running version 4.1 and later, and you'll need to enable IPv6 in order to do it. To enable IPv6 and add an address through vCenter, do the following:

1. Select an ESX/ESXi host, then click the Configuration tab. Select the Networking link on the left-hand side.

2. Then, on the right-hand side, click Properties. You'll get a simple pop-up window. Click the check box labeled Enable IPv6 Support On This System and click OK.

3. Now you'll need to reboot the host, which means you'll need to migrate VMs from it first. Once this is done, you can set IPv6 addresses on adapters for the various network connections set up on the host. Return to the Networking section of the Configuration tab.

4. For each vSwitch, click Properties. Select a port group and either double-click or click the Edit button, and then click the second tab (IP Settings). You should now be able to configure one or more IPv6 addresses easily.

Once you have IPv6 addresses set up, you are ready to configure IPSec. IPSec can be configured with the vSphere CLI vicfg-ipsec command. The following are the parameters you need to set:

--server <host>	The host on which you're configuring IPSec
--add-sa	Adds an IPSec security association (SA)
--sa-src	The IPv6 address of the vCenter server
--sa-dst	The IPv6 address of the ESX/ESXi host
--sa-mode	The IPSec mode, usually transport

`--spi`	The Security Parameter Index (SPI), or SA identifier
`--ealgo`	Encryption algorithm to use
`--ekey`	Encryption key for the SA
`--ialgo`	The authentication algorithm to use
`--ikey`	The authentication encryption key to use
`<SA name>`	A unique name for the SA

Seems like a lot, and it is! Here's an example where I configure a simple transport-mode SA for the host `esx.abc.com`, using the aes128-cbc (AES 128-bit encryption with Cipher Block Chaining) encryption for the SA, HMAC-SHA2 encryption for authentication, and the SA name of TestSA:

```
vicfg-ipsec --server esx.abc.com
--add-sa --sa-src 2001:FFFF::1111:2222 --sa-dst
2001:AAAA::1111:2222 --sa-mode transport --spi 0x9999 --ealgo aes128-cbc
--ekey 0x2038975092830239876490729874092789841201l --ialgo hmac-sha2
--ikey 0x3287648762876287628763487268476827 6287633 TestSA
```

The next step, after creating a security association, is to establish a security policy for encrypting vSphere Client traffic from the management server to the host. This also requires a complex `vicfg-ipsec` command line with numerous parameters:

`--server <host>`	The host on which you're configuring IPSec
`--add-sp`	Adds an IPSec security policy
`--sp-src`	The IPv6 address of the vCenter server
`--sp-dst`	The IPv6 address of the ESX/ESXi host
`--src-port`	Source port for IPSec traffic
`--dst-port`	Destination port for IPSec traffic
`--ulproto`	Upper-layer protocol to encrypt (often TCP)
`--dir`	Traffic direction (in this case, inbound)
`--action`	The action to take for the policy (`ipsec`)
`--sp-mode`	The SP mode; should match the SA mode
`--sa-name`	The SA to associate with the policy
`<SP name>`	A unique name for the SP

Here's an example in keeping with the preceding one, where I apply the policy to host `esx.abc.com`, with the same IPv6 addresses (you'll need to add the /128 subnet mask at the end for a single IPv6 host), for TCP traffic coming to port 443 and the SP name of `TestSP`:

```
vicfg-ipsec --server esx.abc.com --add-sp --sp-src 2001:FFFF::1111:2222/128
--sp-dst 2001:AAAA::1111:2222/128 --src-port 0 --dst-port 443 --ulproto tcp
--dir in --action ipsec --sp-mode transport --sa-name TestSA TestSP
```

There are plenty of other options for configuring IPSec, including configuration options that allow IPSec to act as a true traffic filtering mechanism (more like a firewall). You should explore the options that work best in your organization; keep in mind that this is a complex protocol that can cause you serious headaches if you misconfigure anything.

In addition, you'll need to set up IPSec on the vCenter server the host is communicating with. I'll include a Windows 2008 IPSec example when I cover Hyper-V later in the chapter.

Change and Remove Default Settings on VMware ESXi

By default, a number of services are running on the ESXi platform with the master service daemon hostd acting as a proxy for them. In some cases, you may be able to turn some of these off.

There are three services that many choose to disable:

◆ Web Access login page

◆ Managed Object Browser

◆ Host Welcome login page

All of these are somewhat tied to accessing ESXi information through a web browser, which is enabled by default by pointing the browser to the IP address of the management interface on the ESXi system. The Managed Object Browser is used primarily by the vSphere software development kit (SDK) to peruse the host's management object model. The login pages can almost always be disabled with little to no impact. However, the Managed Object Browser may be used by a variety of programs, and you should test carefully before disabling this.

An additional measure you can take for any of the hostd services listed is to force the use of HTTPS instead of HTTP. This should be carefully considered depending on the environment the platform is in and the use cases you have because HTTPS does have a slightly higher impact on performance, although not usually significant in enterprise environments.

TIP Disabling these services should have minimal impact on an enterprise environment managed through vCenter or even the vSphere Client. Be sure you test this first though! VMware recommends *not* disabling the Web Access login page on ESXi v5.*x* because this can break High Availability (HA) services.

Follow these steps to turn off unneeded services:

1. To determine what services are running, execute the following command via SSH or at the direct ESXi console:

```
vim-cmd proxysvc/service-list
```

You should see output similar to that in Figure 2.13.

FIGURE 2.13

Listing ESXi hostd
services

```
~ # vim-cmd proxysvc/service_list
(vim.ProxyService.EndpointSpec) [
    (vim.ProxyService.LocalServiceSpec) {
        dynamicType = <unset>,
        serverNamespace = "/",
        accessMode = "httpsWithRedirect",
        port = 8309,
    },
    (vim.ProxyService.LocalServiceSpec) {
        dynamicType = <unset>,
        serverNamespace = "/client/clients.xml",
        accessMode = "httpAndHttps",
        port = 8309,
    },
    (vim.ProxyService.LocalServiceSpec) {
        dynamicType = <unset>,
        serverNamespace = "/fdm",
        accessMode = "httpsOnly",
        port = 9089,
    },
```

2. Disable unneeded services using the following commands (substitute `vim-cmd` with `vmware-vim-cmd` for ESX platforms):

Web Access login page
```
vim-cmd proxysvc/remove_service "/ui"
"httpsWithRedirect"
```

Managed Object Browser
```
vim-cmd proxysvc/remove_service "/mob"
"httpsWithRedirect"
```

Host Welcome login page
```
vim-cmd proxysvc/remove_service "/"
"httpsWithRedirect"
```

3. For each service listed, note the `<accessMode>` variable. There are several options you'll see configured, depending on the service. To use HTTPS, configure one of the following:

`httpsOnly` — Forces the use of HTTPS. Connections using HTTP will not get a response

`httpsWithRedirect` — Redirects HTTP attempts to the appropriate port/resource.

4. The settings should take effect immediately, but run `/etc/init.d/hostd restart` and then run the `/sbin/autobackup.sh` script just to be sure.

Enable Operational Security on VMware ESXi

There are several support services that should ideally be configured for optimal virtualization operations. Some of these will be covered separately in later chapters (syslog, for example, is covered in Chapter 7, "Logging and Auditing"), but two in particular warrant mention here:

Network Time Protocol (NTP) NTP is a critical support service for security because it provides a sound means to correlate time stamps between events on different systems. Without NTP, log data from multiple systems (including VMs, hypervisors, and management platforms) cannot be accurately linked together to reconstruct events and incidents.

Simple Network Management Protocol (SNMP) SNMP allows administrators to monitor systems within the environment for configuration and event details. For SNMP, you'll need to configure community strings, which identify the SNMP services both polling and responding in your environment. Many think of SNMP community strings as shared passwords for SNMP services, and this is a reasonably close approximation. The default community strings used by many SNMP implementations and products are public and private. Since these are so common, most attackers trying to enumerate or change configuration settings via SNMP will try these. You should most definitely plan to change them!

Both NTP and SNMP are really operational support services for security but are nonetheless critically important. NTP should always be configured, whereas SNMP configuration will depend on your environment.

CONFIGURING NTP

Enabling and configuring both NTP and SNMP on VMware platforms is actually fairly straightforward. To enable NTP on an ESX or ESXi host, the simplest method is using the vSphere Client with vCenter:

1. Log in to vCenter and access the Inventory ➢ Hosts And Clusters area.

2. Choose a host; then click the Configuration tab along the top. Click the Security Profile link along the left-hand side to show the Services and Firewall settings.

3. Click the Properties link next to the Services listing. You should see an entry for NTP Daemon. Highlight this entry, then click the Options button in the lower-right corner.

   You'll see the options screen for the NTP daemon. There are two categories of options available to choose from. The default screen, General (Figure 2.14), allows you to start the daemon and choose how it will start in the future (automatically, manually, or only when specific ports are opened ahead of time).

FIGURE 2.14
NTP daemon
options

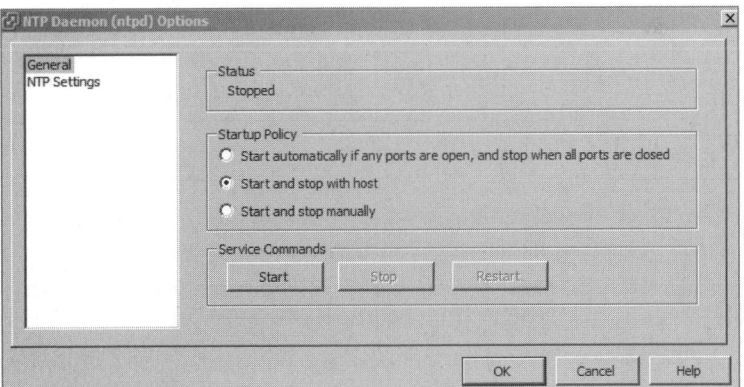

For most enterprises, the NTP daemon should start and stop with the host, but you can choose to start and stop with open and closed ports if the host is exposed in a DMZ or more public-facing subnet.

4. Click the Start button to start the daemon now, or you can start it in a moment after adding NTP servers.

5. Select the second category of NTP daemon settings, aptly titled NTP Settings. There's really only one option here, and that's to add NTP servers from which you want the ESX/ESXi host to get its time. Click the Add button, enter the IP address or hostname of a single NTP server, and finish by clicking OK. You should see a screen similar to Figure 2.15.

FIGURE 2.15
Adding NTP servers to the host NTP configuration

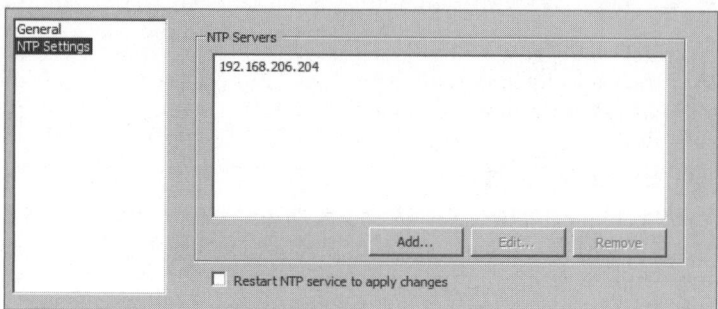

A good rule of thumb is to add at least three NTP servers. There are many external time servers to choose from, but a good list of reliable time services (for those in the United States) can be found at the National Institute of Standards and Technology (NIST):

`http://tf.nist.gov/tf-cgi/servers.cgi.`

6. If the NTP daemon is already started, you can check the box labeled Restart NTP Service To Apply Changes and then click OK.

   If you did not start the service in step 4 before adding NTP servers, click the General category on the left-hand side again, and then click Start before clicking OK.

7. When you are back at the Security Profile Configuration screen, note that you can also configure the firewall ports and recognized services below the standard Services options. When you click Properties for the firewall, you can also enable the NTP daemon here by selecting it and clicking the Options button in the lower-right corner.

Enabling NTP via the command line is also simple with the `vicfg-ntp` command! Here are the steps to take:

1. First, access the vSphere CLI, and add servers:
   ```
   vicfg-ntp -a <NTP server IP> --server <host IP or name>
   --username <username>
   ```

2. Repeat this for each NTP server you would like to add.

3. Then, start the NTP service on the host as follows:
   ```
   vicfg-ntp --start --server <host IP or name> --username <username>
   ```

That's all there is to it for remote command-line control of NTP services on ESXi hosts. For ESX hosts, the syntax is similar but you'd use the `esxcfg-ntp` command instead.

CONFIGURING **SNMP**

To configure SNMP on ESX and ESXi hosts, the most reliable and simple method is to use the `vicfg-snmp` script from the vSphere CLI. You'll also need to ensure that the SNMP port (UDP 161) is open on the ESX/ESXi host.

1. Run the following command to determine whether SNMP is enabled on the host:

   ```
   vicfg-snmp --server <server IP/name> --user <user> --show
   ```

   You'll get back information on whether the SNMP agent is enabled (0 or 1) and the port that SNMP will use.

2. To check whether the SNMP port is open, you will need to check the firewall configuration on the host. This can be done using the vSphere Client or the `esxcli` command for ESXi v5 hosts.

   To use the vSphere Client, connect to the host or to vCenter, navigate to the Hosts And Clusters area, and select a host. Click the Configuration tab in the right-hand pane, and then select the Security Profile link in the list on the left-hand side. Look at the section labeled Firewall. You should see SNMP Server or snmpd listed for incoming (UDP port 161) and potentially outgoing (UDP port 162) on the host if the ports are open. If they're not listed, click the Properties link, find the entry with the same name in the Firewall Properties window, check the box next to it, and then click OK (Figure 2.16).

FIGURE 2.16
Enabling SNMP ports in the ESX/ESXi firewall

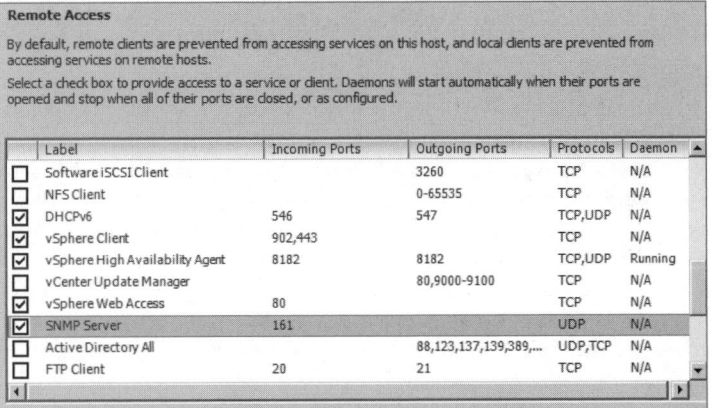

To check the firewall status from the command line, use the `esxcli` command in the vSphere CLI as follows:

```
esxcli --server <server IP/name> --username <user>
network firewall ruleset list
```

3. After being prompted for a password, you should retrieve a list of the services known to the firewall as well as their status (enabled/disabled). To enable a firewall service using the `esxcli` command, run the following (admittedly complicated) command:

```
esxcli --server <server IP/name> --username <user>
network firewall ruleset set -e 1 --ruleset-id=snmp
```

This command will enable (via the option -e 1) the known SNMP rule in the ESXi firewall.

4. Once you have the firewall ports open and the service enabled, you can enable and configure the SNMP services with the `vicfg-snmp` command. Start the SNMP service (if it's not running) by using the following command:

```
vicfg-snmp --server <server IP/name> --username <user> --enable
```

This command will run as is on ESXi, but for ESX systems you will need to add community strings associated with the SNMP service:

```
vicfg-snmp --server <server IP/name> --username <user>
--communities <community strings> --enable
```

6. You can optionally point to SNMP trap targets:

```
vicfg-snmp.pl --server <hostname> --username <username>
--password <password> -t <target hostname>@<port>/<community>
```

This is shown in Figure 2.17.

FIGURE 2.17
Setting SNMP traps on ESXi

While not a hypervisor security control, another place you can configure SNMP within the vSphere infrastructure is on vCenter itself. This is where you can control the community strings used for communication between external SNMP receivers and vCenter and control the ports and URLs needed to send SNMP alerts. To configure these settings, log into vCenter and select the Administration menu at the top. Then choose the vCenter Server Settings menu item, and click the SNMP option in the new window that appears. You'll see a list of SNMP receivers that can be configured with a URL, port, and community string, as shown in Figure 2.18.

Be sure to download any Management Information Base (MIB) files that correspond to vCenter and ESX/ESXi from VMware's Download Center.

Secure and Monitor Critical Configuration Files in VMware ESXi

There are a number of files on ESXi hosts that are considered critical from a security configuration standpoint. Some of these are somewhat static in nature, staying consistent over time unless system changes are made and preserved. Others are much more dynamic in nature, changing date and time stamps regularly, with some also fluctuating in size as well. The base list of files you will typically want to monitor can usually be found at `https://<hostname or IP>/host`. You will likely need to authenticate to get this list. You'll also notice that the files do not have specific directory attributes associated with them, so you won't be able to identify exactly where they reside on the ESXi file system. While you could track them down, we won't need to do this for monitoring file integrity because you'll simply specify the `/host/<filename>` syntax just as you see it in this listing.

FIGURE 2.18
vCenter Server
SNMP settings

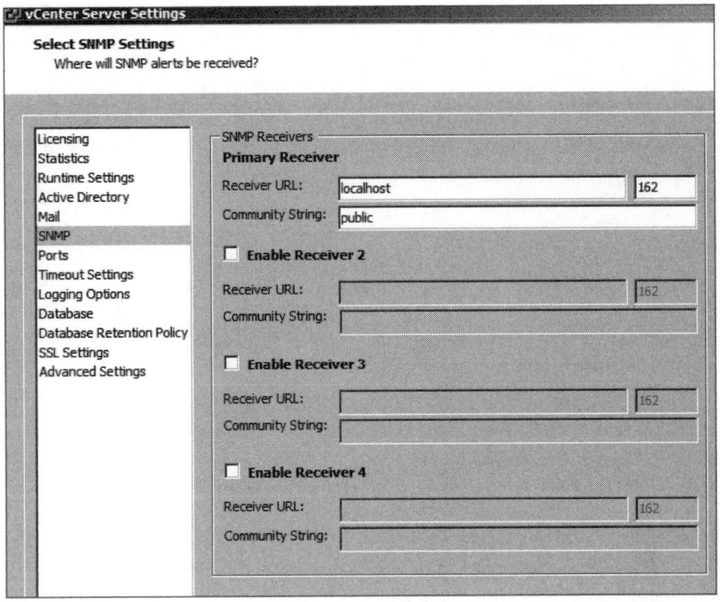

The following are additional files that tend to stay somewhat static and change only when the system is deliberately updated. These files should be considered critical and you should keep track of them by monitoring their integrity (covered shortly):

```
/etc/vmware/esx.conf
/etc/vmware/snmp.xml
/etc/vmware/vmware.lic
/etc/vmware/hostd/proxy.xml
/etc/hosts
/etc/motd
/etc/openwsman/openwsman.conf
/etc/sfcb/sfcb.cfg
/etc/syslog.conf
/etc/vmware/hostd/config.xml
/etc/vmware/ssl/rui.crt
/etc/vmware/ssl/rui.key
/etc/vmware/config
/etc/vmware/configrules
```

Other files that are important to track include security-related configuration files in the /etc directory, such as these:

```
/etc/passwd
/etc/shadow
/etc/ntp.conf
/etc/inittab
/etc/profile
/etc/rc.local
```

```
/etc/resolv.conf
/etc/vmsyslog.conf
/etc/security/access.conf
```

There are also a number of files that are considered important as part of ESXi's /host listing but are updated more regularly, which results in changes to the Date Modified setting. The size of the files should not change regularly, though. These are as follows:

```
/etc/vmware/license.cfg
/etc/opt/vmware/vpxa/vpxa.cfg
/var/log/ipmi/0/sdr_content.raw
/var/log/ipmi/0/sdr_header.raw
/var/log/ipmi/0/sensor_readings.raw
```

Finally, there are several more files listed in /host that change very frequently and may be difficult to monitor on a regular basis. Because these are important log files, you should be cognizant of them, but log files rarely stay static for long:

```
/var/log/messages
/var/log/vmware/hostd.log
/var/log/vmware/vpx/vpxa.log
```

So, now that I've defined the files you'll likely want to monitor for integrity, how can you go about getting and monitoring them? The simplest way on ESXi systems is to download the files to a trusted storage location using the vSphere CLI, then perform a hashing operation on them using a variety of tools for Windows or other systems.

The command to download the files is simple:

```
vifs --server <server name or IP> --username <user> --get /host/<filename>
```

Once those files are stored in a central location, you can run a quick integrity check using the common tools md5sum or sha1sum. The latter is actually a viable command on ESXi systems by default, but you'll typically want to download the files first and then run the hashing command versus the other way around.

Simply run the executable as follows:

```
sha1sum <filename> > filename_sum.txt
```

TIP   Windows versions of hashing tools are plentiful, but a tried-and-true Windows sha-1sum binary can be downloaded from GnuPG at ftp://ftp.gnupg.org/gcrypt/binary/sha1sum.exe.

This is not the most efficient way to do this, however. Scripting the entire process makes a lot more sense, and a batch script is simple to create.

Secure Local Users and Groups on VMware ESXi

ESX and ESXi platforms have local users that can be accessed from the command line locally (using the ESX Console or ESXi Direct Console User Interface, or DCUI) or by using a variety of remote tools (SSH is the one most commonly used). These users are listed in the file /etc/passwd on both platforms. The passwords associated with the users are listed in the /etc/shadow file, just as you'd expect on any modern Unix/Linux platform. There are four security guidelines you should follow related to local users on ESX and ESXi hypervisor systems:

1. Limit the number of local users present on the system as much as possible.

2. Restrict use of the all-powerful root account whenever possible.

3. Implement local password policies for complexity and rotation.

4. Implement Active Directory authentication if at all possible.

LIMITING LOCAL USERS

For vSphere 4.x and 5.x systems, there are a small number of local users present on the system. The following users are present by default in most environments:

root: The root user is the system's most powerful administrator account.

vpxuser: The vpxuser account is a very important user created on each ESXi host when it is connected to (and thus managed by) the VMware vCenter management platform. This account is generated by vCenter with a random 32-character password and is added to the vCenter Administrator role.

dcui: The Direct Console User Interface (DCUI) account is a privileged account for local console access at the system within a datacenter.

daemon: The daemon account is a "catch all" account for ESXi services and is noninteractive.

nfsnobody: The nfsnobody account can be configured as a delegate user for NFS storage if needed. On older versions of ESX and ESXi, this account was named vimuser.

The number of groups on a modern ESXi platform is also much smaller than previous ESX and ESXi versions. The root group contains only the root user, and the daemon group only contains the daemon user. Both the users and nfsnobody groups are empty by default.

With the exception of the nfsnobody account, all of the default accounts on ESXi are needed. The key is to not add any new ones unless they are absolutely needed! The ESX platform's Service Console offered standard Linux commands for controlling privilege use (such as su and sudo), but ESXi offers only su. In general, the fewer interactive user accounts you have on a system, the better.

There are numerous ways to add, delete, and modify local users on ESXi systems. First, though, you should check to see what users exist. This can be done as follows:

1. From the local DCUI or via SSH, simply type **cat /etc/passwd**. All local users should be listed here, as shown in Figure 2.19.

FIGURE 2.19

Contents of ESXi /etc/passwd file

```
root:x:0:0:Administrator:/:/bin/sh
daemon:x:2:2:System daemons:/:/sbin/nologin
nfsnobody:x:65534:65534:Anonymous NFS User:/:/sbin/nologin
dcui:x:100:100:DCUI User:/:/sbin/nologin
vpxuser:x:500:100:VMware VirtualCenter administration account:/:/sbin/nologin
```

2. Use one of the following methods to get information about users and groups:

   ◆ Using the vSphere CLI, you can list all local groups, as well as the users present in each, with the following command:

   ```
   vicfg-user --server <server IP/name> --username <user> -e group -o list
   ```

   ◆ An alternative that lists only the local users as well as their full names and User ID (UID) numbers and whether they have shell access or not (0 or 1) is the following:

   ```
   vicfg-user --server <server IP/name> --username <user> -e user -o list
   ```

   ◆ As a final option, you can connect directly to the ESXi host using the vSphere Client. Once connected, select the Local Users & Groups tab on the right-hand side. You will have two View tabs in this pane, one for users and the other for groups. Double-clicking any of the users or groups will bring up an editing screen, where you can modify attributes, settings, passwords, and membership. A user editing screen is shown in Figure 2.20.

FIGURE 2.20
Local ESXi user properties in the vSphere Client

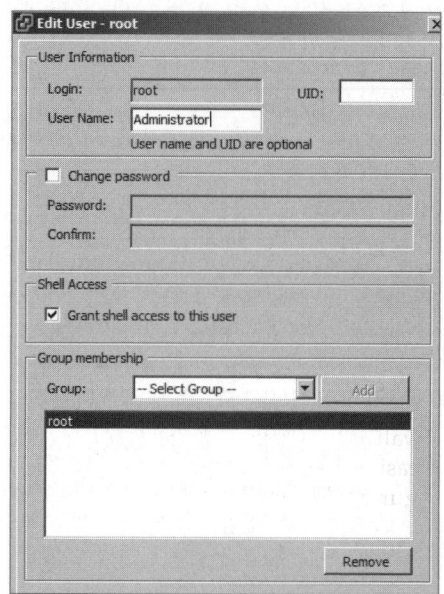

Users can also be managed with the vSphere CLI (remember that the `--username` parameter refers to the admin user for the ESXi host, not the local user you're editing).

   ◆ To add a new local user, run the following command:

   ```
   vicfg-user --server <server IP/name> --username <user> --entity user
   --login <Login Name> --operation add
   ```

   ◆ Groups can be created with a similar command:

   ```
   vicfg-user --server <server IP/name> --username <user> --entity group
   --group <Group Name> --operation add
   ```

◆ To delete users and groups, the `vicfg-user` syntax is similar. To delete a single user, run the following:

```
vicfg-user --server <server IP/name> --username <user> --entity user
--login <Login Name> --operation delete
```

◆ Deleting groups is also simple, with the caveat that all users in the group must be removed first (covered next):

```
vicfg-user --server <server IP/name> --username <user> --entity group
--group <Group Name> --operation delete
```

◆ Modifying users is also performed with the `vicfg-user` command, adding new parameters and changing the operation to `modify` like this:

```
vicfg-user --server <server IP/name> --username <user> --entity user
--login <Login Name> --newpassword <user password> --operation modify
```

◆ Adding and removing users from groups can be done in the same command:

```
vicfg-user --server <server IP/name> --username <user> --entity group
--group <Group Name> --operation modify --adduser <username>
--removeuser <username>
```

RESTRICTING THE LOCAL ROOT ACCOUNT

The second major step to securing local users on ESXi hosts is to restrict the local root account if possible. With ESX, this was easily done using the `sudo` command and the `/etc/sudoers` file where explicit restrictions for user accounts and groups could be defined. Unfortunately, `sudo` doesn't exist on the latest versions of ESXi. You have two options available to you:

◆ Enable lockdown mode, which restricts all remote access other than vCenter. Local access is available to disable lockdown mode as well.

◆ Restrict SSH root logins in the `/etc/ssh/sshd_config` file.

We will walk through both of these procedures.

You can easily enable lockdown mode during the process of adding a host into vCenter, as shown in Figure 2.21.

You can also enable lockdown mode using vCenter in the following manner:

1. Select the Inventory area, then Hosts And Clusters, and finally, choose a specific ESXi host.

2. Click the Configuration tab in the right-hand pane, then choose the Security Profile link on the left side.

3. Once there, scroll down to the Lockdown Mode category and click the Edit link. A small window will pop up with a single check box for enabling lockdown mode.

A final option is to use the local DCUI console at the host itself by choosing Configure Lockdown Mode at the console and then selecting the Enable Lockdown Mode toggle when the windows appears, as shown in Figure 2.22.

Although this doesn't truly rescind all root access to the host, it accomplishes much of the same goal — restricting administrative access.

FIGURE 2.21
Configuring lockdown mode when adding a vCenter host

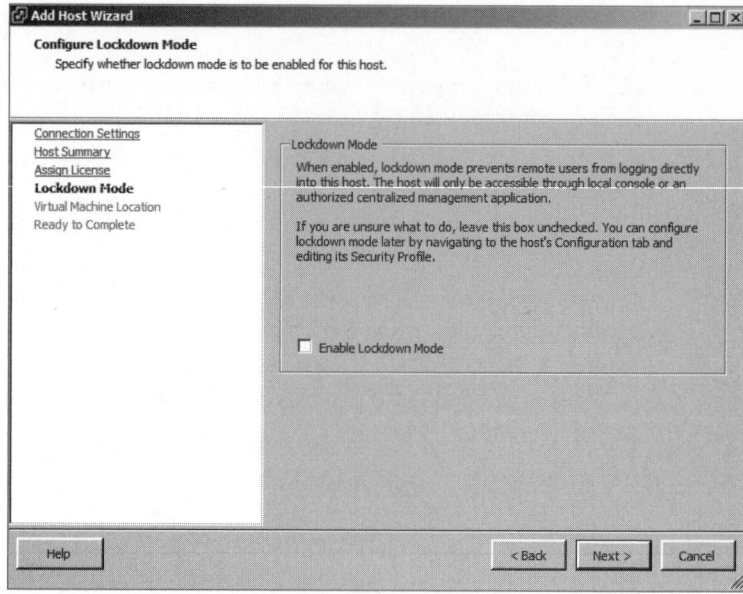

FIGURE 2.22
Configuring lockdown mode using the DCUI

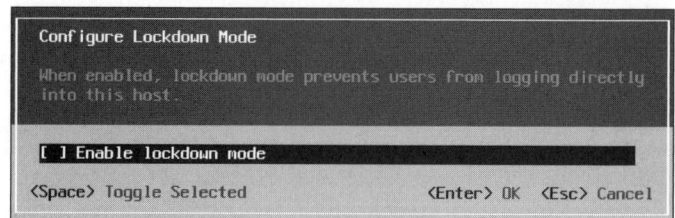

The other method, more familiar to most Linux users, is to restrict SSH root logins in the /etc/ssh/sshd_config file. Open this with the Vi editor, then scroll down to the line that reads PermitRootLogin and ensure that it is set to no, as shown in the bottom line of Figure 2.23.

FIGURE 2.23
Restricting root SSH logins

The last step you can do is create and enforce a policy requiring the use of regular logins and then using the su utility to change to root. This creates a log entry in the /scratch/log/auth.log and /scratch/log/shell.log files. These same log entries are mirrored in /var/log/auth.log and /var/log/shell.log. Logging will be covered in more depth in Chapter 7.

IMPLEMENT AND ENFORCE PASSWORD POLICIES

The third key aspect of local user control is enforcing password policies. With ESXi, establishing and modifying password policies is actually pretty simple. ESXi uses a modified version of the Linux pluggable authentication module (PAM) system that allows for fairly granular control over the most common configuration options. The following can be easily set:

Password entry retries: The number of times a user can fail to enter their password in the ESXi Shell before being denied access.

Complexity: There are four character classes used to define passwords in PAM. These are uppercase letters, lowercase letters, numbers, and special characters like exclamation points and other punctuation. You can define how many characters are required for the password depending on the number of character classes used.

To modify these settings, modify the file /etc/pam.d/system-auth-generic (ESXi 4.*x*) or /etc/pam.d/passwd (ESXi 5.*x*). Once the file is opened, look for the following line:

```
password    requisite    /lib/security/$ISA/pam_passwdqc.so
retry=3 min=A,B,C,D,E
```

Here's how to break down this line. The retry= value represents the number of failed password entry attempts that are tolerated before the user is denied access. The default value is 3, and this is reasonable for most organizations. The next section, min=A,B,C,D,E, takes a bit more to understand. Here's what each of those digits represent:

A   Minimum number of characters required for a password using only one character class (default is 8)

B   Minimum number of characters required for a password using two character classes (default is 8)

C   Minimum number of characters required for a passphrase (default is 8)

D   Minimum number of characters required for a password using three character classes (default is 7)

E   Minimum number of characters required for a password using all four character classes (default is 6)

A key point to note is that the first and last character of the password won't count toward the character class count (which makes sense, because people would try to use horrible passwords like Password).

So, what's the best way to set password policy for optimal security? Here's what I recommend, and this will usually stand up to scrutiny:

```
password    requisite    /lib/security/$ISA/pam_passwdqc.so
retry=3 min=15,12,10,8,8
```

Some of you may be thinking that this looks a bit draconian. Unfortunately, passwords are pretty easy to guess and crack when less-stringent standards are used. As mentioned earlier, you should be limiting local account use in the first place, which may leave you with only the root account and a "regular" user account for each administrator. All of these should be considered incredibly important accounts, and thus more restrictive password policies will help to deter unauthorized access.

IMPLEMENTING ACTIVE DIRECTORY AUTHENTICATION

The fourth consideration for controlling user access to and interaction with the ESXi hosts is by implementing Active Directory authentication and authorization. Enabling Active Directory authentication should be considered mandatory, and most auditors and security teams will ask to see this in place. This can greatly simplify the administration of ESXi hosts, especially in a large, complex environment with multiple admins. The beauty of AD is the ability to add and remove administrative users from a centralized AD group, which is much simpler than logging in to each ESXi platform and making user-related changes there. In some cases, the simplest solution is also the most secure, and this definitely qualifies!

Before enabling Active Directory, ensure that the following prerequisites are in place:

◆ A specially named group, ESX Admins, must be created in Active Directory. It must contain all user accounts you want to have access to the hosts.

◆ NTP should be enabled, and time should be synced to the same time servers as the Active Directory domain controllers.

◆ DNS on each hypervisor host should be able to resolve domain controllers and the domain in general.

◆ ESXi platforms should have the same domain suffix as the domain controllers they'll authenticate to.

Once you have these steps completed, you can configure Active Directory authentication via the vSphere Client. Use the client to connect to vCenter or the host directly. In vCenter, you'll need to navigate to the Inventory section, select Hosts And Clusters, and then choose a specific host. Once you have the host selected, select the Configuration tab in the right-hand pane, and then choose Authentication Services from the list on the left side. You'll see two options listed in this section, Directory Services Configuration and Domain Settings. Both can be edited by clicking the Properties link in the upper-right corner. Then follow these steps:

1. From the first drop-down menu, select Active Directory.

2. In the Domain Settings section, enter the domain the host will be joining, and optionally check the box to use a vSphere authentication proxy. Then enter the IP address of this proxy server.

   Entering a proxy server is optional, but it's an excellent capability to include because it allows hosts to connect to a domain *without* using or storing domain credentials in their configuration. The proxy can be accessed with vCenter credentials and will then handle all authentication with the domain services.

3. Finally, click Join Domain. If you entered configuration details for the vSphere authentication proxy, the host will attempt to contact it and will pass through your existing credentials. Otherwise, you'll be prompted to enter credentials with privileges for adding hosts to the domain. These configuration options are shown in Figure 2.24.

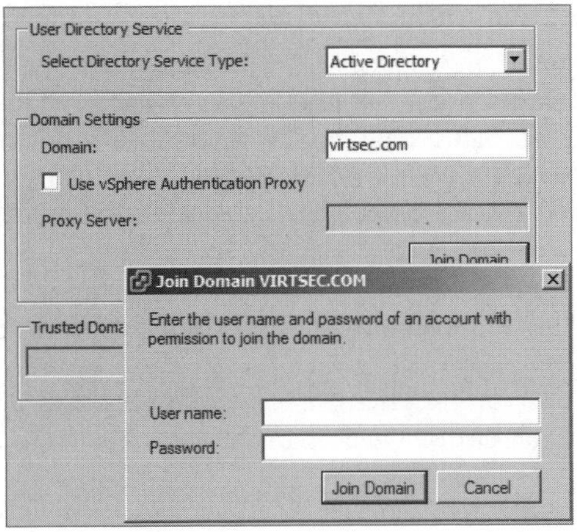

FIGURE 2.24
Adding ESXi hosts
to a domain

Another secure way to communicate with a vSphere authentication proxy is by importing a digital certificate to the ESXi host. This can make communication between ESXi hosts and the proxy simpler to manage without the headache of entering credentials. Follow these steps:

1. In the main Authentication Services configuration screen, click Import Certificate in the upper-right corner

2. You'll be asked to enter the IP address of the proxy as well as the path to the certificate file.

Another way to do this is to use the `vicfg-authconfig` vSphere CLI command to configure Active Directory membership on a specific ESXi host:

1. Run the following command:

```
vicfg-authconfig --server=<host address/name> --username=<host
username> --authscheme AD --joindomain <AD Domain Name>
--adusername=<Active Directory Admin username> --adpassword=<Active
Directory Admin Password>
```

2. You'll be prompted for the ESXi host password. Enter it, and then you should see a "Successfully Joined <Domain>" message.

3. To verify that the host is now a part of the AD domain, use the following command:

```
vicfg-authconfig --server <host address/name> --authscheme AD -c
```

Lock Down Access to Hypervisor Console

There are two ways to generally restrict access to the ESXi console, aside from implementing lockdown mode (which was covered earlier in "Restricting the Local root Account"):

◆ You can configure rules for ESXi's built-in firewall.

◆ You can leverage the modified TCP Wrappers capability in the `/etc/security/access.conf` file.

I've already covered the DCUI shell access (turned on or off through the host interface) and SSH access for remote shell connectivity. These are important to consider as well.

CONFIGURING THE ESXI FIREWALL

The key with firewall rules and services in general is fairly straightforward — allow only those services that are needed, and no more. By default (believe it or not), ESXi firewall settings are configured securely. Be sure to add new services only when they're needed, and audit firewall settings regularly over time to make sure things are still in order.

In ESXi version 5, the ports listed in Table 2.1 are open by default.

TABLE 2.1: Ports open by default in ESXi version 5

PORT/PROTOCOL	DIRECTION	EXPLANATION
8100,8200/TCP,UDP	Inbound/Outbound	Fault Tolerance traffic can come to and exit the ESXi host.
53/UDP	Inbound/Outbound	DNS traffic can come to and exit the ESXi host.
68/UDP	Inbound/Outbound	DHCP traffic can come to and exit the ESXi host.
161/UDP	Inbound	SNMP traffic can come to the ESXi host.
80/TCP	Outbound	Fault Tolerance traffic can exit the host.
80/TCP	Inbound	vSphere Web Access can come to the host.
902/TCP	Inbound/Outbound	Network File Copy (NFC) is allowed inbound and outbound, and this port is also used for the vSphere Client to connect.
443/TCP	Inbound	This port is used to connect the vSphere Client.
427/TCP,UDP	Inbound/Outbound	The Common Information Model (CIM) Service Location Protocol (SLP) can communicate inbound and outbound by default.
5988/TCP	Inbound	CIM Server accepts connections by default.
5989/TCP	Inbound	CIM Secure Server accepts connections by default.
8000/TCP	Inbound/Outbound	vMotion operations are enabled both inbound and outbound.
9/UDP	Outbound	Wake-on-LAN (WOL) is allowed outbound.
31031,44096/TCP	Outbound	Host-Based Replication (HBR) services can communicate outbound by default.
902/UDP	Outbound	The vCenter agent can communicate outbound by default.

There are two ways to effectively manage firewall rules with ESXi hosts. The first, which should come as no surprise, is via the vSphere Client, directly or through vCenter. This is definitely the simplest way to control known services on the ESXi host. However, there's a significant disadvantage to this method: There's no way to define custom services! You can do this at the actual console command line locally or via SSH.

To configure the firewall through the GUI, log in to the host or vCenter with the vSphere Client. Navigate to the Configuration tab for the host (in vCenter, go to Hosts And Clusters in the Inventory section first). Then follow these steps:

1. Click the Security Profile link in the left menu list. Look down in the available options until you see the Firewall section. Click the Properties link on the right-hand side of this section. The Firewall Properties screen open, as shown in Figure 2.25.

FIGURE 2.25

ESXi host firewall properties

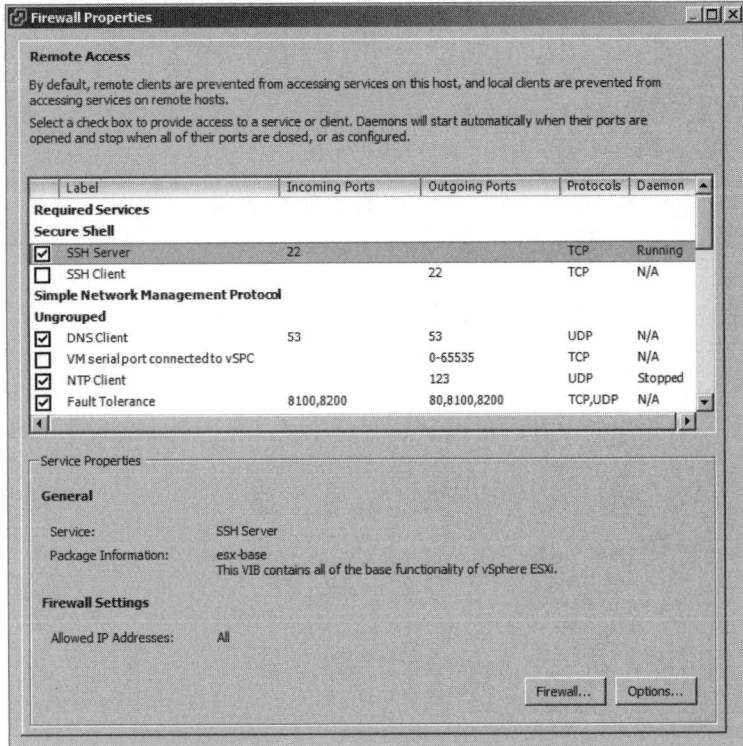

You'll notice a number of defined services listed here. You'll also see the TCP and UDP ports associated with the service and whether they are enabled inbound and or outbound. If the box to the left of the service name is checked, then the service is enabled.

You can highlight some services and then click the Options button in the lower-right corner. Clicking this usually affords you the ability to configure additional options related to the service and its operation, such as how it starts and stops on the host.

2. Check the boxes for any services you want to enable, or uncheck those you don't want enabled (be careful!).

You can also click the Firewall button for any of these services. This allows you to specify IP addresses or subnets that can communicate with the services, offering a more granular method of controlling access to the host and its services (see Figure 2.26).

FIGURE 2.26
Firewall access controls

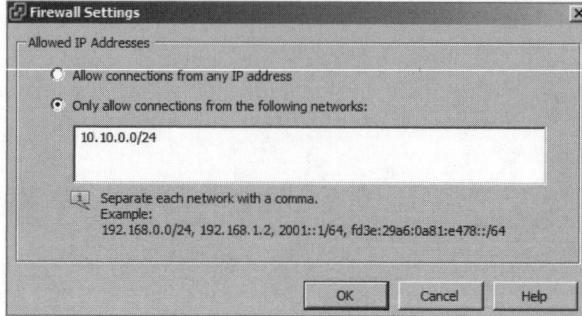

3. When finished enabling and disabling services and their ports, click OK to finish configuring the local host firewall.

4. You can automatically open ports for some services by enabling them in the Services section of the Security Profile configuration area.

To configure custom services or set up firewall access using the local host or SSH, follow these steps:

1. Log in to the local DCUI or use SSH to access the host console shell. Move to the /etc/vmware/firewall directory, and use a text editor to open the file service.xml. You should see a number of XML-tagged sections that look like those shown in Figure 2.27.

FIGURE 2.27
The service.xml firewall rule file

```
<!-- Firewall configuration information -->
<ConfigRoot>

   <!-- Known and blessed servives -->

   <service id='0000'>
     <id>sshServer</id>
     <rule id='0000'>
       <direction>inbound</direction>
       <protocol>tcp</protocol>
       <porttype>dst</porttype>
       <port>22</port>
     </rule>
     <enabled>false</enabled>
     <required>false</required>
   </service>
```

2. To add a new service definition, exit the service.xml file and add a new XML file in the same directory. The following is an example of what the file should look like:

```
<ConfigRoot>
<service id="0099"> <id>YourServiceID</id>
<rule id='0099'>
<direction>inbound</direction>
<protocol>tcp</protocol>
```

```
<porttype>dst</porttype>
<port>
<begin>4444</begin>
<end>5555</end>
</port>
</rule>
<enabled>true</enabled>
<required>true</required>
</service>
</ConfigRoot>
```

The service ID number and name should reflect your own services, as should the rule ID. Direction, protocol, and port type (src or dst) are fairly straightforward. The <begin> and <end> tags are optional if you want to select a range of ports instead of a single port.

3. Once you're finished adding any of these port and service combinations that you want, ensure that the last line of the file is </ConfigRoot>; then save and quit.

4. Now, you'll need to inform the ESXi system of the changes. Refresh the firewall rule set by typing the following command:

```
esxcli network firewall refresh
```

Now, type the following to list the firewall ruleset:

```
esxcli network firewall ruleset list
```

You should see your new service listed in the output.

5. From here, you can add IP address restrictions as well. First, type the following to restrict access from "all":

```
esxcli network firewall ruleset set --allowed-all false
--ruleset-id=<ID Name>
```

Then, enter the following restriction:

```
esxcli network firewall ruleset allowedip add
--ip-address=<IP address or range> --ruleset-id=<ID Name>
```

The key to doing things this way is that you can now see the firewall rules in the vSphere Client as well. You can see an example of this in Figure 2.28, with a new service labeled SybexTest.

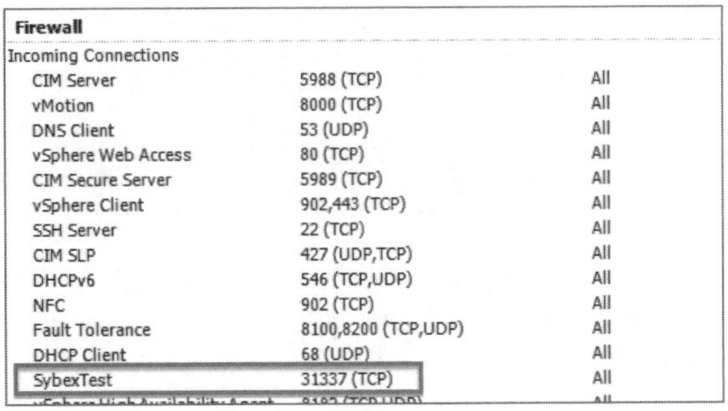

FIGURE 2.28
A new firewall service

Firewall		
Incoming Connections		
CIM Server	5988 (TCP)	All
vMotion	8000 (TCP)	All
DNS Client	53 (UDP)	All
vSphere Web Access	80 (TCP)	All
CIM Secure Server	5989 (TCP)	All
vSphere Client	902,443 (TCP)	All
SSH Server	22 (TCP)	All
CIM SLP	427 (UDP,TCP)	All
DHCPv6	546 (TCP,UDP)	All
NFC	902 (TCP)	All
Fault Tolerance	8100,8200 (TCP,UDP)	All
DHCP Client	68 (UDP)	All
SybexTest	31337 (TCP)	All

CONTROLLING SSH ACCESS USING THE */ETC/SECURITY/ACCESS.CONF* FILE

The second way to control access to the ESXi platform is by creating a regular user account and controlling SSH access to the platform for this account with the `/etc/security/access.conf` file. By default, ESXi will deny access to anyone not explicitly defined in this file.

The first step is to create a new user, which was discussed earlier. Ensure that this user is granted shell access. Next, you can grant access to the user in one of two ways. The first way is simple: Edit the `/etc/security/access.conf` file and add the following line:

```
+:<username>:ALL
```

So for user dave, you'd add `+:dave:ALL`. Save the file, and you can now access the system via SSH using a regular account instead of root. This assumes you've enabled SSH access, of course.

To accomplish the exact same thing via the remote command line, use the `vicfg-user` command in the vSphere CLI. Issue the following command:

```
Vicfg-user --server <host IP/name> --username root --protocol HTTPS
--entity user --login <local user name> --operation modify --role admin
```

Configuring Microsoft Hyper-V on Windows Server 2008

Configuring Microsoft Hyper-V is, believe it or not, a great deal simpler in many ways than locking down some of the other virtualization platforms. The reason for this is simple — it's running on Windows Server 2008! Well, not exactly. Although many believe Hyper-V to be a Type 2 hypervisor because it's running in conjunction with a standard operating system, this is actually not the case. When you install the Hyper-V role on a Windows 2008 platform, the running OS is actually encapsulated and turned into a "parent VM" on top of the hypervisor layer. This parent VM then controls many of the interactions between the other VMs and the hypervisor as well as management functions. A simple depiction of this is represented in Figure 2.29 (the Windows OS is the box labeled "Parent Operating System" in the upper-left corner of the diagram).

FIGURE 2.29
Hyper-V
architecture

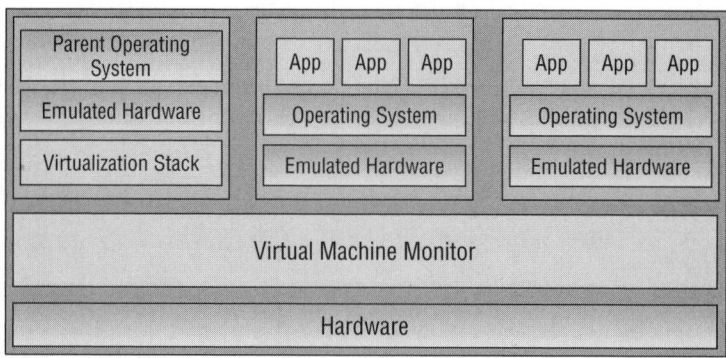

With few exceptions, the standard guidance for locking down a Windows Server 2008 system is the same whether running Hyper-V or not. There are a number of great guides out there for securing Windows Server 2008, and I won't try to replicate the information they contain. Here are a couple of the freely available guides that can be downloaded:

◆ Microsoft's Windows Server 2008 Security Guide

www.microsoft.com/download/en/confirmation.aspx?id=17606

◆ Center for Internet Security Windows Server 2008 Benchmark v1.2.0

www.cisecurity.org

There are plenty of other resources, including the Sybex book *Mastering Microsoft Windows Server 2008 R2* by Mark Minasi et al. (Sybex, 2010).

Before we delve into some of the specifics of securing a Hyper-V platform, there is one very important option that can greatly enhance the overall security posture of any Microsoft Hyper-V system, and that is running the Windows Server 2008 OS in Server Core mode. Running Server Core essentially disables the graphical interface for Microsoft Windows, stripping out all the Windows Explorer interface components that are often the root cause of security issues and vulnerabilities. The aforementioned book by Minasi et al. can get you started, and there are plenty of great resources available from Microsoft as well. This section does not assume you are running in Server Core mode, but keep in mind that much of the general guidance will be the same. Additionally, if you want to *really* restrict the operating platform's footprint, you can install Hyper-V Server 2008, a very specific installation of Server Core just for the Hyper-V role with even less surface area to attack since there's no graphical user interface.

Patching Hyper-V

Patching Hyper-V systems is really no different from patching typical Windows servers. Most organizations are using a centrally managed patching tool like Microsoft Systems Center, Windows Server Update Services (WSUS), and others. This strategy will work fine, with a few caveats:

◆ In most cases, you'll need to migrate running virtual machines to another Hyper-V host when you patch or risk affecting their performance (or worse). This can easily be done with Live Migration and other tools, but patching can't be implemented without a bit of planning.

◆ You'll probably need to disable any automated patching policies you have in place for Hyper-V hosts. Automated patching is not a common configuration setting for most enterprises because testing is usually preferred, but it's incredibly important not to apply patches to virtualization hosts without both testing and preparation beforehand.

◆ You may need to implement a command-line patching capability if you're using Server Core. You can patch systems using one of three methods in this case:

  ◆ Apply patches locally using the msiexec or wusa command.

  ◆ Install patches using WScript or PowerShell scripts.

  ◆ Leverage the built-in SCONFIG tool for Windows Server 2008 R2, which gives you a simple menu-driven interface for controlling the local Windows Update agent.

Securing Communications with Hyper-V

Microsoft Hyper-V uses digital certificates for secure communications with management clients and tools like SCVMM, as well as secure connections to the virtual machines themselves from the hypervisor and from remote clients that are using Remote Desktop Protocol (RDP) and other tools. To ensure that you use secure digital certificates from a trusted third party, you will need to perform two tasks:

1. Disable Hyper-V's generation and use of a self-signed certificate.

2. Replace the default certificate with a separate one of your own.

First, to prevent Hyper-V from generating its own self-signed certificate, you need to run the following command at the command prompt:

```
reg add "HKLM\Software\Microsoft\Windows NT\CurrentVersion\Virtualization"
/v "DisableSelfSignedCertificateGeneration" /f /t REG_QWORD /d 1
```

Then, follow these steps to remove any default certificates:

1. Delete any existing self-signed certificates in the Hyper-V certificate store. Open Microsoft Management Console (MMC) by clicking Start ➢ Run. Enter **mmc**. Click File ➢ Add/Remove Snap-In, and then choose Certificates. Click Add.

2. Choose Service Account, then click Next. Select Local Computer, and then you can choose a specific Hyper-V service account type. There are three from which you can select:

   ◆ Hyper-V Image Management Service

   ◆ Hyper-V Networking Management Service

   ◆ Hyper-V Virtual Machine Management Service

3. Choose Hyper-V Virtual Machine Management Service. You should now have the MMC populated with this Hyper-V service account's certificate store. Select the Personal folder, and then open the Certificates folder within. Delete any certificates in this folder. Then, open the vmms\Trusted Root Certification Authorities folder and click Certificates. Find any certificates matching those from the Personal location and delete these as well.

Now that you've deleted any self-signed certificates, you can start replacing them with your own:

1. Click File ➢ Add/Remove Snap-In again, and then choose Certificates. Click Add. Choose Computer Account and then Local Computer. Finish the wizard.

2. Under Certificates (Local Computer) in the left pane, expand the Trusted Root Certification Authorities location, choose Certificates, and then in the right pane, double-click the certificate you want to use. Select the Details tab, and change the drop-down menu to Properties Only. Highlight the Thumbprint variable, as shown in Figure 2.30. Copy this hexadecimal value into a text file to use later.

3. Open a Windows PowerShell window. Execute the following command:
   ```
   $certs = dir cert:\ -recurse | ? { $_.Thumbprint -eq "thumbprint_value" }
   ```

4. Replace *thumbprint_value* with the hex value you copied in step 2, with no spaces between the numbers (remove them after cutting and pasting). Press Enter, and then enter the following to add the certificate object into an array:
   ```
   $cert = @($certs)[0]
   ```

FIGURE 2.30
Digital certificate
thumbprint

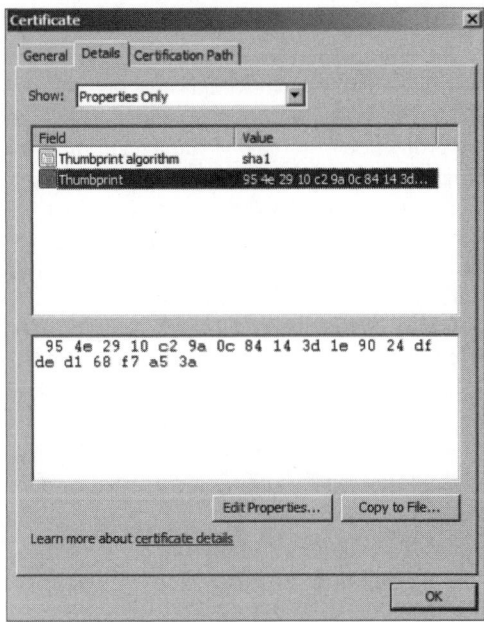

5. Finally, get the private key file name of the certificate:

```
$location = $cert.PrivateKey.CspKeyContainerInfo.UniqueKeyContainerName
```

6. Run the following sequence of commands to modify local access controls to grant read-only access to virtual machines:

```
$folderlocation = gc env:ALLUSERSPROFILE
$folderlocation = $folderlocation + "\Microsoft\Crypto\RSA\MachineKeys\"
$filelocation = $folderlocation + $location
icacls $filelocation /grant "*S-1-5-83-0:(R)"
```

7. Return to the MMC certificates console. Select the local certificate store, and then right-click your trusted certificate in the right side, choosing All Tasks and then Manage Private Keys. Select the Virtual Machines group and ensure that it has Read access allowed. Click OK.

8. Enable the hash value of your certificate in the Registry:

```
$thumbprint = $cert.Thumbprint
reg add "HKLM\Software\Microsoft\Windows NT\CurrentVersion\Virtualization" /v
"AuthCertificateHash" /f /t REG_BINARY /d $thumbprint
```

9. You will need to restart virtual machines to have this take effect.

This is a very convoluted procedure, without a doubt. Microsoft makes more detail available on this procedure, and updates to it, at the following link:

```
http://technet.microsoft.com/en-us/library/ff935311(WS.10).aspx
```

Changing Hyper-V Default Settings

I've already emphasized the importance of hardening the system. Enabling memory protection and BitLocker should be viewed as additional lockdown steps you can take on top of this.

For Hyper-V, you should first consider leveraging the native Windows-based features for memory protection — namely, Data Execution Prevention (DEP) and Address Space Layout Randomization (ASLR). While neither is 100 percent foolproof, they're both valuable. DEP can help protect against buffer overflow attacks by preventing program execution from protected memory space. ASLR constantly changes the memory location of system files, thwarting exploit code and malware that targets a specific memory space. DEP will need to be enabled in hardware with Hyper-V. To see whether your hardware supports DEP, check to see if your processor supports AMD's No Execute (NX) capability or Intel's Execute Disable (XD) functionality. A simple tool that can help you determine whether these features are available is SecurAble, available at the Gibson Research Corporation site:

```
http://www.grc.com/securable.htm
```

For the simplest way to enable DEP, follow these steps:

1. Right-click My Computer or the Computer Start menu item and select Properties. Select the Advanced tab, and then click the Settings button in the Performance area. Select the tab labeled Data Execution Prevention, as shown in Figure 2.31.

FIGURE 2.31
Data Execution
Prevention
configuration

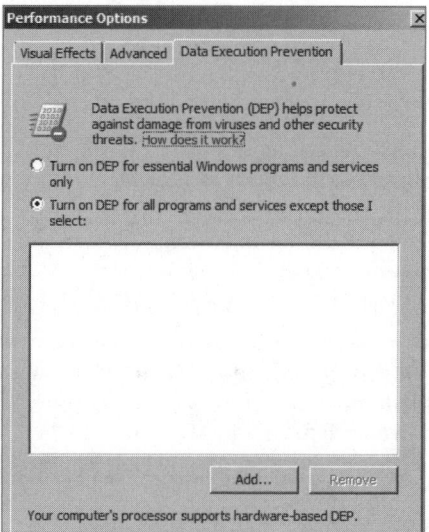

You should see that DEP is supported in hardware, ideally, and you should enable DEP for all programs except those you opt out of, which should only be those for which DEP causes performance or stability problems. Be sure you test carefully on a lab or test system before enabling this in production though!

2. To enable ASLR, manually create the following Registry setting:

```
HKLM\SYSTEM\CurrentControlSet\Control\Session Manager\Memory Management\
MoveImages
```

Set the value to DWORD -1, 0, or 1. A value of -1 will enable ASLR for everything on the system, 0 will disable it, and 1 (or anything other than -1 or 0) will enable it only for specific applications specially marked as compatible with this feature. Again, be very careful with this setting, and test before implementing.

Another change to the default configuration that you should consider is enabling BitLocker encryption (formally known as BitLocker Drive Encryption, or BDE) on Hyper-V volumes. This can help to protect VM disks and configuration files located on the Hyper-V platform. For enterprises storing all virtualization files on a separate storage platform, this will be less applicable overall. I cover virtual machine encryption separately in Chapter 6, "Securing the Virtual Machine." To enable BitLocker, follow these steps:

1. On an existing Hyper-V install, click Start ➢ All Programs ➢ Administrative Tools ➢ Server Manager.

2. When the Server Manager window opens, highlight Features in the left pane, and then click Add Features in the right window. Click BitLocker Drive Encryption, and then click Next.

3. Follow the prompts to complete the installation, and then you'll need to reboot the system. When it reboots, Server Manager will automatically restart to finish BitLocker installation tasks.

4. Once those are finished, you'll likely see errors upon trying to start BitLocker on a standard Hyper-V installation due to perceived drive compatibility issues. The easiest way to get things set up properly is by downloading the Microsoft BitLocker Drive Preparation Tool:

```
http://support.microsoft.com/kb/933246/en-us
```

Install the tool for your Windows 2008 OS, run it, and then reboot when the tool is finished. You should see a screen similar to that in Figure 2.32. In addition to the system drive (usually C:), you'll have a new system drive defined (S:).

5. Reboot your system again.

6. Once it starts back up, navigate to Control Panel and click the icon for BitLocker Drive Encryption. When the BitLocker window opens, select Turn On BitLocker. Follow the prompts until you see a screen to enable the Trusted Platform Module (TPM) in your system's hardware (Figure 2.33).

FIGURE 2.32
BitLocker Drive
Preparation

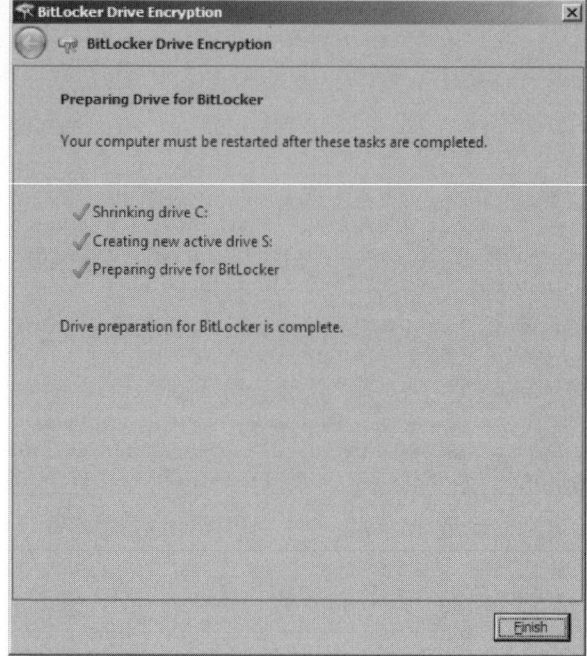

FIGURE 2.33
Enable TPM

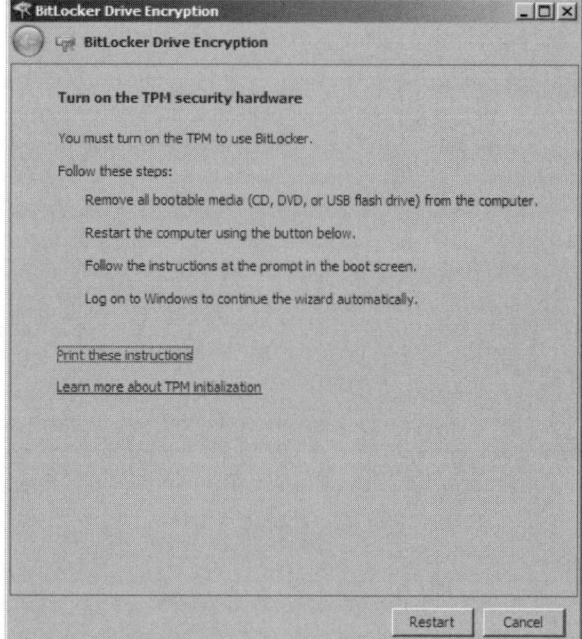

7. Follow the instructions to enable the TPM, and then be sure to archive the recovery password when the wizard is finished. Finish the steps in the wizard to continue the encryption process.

Keep in mind that encryption will impart a slight performance impact to the system in general, so make sure you test this out before deploying in production. This will protect system volumes when they're not booted up, so a system that's running will still be vulnerable to attacks. Consider BitLocker as an additional layer of protection that's nice to have, not your first line of defense.

Enabling Operational Security for Hyper-V

Enabling NTP and SNMP on Hyper-V systems is just as important as on vSphere platforms. Enabling both of these services is fairly simple, thankfully.

It's important to know that member servers in a Windows domain natively sync their time to the domain controllers they communicate with. It is important to align time-sensitive services like Kerberos, which can start acting wacky when it gets about 5 minutes out of sync. For this reason, it's advised to leave the built-in configuration alone and simply ensure that your domain controllers are pointed to the definitive internal and/or external time sources you define. Regardless of how you set up your NTP hierarchy, here's the simplest way to configure NTP on a Windows system:

1. Open a Windows command prompt on the system on which you plan to sync time.

2. Run the following Windows Time command:

```
w32tm /config /manualpeerlist:"ntp1.time.com ntp2.time.com",0x8/
syncfromflags:MANUAL
```

Replace the names of the NTP servers with those you plan to use, and make sure you enclose the names in quotes, with a space between each.

3. Stop and restart the time service to make sure the changes take effect:

```
net stop w32tm
net start w32tm
```

4. To check the status of the time service, including the last sync time, which server was accessed, and more, run the following:

```
w32tm /query /status
```

The second major service you need to configure for operational health in the virtual environment is SNMP. To begin, you will need to install the SNMP service. To do this, click Start ➤ All Programs ➤ Administrative Tools ➤ Server Manager. When the Server Manager window opens, highlight Features in the left pane, and then click Add Features in the right-hand window. Click SNMP Services (you can also enable the SNMP WMI Provider if you like), and then click Next. Let the service install, and then click Close.

Now, follow these steps to configure SNMP:

1. Start the Services console by clicking Start ➤ Run and entering **Services.msc**.

2. Scroll down to SNMP Service and double-click it. You should see a number of tabs across the top of the service configuration window. The three tabs we are concerned with are Agent, Traps, and Security.

3. On the Agent tab, enter contact and location information as well as the types of data that the SNMP agent can access.

4. On the Traps tab, enter community strings that the system will respond to as well as the IP addresses and/or hostnames where the data will be sent. Remember that the strings `public` and `private` are common defaults and should be changed!

5. Finally, on the Security tab, specify what systems can send or receive SNMP information to and from the host.

That's the simplest configuration you can enable for setting up SNMP on your Hyper-V hosts.

Securing and Monitoring Critical Configuration Files for Hyper-V

Monitoring critical files by running cryptographic hashing functions against them is a simple way to determine whether they've been changed anytime recently. Hashing this list of files, and maintaining a baseline that you compare regularly, will give you a basic way to determine if any of the critical Hyper-V files have been modified by malware or other attacks.

Most critical binaries and library files do not change unless patches have been applied, in which case you'll need to develop a new baseline of hash values and start monitoring from there. There are numerous references available online for monitoring critical Windows configuration files. Here, we'll focus on just the files and locations that are directly tied to the operation and functionality of Hyper-V. If these files have changed unexpectedly, you could potentially have an operational issue or a security compromise underway, and you should initiate troubleshooting or incident response processes, as appropriate.

What files do you need to monitor? There are quite a few, and I'll break them down into specific lists where there are numerous files in a single directory.

◆ Individual files
   `C:\ProgramData\Microsoft\Event Viewer\Views\ServerRoles\Virtualization`
   `.Events.xml`
   `C:\ProgramData\Microsoft\Windows\Hyper-V\InitialStore.xml`
   `C:\Users\Public\Documents\Blank floppy disk\Blank.vfd (may not exist)`

◆ Files in `C:\Windows\inf`
   `wnetvsc.inf`
   `ws3cap.inf`
   `wstorflt.inf`
   `wstorvsc.inf`
   `wstorvsp.inf`
   `wvid.inf`
   `wvmbus.inf`
   `wvmbushid.inf`
   `wvmbusvideo.inf`
   `wvmic.inf`
   `wvms_mp.inf`
   `wvms_pp.inf`

◆ Files in `C:\Windows\System32`
   `hvax64.exe (AMD Hyper-V Hypervisor)`

```
hvix64.exe (Intel Hyper-V Hypervisor)
hypervisor.mof
IcCoinstall.dll
nvspwmi.dll
rdp4vs.dll
RemoteFileBrowse.dll
removehypervisor.mof
synthnic.dll
synthstor.dll
vhdsvc.dll
vid.dll
vmbusCoinstaller.dll
vmbuspipe.dll
vmbusvdev.dll
vmbusvideod.dll
vmclusex.dll
vmclusres.dll
vmdCoinstall.dll
vmicheartbeat.dll
vmickvpexchange.dll
vmicshutdown.dll
vmicsvc.exe
vmictimeprovider.dll
vmictimesync.dll
vmicvss.dll
vmms.exe
vmprox.dll
vmsntfy.dll
vmwp.exe
vmwpctrl.dll
vsconfig.dll
WindowsVirtualization.mof
WindowsVirtualizationUninstall.mof
```

◆ Files in C:\Windows\System32\drivers

```
hvboot.sys
isoparser.sys
netvsc50.sys
netvsc60.sys
passthruparser.sys
s3cap.sys
storflt.sys
storvsc.sys
storvsp.sys
vhdparser.sys
vid.sys
vmbus.sys
vmbushid.sys
```

```
vmbusvideom.sys
vmswitch.sys
winhv.sys
```

◆ Files in C:\Windows\System32\drivers\en-US

```
isoparser.sys.mui
hvboot.sys.mui
vmbus.sys.mui
netvsc50.sys.mui
netvsc60.sys.mui
passthruparser.sys.mui
storflt.sys.mui
storvsp.sys.mui
vhdparser.sys.mui
```

◆ Files in C:\Windows\System32\DriverStore\en-US

```
wnetvsc.inf_loc
ws3cap.inf_loc
wstorflt.inf_loc
wstorvsp.inf_loc
wvid.inf_loc
wvmbus.inf_loc
wvmbushid.inf_loc
wvmbusvideo.inf_loc
wvmic.inf_loc
wvms_mp.inf_loc
wvms_pp.inf_loc
```

◆ Files in C:\Windows\System32\en-US

```
nvspwmi.dll.mui
RemoteFileBrowse.dll.mui
SynthNic.dll.mui
SynthStor.dll.mui
vhdsvc.dll.mui
vmclusex.dll.mui
vmclusres.dll.mui
vmicheartbeat.dll.mui
vmickvpexchange.dll.mui
vmicshutdown.dll.mui
vmictimesync.dll.mui
vmicvss.dll.mui
vmms.exe.mui
vmswitch.sys.mui
vmwp.exe.mui
vsconfig.dll.mui
WindowsVirtualization.mfl
WindowsVirtualizationUninstall.mfl
SnapInAbout.dll.mui
virtmgmt.msc
```

◆ Services in C:\Program Files\Hyper-V

```
InspectVhdDialog.exe
InspectVhdDialog.resources.exe
Microsoft.Virtualization.Client.dll
Microsoft.Virtualization.Client.resources.dll
Microsoft.Virtualization.Client.Management.dll
Microsoft.Virtualization.Client.Management.resources.dll
Microsoft.Virtualization.Client.RdpClientAxHost.dll
Microsoft.Virtualization.Client.RdpClientInterop.dll
Microsoft.Virtualization.Client.Settings.dll
Microsoft.Virtualization.Client.Settings.resources.dll
Microsoft.Virtualization.Client.VMBrowser.dll
Microsoft.Virtualization.Client.VMBrowser.resources.dll
Microsoft.Virtualization.Client.Wizards.dll
Microsoft.Virtualization.Client.Wizards.resources
SnapInAbout.dll
virtmgmt.msc
vmconnect.exe
vmbus.cat
vmstorage.cat
vmbusvideo.cat
vmic.cat
netvsc.cat
vmbushid.cat
vmginst.cat
```

As mentioned earlier in this chapter for VMware, a nice hashing tool for Windows systems is the Windows sha1sum binary that can be downloaded from GnuPG at:

```
ftp://ftp.gnupg.org/gcrypt/binary/sha1sum.exe
```

Run the executable as follows:

```
sha1sum <filename> > filename_sum.txt
```

Secure Local Hyper-V Users and Groups

Since Hyper-V local access is managed through the Windows 2008 Server parent partition, there are a few specifics to consider. First, you should strongly consider using only domain groups for managing user access. These can be placed into local groups for providing local, more granular role-based access. Second, you should leverage management console user controls, such as System Center Virtual Machine Manager (SCVMM), if possible. This will allow for more streamlined management, which is often a precursor to improved security and auditing as well.

That said, the best way to assign user and group role-based access to Hyper-V and virtual machines is via Microsoft's Authorization Manager (AzMan) MMC. I'll walk though how to use it and also describe a few standard virtualization tasks to get you started:

1. Start AzMan by clicking Start ➢ Run and then entering **azman.msc**. The console opens.

2. When you first start using AzMan, you won't have an authorization store loaded. Right-click Authorization Manager in the left pane and select Open Authorization Store. Load

the Hyper-V store found at `\ProgramData\Microsoft\Windows\Hyper-V` `\InitialStore.xml`.

3. Right-click the Hyper-V Services icon that appears in the left pane and select New Scope. Give the scope a name and description, then click OK.

A scope can be defined as whatever you want, such as a specific application or cluster, certain network segments, or organizational groups or locations. Once you have a scope defined, you can focus on three specific configuration areas: Task Definitions, Role Definitions, and Role Assignments. Ideally, the first thing to create is a task definition. This is a group of actions that make up a task, such as Manage Virtual Networking Components or Create And Use Virtual Machines.

4. Right-click the `Task Definitions` folder in your scope and select New Task Definition. Add a name and description, then click the Add button in the lower window that allows you to select specific operations, shown in Figure 2.34.

FIGURE 2.34
The AzMan tasks
window

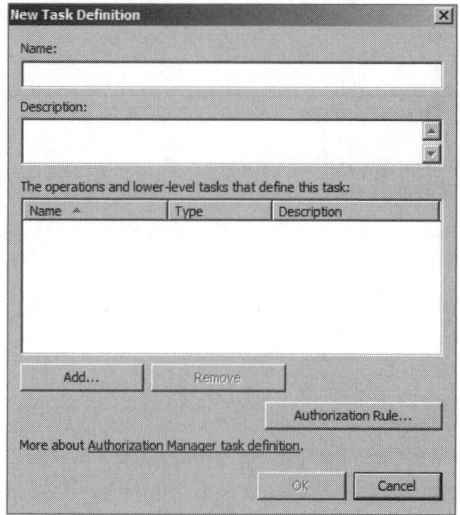

5. You'll now have a new window open up with two tabs, Tasks and Operations. Click Operations, and you can add granular task operations that fit what it is you're trying to accomplish, as shown in Figure 2.35.

6. Check the box next to each task you'd like to add, and then click OK.

7. The next step is to add roles. Role definitions describe types of users such as network engineers, security admins, VM users, and others. Right-click the `Role Definitions` folder and select New Role Definition. You can then provide a name and description, as usual, and click the Add button again. Now, you can choose to add lower-level roles, as well as tasks, to this new role. Alternately, you can add specific operations to the role, much as you did with tasks previously. It's recommended to package all operations into tasks and then assign tasks to roles for ease of management and maintenance. Once you've added tasks, additional roles, and/or operations, click OK. An example of a Network Manager role, with the task Manage Networks, is shown in Figure 2.36.

FIGURE 2.35
Adding specific operations

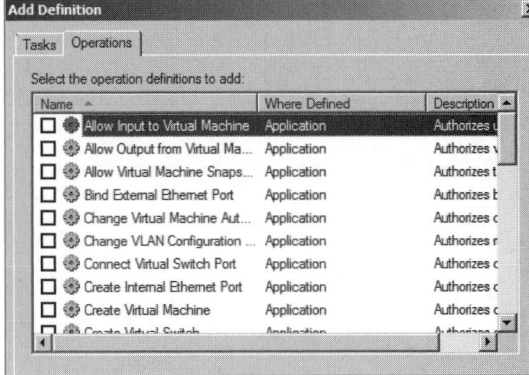

FIGURE 2.36
A simple role example

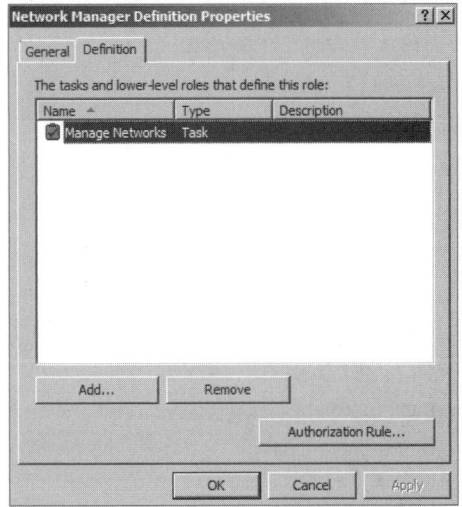

8. Finally, you'll need to assign users and groups to the roles. Right-click the `Role Assignments` folder and select New Role Assignment. You can then select a role that's been defined and click OK. Highlight the role that now appears under this folder, right-click it, and select Assign Users And Groups. You can further select to add users and groups from Windows and Active Directory or directly from AzMan. If you opt to add them from Windows or Active Directory, you'll get a fairly standard window that allows you to select object types, locations, and names of the users and/or groups you're looking to associate with the role.

That's really all there is to it! The following is a list of operations and descriptions for key categories of operations that you can select to provide Hyper-V role-based access:

- Hyper-V Service Operations
    - *Read Service Configuration* (Authorizes reading configuration of the Virtual Machine Management Service)
    - *Reconfigure Service* (Authorizes reconfiguration of Virtual Machine Management Service Hyper-V Network Operations)
    - *Bind External Ethernet Port*
    - *Connect Virtual Switch Port*
    - *Create Internal Ethernet Port*
    - *Create Virtual Switch*
    - *Create Virtual Switch Port*
    - *Delete Internal Ethernet Port*
    - *Delete Virtual Switch*
    - *Delete Virtual Switch Port*
    - *Disconnect Virtual Switch Port*
    - *Modify Internal Ethernet Port*
    - *Modify Switch Port Settings*
    - *Modify Switch Settings*
    - *Change VLAN Configuration on Port*
    - *Unbind External Ethernet Port*
    - *View External Ethernet Ports*
    - *View Internal Ethernet Ports*
    - *View LAN Endpoints*
    - *View Switch Ports*
    - *View Switches*
    - *View Virtual Switch Management Service*
    - *View VLAN Settings*
- Hyper-V Virtual Machine Operations
    - *Allow Input to Virtual Machine* (Authorizes user to give input to the virtual machine)
    - *Allow Output from Virtual Machine* (Authorizes viewing the output from a virtual machine)

- *Change Virtual Machine Authorization Scope*
- *Create Virtual Machine*
- *Delete Virtual Machine*
- *Pause and Restart Virtual Machine*
- *Reconfigure Virtual Machine*
- *Start Virtual Machine*
- *Stop Virtual Machine*
- *View Virtual Machine Configuration*

Here are a few examples of common tasks and the operations that go along with them:

- Task: Add an External Network to a Server
  - Bind to External Ethernet Port
  - Create Internal Ethernet port
  - Connect Virtual Machine
  - Create Virtual Switch
  - Create Virtual Switch Port
  - View External Ethernet Ports
  - View Internal Ethernet Ports
  - View LAN Endpoints
  - View Switch Ports
  - View Switches
  - View Virtual Switch Management Service
  - View VLAN Settings

- Task: Modify a VM
  - Allow Output from a Virtual Machine
  - Read Service Configuration
  - Reconfigure Virtual Machine
  - View Virtual Machine Configuration

- View Hyper-V Settings (for an audit role, perhaps):
  - Allow Output from Virtual Machine
  - Read Service Configuration

- ◆ Reconfigure Service

- ◆ View Virtual Machine Configuration

More examples of tasks and operations can be found on Microsoft's site here:

```
http://technet.microsoft.com/en-us/library/dd282980(WS.10).aspx
```

After all that, what are the best practices from a security standpoint? Simple, really — you are striving to adhere to the principle of *least privilege*. Roles should be as granular as you can get them, and each role should have only the specific tasks and operations needed to get the job done, and nothing more. This helps prevent deliberate malicious activities from insiders as well as accidents that could have significant impact if more privileges are granted.

Lock Down Access to the Hyper-V Hypervisor Platform

Most administrators accessing Hyper-V platforms will do so in one of two ways. The first is by leveraging a centralized management console like SCVMM or Hyper-V Manager. The other is by using Remote Desktop Services. We'll cover SCVMM in Chapter 5 on management platforms. Here, we'll discuss the changes you'll need to enact on the local Hyper-V system to allow a remote Hyper-V Manager MMC to connect and manage the application:

1. First, following the same steps discussed earlier, add the remote user or group to the Administrator Role Assignment for Hyper-V in AzMan.

2. Second, access the local Computer Management console by selecting Start ➢ All Programs ➢ Administrative Tools ➢ Computer Management. Open System Tools, then Local Users And Groups. Double-click the Distributed COM Users group, and use the Add button to add the remote user/group to this local group. Click OK.

3. Now, open the Services And Applications section, right-click the WMI Control option, and select Properties. Click the Security tab, expand the Root directory, and highlight CIMV2. Now click the Security button at the bottom, shown in Figure 2.37.

4. Make sure the remote user/group is added here. Then, under the Permissions box, click Advanced.

5. You need to make a few small modifications to the permissions set of this user or group. Highlight the user or group in the Advanced Permissions box and click Edit. Now make the following changes (shown in Figure 2.38):

   - ◆ Make sure Apply To is set to This Namespace And Subnamespaces.

   - ◆ Change Permissions to Allow Remote Enable (check the box)

   - ◆ Check the box labeled "Apply these permissions to objects and/or containers within this container only."

   Click OK to make the changes and return to the WMI Control Properties window.

6. Scroll down from CIMV2 to reach a similar section labeled Virtualization. Click the Security button as before, and follow the exact same steps (steps 4 and 5) to add the

user/group and modify the permissions for Remote Enable. Click OK to complete the changes, and then exit the WMI Control Properties section. You'll need to reboot the server for these changes to take effect.

FIGURE 2.37
Modifying the
WMI properties for
Hyper-V access

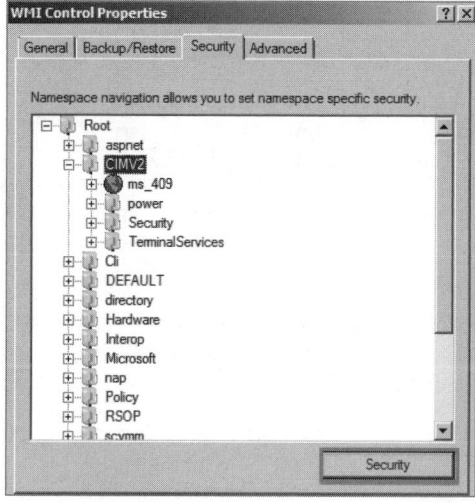

FIGURE 2.38
Permissions set-
tings for WMI
CIMV2 access

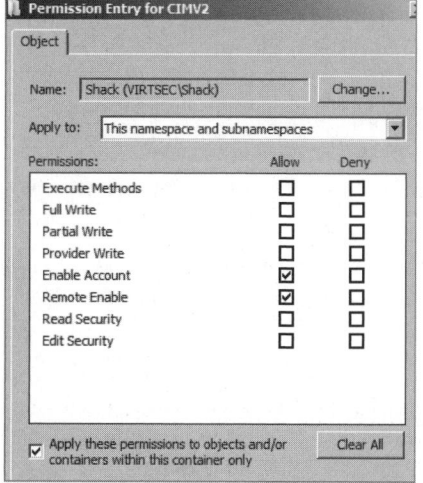

You'll also need to ensure that the local firewall on your Hyper-V server has been configured properly to allow the remote WMI interaction. By default, the rules listed in Table 2.2 are in place when you install Hyper-V.

TABLE 2.2: Default rules in place when Hyper-V is installed

RULE NAME	DESCRIPTION	PORT(S)	PATH TO PARENT SERVICE
Hyper-V - WMI (Async-In)	Inbound rule for Hyper-V to allow asynchronous WMI traffic	TCP any	%systemroot%\system32\wbem\unsecapp.exe
Hyper-V - WMI (DCOM-In)	Inbound rule for Hyper-V to allow WMI management using DCOM	TCP 135	%SystemRoot%\system32\svchost.exe
Hyper-V - WMI (TCP-In)	Inbound rule for Hyper-V to allow remote WMI traffic	TCP any	%SystemRoot%\system32\svchost.exe
Hyper-V - WMI (TCP-Out)	Outbound rule for Hyper-V to allow remote WMI traffic	TCP any	%SystemRoot%\system32\svchost.exe
Hyper-V (RPC)	Inbound rule for Hyper-V to allow remote management using RPC/TCP	Dynamic RPC	System
Hyper-V (RPC-EPMAP)	Inbound rule for RPCSS service to allow RPC/TCP traffic for Hyper-V	RPC Endpoint Mapper	System
Hyper-V (REMOTE_DESKTOP_ TCP_IN)	Inbound rule for Hyper-V to allow remote connection to virtual machine.	TCP 2179	%systemroot%\system32\vmms.exe
Hyper-V Management Clients - WMI (Async-In)	Inbound rule for Hyper-V Clients to allow asynchronous WMI traffic	TCP any	%systemroot%\system32\wbem\unsecapp.exe
Hyper-V Management Clients - WMI (DCOM-In)	Inbound rule for Hyper-V Clients to allow WMI management via DCOM	TCP 135	%SystemRoot%\system32\svchost.exe
Hyper-V Management Clients - WMI (TCP-In)	Inbound rule for Hyper-V Clients to allow remote WMI traffic	TCP any	%SystemRoot%\system32\svchost.exe
Hyper-V Management Clients - WMI (TCP-Out)	Outbound rule for Hyper-V Clients to allow remote WMI traffic	TCP any	%SystemRoot%\system32\svchost.exe

Note that the first four rules are enabled by default for standard WMI interaction with Hyper-V. To enable the last four WMI-related rules (required for remote management), you'll need to run the following at the command prompt:

```
netsh advfirewall firewall set
  rule group="Windows Management Instrumentation (WMI)" new enable=yes
```

This will enable the firewall rules allowing remote MMC access to Hyper-V.

The second method for administering Hyper-V is via Remote Desktop Services. Although fully securing Remote Desktop is beyond the scope of this book, here are several key suggestions for locking this down appropriately:

◆ Use strong passwords for accessing the system. This is a fundamental best practice in security overall but still a problem for many.

◆ Restrict access to specific users and systems. This can be accomplished by navigating to Control Panel, clicking System, and then clicking Remote Settings. First, select the last option, "Allow connections only from computers running Remote Desktop with Network Level Authentication (more secure)." Then click the Select Users button. These options are shown in Figure 2.39.

FIGURE 2.39
Remote Desktop user and computer selection

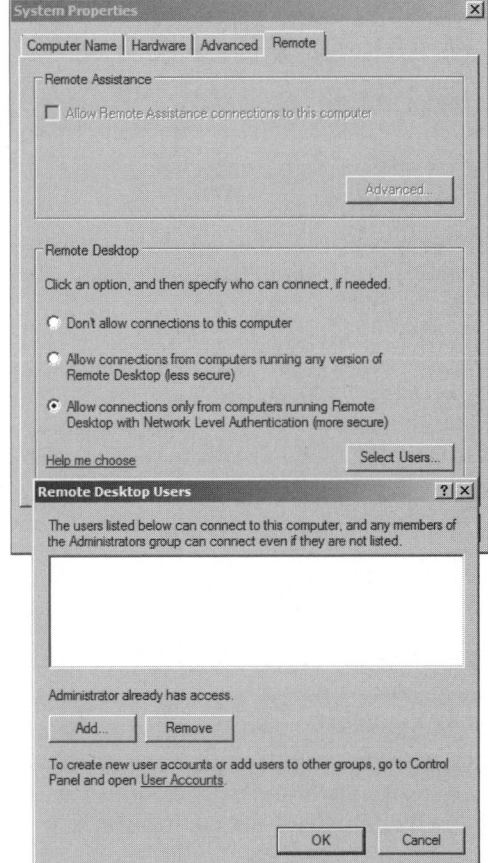

Click Add and select users who can access the system with Remote Desktop, and then click OK three times to finish.

◆ Modify security settings for the host. Navigate to Start ➢ All Programs ➢ Administrative Tools ➢ Remote Desktop Services ➢ Remote Desktop Session Host Configuration. Now double-click the RDP-Tcp connection in the box on the screen. You should now see a window pop up called RDP-Tcp Properties. On the General tab, choose SSL (TLS 1.0) for the Security layer. This is a strong option that establishes certificate-based negotiation for connections. For Encryption Level, choose High or FIPS-140. Ensure that the check box is checked for requiring network-level authentication. Also, replace the default self-signed certificate with a signed one from a trusted certificate authority. On the Log On Settings tab, check the box labeled Always Prompt For Password.

It's definitely preferred to use a Hyper-V management tool to administer the system, but securing Remote Desktop is a good practice to follow regardless.

Configuring Citrix XenServer

The good thing about XenServer is that it is a *lot* like Linux. For some virtualization administrators, this is also a bad thing, because they may not have the command-line chops to manage and configure these systems properly. While there's a lot you can accomplish using XenCenter, you will still need to leverage the command line for many specific tasks. It's important to make one other point here — XenServer is not a standard Linux kernel or OS. It's modified enough that you should be careful to consider what may be negatively affected by running standard OS commands.

Patching XenServer

All patches for XenServer are known as *hotfixes*, a term many associate with Microsoft patching. To illustrate one of the major differences between XenServer and major Linux distributions (particularly Red Hat and CentOS), the system's console OS comes with a copy of the well-known update utility yum. However, Citrix recommends against enabling or using it because it will cause standard CentOS packages to be downloaded and installed, which may conflict with the system's customized package operation.

All hotfixes issued by Citrix are cryptographically signed, and these signatures are checked when uploaded to a hypervisor host. Each hotfix also contains the following metadata components:

◆ A unique hotfix identifier number

◆ A simple evaluation check that determines the hotfix applicability to the individual host it's being installed on

◆ Guidance for post-install configuration and activation, where applicable

PATCHING VIA XENCENTER

The first way to update XenServer is via XenCenter. The update process is simple, and there's a wizard that walks you through the process. You have two options for upgrading through XenCenter: software updates and Rolling Pool Upgrades.

To get started with a standard software update, you first need to acquire hotfix files and store them on a centrally located platform or local system. Then follow these steps:

1. In XenCenter, click Tools, then Install Software Update. The wizard opens.

2. Click Next, and then click Add to add hotfix files. Click Next, and then select the server(s) you want to update. Click Next again.

3. The update evaluation checks are then performed. XenCenter will inform you of any issues that may prevent the hotfix from installing properly, such as version mismatch. An example is shown in Figure 2.40.

FIGURE 2.40
XenServer update issues

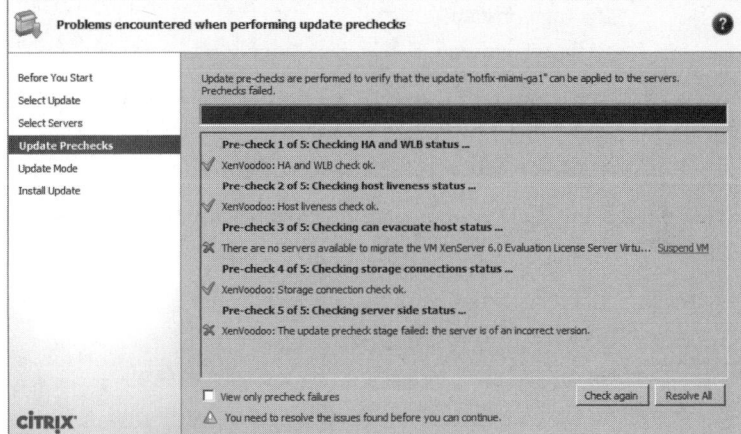

4. After all issues are resolved, click Next to proceed.

5. The next stage of the wizard is the update mode. Choose an option for updating XenServer — either Automatic or Manual.

   ◆ Automatic mode lets XenCenter decide how to migrate VMs to other hosts and can migrate them back once the host is updated.

   ◆ Manual mode allows you to pick and choose which updates are sent to which servers (and when) as well as how and when to migrate VMs running on the host to other hosts.

6. Click Next; then finalize the update process.

A Rolling Pool Upgrade is a tool that allows you to upgrade XenServer hosts in a pool to a newer version of XenServer. Services running from the pool will stay available through the process. The steps are very similar to the ones for basic upgrades. You start the process by selecting Tools, then Rolling Pool Upgrade. Then select Pools instead of individual hosts.

PATCHING VIA THE COMMAND LINE

You can also use the command line to update individual XenServers or perform Rolling Pool Upgrades.

You first need to acquire hotfix files and store them on a centrally located platform or local system. Then shut down or suspend any running VMs on the host system. In a pool, you can migrate VMs to other pool hosts. Then follow these steps:

1. Copy the update files to the host. This can be accomplished by using the scp command as follows:

   ```
   scp <hotfix file name> <XenServer IP>:/<directory>
   ```

   So an example might be:

   ```
   scp Update.zip 10.10.0.128:/patches
   ```

2. Next, log in to the target system using SSH or the local or XenServer console. Run the following command:

   ```
   xe patch-upload file-name=<hotfix file name>
   ```

   You should get a universally unique identifier (UUID) for a specific patch returned to you that looks like the following:

   ```
   b11249c7-fcbc-62c5-8178-901def987afd
   ```

3. To apply the patch to an entire pool, run the following:

   ```
   xe patch-pool-apply uuid=b11249c7-fcbc-62c5-8178-901def987afd
   ```

   To apply the patch to a single host, run the following:

   ```
   xe patch-apply host=<host name>
   uuid=b11249c7-fcbc-62c5-8178-901def987afd
   ```

4. Run the xe patch-list command to verify that the host(s) accepted the patch.

There are additional options you could apply, but these are the basics to get started. A simple script could be used to automate the application of XenServer patches from the command line. Follow these steps:

1. First, use the Vi editor to create a new file called xenpatch.sh and enter the following code:

   ```
   #!/bin/bash
   unzip $1
   patchname=`basename $1 .zip`.xsupdate
   echo "Patch $patchname being applied"
   xe patch-pool-apply uuid=`xe patch-upload file-name=$patchname`
   ```

2. Save the script and exit the file. Now change the permissions on the script by typing the following at the command line (you should do this as whatever user will run the script):

   ```
   chmod 700 xenpatch.sh
   ```

3. Run the script at the command line, providing it with the name of the patch file you want to open and run (should be a ZIP file). For example, to install the patch package X010203 .zip, you would execute the following:

   ```
   xenpatch.sh X010203.zip
   ```

Secure Communications with XenServer

Much like VMware ESXi, XenServer relies heavily on SSL certificates for interaction with management consoles and components, primarily XenCenter. XenServer's SSL certificates are tied to the XenAPI network service, which is used by most applications that need to access the system.

It's a good idea to verify the SSL fingerprint on a XenServer host to ensure that you are connecting to the host you think you're connecting to, helping to prevent Man-in-the-Middle (MitM) attacks.

First, access the XenServer interactive console. This can be done by logging in via SSH or within XenCenter by selecting a XenServer host and clicking the Console tab in the right pane. Once you have command-line access, type **xsconsole**. The first option in the menu, Status Display, will display the SSL certificate fingerprint when selected (see Figure 2.41). This fingerprint should match that presented when you connect to the host for the first time in XenCenter.

FIGURE 2.41
XenServer SSL certificate fingerprint

To replace the default SSL certificates on the host, perform the following actions:

1. At the command line, first move the original certificate's file to a different name. If something goes wrong, you can rename the file again and restore the system to the original configuration, as in the following example:

   ```
   mv /etc/xensource/xapi-ssl.pem /etc/xensource/xapi-ssl.pem.orig
   ```

2. Now copy the new certificate (in PEM format) to the system:

   ```
   cp <your file>.pem /etc/xensource/xapi-ssl.pem
   ```

3. An optional configuration step is to include Diffie-Hellman parameters in your certificate with OpenSSL. This can be useful for certain key exchange methods with servers, but it's not required for most XenServer interactions. To do this, run the following command:

   ```
   openssl dhparam 512 >> /etc/xensource/xapi-ssl.pem
   ```

To ensure that XenCenter recognizes any unusual changes in SSL certificates, you can enable alerting for SSL changes detected. To accomplish this, log into XenCenter, click the Tools menu option, and select Options. The first item you'll be presented with is Security. You can check two configuration items; the first is to alert when any new SSL certificates are detected, and the second is to alert when a change is detected with known SSL certificates on XenServer hosts. These settings are shown in Figure 2.42.

FIGURE 2.42
SSL certificate alerting in XenCenter

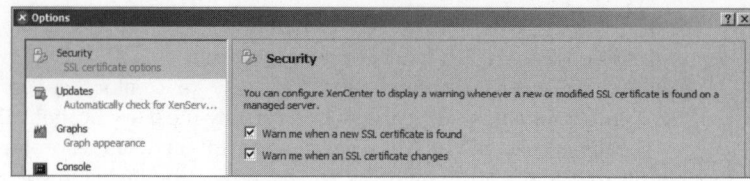

Change XenServer Default Settings

There are many changes you can make to XenServer that likely conform to Linux hardening best practices. Rather than creating Yet Another Linux Hardening Guide (YALHG), I'll list some of the more fundamental configuration steps you should take. These steps have been tested on XenServer's latest versions. Feel free to experiment with other hardening steps that apply to Red Hat Enterprise and CentOS operating systems, but test them all first to ensure that XenServer works properly with them! Good examples of Linux-focused hardening guides can be found at the Center for Internet Security:

```
http://benchmarks.cisecurity.org/en-us/?route=downloads.browse.category
.benchmarks.os.linux
```

LIMIT RUNNING SERVICES

A number of services are running on a default installation of XenServer. To determine which services are running, you can execute the following command:

```
chkconfig --list | grep 3:on | cut -f 1
```

On a default installation, you should see the following services:

```
atd
attach-static-vdis
crond
fe
firstboot
genptoken
iptables
irqbalance
kdump
loadbrsysctl
lwsmd
management-interface
mcstrans
mdmonitor
microcode_ctl
mpathroot
mpp
multipathd
netfs
```

```
network
nfslock
ntpd
openvswitch
perfmon
portmap
rawdevices
rpcgssd
rpcidmapd
set-memory-target
snapwatchd
squeezed
sshd
syslog
unplug-vcpus
v6d
vhostmd
xapi
xapi-domains
xe-linux-distribution
xenservices
```

These services, by default, are usually needed or useful, and I recommend leaving them in place. If you see additional services that you determine you don't need, you can easily shut them down with the following command:

```
chkconfig --level 3 <service name> off
```

CHANGING BOOT BEHAVIOR

XenServer, much like a traditional Linux system, allows users to reboot or log into *single user mode*. Single user mode is a special shell mode that allows root privilege access to the OS for configuration and emergency changes. This is of course a liability! To require the root password to enter single user mode, edit the /etc/inittab file and enter the following line:

```
~~:S:wait:/sbin/sulogin
```

Another boot loader on XenServer is the *extlinux* loader, which should also be protected with a password. Follow these steps to make this change:

1. First, choose a password for the loader, and run it through the sha1sum command to get a 40-character hash:

   ```
   echo <your password> | sha1sum
   ```

2. Edit the /boot/extlinux.conf file and add the following line in the top section with the # location mbr comment:

   ```
   menu master passwd <your hash from Step 1>
   ```

3. Save and exit the file.

DISABLE DEBUG MODE

Debug mode allows users and processes to potentially access sensitive areas of the XenServer file system and also generate and read potentially sensitive log data. I recommend disabling debug mode in two ways. First, disable debug mode for the Xenstored processes, which allow VM storage (and thus VMs) to access debug mode. To disable debug mode for Xenstored, check the file /etc/xensource/xenstored.conf and make sure there are no entries reading allow-debug=true. By default, there should not be any of these entries, but checking intermittently is a good idea.

One other type of debug mode access is the global catalog debug mode used by the XAPI process when XenServer is using Active Directory and LDAP stores. To disable global catalog debugging, edit the /etc/xapi.conf file and find the following line:

```
gc-debug=true
```

Change true to false and then save and exit the file.

LIMIT ACCESS TO *CRON* AND *AT*

Certain users might need to create scheduled jobs and tasks using the cron or at utility. You should restrict these capabilities to specific administrative users to preserve operational integrity and limit resource consumption on the XenServer host. To limit access to these utilities, follow these steps at the XenServer command line:

1. First, create the cron.allow and cron.deny files in the /etc directory:

   ```
   touch /etc/cron.allow
   touch /etc/cron.deny
   ```

2. Change the permissions on cron.allow to prevent tampering with it:

   ```
   chmod 600 /etc/cron.allow
   ```

3. Now, add all users listed in the /etc/passwd file (other than root) using a simple awk script:

   ```
   awk -F: '{print $1}' /etc/passwd | grep -v root > /etc/cron.deny
   ```

4. Repeat the process for the at command using at.allow and at.deny:

   ```
   touch /etc/at.allow
   chmod 600 /etc/at.allow
   awk -F: '{print $1}' /etc/passwd | grep -v root > /etc/at.deny
   ```

   Now, all users except root will be explicitly denied from using cron or at.

RESTRICTING THE XENSERVER NETWORK CONFIGURATION

The XenServer kernel can very capably handle a variety of network traffic and conditions. There are a number of settings in the /etc/sysctl.conf file that should be present and/or set. Most of these settings are intended to disable potentially malicious traffic such as Internet Control Message Protocol (ICMP) traffic, directed broadcasts, and source-routed packets. Others are filtering and denial of service (DoS) mitigation tools.

Listing 2.1 shows the settings you should look for. In this file, 0 (zero) is disabled and 1 (one) is enabled. If the settings don't exist, create them! After adding and changing these settings, run the command `sysctl -p` to enable them. (This listing is also available on the book's web page at www.sybex.com/go/virtualizationsecurity.)

LISTING 2.1:   Settings for the /etc/sysctl.conf file

```
#Don't act like a router and pass traffic between networks
net.ipv4.ip_forward = 0
net.ipv4.conf.all.send_redirects = 0
net.ipv4.conf.default.send_redirects = 0

#Restrict routing table alteration
net.ipv4.conf.all.accept_redirects = 0
net.ipv4.conf.all.secure_redirects = 0
net.ipv4.conf.default.accept_redirects = 0
net.ipv4.conf.default.secure_redirects = 0

#Enable reverse path filtering
net.ipv4.conf.all.rp_filter = 1
net.ipv4.conf.default.rp_filter = 1

#Block source routed packets
net.ipv4.conf.all.accept_source_route = 0
net.ipv4.conf.default.accept_source_route = 0

#Log source routed, redirected, or spoofed packets
net.ipv4.conf.all.log_martians = 1
net.ipv4.conf.default.log_martians = 1

#Enable SYN cookies to mitigate DoS attacks
net.ipv4.tcp_syncookies = 1

#Enable SYN cookies when certain traffic threshold is reached
net.ipv4.tcp_max_syn_backlog = 1280

#Ignore directed broadcasts and prevent SMURF attacks
net.ipv4.icmp_echo_ignore_broadcasts = 1

#Ignore weird ICMP error messages
net.ipv4.icmp_ignore_bogus_error_responses = 1

#Disable the 12 byte TCP timestamp field in the TCP header
net.ipv4.tcp_timestamps = 0
```

Enabling XenServer Operational Security

Enabling NTP and SNMP on XenServer is fairly straightforward, especially for administrators familiar with Linux. Both can be configured by modifying key configuration files and starting up standard services.

To add time servers, use the Vi editor to modify the file /etc/ntp.conf. Add the following lines to the file (they are likely there by default):

```
server 0.xenserver.pool.ntp.org
server 1.xenserver.pool.ntp.org
server 2.xenserver.pool.ntp.org
server 3.xenserver.pool.ntp.org
```

These four NTP servers are those recommended by Citrix, but you should add time servers that you are already familiar with and use within your infrastructure. To ensure that the changes take effect, restart the time service by running the following command:

```
/etc/init.d/ntpd restart
```

This will restart the NTP daemon and should configure the local NTP service to acquire time from the NTP servers specified in the configuration file.

To check the status of NTP on your XenServer host, you can run the `ntpq -p` command. This command will return a number of fields related to NTP synchronization on the XenServer host.

To enable and modify SNMP services, you'll first need to allow the SNMP traffic to the host by modifying the local firewall. To do this, follow these steps:

1. Use the Vi editor to modify the file /etc/sysconfig/iptables. Add the following line somewhere before the last rules entry (which should read -A RH-Firewall-1-INPUT -j REJECT --reject-with icmp-host-prohibited):

    ```
    -A RH-Firewall-1-INPUT -p udp --dport 161 -j ACCEPT
    ```

2. Save and close the file, and then restart the firewall service by running this command:
    ```
    service iptables restart
    ```

3. Now, modify the SNMP configuration file at /etc/snmp/snmpd.conf. A number of settings can be configured here. By default, only the `systemview` subtree of the Xen Management Information Base (MIB) is presented, and this should be left alone unless you have a specific reason to allow more access. You should, however, change the default community string from `public` to something more secure. Do this by changing `public` in the following line to the SNMP community string set up within your infrastructure monitoring systems.

    ```
    com2sec notConfigUser     default     public
    ```

4. After making any other changes you need, save the file and close it. Now, start up the SNMP service by typing **service snmpd start**.

5. To enable SNMP as a service that automatically starts, run the following command:

    ```
    chkconfig snmpd on
    ```

You should now have functional NTP and SNMP services running on the XenServer host.

Secure and Monitor Critical XenServer Configuration Files

A number of configuration files should be monitored on a XenServer platform. As with both ESXi and Hyper-V, the key to monitoring these files for changes and overall integrity is to perform a hashing function against the files at a given point in time, recording the output values. These values become the baseline you can compare against later when performing the same hashing algorithm operation. If a value changes, the file has changed in some way. If the hashes are the same, the file has not changed.

TIP   Keep in mind that updating and upgrading the system will likely change a number of files, so be sure to create a new baseline after performing those operations.

There are many different approaches to monitoring important files and directories on Linux platforms. For a simple starting point, the following directories should be monitored on XenServer implementations:

/etc

/usr/bin

/usr/sbin

/bin

/sbin

/opt/xensource/

The distribution comes with a number of hashing tools built in. These include md5sum, sha-1sum, sha256sum, and sha512sum. I recommend using sha512sum because it's the most secure of these hashing algorithms. The following is a simple script that can easily be used in the XenServer command shell to do this on a regular basis:

```
#!/bin/bash
while read line
do
    find $line -type f -print0 | xargs -0 sha512sum > /tmp/checksums.txt
done < $1
```

Add these lines of code to a script file (named, for example, hashing.sh), make the script executable with chmod +x, and then create a text file that includes all of the directories listed earlier (as well as any others you want to monitor). Run the script like this:

```
./hashing.sh <text file name>
```

You should be able to pick up your file of hashes in the /tmp directory when it's done. You can then use the diff function to compare this to a new file. Do this daily, or however often you want to perform simple file integrity monitoring.

Secure Local Users and Groups

The processes for adding, deleting, and modifying local users and groups on XenServer are essentially similar to a standard Linux approach. There are also a number of simple roles defined with role-based access controls that can be applied.

Changing the Format of the Password File

Unfortunately, there is one significant weakness in XenServer's local user security configuration from the very start — the password hashes are stored in the /etc/passwd file, to which all users have read access! This has been deprecated in many Linux distributions today in favor of a more secure system using both the /etc/passwd user file and the restricted /etc/shadow file with password hashes. You can change this behavior with the pwconv command, which will convert the system to use the /etc/shadow format. You can also tie the shadow file into pluggable authentication modules by editing the /etc/pam.d/system-auth file. Look for the following line:

```
password     sufficient     pam_unix.so try_first_pass use_authtok nullok md5
```

Modify the file to include the word shadow at the end, so it looks like this:

```
password     sufficient     pam_unix.so try_first_pass use_authtok nullok md5 shadow
```

Save the file and exit.

WARNING   XenServer does not officially support the use of shadowed passwords. If you convert the system to use /etc/shadow files, you may break system compatibility within pools! Test carefully in a test lab and see if your configuration still works properly before enabling shadowed passwords in a production setting.

Setting Up Users and Groups

The adduser and useradd commands (they both work the same) can be used to create a new, lower-privilege user. In the following example, the entity named RegularUser is given a User ID of 525 (any unique number over 500 is acceptable; you can also let useradd pick a value for you), a group ID of 200, a home directory of /home/reguser, a shell of /bin/bash, and the username of reguser:

```
useradd -c "RegularUser" -u 525 -g 200 -d /home/reguser -s /bin/bash reguser
```

To set a password for this user, you can use the passwd command and follow the prompts:

```
passwd <username>
```

To delete a user, use the userdel command:

```
userdel -r <username>
```

To add a specific group, use groupadd as shown:

```
groupadd -g <group ID number> <groupname>
```

One additional step you should take is to ensure that all user accounts have passwords associated with them. Look in the /etc/passwd or /etc/shadow (if you're using shadowed passwords) file and ensure that the first field after the username has a hash value or the !! symbols, which means the account can't be logged in.

Configuring Password Aging and History

Password aging default settings can be configured in the /etc/login.defs file. There are four setting you can edit in this file. The recommendations are shown in Table 2.3.

TABLE 2.3: Configuring password aging settings

NAME	SETTING	DEFAULT VALUE	RECOMMENDED VALUE
PASS_MAX_DAYS	The maximum number of days a password may be used	99999	90
PASS_MIN_DAYS	The minimum number of days allowed between password changes	0	4
PASS_MIN_LEN	The minimum accept-able password length	5	10
PASS_WARN_AGE	The number of days' warning given before a password expires	7	7

Another common password security control is password history. This control keeps track of a certain number of user passwords, preventing users from the using the same passwords over and over again. Many feel that this control can help if someone's commonly used password is compromised elsewhere because attackers will often try this same password on other systems. To configure password history, you'll need to modify the /etc/pam.d/system-auth file. Add the following line into the file to remember the previous six passwords, which is the minimum I recommend:

```
password    required    pam_unix.so    remember=6
```

Now save the file and exit. Users will be forced to use a new password for the next six password cycles.

CONFIGURING THE *SUDOERS* FILE

The great thing about local user control on the XenServer platform is the presence of sudo. This is by far the simplest way to restrict and control the kinds of activities that individual users and/or groups can perform. Edit the /etc/sudoers file with the command visudo. You can then create groups of command aliases that are assigned to users — in other words, groups of privileged commands that certain users and groups can run without being root. For a XenServer platform, you may want to create a new Command Alias group for Xen admin commands by adding the following line:

```
## Administration of the XenServer platform
#Cmnd_Alias XENADMIN = /opt/xensource/bin/xe, /opt/xensource/bin/xapi, /opt/
xensource/bin/xstored, /opt/xensource/bin/xsh
```

You can then control which users can access and run these commands. For example, if you had a special group called xenadmins defined, you could add this line to the sudoers file:

```
%xenadmins    ALL=XENADMIN
```

This would grant the group sudo access to the executables for XenServer administration.

Working with PAM Files

Additional user control can be managed with pluggable authentication module (PAM) files, although the modules on XenServer do not appear to be as full featured as those on ESXi or modern Linux variants. You can, however, use PAM to restrict access to the XenAPI set to a group of users. First, create the list of users you want. For example, you could create a file called /etc/localadmins. Add one username per line. Then you can edit the PAM configuration to use PAM for restricting this access. For XenServer, all the necessary policies are configured in a single file, /etc/pam.d/system-auth. Use Vi to edit this file, and make the following change (the highlighted line):

```
#%PAM-1.0
auth          required      pam_env.so
auth          required      pam_listfile.so item=user sense=allow file=
/etc/localadmins
auth          sufficient    pam_unix.so try_first_pass nullok
auth          required      pam_deny.so
;
account       required      pam_unix.so
;
password      required      pam_cracklib.so try_first_pass retry=3
password      sufficient    pam_unix.so try_first_pass use_authtok nullok md5
password      required      pam_deny.so
;
session       optional      pam_keyinit.so revoke
session       required      pam_limits.so
session       [success=1 default=ignore] pam_succeed_if.so service in crond quiet
use_uid
session       required      pam_unix.so
;
```

Now, you'll need to enable external PAM authentication for the host with this xe command:

```
xe pool-enable-external-auth auth-type=PAM service-name=pam
```

Enabling Active Directory Authentication

An alternative to using PAM to restrict access is to enable Active Directory authentication for the XenServer. This is usually the preferred mode of authentication for enterprise environments.

First, make sure the following firewall ports are open on the XenServer host to allow communication with domain controllers (accomplished by running the iptables -L command):

UDP/TCP 53 (DNS)

UDP/TCP 88 (Kerberos 5)

UDP 123 (NTP)

UDP 137 (NetBIOS Name Service)

TCP 139 (NetBIOS Session (SMB))

UDP/TCP 389 (LDAP)

TCP 445 (SMB over TCP)

UDP/TCP 464 (Machine password changes)

TCP 3268 (Global Catalog Query)

Now you'll need to enable external authentication just as described for PAM but instead pointing to the AD domain:

```
xe pool-enable-external-auth auth-type=AD service-name=<FQDN> config:user=<domain
admin username> config:pass=<domain admin password>
```

An alternative is to add the host to Active Directory through XenCenter. Follow these steps:

1. Log in to XenCenter and select the host or pool you would like to add to the domain.

2. Click the Users tab on the right side.

3. Click the Join Domain button. Enter the domain name, a domain admin user, and the user's password. Then click OK.

4. You should now see a list of the users and groups with access in the pane below, as shown in Figure 2.43.

FIGURE 2.43
Domain authentication via XenCenter

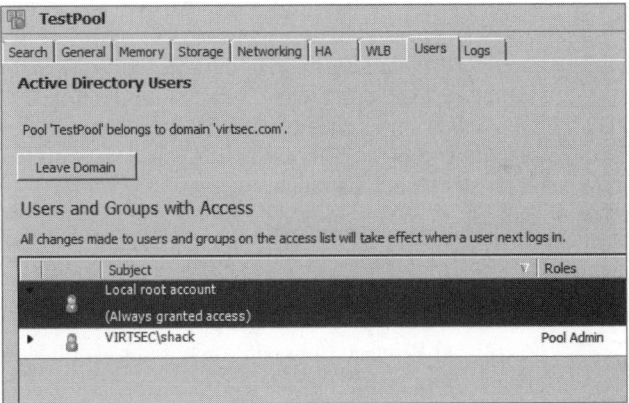

TIP For either PAM or AD authentication, you can disable external authentication on a XenServer host with this command: `xe pool-disable-external-auth`.

You can now leverage XenServer's built-in role-based access control (RBAC) system. To see the roles defined on a XenServer host, run the command `xe role-list`. You should see output similar to that shown in Figure 2.44.

FIGURE 2.44
Standard XenServer
roles

```
[root@XenVoodoo ~]# xe role-list
uuid ( RO)          : 7955168d-7bec-10ed-105f-c6a7e6e63249
          name ( RO): vm-power-admin
    description ( RO): The VM Power Administrator role has full access to VM and template managem
ent and can choose where to start VMs and use the dynamic memory control and VM snapshot features


uuid ( RO)          : aaa00ab5-7340-bfbc-0d1b-7cf342639a6e
          name ( RO): vm-admin
    description ( RO): The VM Administrator role can manage VMs and templates


uuid ( RO)          : fb8d4ff9-310c-a959-0613-54101535d3d5
          name ( RO): vm-operator
    description ( RO): The VM Operator role can use VMs and interact with VM consoles


uuid ( RO)          : 7233b8e3-eacb-d7da-2c95-f2e581cdbf4e
          name ( RO): read-only
    description ( RO): The Read-Only role can log in with basic read-only access


uuid ( RO)          : b9ce9791-0604-50cd-0649-09b3284c7dfd
          name ( RO): pool-operator
    description ( RO): The Pool Operator role manages host- and pool-wide resources, including se
tting up storage, creating resource pools and managing patches, high availability (HA) and worklo
ad balancing (WLB)


uuid ( RO)          : 0165f154-ba3e-034e-6b27-5d271af109ba
          name ( RO): pool-admin
    description ( RO): The Pool Administrator role has full access to all features and settings,
including accessing Dom0 and managing subjects, roles and external authentication
```

These roles have the capabilities described in the following list:

- **Pool Admin**: Assign/modify roles, Log in to server consoles with SSH and XenCenter, server backup/restore, Log out active user connections, Create and dismiss alerts, Cancel task of any user, Pool management, VM advanced operations, VM create/destroy operations, VM change CD media, View VM consoles, XenCenter view mgmt ops, Cancel own tasks, Read audit logs, Configure and manage WLB, Apply WLB Optimization Recommendations, Modify WLB Report Subscriptions, Accept WLB Placement Recommendations, Display WLB Configuration, Generate WLB Reports, Connect to pool and read all pool metadata

- **Pool Operator**: Log out active user connections, Create and dismiss alerts, Cancel task of any user, Pool management, VM advanced operations, VM create/destroy operations, VM change CD media, View VM consoles, XenCenter view mgmt ops, Cancel own tasks, Read audit logs, Configure and manage WLB, Apply WLB Optimization Recommendations, Modify WLB Report Subscriptions, Accept WLB Placement Recommendations, Display WLB Configuration, Generate WLB Reports, Connect to pool and read all pool metadata

- **VM Power Admin**: VM advanced operations, VM create/destroy operations, VM change CD media, View VM consoles, XenCenter view mgmt ops, Cancel own tasks, Read audit logs, Accept WLB Placement Recommendations, Display WLB Configuration, Generate WLB Reports, Connect to pool and read all pool metadata

- **VM Admin**: VM create/destroy operations, VM change CD media, View VM consoles, XenCenter view mgmt ops, Cancel own tasks, Read audit logs, Display WLB Configuration, Generate WLB Reports, Connect to pool and read all pool metadata

- **VM Operator**: VM change CD media, View VM consoles, XenCenter view mgmt ops, Cancel own tasks, Read audit logs, Display WLB Configuration, Generate WLB Reports, Connect to pool and read all pool metadata

◆ **Read Only**: Cancel own tasks, Read audit logs, Display WLB Configuration, Generate WLB Reports, Connect to pool and read all pool metadata

To take advantage of XenServer RBAC, you'll need to add users (local or AD based) into the system as *subjects*. Subjects are the object type understood by RBAC, so you'll need to match these up before taking advantage of the RBAC system. The command to add a user as a subject is as follows:

```
xe subject-add subject-name=<username>
```

For example, Figure 2.45 shows a host joined to the Virtsec.com domain shown adding a domain user named shack. This is verified with the xe subject-list command afterward (some output is truncated in the figure).

FIGURE 2.45

Adding a domain-based RBAC subject

```
[root@XenVoodoo bin]# xe subject-add subject-name=shack
cfb800ec-e78e-80ed-99d8-2cda29927eee
[root@XenVoodoo bin]# xe subject-list
uuid ( RO)                    : cfb800ec-e78e-80ed-99d8-2cda29927eee
    subject-identifier ( RO): S-1-5-21-1967180877-440539018-685507964-1000
            other-config (MRO): subject-name: VIRTSEC\shack; subject-upn: shack@VIRTSEC.COM; su
1000; subject-gecos: ; subject-displayname: VIRTSEC\shack; subject-is-group: false; subject-
word-expired: false
                    roles (SRO): pool-admin
```

SETTING UP ROLE-BASED ACCESS CONTROL

Now the user can be added to one or more roles on the system. To do this with PAM, follow these steps:

1. Stop the XenAPI service (xapi):

   ```
   /etc/init.d/xapi stop
   ```

2. Make a copy of the file /var/xapi/state.db and then edit the file with Vi. Search for the username you added as a subject. You should see something similar to the following (assuming username of XenAdmin1):

   ```
   other_config="(('subject-name' 'XenAdmin1') ('subject-uid' 'u520')
   ('subject-gid' 'g520') ('subject-gecos' '') ('subject-displayname'
   'XenAdmin1') ('subject-is-group' 'false') ('subject-account-disabled'
   'false') ('subject-account-expired' 'false') ('subject-account-locked'
   'false') ('subject-password-expired' 'false'))" subject_identifier="u520"
   uuid="cfb800ec-e78e-80ed-99d8-2cda29927eee" roles="
   ```

3. By default, new subjects are added to the Pool Admin role. However, you may want to apply a different role for a variety of reasons. To do this, get the UUID of the role that you obtained after running xe role-list. In the example provided earlier (shown in Figure 2.44), the Vm Admin role has the UUID of aaa00ab5-7340-bfbc-0d1b-7cf342639a6e. Modify the line in the state.db file to read:

   ```
   roles="('OpaqueRef:aaa00ab5-7340-bfbc-0d1b-7cf342639a6e')"
   ```

4. Save and exit the state.db file, and then restart the XenAPI service:

   ```
   /etc/init.d/xapi start
   ```

So, that's the process in a nutshell for adding RBAC with PAM.

Adding RBAC with AD is a bit simpler! Use one of the following commands to add AD users or groups to a specific role (these accomplish the same thing):

```
xe subject-role-add uuid=<subject UUID> role-uuid=<role UUID>
xe subject-role-add uuid=<subject UUID> role-name=<role name>
```

To change a subject's role, you will first need to remove an existing role, then add the new one:

```
xe subject-role-remove uuid=<subject UUID> role-name=<role you're removing>
xe subject-role-add uuid=<subject UUID > role-name=<role you're adding >
```

After adding AD users, you should be able to log in to the system using domain credentials. Figure 2.46 shows an example of logging in to the XenServer host via SSH with the domain admin account shack@virtsec.com. As you can see, the user is granted full privileges on the system due to the RBAC Pool Admin role assignment:

FIGURE 2.46

AD XenServer login
and role assignment

```
Shacks-iMac:.ssh root# ssh shack@virtsec.com@10.10.0.128
shack@virtsec.com@10.10.0.128's password:
Last login: Sat Feb  4 10:16:53 2012
Type "xsconsole" for access to the management console.
[root@XenVoodoo ~]# whoami
root
```

There are many, many benefits to using RBAC, chief among them being the granular control of privilege sets and detailed audit log generation for all user activity. I'll cover audit logs and logging in general later in the book in Chapter 7.

Lock Down Access to the XenServer Platform

XenServer has a number of methods available to control remote access to the system and its services. The first, and a standard Linux component for many distributions, is TCP Wrappers. TCP Wrappers consists of two files, /etc/hosts.allow and /etc/hosts.deny, which can be configured to explicitly allow and deny access to certain INET services found in /etc/xinetd.d. Both files have similar syntax, and a specific order is followed when placing entries into the files for access control:

1. Access will be granted when a service/client pair matches an entry in the /etc/hosts.allow file.

2. Access will be denied when a daemon/client pair matches an entry in the /etc/hosts.deny file.

3. Otherwise, access is granted (if no entry exists at all).

Many organizations simply choose to put all entries (both allow and deny) in the /etc/hosts.allow file. The following demonstrates both an allow and a deny entry for the SSH daemon:

```
sshd : 10.10.* : allow
sshd : 10.10.0.200 : deny
```

In addition to TCP Wrappers, standard SSH root login restriction and overall user restrictions can be managed in the /etc/ssh/sshd_config file. Open this file with the Vi editor and ensure that the following line is there:

```
PermitRootLogin no
```

You can also control who can access the system via SSH using the `AllowUsers` directive. Just include this keyword followed by usernames separated by spaces, as shown here:

```
AllowedUsers dave bob john
```

This is a simple and effective way to control SSH access if you need to have it enabled. Be sure to restart the SSH service after making these changes.

When using XenCenter to connect to and manage XenServer, the use of the XenServer console allows automatic access to the system with root privileges on certain versions of XenServer. To force a root password prompt within the XenCenter console, edit the file `/usr/lib/xen/bin/dom0term.sh`. Find the following line:

```
exec /bin/login -f root
```

Change this file to read as follows, and save and exit the file:

```
exec /bin/login -p
```

Finally, you can control most traffic to and from the XenServer by configuring the built-in IPTables firewall. The default firewall rules on a XenServer 6.*x* host include the following:

```
-A RH-Firewall-1-INPUT -i lo -j ACCEPT
-A RH-Firewall-1-INPUT -p icmp --icmp-type any -j ACCEPT
-A RH-Firewall-1-INPUT -p 50 -j ACCEPT
-A RH-Firewall-1-INPUT -p 51 -j ACCEPT
-A RH-Firewall-1-INPUT -p udp --dport 5353 -d 224.0.0.251 -j ACCEPT
-A RH-Firewall-1-INPUT -p udp -m udp --dport 631 -j ACCEPT
-A RH-Firewall-1-INPUT -p tcp -m tcp --dport 631 -j ACCEPT
-A RH-Firewall-1-INPUT -p udp -m udp --dport 67 --in-interface xenapi -j ACCEPT
-A RH-Firewall-1-INPUT -m state --state ESTABLISHED,RELATED -j ACCEPT
-A RH-Firewall-1-INPUT -m state --state NEW -m udp -p udp --dport 694 -j ACCEPT
-A RH-Firewall-1-INPUT -m state --state NEW -m tcp -p tcp --dport 22 -j ACCEPT
-A RH-Firewall-1-INPUT -m state --state NEW -m tcp -p tcp --dport 80 -j ACCEPT
-A RH-Firewall-1-INPUT -m state --state NEW -m tcp -p tcp --dport 443 -j ACCEPT
-A RH-Firewall-1-INPUT -j REJECT --reject-with icmp-host-prohibited
```

Looking at this list, you may notice some unusual ports listed, such as Internet Printing Protocol (IPP, port 631). Why in the world is that there? Great question. The good news is that most of these ports are not enabled and passing traffic by default. The firewall is just set up this way. The following are the most common ports in use by enterprise XenServer platforms:

- XenCenter ports
  - TCP 22 (SSH)
  - TCP 443 (XenAPI management)
  - TCP 5900 (VNC for Linux guests)
  - TCP 3389 (RDP for Windows guests)
- Resource pool ports
  - TCP 22 (SSH)
  - TCP 443 (XenAPI management)

- ◆ Internal infrastructure ports

    - ◆ TCP/UDP 123 (NTP)

    - ◆ TCP/UDP 53 (DNS)

    - ◆ TCP 389 (Active Directory or LDAP)

    - ◆ TCP/UDP 139 (NetBIOS Session Service)

    - ◆ TCP/UDP 445 (Microsoft-DS)

- ◆ Storage ports

    - ◆ TCP 3260 (iSCSI)

    - ◆ TCP 2049 (NFS)

    - ◆ TCP 21605 (Simple Object Access Protocol [SOAP] over HTTP StorageLink Gateway traffic)

There are many ways to configure the local IPTables firewall. One simplified method is to type the command `lokkit` at the command prompt. You'll then be presented with a curses interface like that shown in Figure 2.47.

FIGURE 2.47
XenServer firewall
configuration

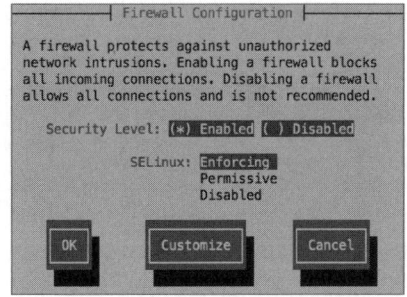

You've got the option to enable SELinux (Security Enhanced Linux) on this screen, too. There are three options:

`Enforcing`: Enables SELinux

`Permissive`: Only issues warnings without actually controlling behavior on the platform

`Disabled`: Turns off SELinux

SELinux can be very complex to configure and is outside the scope of this book. Just know that it can be more problematic than it's worth in most environments!

To perform a quick and dirty configuration on the local firewall, select Customize. You should see a screen like that in Figure 2.48.

Here, you can easily enable or disable incoming firewall rules. Click OK and then OK again when finished. To see what rules are actually in place, run the following:

```
iptables -L
```

FIGURE 2.48
XenServer firewall
customization

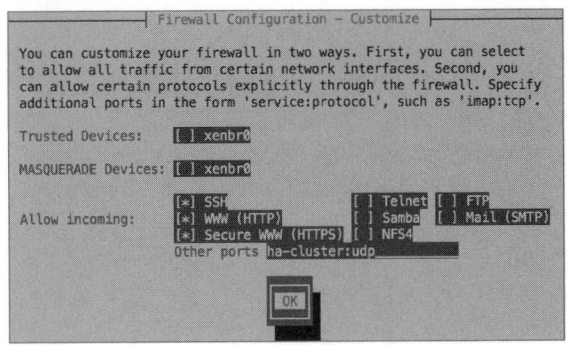

You can easily add new firewall rules as well. For example, to add a new rule that allows TCP port 31337 on the INPUT chain, you can use the following syntax:

```
iptables -A INPUT -p tcp --dport 31337 -j ACCEPT
```

This adds TCP 31337 as a viable and accepted destination port on the host. For most organizations, it's best to keep this as simple as possible. An excellent tutorial on IPTables can be found here:

www.frozentux.net/documents/iptables-tutorial/

Chapter 3

Designing Virtual Networks for Security

Virtual networks are a key element in designing a secure virtualized infrastructure. All major hypervisor platforms have virtual networking elements, and their design and configuration can play a significant role in how well the environment functions as well as the overall network security design you'll employ. There are numerous considerations for configuring virtual networks, ranging from connectivity to physical networks to Layer 2 VLAN segmentation, and each platform has its own set of capabilities and limitations. This chapter will cover the fundamentals of secure virtual network design as well as the major options available to securely configure Microsoft, VMware, and Citrix virtual switches.

In this chapter, you will learn about the following topics:

◆ Similarities and differences of virtual and physical networks

◆ Configuring virtual switches securely

◆ Integrating with physical networking

Comparing Virtual and Physical Networks

All virtualization platforms have a native set of virtualized networking components that need to be configured for performance, availability, and security. In addition, there are certain critical elements of the physical networking infrastructure that should be evaluated. When designing network security within and for the virtualization platforms and virtual machines (VMs) in your environment, the following are all key components:

Physical switches Physical switches are those already within your network. There are many different varieties of physical network switches and lots of vendors to choose from, like Cisco, Juniper, and others. When connecting physical switches to virtual platforms hosting VMs, you'll need to ensure that you plan appropriately for the volume and types of traffic that will need to be carried.

Virtual switches Virtual switches (often called vSwitches, in VMware parlance) are software-based representations of a physical switch and carry numerous types of traffic. This can include management traffic to the virtualization platform, production traffic to and from

VMs, and specialized traffic like iSCSI and NFS storage traffic and dynamic memory migration from one platform to another.

Physical network interface cards (NICs)   A hypervisor platform will have a certain number of physical NICs, and it's important to plan appropriately for how they'll be utilized. Considerations include redundancy, speed and performance needs, and appropriate segregation of traffic types.

Virtual NICs   Virtual NICs can take two primary forms. The first type is those present on virtual machines hosted on the hypervisor platform. As with any production system, the number and type of NICs needed will vary widely. The second type of virtual NIC is represented on the hypervisor itself, linking the hypervisor and its virtual switches to any physical NICs present on the hardware platform.

Physical network security devices   These can include firewalls, intrusion detection sensors, and any other common network security platforms that enterprises tend to run. In many cases, these can still be leveraged to their full capabilities with virtual platforms within the environment, but some architecture changes and traffic monitoring and filtering enhancements may be needed.

Virtualized network security devices   Most vendors of enterprise-class network security devices have created virtualized models that can be integrated into the virtual environment easily as specialized virtual machines (often called *virtual appliances*). In some cases, these virtual appliances can afford organizations significant benefits and advantages versus their physical counterparts. Examples of such benefits include virtualization-specific functionality like virtualization application traffic monitoring and integration with virtualization management platforms, performance improvements, and enhanced visibility to VM traffic.

All of these devices and components play a role in your overall architecture. An example of how physical switches and NICs interact with virtual switches and NICs is depicted in Figure 3.1.

FIGURE 3.1
Virtual and physical network components

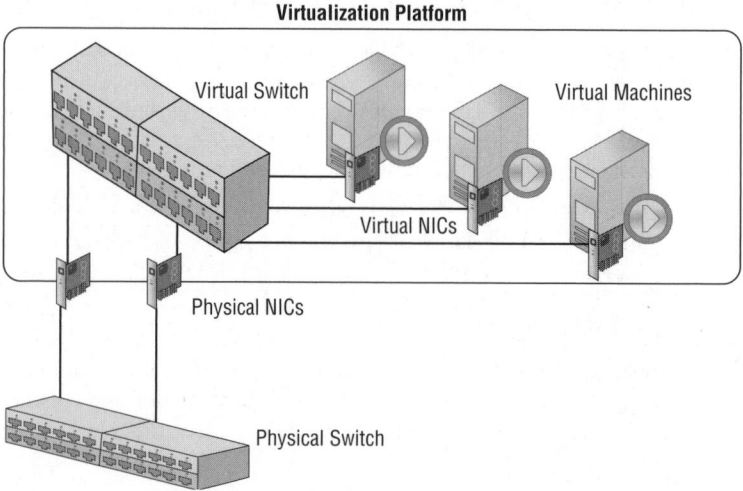

Virtual Network Design Elements

There are numerous types of virtual switch designs that can be implemented. Which design is most effective and efficient is a function of what the system's intended use cases are (criteria include sensitive data vs. nonsensitive, level of overall criticality, hardware resources, etc.). However, there are several simple types of designs that can be considered and are often used in a variety of combinations.

PHYSICAL NICS

The first key design consideration is the number of physical NICs. There are really three different types of traffic that you'll consider in any virtual network environment:

Virtual machine traffic   Production VM traffic will usually make up the majority of the traffic coming into and out of your hypervisor platform. At least one virtual switch, and likely more, will need to be allocated for this traffic, with at least a single physical NIC.

Management network traffic   Management traffic can be as simple as Secure Shell (SSH) traffic to a virtualization administrator's workstation or customized traffic to and from a virtualization management platform like VMware vCenter or Citrix XenCenter. This traffic may contain sensitive data and should ideally be segmented from production traffic if possible.

Specialized operations traffic   Storage network traffic, dynamic memory migration, and other specialized types of operational traffic are also vitally important to the proper operation of the virtual environment. These types of traffic should also be isolated from typical production segments whenever possible because they may be carrying sensitive data in cleartext and an attacker could potentially sniff this traffic if they gain access to the local subnet.

Ideally, all three of these traffic types will be physically and logically isolated, with separate virtual switches and separate physical NICs allocated for each. This gives an administrator the most flexibility in securing the system and may also be ideal from an availability perspective. However, you may not have enough physical NICs in your system to allocate one or more physical NICs to each traffic type, especially with blade systems in a chassis that accommodates only a single quad card (four NICs) per blade. While having three distinct types of traffic and four NICs may sound like enough, this doesn't account for redundancy and improved performance with NIC aggregation.

The following includes some simple guidelines to follow that allow for maximum availability, redundancy, and traffic segmentation:

Two physical NICs   With two physical NICs, you're not likely to have the option of redundancy and availability unless you carry all the traffic over both NICs. While this is an option, it's important to properly segregate traffic for the reasons discussed earlier. Availability aside, the "best practice" from a security perspective is to dedicate a single physical NIC to production VM traffic and combine management traffic and specialized operational traffic on the second physical NIC. These can both connect to the same physical switch but should have separate virtual LAN (VLAN) tags assigned to them, which will be discussed later in this chapter. This design is shown in Figure 3.2.

Again, it's important to reinforce that this is not an ideal design by any means. There is no redundancy built in, and this design should be considered only if hardware resources are extremely limited or in a lab or testing environment. Buying more physical NICs, even 10 Gb NICs, is fairly inexpensive and should be considered if at all possible.

FIGURE 3.2
A simple two-NIC design

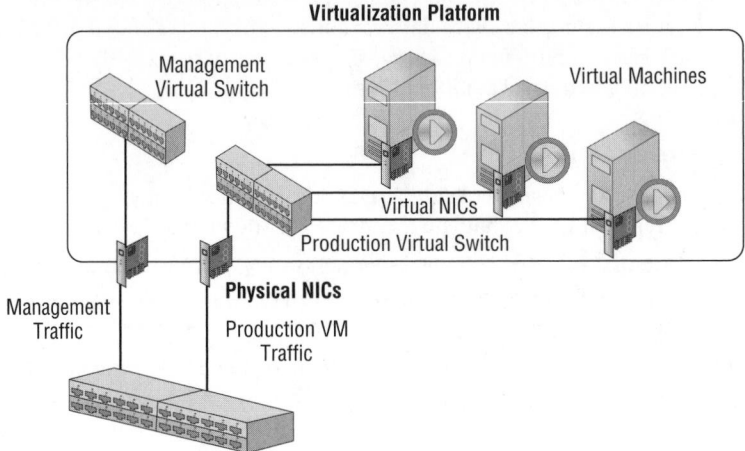

NOTE With most of today's modern hardware, it's highly unlikely that you'll be limited to just two physical NICs.

Four physical NICs With four physical NICs in the hardware platform (a surprisingly common configuration due to the prevalence of lower-cost blade architectures), there are multiple design options, some focused on availability and others on segmentation. For a more available design with four NICs, simply double the NIC allocation used in the two-NIC design; thus, you end up with two NICs for production VM traffic and two NICs for combined operations and management traffic. This is a much more reasonable approach than the two-NIC option that allows for some redundancy and failure scenarios without a devastating impact on any one traffic type (in the short term, anyhow). This design is depicted in Figure 3.3.

FIGURE 3.3
A redundant, four-NIC design

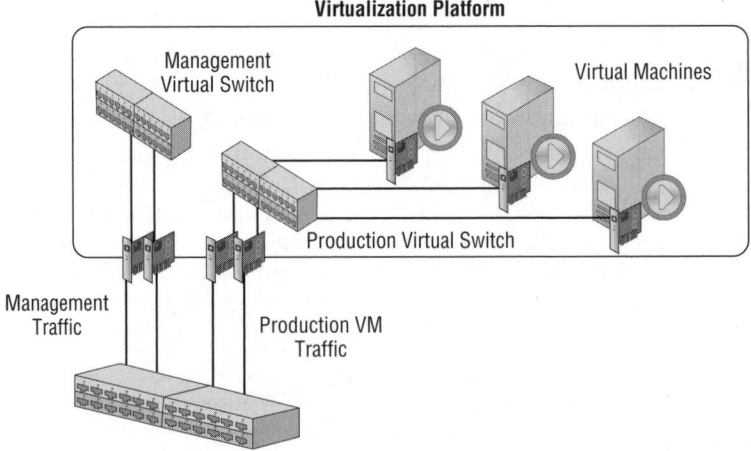

Another design that allows for more redundancy in production traffic with additional segmentation would dedicate two NICs for production VMs, one NIC for management traffic, and another NIC for operations traffic. This makes a trade-off between full redundancy and additional segmentation, as shown in Figure 3.4.

FIGURE 3.4

A more segregated four-NIC design

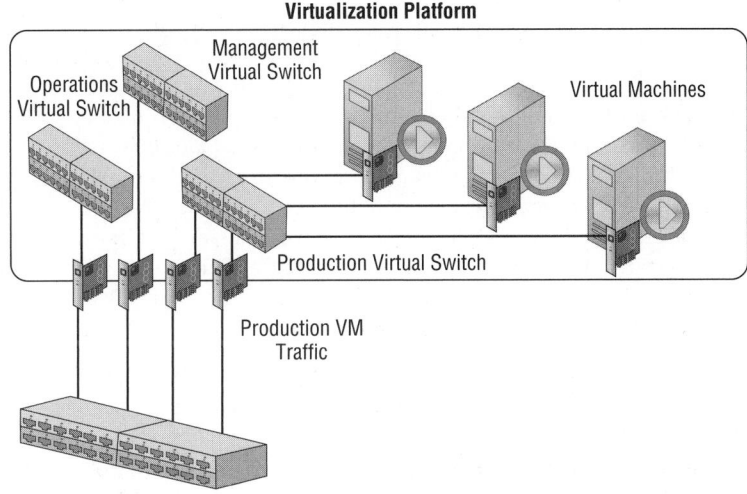

Six physical NICs With six physical NICs in the hardware platform, full measures of redundancy and segregation can be included. A simple design might be two distinct physical NICs to carry each specific traffic type. This is shown in Figure 3.5.

FIGURE 3.5

A basic six-NIC design

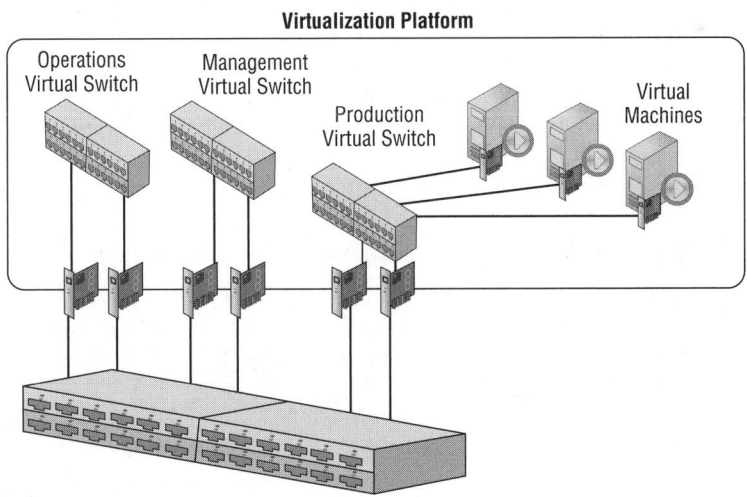

VIRTUAL SWITCHES

The key component in a virtual network configuration is the virtual switch. Virtual switches are used to connect everything within a virtual environment—virtual machines, physical hardware for connectivity, management networks, storage connectors, and so on. All major hypervisor platforms have virtual switches that are integrated into the kernel of the hypervisor OS to some degree, which allows the virtual switches to carry internal VM communications (as well as other types) very quickly. How this is designed depends on the particular hypervisor product as well as the type of virtualization in place. VMware vSphere, for example, uses *full virtualization*, which makes the virtualization technology completely transparent to the VMs. Citrix XenServer, on the other hand, leverages *paravirtualization*, where the VMs are aware that they're virtualized and may need special drivers to properly interact with the hypervisor OS and native hardware. In general, most virtualization solutions have the virtual switch integrated directly with the hypervisor OS at the kernel level or leverage a specialized VM for management purposes that assists with virtual networking functionality.

Physical vs. Virtual Networks

It's important to differentiate between some common capabilities and core functionality of physical and virtual network devices.

SIMILARITIES BETWEEN PHYSICAL AND VIRTUAL NETWORKS

Physical and virtual switches have much in common. There are a number of prevalent features for any switch that should be supported by a virtualized version, regardless of vendor chosen.

First, all switches should have VLAN support. VLAN tags allow traffic to be broken down into different broadcast domains, hypothetically allowing a single switch's traffic to be broken up by specific ports depending on what VLAN identification numbers are associated with those ports.

The second common feature that should generally be found in a switch, whether physical or virtual, is the ability to vary traffic throughput and speeds per port. This is usually a capability found on physical switches, although you'll find wide variation in how much configuration can be done on virtual switches. Most virtual switches also don't afford administrators much granularity in this department, unfortunately.

DIFFERENCES BETWEEN PHYSICAL AND VIRTUAL NETWORKS

Numerous differences can be found between physical and virtual switches.

Virtual switches can have significantly more ports than physical switches, for one. Most virtual switches can support hundreds of ports (or even over a thousand), although this can be difficult to manage.

One major difference is the lack of ability to cascade, or interlink, switches together in virtual environments. This is something every enterprise does with physical switches, extending the reach of a network's core out to offices, remote locations, and so on. This also requires the use of protocols like Spanning Tree Protocol (STP) to prevent traffic from looping endlessly. Virtual switches cannot be connected within a hypervisor environment, requiring some architectural changes to connect multiple traffic segments together.

A consistent theme you'll find is that virtual switches (at least the defaults that are vendor supplied) tend to have fewer configuration options (including security options) than their physical counterparts. Most enterprise-class physical switches support MAC address "stickiness" for individual ports (to prevent Address Resolution Protocol [ARP] spoofing and man-in-the-middle attacks), and many also support monitoring Dynamic Host Configuration Protocol (DHCP) servers to keep track of leases offered. These features are not found natively on any "out-of-the-box" virtual switches, but there are still a number of security configuration options and design variations that should be evaluated when looking to secure virtual networks.

Virtual Network Security Considerations

Most of your existing architecture and security devices will still play a role within the virtual environment, but there are some specific nuances to designing and configuring security for virtual switches and networks that warrant mention.

Important Security Elements

Following is a list of the most important things to evaluate:

Management network isolation   Isolating the network connections to virtualization management platforms and/or administrators' workstations is a simple and effective security measure to employ. This prevents sensitive commands from being executed, data from being transferred, or other information useful to attackers from intermingling with production network traffic.

You may question why this is so critical, and rightly so. To many administrators, it might look like overkill, but I can assure you it's not, and the reason is simple. It is no longer safe to assume that attackers have not compromised your network. Your attackers would love nothing more than to compromise entire virtualization infrastructures by hijacking your management credentials or other useful information. Although management connections are likely encrypted using Secure Sockets Layer (SSL) or Transport Layer Security (TLS), a simple configuration error could result in this information being sent in a less-than-secure manner, and any attacker able to eavesdrop on your network traffic could see this, or at least some of it. By specifically isolating the management network connections, preferably with physically separate connections, you're minimizing the potential for this security breach to occur.

Virtual switch isolation   Another simple tactic for controlling who can see what traffic is using distinct virtual switches (or port groups) to control and to isolate the physical NIC connections that pass traffic into and from the hypervisor. By using the three distinct groups mentioned earlier in the chapter (production VMs, management connections, and specialized operations and storage), it's not only easier to manage your environment, it's also easier to keep it secure. Again, this is a simple network architecture best practice, with relevance to security as well.

Monitoring capabilities   Network administrators need to monitor their environment for many reasons, ranging from operational management and troubleshooting to security and intrusion analysis. Tools like sniffers and intrusion detection sensors are commonly employed to analyze traffic, but before any monitoring can be done, the traffic must be visible and available to the administrators and their tools. On physical switches, this is commonly accomplished by creating what is known as a mirror port (or a SPAN port in Cisco terminology), where traffic from one or more production ports is copied to a different port for analysis. Virtual switches usually don't provide this sort of functionality, so other methods may need to be employed to allow for proper traffic monitoring and analysis.

Security policies   As mentioned earlier, most enterprise switches today come with a host of security configuration options, ranging from MAC address filtering and access controls to DHCP monitoring and others. Some switches are capable of tying into larger Network Access Control (NAC) architectures, which can evaluate network endpoints for specific security attributes before passing traffic. Virtual switches don't offer these kinds of capabilities natively, but they may have some simple security policies that can be enabled to accomplish certain administrative goals. Third-party switches like the Cisco Nexus 1000v or the Open vSwitch include much more in the way of security features, and we'll touch on these in this and subsequent chapters.

Management and access controls   A number of types of access controls can be implemented to control access to and from virtual environments. Some are located on the hypervisor platform itself, as covered in Chapter 2, "Securing Hypervisors." Some are located on the virtualization management platform, which we'll discuss in Chapter 5, "Virtualization Management and Client Security." Aside from VLANs, there are not usually any access controls present in the default virtual switches from hypervisor vendors.

Architecture Considerations

For virtual networks, there are lots of different architectural models to explore. One of the most common questions I'm asked with regard to designing secure virtual networks is, Can we still use our existing security infrastructure? In almost every case, my answer is yes. There are three basic types of virtual network designs, each of which has its own pros and cons. Any of them can be expanded or used interchangeably depending on where in the network it lives. As this is a book specifically on virtualization security, I'll explain the models in simple terms and lay out the security considerations that should factor into your decision to use one over the other.

PHYSICAL SEPARATION OF TRUST ZONES

The first and simplest model conceptually leverages complete physical separation of different trust zones. Each zone is hosted on a distinct hypervisor platform, and each of these platforms is connected to a separate physical switch that then connects to a network access control mechanism like a firewall. This design is shown in Figure 3.6.

An alternative to this design would be two different VLANs connected to the same physical switch and these VLANs in turn connecting to different firewall ports. That variation assumes that the VLANs themselves provide adequate segmentation, however, and there are several known ways to circumvent this.

The obvious security benefits of this model are complete physical separation and enhanced control over what systems and applications are running, and where. The one significant downside is cost—both capital costs for hardware and software and operational costs in configuring and managing the infrastructure.

FIGURE 3.6
Simple virtualiza-
tion architecture

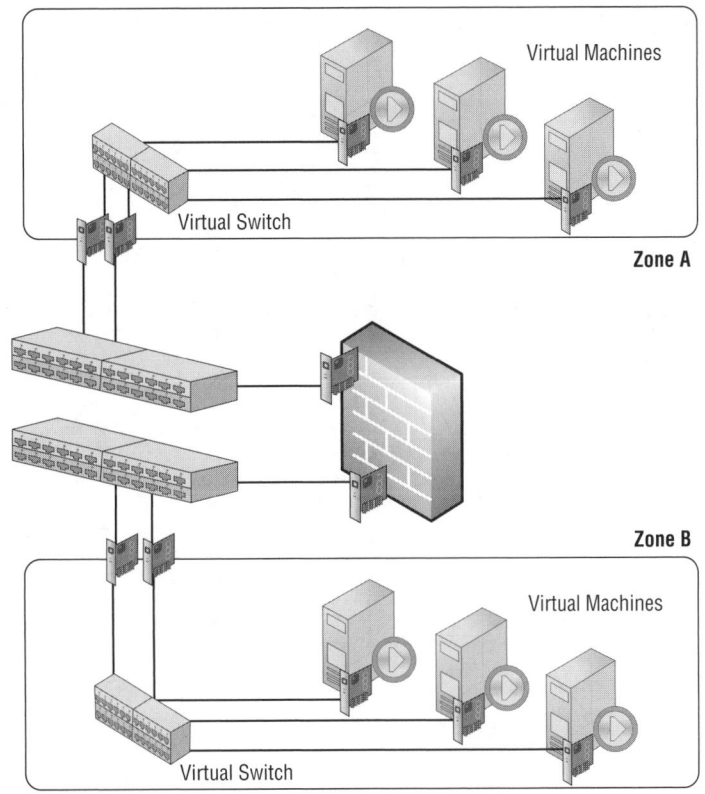

SINGLE VIRTUAL PLATFORM WITH PHYSICAL FIREWALL

The second model takes the concept of physical segmentation and builds on it a bit by collapsing the different zones into a single virtual platform. As you can see in Figure 3.7, the zones are now isolated by way of virtual switches in a single hypervisor platform, but the physical firewall still segments the traffic in the physical realm.

In this figure, I've left the separate physical switches in place, but the same concept from the previous model could be applied using VLANs to segment at Layer 2 from a single physical switch. There are numerous benefits to this model operationally and financially—less hardware to purchase, less software to configure and manage, and segmentation controlled by the hypervisor. This is a good balance of security and efficiency. However, there's an Achilles' heel in this model, and it's the hypervisor itself. If the hypervisor gets compromised, the segmentation in place could hypothetically be breached, leading to data intermingling and other negative security effects.

FIGURE 3.7
More collapsed
virtualization
architecture

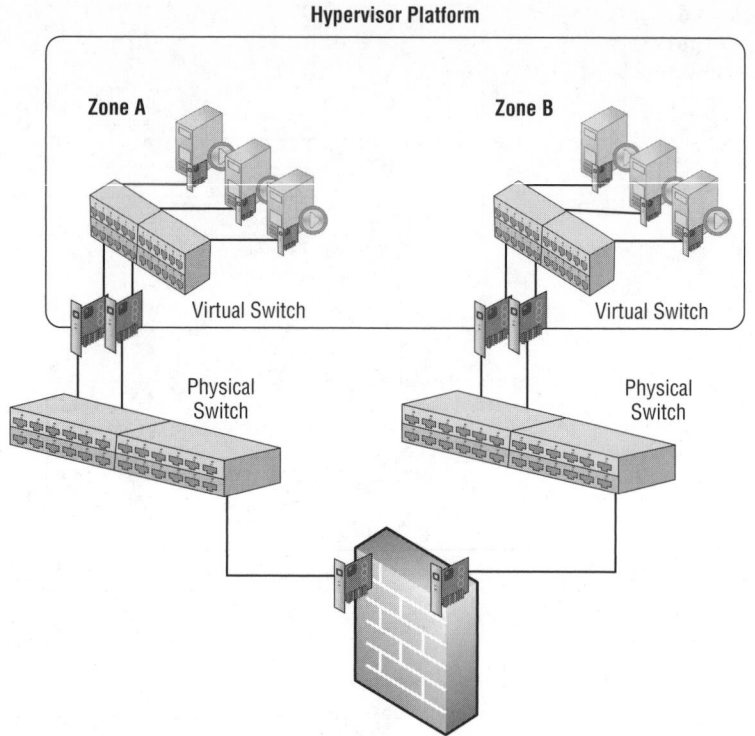

FIGURE 3.7
More collapsed
virtualization
architecture

FULLY VIRTUALIZED SECURITY

The final model starts integrating fully virtualized security components, namely the network access controls that previously resided only in the physical network. In this model, all security zones are contained on the same hypervisor, and more robust access controls are also included as virtual systems that traffic flows through, as shown in Figure 3.8.

There are many benefits to this model—lower costs for hardware and operational overhead, simpler administration in some cases, and deeper monitoring and control capabilities that are more tightly integrated into the virtual environment. However, these benefits can come at a cost. Now all of your security is baked into a single platform, creating the potential for a single point of failure. With this model, the security tools are using the same pool of resources (memory, disk, etc.) that the virtual machines depend on, and all sorts of conflicts can arise. For these reasons alone, many organizations choose to continue using physical security devices and controls in addition to some newer virtualized appliances and controls.

Configuring Virtual Switches for Security

There are surprisingly few security configuration options available within the stock virtual switches from VMware, Microsoft, and Citrix. VMware currently has the most native options available, although there are more options in the Hyper-V release integrated with Microsoft's new server operating system, Windows Server 2012. For all the major platforms, there are about a half-dozen options you'll want to ensure that you can configure to some extent.

FIGURE 3.8
Completely
collapsed virtual-
ization architecture

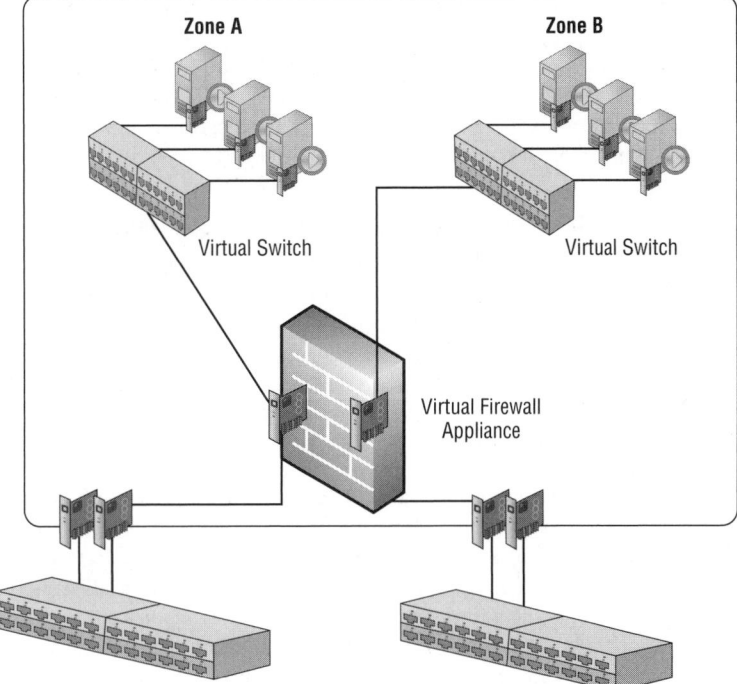

Defining Separate vSwitches and Port Groups

Defining separate virtual switches and port groups for different traffic types is a simple way to control what information is carried over which network segment.

Why you should do this   You may be required to separate certain types of traffic for compliance reasons, first of all. For example, the Payment Card Industry Data Security Standard (PCI DSS) specifically states that network segmentation is one of the key techniques used to define scope for compliance purposes, and the virtualization supplement for the PCI DSS also states that simple network isolation should be regarded as good practice.

RESOURCES

The PCI DSS is available at:

    https://www.pcisecuritystandards.org/documents/pci_dss_v2.pdf

The virtualization supplement is available at:

    https://www.pcisecuritystandards.org/documents/Virtualization_InfoSupp_
    v2.pdf

Security benefits Hypothetically, two virtual switches cannot pass traffic between themselves. By creating separate virtual switches for major traffic types or sensitive data types, you should see true data isolation unless you've bridged the virtual switches through a VM (such as a firewall VM, mentioned in the previous section), or unless you have connected both virtual switches to the same physical network and allowed traffic to mingle there. But this does *not* mean that you should feel completely safe placing sensitive and nonsensitive network segments on the same hypervisor platform. There is never a guarantee that a flaw in the hypervisor platform itself couldn't lead to a compromise. In general, however, creating separate virtual switches is a best practice to start off your virtual network security.

DEFINING SEPARATE VIRTUAL SWITCHES AND PORT GROUPS WITH VMWARE VSPHERE

There are two ways to create virtual switches and port groups within a VMware vSphere 5 environment (and some variations, but we'll stick with the two primary ways). The first is using the vSphere Client, either through the vCenter Server (the vSphere management platform) or by connecting to an ESX or ESXi host directly. The second is through the command line using the local esxcfg-vswitch command or the remote vSphere CLI vicfg-vswitch command. There are other options using different remote administration tools and command sets, but these are the most common.

NOTE When working with an ESX host, you have the choice of three network connection types to create: Virtual Machine, VMkernel, and Service Console. If you are working with ESXi, you have two options, Virtual Machine and VMkernel. On the ESXi platform, the management connection has been incorporated into the same networking construct as the specialized operations type instead of being a completely separate defined network connection. You should still consider a separate VMkernel connection on ESXi for management however! When you create a new VMkernel vSwitch or port group, you can choose to dedicate it as a management connection.

Using the vSphere Client

To define virtual switches or port groups using the vSphere Client, start the client, then enter the IP address or hostname of the vCenter server or individual ESX/ESXi host you want to connect to along with a user account with appropriate privileges to make networking changes to the platform. Once you establish a connection, you'll be at the vSphere Home screen. If you're connecting directly to a single ESX or ESXi host, click the Inventory icon in the Inventory section. If you're connecting through vCenter, select the Hosts And Clusters icon within the Inventory section as shown in Figure 3.9, then highlight the ESX/ESXi server for which you want to configure networking.

Once you're on the initial hypervisor host screen in the client, follow these steps.

1. Select the Configuration tab, and then highlight the Networking option along the left side.

2. On the Networking screen, select Add Networking on the upper-right side.

3. The Add Network Wizard appears. If you are working with an ESX host, you will be given the choice of three network connection types to create: Virtual Machine, VMkernel, and Service Console, as shown in Figure 3.10. If you are working with ESXi, you should have only two options, Virtual Machine and VMkernel.

FIGURE 3.9

Hosts and Clusters
in the vCenter
Inventory

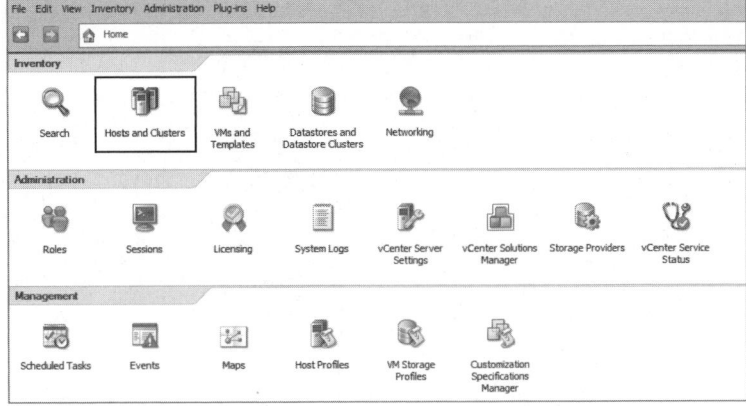

FIGURE 3.10

ESX network
Connection Types

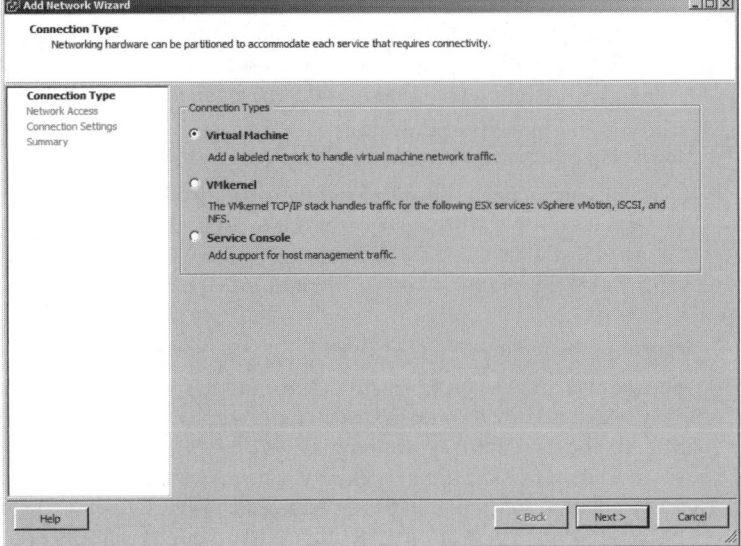

Select the type of network you want to define and click Next. On ESX, the three major types of traffic are automatically aligned with the virtual switch selection options. On ESXi, you'll need to differentiate the VMkernel type in just a moment.

4. On the Network Access screen, choose to create a new virtual switch or select an existing one on which to create a new port group. Click Next.

5. On the Connection Settings screen, define a network label (the name you ascribe to the switch or port group) and any VLANs that need to be defined for access to and from the virtual switch. On ESXi platforms, you also need to select the type of network traffic a VMkernel network type will carry (vMotion, fault tolerance logging, and/or management traffic), as shown in Figure 3.11. When finished, click Next.

FIGURE 3.11
ESXi VMkernel
traffic types

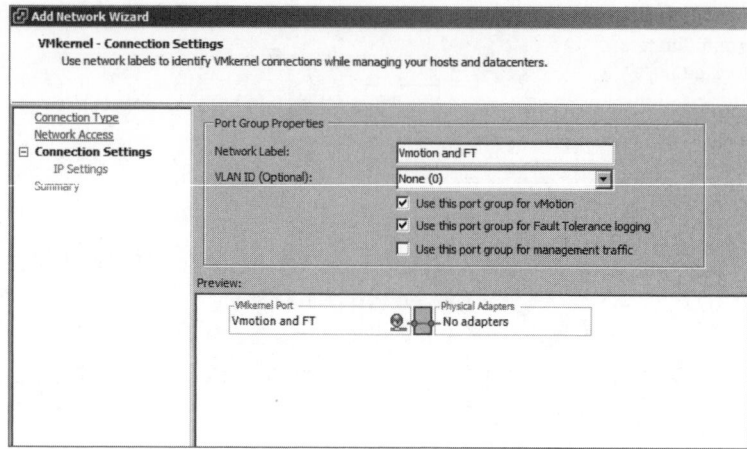

6. If you chose VMkernel, Service Console switch, or port group types, you'll now be able to configure IP address information; otherwise you'll be at the Summary screen. Click Next after finalizing these steps and you're done!

Modifying an Existing Virtual Switch or Port Group

If you are simply modifying an existing virtual switch or port group, visit the same Configuration ➢ Networking screen for the ESX/ESXi host, and select Properties next to the relevant virtual switch. Click the Add button on the lower left to open the Add Networking Wizard. A simple segregated network using different virtual switches is shown in Figure 3.12.

Creating a Distributed Virtual Switch

VSphere also allows you to create a distributed virtual switch (commonly called a dvSwitch or VDS), which allows one consistent virtual switch configuration to be spanned across multiple ESX/ESXi hosts within a specific cluster. To create one of these through the graphic interface using vCenter, first click the Inventory icon, and then choose Networking. Right-click a datacenter object in the tree view on the left side and select the option New vSphere Distributed Switch. The Create vSphere Distributed Switch Wizard appears. When it does, follow these steps:

1. Depending on the version of vSphere you're running, you'll have one or several options as to the version of the VDS you want to create.

    ◆ Version 4 is a standard VDS.

    ◆ Version 4.1 adds in load-based NIC teaming and network I/O control.

    ◆ Version 5 adds a number of capabilities relevant to security, namely NetFlow and port mirroring.

    If at all possible, choose version 5 and later because these capabilities are not insignificant (They will be covered in more detail in later chapters.) Select the version of the VDS you want to create and click Next.

FIGURE 3.12
A simple isolated
virtual network

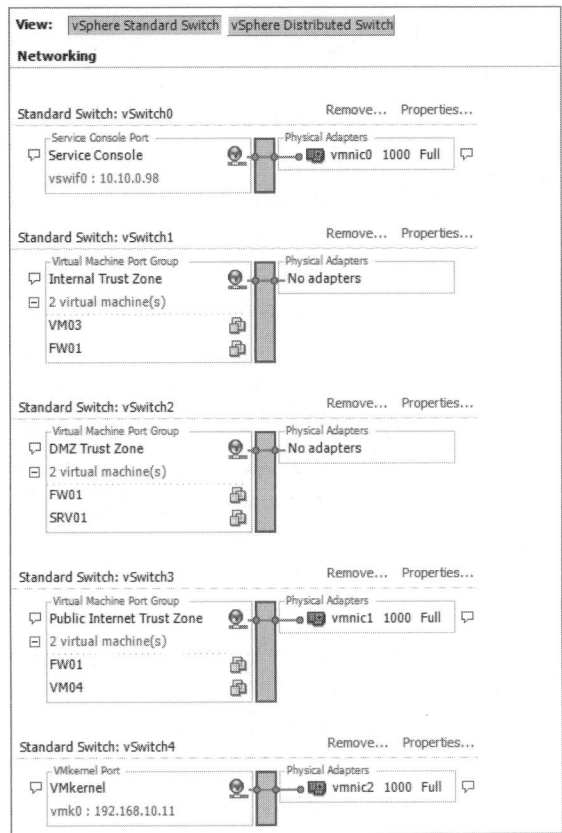

2. On the next screen, select the VDS name and the number of physical NICs (uplinks) that can be associated with the VDS per physical hypervisor host. Click Next.

3. Add existing compatible ESX/ESXi hosts and physical adapters to be associated with the VDS. Click Next and then Finish to create the VDS.

After the VDS is created, you can modify Port Group settings by right-clicking it in the tree view and selecting New Port Group or Manage Port Groups. VDS security policy settings will be covered later in this chapter in the section "Implementing Native Virtual Networking Security Policies."

Using the Command Line

Another way to create virtual switches and port groups is through the command line. For many vSphere implementations, this will be done in one of two ways. The first way is the simplest overall; it leverages the built-in esxcfg-vswitch command on both ESX and ESXi platforms. By accessing the ESX Service Console (through SSH or another means) or the ESXi Console (via ESXi Shell or SSH), this command can be easily used to create and configure standard vSwitches.

NOTE For ESXi systems, there is no longer any concept of the vswif interface type; this represented the Service Console, which has been deprecated.

First, assuming you have accessed the ESX or ESXi command line, the commands you run to create and configure a new virtual switch are as follows:

1. To add a new virtual switch, use the -a flag and specify the name of the virtual switch:

   `esxcfg-vswitch -a <vSwitch name>`

2. Add a port group to the vSwitch. By default, when you create a new port group, it's classified as a Virtual Machine network type.

   `esxcfg-vswitch -A <port group name> <vSwitch name>`

3. Now you have the option to create two different types of port groups (management connectivity and VMkernel connectivity). On ESX platforms, there are two specific commands that can be run to accomplish this.

   For management connections, execute the `esxcfg-vswif` command as follows:

   `esxcfg-vswif -a -i <IP address> -n <netmask> -p <portgroup name> <management port name>`

   For creating VMkernel operations ports, use the `esxcfg-vmknic` command:

   `esxcfg-vmknic -a -i <IP address> -n <netmask> <port group name>`

   To establish VMkernel port group types on ESXi, simply use the `esxcfg-vmknic` command in the same way, but specify separate virtual switches and port groups for management traffic and VMkernel operations.

Using vSphere CLI

The final way to configure virtual switches at the command line is by using remote command options. The two most popular remote command tools for VMware are the vSphere CLI and PowerCLI. Here, we'll use the VMware vSphere CLI, which VMware makes available for free. (I'll cover PowerCLI in more detail in Chapter 10, "Scripting Tips and Tricks for Automation.")

The great thing about the vSphere CLI is the ease of use—almost all of the commands align with existing command sets on individual hosts. This means that administrators familiar with commands like `esxcfg-vswitch` and `esxcfg-vmknic` can use the vSphere CLI commands without many changes. Many of the commands will also run against a centralized vCenter Server, allowing configuration of any ESX/ESXi hosts managed by that system.

To run the `vicfg-` commands, simply use the equivalents to those just discussed in the previous section (i.e., `vicfg-vswitch.pl` for `esxcfg-vswitch`) and add the hostname or IP, a username, and a password. For example, to list the virtual switches on ESXi host 10.10.0.99, you'd run the following command:

`vicfg-vswitch.pl --server 10.10.0.99 --username root --password <password>`

Just add the command options at the end of the statement, and you should be good to go!

One point to note here—the password is included in the command line for simplicity and for fully automated scripting control in this and other vSphere CLI examples. There is a chance that this will be logged or recorded somehow, and security-conscious organizations will likely want other options. If you exclude the `--password` option in the command line, you'll be prompted to enter it manually.

TIP   Remember, for all of these commands, you should be specifying separate physical NICs for true segmentation whenever possible. This can be accomplished by adding the -L flag and a physical NIC (uplink) name afterward.

DEFINING SEPARATE VIRTUAL SWITCHES AND PORT GROUPS WITH MICROSOFT HYPER-V

Hyper-V virtual switches are defined a bit differently than VMware's. Instead of two to three distinct virtual switches, Microsoft allows you to create one of the three virtual switch types:

◆ External virtual switches can be bound to a physical NIC and allow VMs to be connected to a physical network.

◆ Internal virtual switches do not connect to a physical NIC and allow VMs to communicate with other internal VMs as well as the Hyper-V host operating platform.

◆ Private vSwitches are similar to internal vSwitches, where VMs can communicate only with other VMs on the same virtual network. However, private vSwitch VMs *cannot* communicate with the Hyper-V host.

Creating a Switch Using Hyper-V Manager

This is a limited set of options for virtual network definition. For most operations, you'll likely have to create the generic external virtual switch type, and that would apply for the three traffic types just defined. Follow these steps:

1. To create a new virtual switch, open the Hyper-V Manager on a Hyper-V host.

2. Highlight a Hyper-V host in the list on the left side. Select the Virtual Network Manager or Virtual Switch Manager link on the right side under Actions. You'll see a list of existing virtual networks along with the option to create a new one on the right side, as shown in Figure 3.13.

FIGURE 3.13
Hyper-V virtual
networks

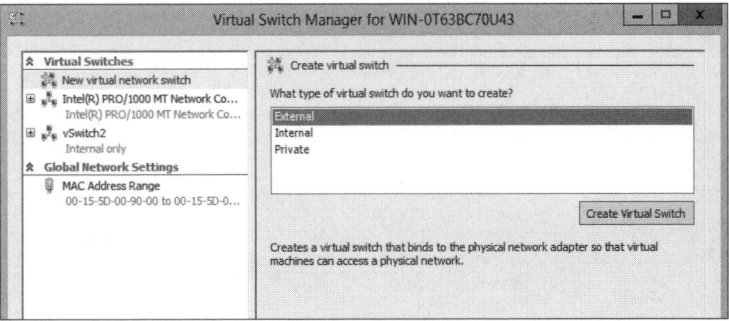

3. Select the type of virtual network you want to create, then click the Add or Create Virtual Switch button, depending on the version of Hyper-V you have. You'll now be able to enter a name for the virtual network, any notes you care to add that describe it in more detail, and the appropriate network type and physical NICs for connectivity, where appropriate.

4. Click OK to finish, and then close the Virtual Network Manager window.

Creating a Switch Using SCVMM

Most enterprises running Hyper-V will be using more robust management tools than the stand-alone Hyper-V Manager tool on each host. A common management platform for Hyper-V operations is Microsoft's System Center Virtual Machine Manager (SCVMM). Here's how to create a new virtual switch using SCVMM:

1. Log in to SCVMM. If you have SCVMM 2008, highlight the Hosts tab in the left-hand column. If you have SCVMM 2012, highlight the Fabric tab and then select All Hosts. Choose the appropriate Hyper-V host, and it should be highlighted in the top pane on the right side.

2. Double-click the Hyper-V host in the right-hand pane. The Host Properties window appears.

3. Click the Networking tab along the top (in SCVMM 2008) or the Virtual Networks tab on the left side (for SCVMM 2012) and you'll be presented with a list of existing virtual networks on the left side of the window. Click the Add button on the top.

4. In the right-hand pane, enter a name for the virtual network, a network tag, and a description. In the Network Bindings section, choose the type of switch (Private Network or Internal Network). This is shown in Figure 3.14.

FIGURE 3.14
Creating a new
virtual network
with SCVMM

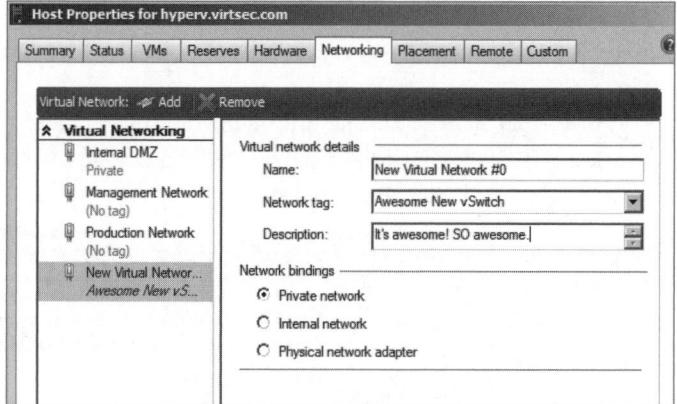

Many administrators also use PowerShell scripts to manage Hyper-V. There will be more on this in Chapter 10 where scripting is covered.

DEFINING SEPARATE VIRTUAL SWITCHES AND PORT GROUPS WITH CITRIX XENSERVER

There are several ways to configure virtual networks for XenServer, but the most common by far is through the XenCenter management platform, and that's what I'll cover here:

1. Connect to your XenCenter implementation, then select either a XenServer pool or an individual XenServer instance.

2. On the right side, click the Networking tab along the top, and you are presented with two panes: Networks and Management Interfaces.

3. Click the Add Network button below the top window to add a new vSwitch. You have four network types that can be created, depending on the XenServer architecture implementation you have in place:

External network A network that is connected to a physical NIC and usually passes VLAN-based traffic (covered shortly).

Single-server private network This type of virtual switch will pass only traffic between VMs on the same XenServer host.

Cross-server private network If more advanced switching capabilities are installed on XenServer (meaning you've installed the Open vSwitch), this type of network can be installed. This connection type allows the creation of private connections between different VMs in a single pool (on one or multiple hosts).

Bonded network This simply bonds two physical NICs for a network, providing improved performance.

4. Select the type of network you would like to create. Click Next.

5. Provide a network name and description in the fields provided. The more descriptive, the better. Click Next.

6. Configure the network to use a particular NIC and configure any VLANs and maximum transmission unit (MTU) settings. Click Finish.

7. To add specific management interfaces, or link them to your vSwitches, click the Configure button below the bottom window under the Networking tab.

8. You'll be presented with existing management interfaces in the left-hand pane. Highlight one of these and configure it, or click the New Interface button at the bottom to set up a new one. This screen is shown in Figure 3.15.

FIGURE 3.15
XenServer
Management
Interfaces

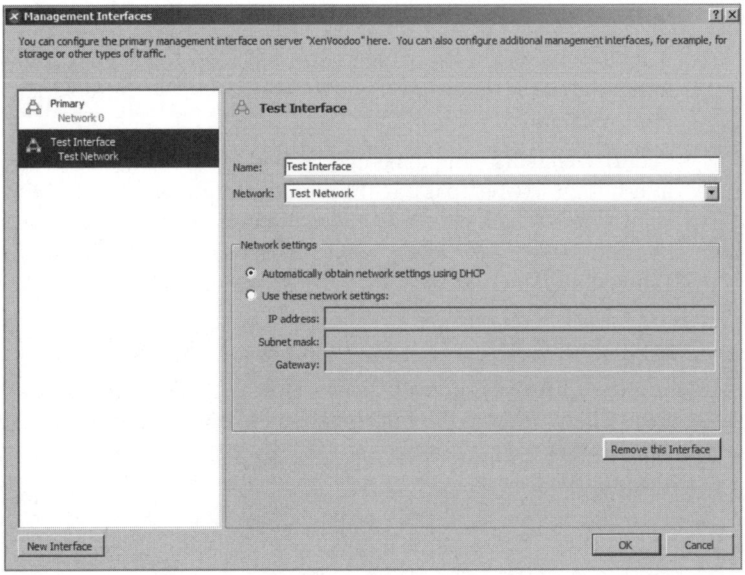

9. Enter the interface name, the network to associate with, and any addressing information. Click OK when finished.

To create a new XenServer network at the command line, use the `xe` command as follows:

```
xe network-create name-label=<vSwitch name>
```

This will create a new internal network (single-server private network).

Keep in mind that separating different network types is a security best practice in both physical and virtual environments. By following these steps, you can ensure that the management network is also segmented appropriately. But be sure also to connect it to a separate physical NIC (uplink), if at all possible! If it's not possible in your environment, then you're likely going to need to use virtual LANS (VLANs), which I'll cover next.

Configuring VLANs and Private VLANs for Network Segmentation

Virtual LANs are likely already set up in your environment. It's important to ensure that VLAN-tagged traffic flows smoothly from physical segments into virtual ones.

Most security professionals agree that VLANs are not really an adequate security measure to properly restrict traffic between systems and network segments. VLAN hopping attacks using techniques like switch spoofing and double tagging are possible in some older switches, and implementing more VLANs can lead to more configuration complexity, which is a major cause of security issues if things are not managed properly.

That said, organizations use VLANs as a simple network segmentation measure all the time, and so should you.

Why you should do this   There are several pragmatic reasons to configure VLANs and private VLANs in your virtual environment. First, from an availability standpoint, you'll need to match the configuration of your physical network VLANs to keep traffic flowing into and out of the virtual environment. Second, VLANs provide a reasonable way to break up broadcast domains and also provide an added measure of isolation between traffic passing across the same physical (or virtual) medium.

Another reason you should implement VLANs in your virtual environment—sad but true—is that they may be all you have for security and isolation in a native virtual switch implementation.

Security benefits   Implemented properly, VLANs keep packets on different VLANs from intermingling when passing through the same switches. If these varied VLAN traffic types have different data-classification levels, mingling traffic can be a major issue because sensitive data will be flowing alongside nonsensitive traffic and may be more exposed to attacks. While not a panacea, every little thing helps!

CONFIGURING VLANs ON A VMWARE vSPHERE vSWITCH

Configuring VLANs is actually very simple with VMware. You can configure VLANs using the vSphere Client or using the command line within the Service Console. You can also configure private VLANs.

Configuring VLANs in vSphere Client

Follow these steps to configure VLANs with the vSphere Client:

1. Within the vSphere Client (connected to an individual hypervisor platform or vCenter Server), select the ESX/ESXi host on which you want to configure VLANs, and choose the Configuration tab in the right-hand pane. Then select the Networking option in the list on the left side.

2. Assuming you are modifying an existing virtual switch and port group, select the Properties link directly to the right of the virtual switch you want to modify.

3. Highlight the port group you wish to modify in the vSwitch Properties box that pops up, and then click the Edit button at the bottom of the window.

4. In the port group Properties window that pops up, you have two options for virtual machine port groups: the network label and the VLAN ID, as shown in Figure 3.16.

FIGURE 3.16
Modifying port group VLANs

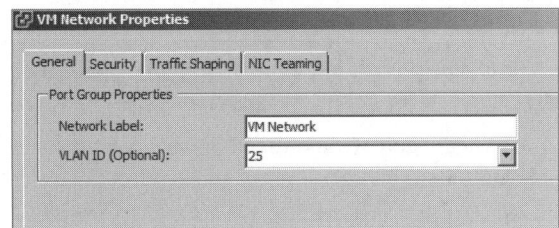

NOTE   For VMkernel port groups, you have these two options and several others, such as check boxes for enabling vMotion and management traffic. I'll cover these later.

Adding or changing a VLAN is as simple as selecting an option in the drop-down box or entering a new value. Click OK to save the changes, and then click Close to exit the vSwitch Properties window.

Configuring VLANs Using the Command Line

To add or modify VLANs at the command line, use the `esxcfg-vswitch` command (within the Service Console or at the ESXi command line) or the `vicfg-vswitch.pl` vSphere CLI script. Specify the port group you want to modify with the -p flag and the VLAN tag with the -v flag, as follows:

```
esxcfg-vswitch -p <port group> -v <VLAN ID> <vSwitch name>
```

Configuring Private VLANs

VMware has added with its vNetwork Distributed Switch (vDS) the ability to implement private VLANs (PVLANs) in addition to standard ones. What exactly are private VLANs, and what's the benefit of using them? In a nutshell, private VLANs give you the ability to further subdivide VLANs into additional segments. For example, if VLAN 20 is the main production VM network but you'd like to keep database servers on one port group separate from web servers on a different port group, you could leverage private VLANs on a vDS to accomplish this.

Two types of private VLANs can be created, called primary and secondary PVLANs. The primary VLAN tag is used for carrying traffic *to* the ESX/ESXi host, whereas secondary VLANs carry traffic *from* ESX/ESXi hosts and can be subdivided into three types:

Promiscuous ports can send and receive Layer 2 frames from any other ports in the entire VLAN. These are usually designated as the *virtual uplinks* for all other PVLAN ports because they can communicate with all ports both in and out of the PVLAN.

Isolated ports can communicate only with promiscuous ports in the same secondary PVLAN and are the most restrictive type of PVLAN port.

Community ports can communicate with promiscuous ports and other ports in the same secondary PVLAN. These are used when multiple separate ports in a PVLAN need to communicate with one another as well as systems external to the PVLAN.

PVLANs can be configured within the Properties window of a vDS but only on vCenter management systems. Here's how:

1. Select the Inventory link, then Networking, and then highlight the vDS on which you want to make changes.

2. On the Summary tab for the VDS, click the Edit Settings link on the left side. When the VDS Settings window opens, select the Private VLAN tab along the top, as shown in Figure 3.17.

FIGURE 3.17
VDS private VLAN configuration

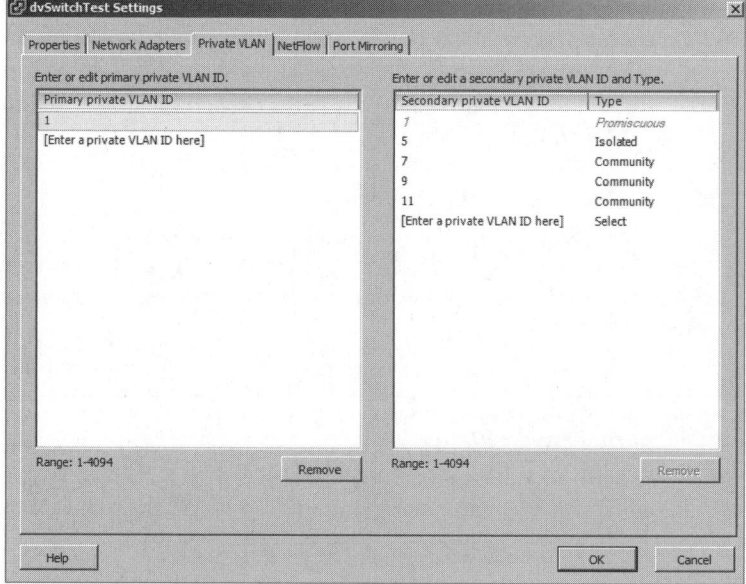

3. Here, you can configure primary PVLANs on the left side and associated secondary PVLANs on the right side. In Figure 3.17, the primary PVLAN tag is 1, and secondary tags of 5, 7, 9, and 11 are designated with various port types (Isolated or Community). The promiscuous type is automatically assigned to PVLAN 1 because it connects everything in the secondary PVLANs to other virtual and physical network segments. Simply click in either the left or right pane where you see the label Enter A Private VLAN ID Here and manually enter primary and secondary PVLAN tags. When finished, click OK.

4. Now that you're back at the main vDS configuration screen, assign the PVLAN tags that you've defined to VDS port groups. Right-click one of the port groups for the vDS in the left pane and select Edit Settings.

5. On the dvPortGroup Settings screen, select VLAN from the list on the left side, and then choose Private VLAN from the drop-down menu on the right side. In the Private VLAN Entry drop-down menu, select any of the primary or secondary PVLANs you defined. (See Figure 3.18.)

FIGURE 3.18
Private VLAN
selection for VDS
port groups

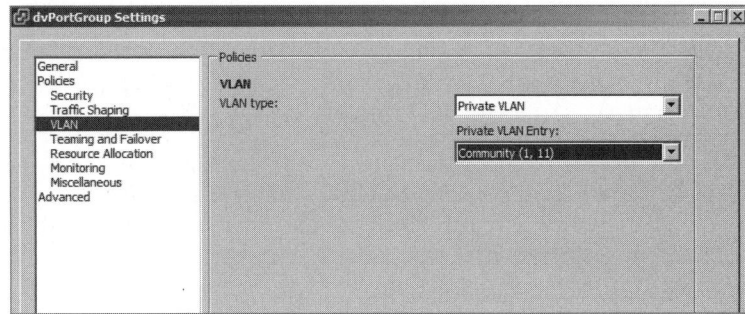

6. Click the Close button to finish.

CONFIGURING VLANS ON A MICROSOFT HYPER-V vSWITCH

Given the fairly limited functionality of Microsoft's virtual networking capabilities, configuring VLANs is not particularly complex, and there's no way to configure private VLANs at all. Let's take a look at the first way.

To configure a VLAN using either Hyper-V Manager or SCVMM, follow these steps:

1. If you're using the Hyper-V Manager, click the Virtual Network Manager link (or Virtual Switch Manager in Server 2012) for a specified Hyper-V host. If you're using SCVMM, double-click the host to access its Properties window, and then select the Networking tab (or Virtual Networks in SCVMM 2012). Both of these methods will bring you to the same window, where you can add or modify virtual networks.

2. For a given virtual switch that is in External or Internal mode, you should see a check box on the right-hand side that is labeled "Enable virtual LAN identification for management operating system" for Hyper-V Manager or "Access host through a VLAN" in SCVMM (Figure 3.19).

FIGURE 3.19
Hyper-V vSwitch
VLANs

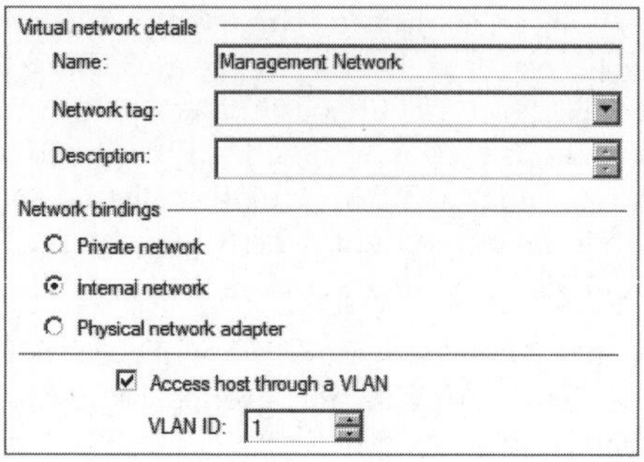

3. Click to check the check box, and then modify the VLAN ID in the box below. Click OK and you're done! This sets the VLAN for the entire vSwitch.

You may want to have VMs with multiple VLANs on a vSwitch instead. For this configuration, you'll need to leave the previous box unchecked and pass through VLAN traffic directly to the VMs themselves. Setting the VLANs on the individual VMs is a simple task as well:

1. In either Hyper-V Manager or SCVMM, right-click any VM and select Properties in SCVMM or Settings in Hyper-V Manager.

2. You're looking for the Network Adapter hardware configuration. In Hyper-V Manager, simply look in the left-hand pane under the Hardware section (the NICs will be listed underneath). In SCVMM, click the Hardware Configuration tab along the left side in the VM's Properties menu.

3. Select the VM NIC that you want to modify. In the right-hand pane, you will see a check box labeled Enable VLAN (or Enable Virtual LAN Identification in Hyper-V Manager, as shown in Figure 3.20).

4. Check this box and select a VLAN ID from the drop-down menu. Then click OK, and you'll be set.

Configuring VLANs on a Citrix XenServer vSwitch

Much as with Hyper-V, setting simple VLAN tags for an entire XenServer vSwitch is very simple.

NOTE　Keep in mind is that these VLAN settings, much like those on Hyper-V vSwitches, are applied to the entire vSwitch!

Here are the steps:

1. While logged into XenCenter, select a pool or XenServer host, and then choose the Networking tab in the right-hand pane.

2. Select the network for which you'd like to add or modify a VLAN tag, and click the Properties button (or right-click the network and choose Properties from there).

3. Select the Network Settings category in the left-hand list pane. The configuration options should appear on the right side, as shown in Figure 3.21.

FIGURE 3.20
Virtual machine
VLANs in Hyper-V

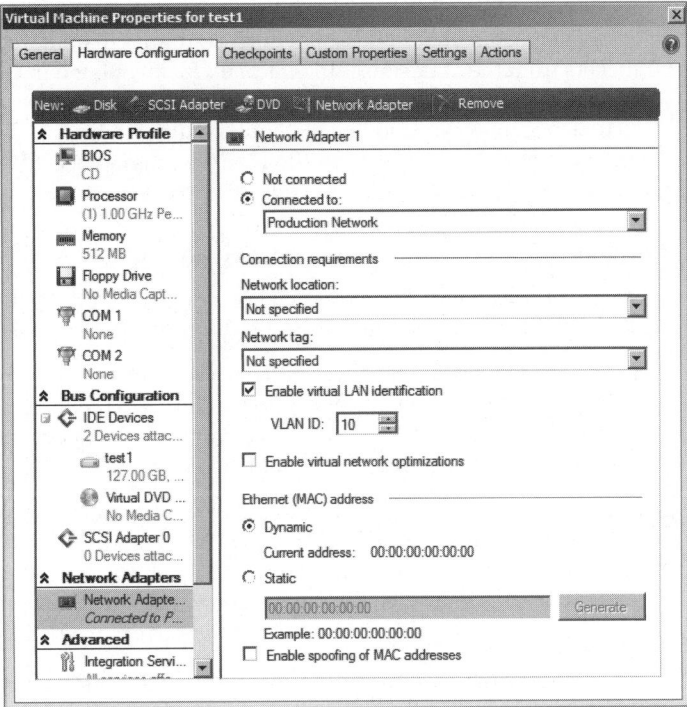

FIGURE 3.21
XenServer vSwitch
VLAN settings

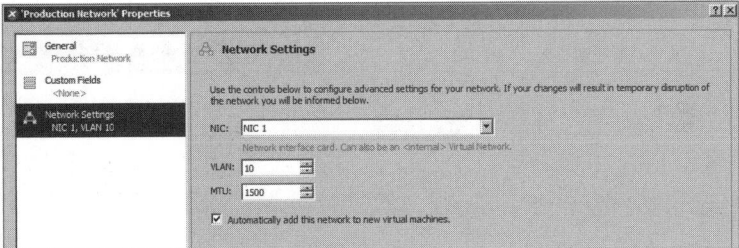

4. Modify the VLAN parameter to the desired value, and then click OK.

Limiting Virtual Network Ports in Use

As with any switch, it's prudent to limit the ports in use so that they don't inadvertently get used for something else.

Why you should do this   As much for datacenter housekeeping and sound operational control as it is a security measure, limiting ports in use can help to keep your infrastructure a bit more organized and prevent new or rogue VMs from being introduced to the environment (whether inadvertently or purposefully). On physical switches, ports can be disabled when not in use and turned on when they're needed. On virtual switches, a bit more planning and monitoring needs to take place.

Security benefits Many of the security issues that tend to arise in virtual environments stem from poor operational practices rather than more sensational threats like evil hackers from the dark side of the Internet. As mentioned in Chapter 1, "Fundamentals of Virtualization Security," virtual sprawl and the proliferation of rogue or misconfigured virtual machines can lead to a plethora of vulnerabilities and issues. Reducing potential security issues by strictly controlling the systems connected to virtual switches will easily improve the security posture of your infrastructure more than you realize.

CHECKING VIRTUAL SWITCH PORTS IN VMWARE VSPHERE

The simplest way to check what switch ports are in use on a standard VMware vSwitch is by manual verification. There are really only two steps to this when using the vSphere Client:

1. For each ESX/ESXi host, access the Configuration tab and then click the link for Networking on the left side. This should reveal the virtual switches and port groups in place. Look at the VMs listed for each standard vSwitch and ensure that they are legitimate virtual machines that should be connected.

2. Click the Properties link next to each vSwitch, and notice the first parameter listed on the right side, labeled Number Of Ports. This should match the number of virtual machines in use. If you need to remove ports, double-click the vSwitch icon. In the vSwitch Properties window, you'll have a configuration option to modify the total number of ports on the vSwitch. Change this, and click OK when finished.

For distributed virtual switches, the process is also fairly straightforward:

1. In the Inventory section, select Networking, and then select either a VDS or a port group. Then, in the right-hand pane, select the Ports tab, as shown in Figure 3.22.

FIGURE 3.22
VDS ports

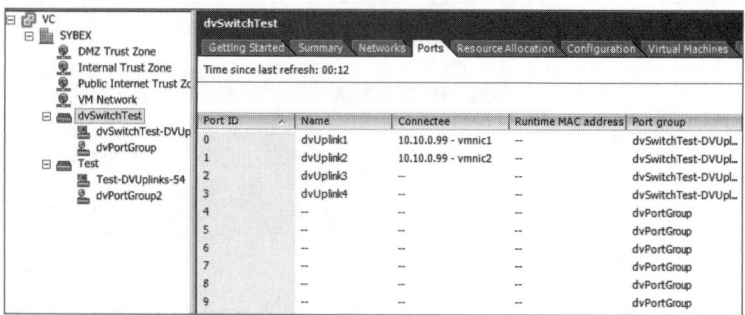

2. Compare the number of ports in use on this tab with the total number defined in the VDS port groups. Select any port group, right-click, and choose Edit Settings. The total number of ports defined in the port group can be modified on the first screen.

Another very simple way to verify the ports defined versus the ports in use is by using the esxcfg-vswitch or the remote vicfg-vswitch command-line tools. By simply running these commands with the -l option (that's a lowercase l, which stands for *list*), each switch and port group will be listed per host with the number of configured ports and the number of used ports, as shown in Figure 3.23.

FIGURE 3.23
Command-line verification of ports in use

```
~ # esxcfg-vswitch -l
Switch Name       Num Ports   Used Ports   Configured Ports   MTU    Uplinks
vSwitch0          128         3            128                1500   vmnic0

   PortGroup Name         VLAN ID   Used Ports   Uplinks
   VM Network             99        0            vmnic0
   Management Network     0         1            vmnic0

DVS Name          Num Ports   Used Ports   Configured Ports   MTU    Uplinks
Test              256         1            256                1500

   DVPort ID          In Use      Client
   0                  0
   1                  0
   2                  0
   3                  0
   4                  0
   5                  0
   6                  0
   7                  0

DVS Name          Num Ports   Used Ports   Configured Ports   MTU    Uplinks
dvSwitchTest      256         3            256                1500   vmnic2,vmnic1

   DVPort ID          In Use      Client
   0                  1           vmnic1
   1                  1           vmnic2
   2                  0
   3                  0
```

CHECKING VIRTUAL SWITCH PORTS IN MICROSOFT HYPER-V

Within either of the Microsoft virtualization management consoles mentioned, it's simple to look at a particular host and see what the physical NICs and VM NICs are connected to. Simply highlight a host and select the View Networking option from the right side within SCVMM 2008, or right-click the host and choose View Networking In SCVMM 2012. You should see a screen similar to that in Figure 3.24.

As you can see, the interface is not ideal for examining individual VM ports in use. To be more accurate, you're looking to see if any virtual switches are defined with no active VMs or connections—in other words, unused virtual networking assets, which should ideally be removed (especially if they are defined as external networks!). Later, when I cover scripting tools and techniques in Chapter 10, we'll look at some other ways to assess this.

FIGURE 3.24

Hyper-V vSwitch
usage

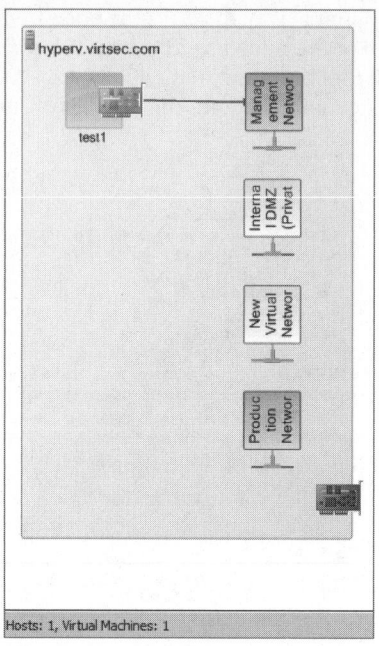

CHECKING VIRTUAL SWITCH PORTS IN CITRIX XENSERVER

XenServer does not offer any native options to list the specific VMs connected to each virtual switch, or the connections to them. Instead, you need to run several commands and piece together the information each provides:

1. Run the xe vm-list command to get a current list of the VMs associated with the host. Each VM will have a unique ID number (a universally unique identifier, or UUID), as seen in Figure 3.25.

FIGURE 3.25

XenServer VM list

```
[root@xenvoodoo ~]# xe vm-list
uuid ( RO)           : b90056c9-2b79-3596-fe6b-5da0b51fd0d4
    name-label ( RW): CentOS
    power-state ( RO): halted


uuid ( RO)           : 5e295b12-6476-4192-b7ec-3e7ba6cb2300
    name-label ( RW): Control domain on host: XenVoodoo
    power-state ( RO): running
```

2. Note the unique UUID for a VM (for example, in Figure 3.25, the CentOS VM has the UUID of b90056c9-2b79-3596-fe6b-5da0b51fd0d4).

3. Run the xe vif-list command, which returns a list of the virtual interfaces defined for VMs. Each virtual interface has its own unique ID (UUID) but also lists the VM UUID that it's associated with as well as the network it's connected to (network-uuid). This is shown in Figure 3.26.

FIGURE 3.26
XenServer virtual
interface list

```
[root@xenvoodoo ~]# xe vif-list
uuid ( RO)          : 478cf54d-c65a-417d-83ce-2f2d0932fe6b
        vm-uuid ( RO): b90056c9-2b79-3596-fe6b-5da0b51fd0d4
         device ( RO): 1
   network-uuid ( RO): c9f30d95-a4ff-3ad0-d2e5-baaf4b940d70


uuid ( RO)          : aae91eec-69bd-6cc6-09d3-3a0696b818c3
        vm-uuid ( RO): b90056c9-2b79-3596-fe6b-5da0b51fd0d4
         device ( RO): 0
   network-uuid ( RO): 3845ee3e-23c3-3f1c-db8d-f4aacfe0db5b
```

4. Run the commands `xe network-list` and `xe pif-list`. This will list the physical NICs in the XenServer platform as well as the defined networks. Each physical NIC is shown to be associated with a network.

5. You can now cross-associate the UUIDs for VM NICs, physical NICs, and defined networks—simple, right? See the output of the `xe pif-list` command in Figure 3.27.

FIGURE 3.27
XenServer physical
interface list

```
[root@xenvoodoo ~]# xe pif-list
uuid ( RO)                : eb6ed096-0031-09f4-9d6f-99b0319f2af7
             device ( RO): bond0
   currently-attached ( RO): true
               VLAN ( RO): -1
       network-uuid ( RO): 6f75c8aa-170d-4789-6502-5dc369681183

uuid ( RO)                : 184d95d8-5e48-3010-be12-815cb6e9776c
             device ( RO): eth1
   currently-attached ( RO): false
               VLAN ( RO): -1
       network-uuid ( RO): c94e7b3a-1847-8ed4-f97e-f5f2e9e841f6

uuid ( RO)                : e2e85651-bea2-5443-e270-7c76a1ca974a
             device ( RO): eth0
   currently-attached ( RO): true
               VLAN ( RO): -1
       network-uuid ( RO): 3845ee3e-23c3-3f1c-db8d-f4aacfe0db5b

uuid ( RO)                : 3e52cad5-3913-3d17-27bb-d0f55856f9ec
             device ( RO): eth2
   currently-attached ( RO): false
               VLAN ( RO): -1
       network-uuid ( RO): e13b2969-5db8-4240-4aac-2f36bdbe5d18

uuid ( RO)                : 154ffdd0-b85e-c2b1-c06c-211b5621201e
             device ( RO): eth0
   currently-attached ( RO): true
               VLAN ( RO): 1
       network-uuid ( RO): 8a4a2665-9f3e-67ec-1750-d32428ba7e55

uuid ( RO)                : 35b01214-8e14-6ac4-b2da-0b6736a7a2ed
             device ( RO): eth0
   currently-attached ( RO): true
               VLAN ( RO): 5
       network-uuid ( RO): c9f30d95-a4ff-3ad0-d2e5-baaf4b940d70
```

To say that this is nonintuitive and clumsy would be a severe understatement.

Implementing Native Virtual Networking Security Policies

Although the built-in virtual switches from major virtualization vendors leave much to be desired, there are a few things you can implement to improve security without installing third-party and vendor products.

Why you should do this   Any time you have security options natively built in, it's worth investigating what benefits they bring. In some cases, they'll impose an operational burden on your virtual environment that's unacceptable. In others, they won't cause any impact whatsoever and it will make great sense to put them in place.

Security benefits   Most of the basic virtual switches provided by the virtualization vendors do not have much to offer in the way of security controls. Even VMware, with the most built-in security options, leaves much to be desired. However, there are several options that warrant mention, and these should be configured carefully.

VMware vSphere Virtual Switch Security Policies

VMware virtual switches and port groups have three fundamental security policies that can be configured:

Promiscuous Mode: If this is enabled, the port group will allow all traffic to reach all VMs associated with the port group.

MAC Address Changes: If this is set to Accept, inbound traffic to VMs is allowed to systems that have changed their MAC address in some way.

Forged Transmits: If this is set to Accept, outbound traffic from VMs is allowed when these virtual systems have changed their MAC address in some way.

The Promiscuous Mode setting can actually have some benefit (I'll discuss this in more detail in Chapter 4, "Advanced Virtual Network Operations"). The other two settings, MAC Address Changes and Forged Transmits, are directly related to the fact that all VMware VMs have two MAC addresses by default—one initial MAC address, set by VMware, and the other that is established within the VM platform settings. Initially, these are identical and will have one of four VMware MAC organizationally unique identifier (OUI) prefixes:

```
00:50:56
00:05:69
00:0C:29
00:1C:14
```

The MAC Address Changes and Forged Transmits settings both deal with changes to the *effective* MAC address, which can be changed within the VM guest OS.

The best practice for most implementations is to set the following:

◆   Promiscuous Mode: Reject

◆   MAC Address Changes: Reject

◆   Forged Transmits: Reject

These can easily be set using the vSphere Client. Click the Properties link for any vSwitch or port group, and there will be a tab labeled Security along the top, as shown in Figure 3.28.

FIGURE 3.28
Virtual Switch
Security Policies

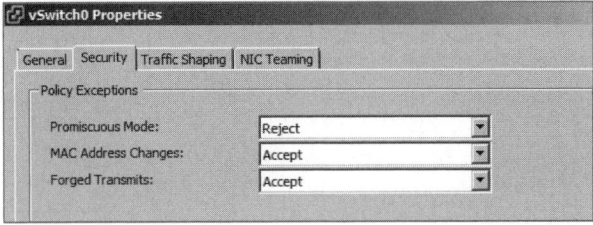

By default, the Promiscuous Mode setting is Reject, while the other two are Accept. Individual port groups can have different settings than the vSwitch, and their settings will override those of the vSwitch.

For distributed virtual switches, there are several places where security policy changes can be made. The first is at a global VDS level. If you are in the Inventory section of vCenter, select Networking and then right-click a distributed virtual switch port group. In the left-hand pane, you should see a configuration option for Security, which can be selected to configure the three major policies. One interesting feature in VDS is the option to selectively override specific port groups and ports. By selecting the Advanced option, you'll see a link labeled Edit Override Settings. By selecting this, you'll be presented with the options shown in Figure 3.29.

FIGURE 3.29
VDS port security
override settings

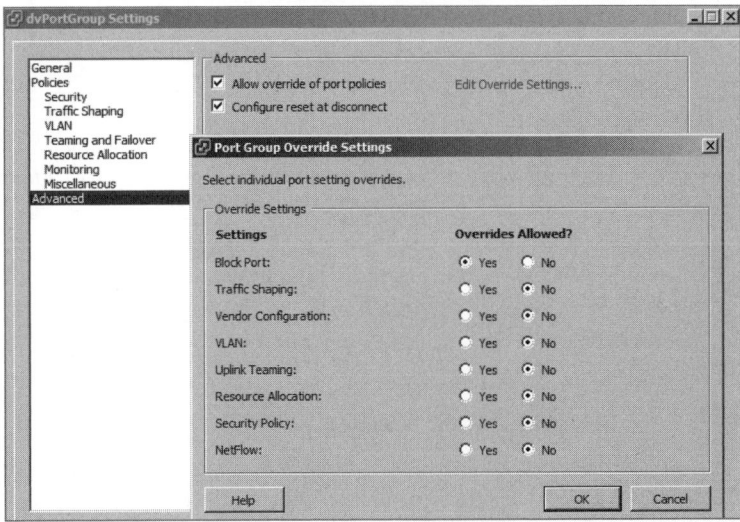

Another option for VDS security policy settings is more global in nature. You can set the policy for all port groups on a VDS by right-clicking the VDS and selecting Manage Port Groups. You will see a screen similar to Figure 3.30.

FIGURE 3.30
VDS global security
policy selection

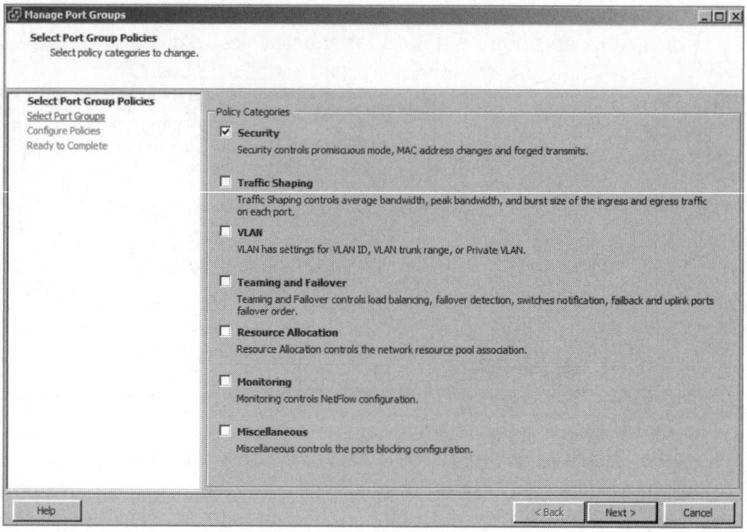

Select Security, choose which VDS port groups you want to configure, and set the overall policy for them all in one fell swoop. Convenient!

To set these security policies at the command line, you've got a few different options. The first thing to know is that there's no native, simple way to do this remotely on ESX platforms. For ESXi, the vSphere CLI has commands that will work, but this is not the case for ESX because it's being phased out.

For ESX hosts, access the Service Console locally or via SSH, and use the `vmware-vim-cmd` command as follows:

```
vmware-vim-cmd hostsvc/net/vswitch_setpolicy --securepolicy-promisc=false -v <vSwitch name>
vmware-vim-cmd hostsvc/net/vswitch_setpolicy --securepolicy-macchange=false -v <vSwitch name>
vmware-vim-cmd hostsvc/net/vswitch_setpolicy --securepolicy-forgedxmit=false -v <vSwitch name>
```

For ESXi hosts, you can use the `esxcli` command set to query and change security policies for both vSwitches and port groups. At the console command line, execute the following to list the policies in place for a vSwitch:

```
esxcli network vswitch standard policy security get -v <vSwitch name>
```

To get the security settings for a port group instead, execute the following:

```
esxcli network vswitch standard portgroup policy security get -p <port group name>
```

This command not only shows the policies set for the port group, it also shows whether the settings can override those of the port group's vSwitch. To set the policies instead of simply listing them, change the `get` parameter to `set`, and add one of the following parameters and 0/1 values (0 is Reject, and 1 is Accept):

```
-m 0/1 #This sets the MAC Address Change value to Reject or Accept
-f 0/1 #This sets the Forged Transmits value to Reject or Accept
-p 0/1 #This sets the Allow Promiscuous value to Reject or Accept
```

So, for example, if you wanted to set the Forged Transmits value to Reject for vSwitch0, you'd run the following:

```
esxcli network vswitch standard policy security set -f 0 -v vSwitch0
```

The `esxcli` commands work exactly the same with the remote vSphere CLI; you'll just need to include the `-s` or `-h` switch to point to a host or vCenter, the `-u` switch to specify a username, and the `-p` switch with a password.

MICROSOFT HYPER-V VIRTUAL SWITCH SECURITY POLICIES

With Hyper-V on Server 2008 R2 and SCVMM 2008, there were no native security options available for Microsoft's virtual switches. However, in Windows Server 2012, you can implement several simple policies.

NOTE   One of the most fundamental changes for Microsoft Hyper-V is the new extensibility of the virtual switch, which allows third-party vendors to integrate with Microsoft's virtual switch to provide more advanced monitoring and security control over VM traffic. This topic is outside the scope of this book, however.

For VMs defined on a Windows 2012 Server Hyper-V installation, there are three security and monitoring settings that can be enabled. Within Hyper-V Manager or SCVMM, highlight the VM you would like to protect, then right-click and select Properties. Now follow these steps:

1. In the left-hand pane, find the network adapter connected to the vSwitch that you'll be editing. Expand the network adapter's information, and then select the Advanced Features item.

2. The first option you'll see is labeled DHCP Guard. Check the box next to Enable DHCP Guard if you want to prevent the VM from ever responding to DHCP requests and posing as a DHCP server.

3. The second option, right below the DHCP Guard option, is Router Guard. Check the option labeled Enable Router Advertisement Guard if you want to prevent this VM from advertising itself as a router to other VMs or systems.

   The third option is very useful for network traffic monitoring, and is labeled Port Mirroring. This will be covered in more detail in Chapter 4.

These options are shown in Figure 3.31.

CITRIX XENSERVER VIRTUAL SWITCH SECURITY POLICIES

There are no built-in security settings for XenServer virtual switches and networking capabilities at this time (up to and including version 6.*x*). The Open vSwitch, covered briefly in Chapter 4, has many more options, and serious Xen shops will likely want to implement this without fail.

Securing iSCSI Storage Network Connections

Most enterprise virtualization deployments will have some sort of large-scale storage in place. The most common types in place are Network File System (NFS), Network Attached Storage (NAS), Fibre Channel storage area network (SAN), and iSCSI SAN. The topic of storage security is beyond the scope of this book, and the vast majority of the topics and controls associated with enterprise storage security aren't configured or managed from within the virtualization environment in any case. However, there is a simple means to authenticate iSCSI storage endpoints by implementing the Challenge Handshake Authentication Protocol (CHAP) on iSCSI storage adapters, and it's generally recommended to do so if possible.

FIGURE 3.31
Windows Server
2012 vSwitch secu-
rity policies

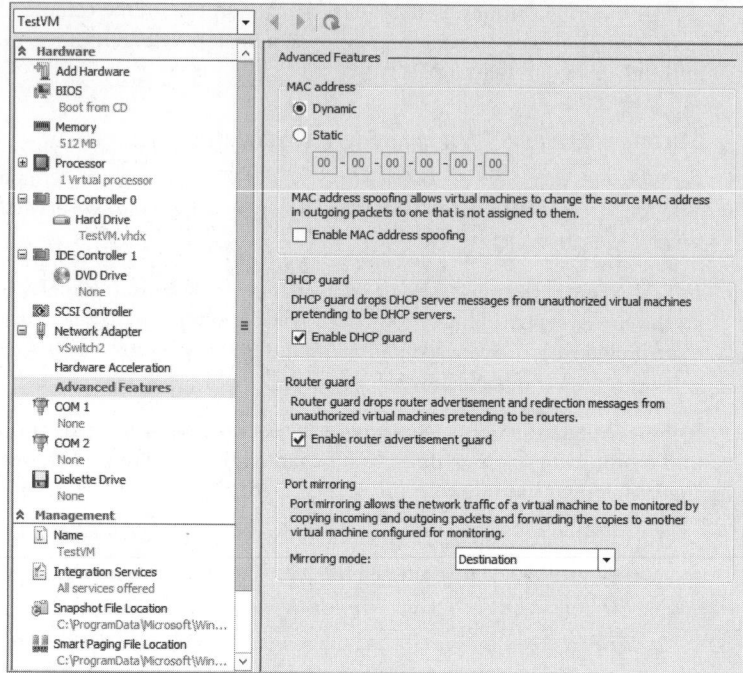

Why you should do this   Although there are known weaknesses with CHAP, it's simple to implement and is a built-in component of the iSCSI standard. For organizations lacking the ability to implement more robust controls, CHAP is a reasonable way to secure an iSCSI implementation.

NOTE   For information about CHAP weaknesses, see www.rootsecure.net/content/downloads/pdf/cheating_chap.pdf.

Security benefits   Because most (or all) of the virtual machine disks are stored on separate large-scale storage media, there's a good chance some sensitive data will pass between the hypervisor platform and your SAN or NAS. Protecting this data in transit, using various encryption mechanisms, is a good idea. However, another important aspect of securing your storage traffic is ensuring that the traffic is communicating with only a valid storage end-point. Many of the most sophisticated storage attacks take the form of man-in-the-middle (MITM) techniques or spoofing. CHAP can help to prevent this from happening.

IMPLEMENTING iSCSI CHAP WITH VMWARE vSPHERE

To enable CHAP for iSCSI, follow these steps:

1. Use the vSphere Client to connect to vCenter or an individual ESX/ESXi host. Select an individual host and navigate to the Configuration tab.

2. Click the Storage Adapters link on the left-hand side in the Hardware section.

3. Select the iSCSI Initiator, right-click, and select Properties.

4. Click the CHAP button in the lower left of the Properties window. A screen similar to Figure 3.32 will appear.

FIGURE 3.32
iSCSI CHAP con-
figuration screen

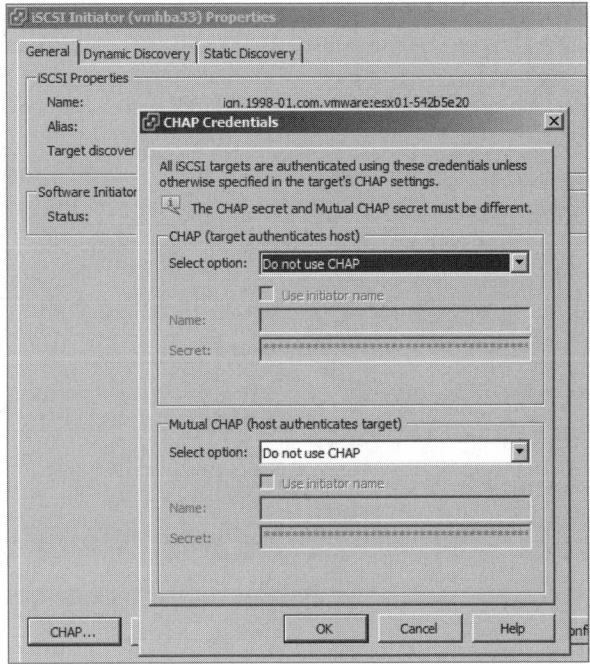

5. Select one of the four drop-down options under CHAP (Target Authenticates Host). These four options are fairly straightforward:

- Do Not Use CHAP

- Do Not Use CHAP Unless Required By Target

- Use CHAP Unless Prohibited By Target

- Use CHAP

Ideally, you'll select Use CHAP if you can.

6. You can check the Use Initiator Name box or enter a different iSCSI identifier for use with CHAP. In essence, the initiator name is the unique footprint of the iSCSI adapter. Now, in the Secret box, enter a password that will also be configured on the iSCSI storage device you'll be connecting to.

7. If you want to perform two-way authentication (where the ESX/ESXi host validates the identity of the iSCSI storage device), repeat steps 4 and 5 using the Mutual CHAP box. Be sure to use a different Secret value than the one you used in the first box.

8. That's it! Click OK and then Close.

After finishing CHAP setup, you'll be prompted to rescan the adapter to incorporate the changes.

IMPLEMENTING iSCSI CHAP WITH MICROSOFT HYPER-V

Because Hyper-V runs on Windows Server 2008, the process for enabling iSCSI interfaces using CHAP on Hyper-V is the same as that for the OS. Details are beyond the scope of this book, but the simplest way to implement it is to use Windows Server 2008's iSCSI Initiator tool. On the Configuration tab, you can configure CHAP secrets, as shown in Figure 3.33.

FIGURE 3.33
Microsoft iSCSI
CHAP configuration

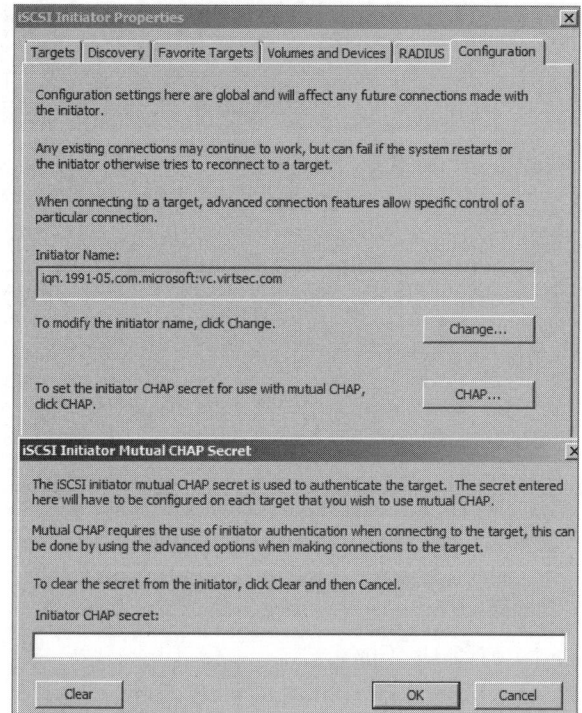

Another option is to use the `iscsicli` command-line tool, which is more granular.

IMPLEMENTING iSCSI CHAP WITH CITRIX XENSERVER

In XenCenter, configuring CHAP for iSCSI storage connections is simple.

1. Highlight a Pool or individual XenServer system, and then select the Storage tab in the right-hand pane.

2. If you have iSCSI storage defined already, right-click it and select Properties. Otherwise, click the button labeled New SR under the storage window. You can then define a Software iSCSI connection, provide a name and description, and click through to the Location section.

3. Here, you'll have the Use CHAP check box option, providing a username and CHAP secret (labeled as Password). This is shown in Figure 3.34.

FIGURE 3.34
XenServer iSCSI
CHAP configuration

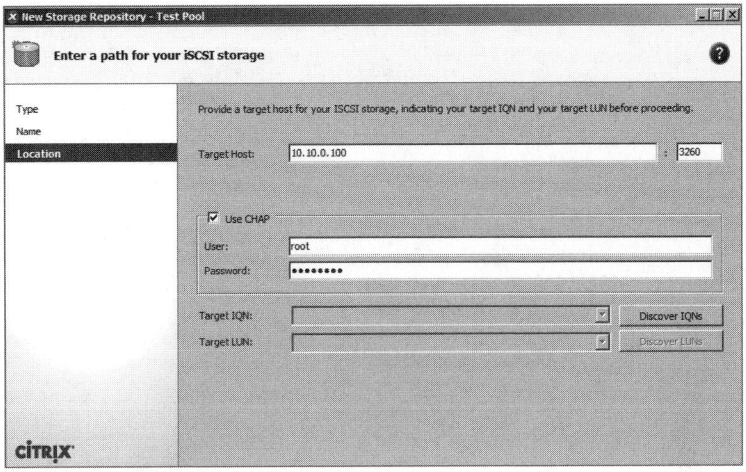

5. Click Finish or OK to finalize the configuration.

Integrating with Physical Networking

Connecting vSwitch ports and NICs to the physical LAN is necessary at some point (at least for most environments). The major consideration here is to ensure that trunk ports are configured properly for VLAN tagging between physical and virtual switches. If a native VLAN is set up in the physical environment, be sure to accommodate for this when configuring physical switch trunk ports to vSwitches! Virtual switches do not handle native VLAN packets properly, and you'll lose traffic or cause DoS scenarios to occur.

There are really only a few major considerations for security when configuring the physical switch ports to connect to a virtual infrastructure:

Disable Spanning Tree The Spanning Tree Protocol (STP) prevents infinite loops of frames from passing between switches in a network. In general, virtual switches maintain lists of MAC addresses in use and frame information without needing actual packet details, so STP is unnecessary. In fact, enabling it can cause some performance issues or loss of availability.

Be careful with dynamic trunking VMware vSwitches can run in Virtual Switch Tagging (VST) mode, giving the vSwitches the wherewithal to manage VLANs for connected VMs within various port groups. If Dynamic Trunking Protocol (DTP) is enabled on the physical switch, it can cause issues when communicating with VMware vSwitches in VST mode.

Ensure that physical NICs with multiple VLANs are connected to trunk ports When multiple vSwitches or port groups with various VLANs are accessing a physical NIC in the hypervisor host, it's critical to ensure that the physical switch port it connects to is a trunk port that's properly configured.

SIMPLE CISCO SWITCH EXAMPLE

The following example illustrates the basic configuration options you'd want to consider when connecting your physical switches to a hypervisor host. This example configures two Gigabit Ethernet NICs as trunk ports using native VLAN 10 (which you should change to your own native VLAN value). 802.1Q encapsulation is generally considered the accepted standard for trunking these days too.

```
(config)#int gi0/1
(config-if)#channel-group 1 mode on
(config-if)#switchport trunk encapsulation dot1q
(config-if)#switchport trunk allowed vlan all
(config-if)#switchport mode trunk
(config-if)#switchport trunk native vlan 10
(config)#int gi0/2
(config-if)#channel-group 1 mode on
(config-if)#switchport trunk encapsulation dot1q
(config-if)#switchport trunk allowed vlan all
(config-if)#switchport mode trunk
(config-if)#switchport trunk native vlan 10
```

Chapter 4

Advanced Virtual Network Operations

There are a number of operations, tasks, and technologies related to security that administrators and engineers working with virtualization environments need to be familiar with. Of the three fundamental tenets of information security—confidentiality, integrity, and availability—most security professionals focus on confidentiality and integrity, whereas operations teams focus on availability first and integrity second. Many network operations within the virtual environment are concerned primarily with availability and continuous network connectivity. In this chapter, we'll dive into several additional aspects of network operations that impact security and compliance.

In this chapter, you will learn about the following topics:

◆ Load balancing in virtual environments

◆ Traffic shaping and network performance

◆ Creating a sound network monitoring strategy

◆ Controls and processes for monitoring network traffic

Network Operational Challenges

Network engineers and administrators face a number of common operational challenges in the physical environment. Switches, routers, load balancers, proxies, firewalls, and network monitoring tools are all common elements of any robust enterprise network, and these same tools and concepts need to carry over to virtual networks too. This chapter covers the following topics on the VMware, Microsoft, and Citrix virtualization platforms:

Load balancing in virtual environments Network load balancing is a topic unto itself and intersects with routing and general network-optimization strategies and technologies. We'll focus specifically on a few simple tactics to manage network load balancing in virtual environments, but keep in mind that your existing enterprise load balancers and clustering technologies can (and will) still come into play. The primary concern here is ensuring that traffic is properly balanced between multiple NICs, both physical and virtual.

Traffic shaping and network performance Traffic shaping and network performance are closely tied to load balancing but usually focus on bandwidth controls and shaping. Some of this can be performed at the individual NIC level, other configuration options can be set within operating systems, and still others are controlled at the virtual switches. In addition, there are many cases where performing traffic shaping at the physical switch and load balancer makes the most sense, and network engineering teams will need to decide where to implement specific controls and configuration options.

Creating a sound network monitoring strategy   The final operations challenge is monitoring network traffic, which is something any security-conscious enterprise will want to do, for intrusion detection and prevention as well as auditing and network behavioral profiling. In most cases, organizations today employ one or more of the following network monitoring strategies and techniques:

♦ Enabling promiscuous mode on individual server NICs to sniff traffic that passes by on a local switch. In most switched environments, this will not be sufficient by itself because the switch will pass traffic to only the device that it is destined for. This is often a starting point for monitoring, however, especially if you have dedicated a server or VM to providing intrusion detection and sniffing functions, using the open-source Snort intrusion detection system (IDS), for example.

♦ Enabling a Switched Port Analyzer (SPAN) port on switches to map traffic from one port to another that is dedicated for monitoring only. In essence, you are "copying" traffic from a port (or multiple ports) to a dedicated monitoring port where a sniffer or intrusion detection sensor is online. This is sometimes referred to as *mirroring* a port.

♦ Leveraging a network tap, which is a hardware device that allows traffic to be copied and split into two (or more) segments. One is the original traffic segment, while the other is set up for traffic capture and monitoring.

♦ Implementing inline devices, where all traffic flows through a sensor that can both sniff traffic and potentially block attacks.

OTHER RESOURCES FOR VIRTUAL SWITCH MONITORING AND CONTROL

This chapter introduces some of the more common methods for the major platforms, but there are plenty of others, especially with the advent of vendor solutions that integrate natively with virtualization technologies. Some are listed here:

♦ VMware Distributed vSwitch Migration and Configuration Guide (available at www.vmware.com)

♦ Microsoft Guide to Configuring Virtual Networks for Windows Server 2008 R2 (available at http://technet.microsoft.com)

♦ Microsoft Windows Server 2012 Information (available at http://technet.microsoft.com)

♦ Hyper-V 2012 Overview (available at http://technet.microsoft.com)

♦ Citrix XenServer vSwitch Controller Guide (for XenServer 5.6, available at http://support.citrix.com)

Network Operations in VMware vSphere

VMware has provided a number of capabilities in its vSphere 5 product line, allowing for reasonably granular traffic control and management, network redundancy, and monitoring for security and operational health. Most of these capabilities are fairly simple to implement.

Load Balancing in vSphere Virtual Environments

NIC teaming is a simple concept: Multiple physical NICs are bound to a virtual switch, and the NICs all carry the same type of traffic to provide redundancy and failover capabilities. These NICs are then referred to as a *NIC team* for the virtual switch in question. To provide true failover and redundancy, these NICs should be connected to separate physical switches. A simple representation of this is shown in Figure 4.1.

FIGURE 4.1
NIC teaming for a
virtual switch

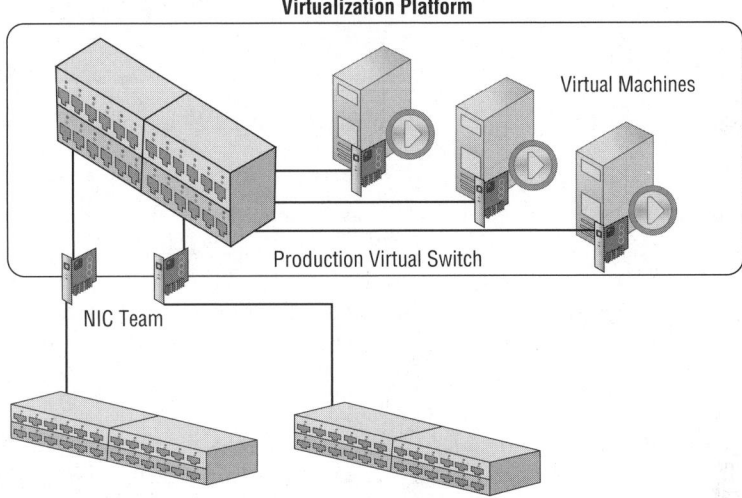

A NIC team can be set up easily as long as there are enough physical adapters in the hardware platform running ESX or ESXi. In the vSphere Client, a vSwitch with multiple adapters in a NIC team is shown in Figure 4.2.

FIGURE 4.2
A vSwitch with
multiple physical
NICs in the vSphere
Client

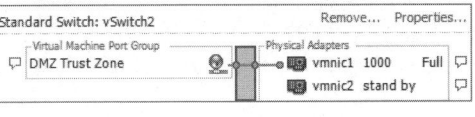

To set up NIC teaming, use the vSphere Client to connect to vCenter or a single ESX or ESXi host. Then follow these steps:

1. In vCenter, select Inventory, then Hosts And Clusters. Then choose a single ESX or ESXi host in the left-hand pane. For a direct connection, just highlight the host. Choose the Configuration tab in the right-hand pane, and then choose Networking.

2. For the virtual switch to which you'd like to assign a NIC team, click the Properties link to the right of the vSwitch.

3. Choose the Network Adapters tab, and select Add to add the physical NICs you want to include in the NIC team. You can adjust the policy failover order of the NICs as well, selecting which NIC(s) will be active and which will be standby. This is shown in Figure 4.3.

FIGURE 4.3
Setting active and standby NICs

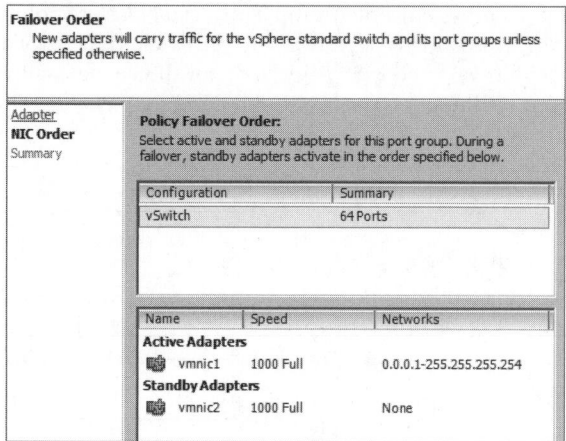

4. Finish the wizard, then choose the Ports tab in the vSwitch properties. Select the NIC Teaming tab on the far right.

    Here, you can set the NIC team policy, as shown in Figure 4.4.

FIGURE 4.4
NIC team policies

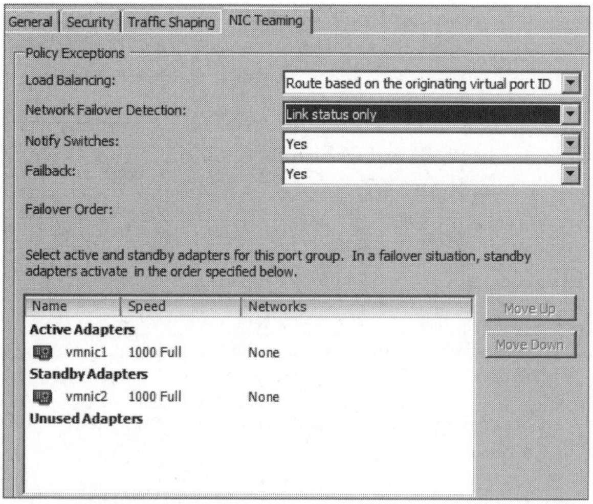

The NIC team can have one of four load balancing policies configured. These are briefly described here:

Originating Virtual Port ID   This is essentially vSwitch NIC round-robin. Each virtual guest will use the next available physical NIC mapped to the switch. For example, if a vSwitch has two physical NICs, VM1 would use vmnic1 and VM2 would use vmnic2. Then VM3 would use vmnic1 again and VM4 would use vnmic2. And so on.

Source MAC   Physical NICs are mapped to source MAC address hashes from virtual NICs within virtual machines.

IP Hash   The source and destination IP addresses are leveraged in this algorithm to determine what physical NIC is used for communication. This is the only NIC team load balancing method that allows virtual machines with a single virtual NIC to employ multiple distinct physical NICs in the host system.

Explicit Failover   With this method, you can specify the active and standby adapters of your choosing. If an active NIC fails, a standby NIC will immediately be chosen to take its place. There are several other options here that can be set:

> **Network Failover Detection**   This setting controls how the NIC team will detect NIC failure and perform failover. The first option, Link Status Only, looks for an electrical signal from the NIC itself and is ideal for detecting a physical switch failure or the network cable being unplugged. This option is not good at detecting configuration issues, however. The second option, Beacon Probing, sends Ethernet broadcast frames out on a regular basis and detects both link failure and other types of configuration problems.

> **Notify Switches**   This option sends Reverse Address Resolution Protocol (RARP) messages to the physical switch when a failover occurs. This allows the physical switch to update its Content Addressable Memory (CAM) tables for which MAC addresses are connected to which ports. This can backfire for VMs running load balancing software like Microsoft's NLB, however. (NLB is covered in the section "Load Balancing in Hyper-V Virtual Environments" later in the chapter.) You should set this to No for vSwitches that host Microsoft VMs running NLB in unicast mode because they'll try to manipulate MAC addresses, which can cause issues.

> **Failback**   If this is set to Yes, failed NICs that come back up will replace the NICs that took their place, returning them to a lower priority or standby mode.

Traffic Shaping and Network Performance in VMware vSphere

Traffic shaping with vSphere is simple to configure, but it shouldn't be used as a replacement for a sound NIC teaming and load balancing configuration. All VMs share equal bandwidth and NIC capacity by default. If you have very specialized circumstances where VMs need granular traffic control, then traffic shaping offers another option.

To set up traffic shaping, follow these steps:

1. In vCenter, select Inventory, then Hosts And Clusters. Then choose a single ESX or ESXi host in the left-hand pane. For a direct connection, just highlight the host. Choose the Configuration tab in the right-hand pane, and then choose Networking.

2. For the virtual switch you'd like to set up traffic shaping for, click the Properties link to the right of the vSwitch.

3. On the Ports tab, double-click the vSwitch or select it and choose Edit. Then choose the Traffic Shaping tab along the top.

4. Enable traffic shaping by changing the Status drop-down box to Enabled.

5. Configure the three primary traffic-shaping policies, as shown in Figure 4.5:

   Average Bandwidth: This setting controls the data transfer (in kilobytes/second) on the virtual switch.

   Peak Bandwidth: Peak bandwidth is the maximum traffic volume (in kilobytes/second) the vSwitch can sustain before dropping packets.

   Burst Size: Burst size is the maximum size in kilobytes of a traffic burst, which is a function of bandwidth over time. Packets will be dropped if this threshold is met during peak periods, but packets can be queued as well.

FIGURE 4.5
Traffic-shaping
policies

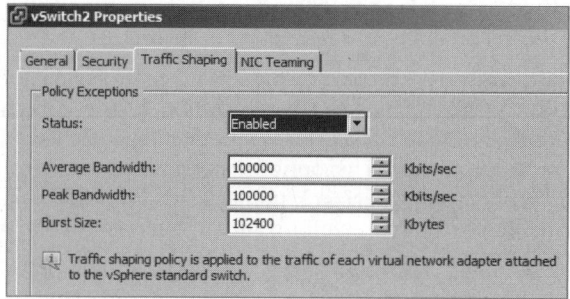

WARNING   Again, be careful with the traffic-shaping settings because you can cause more harm than good unless you are sure you need to set them.

Creating a Sound Network Monitoring Strategy in VMware vSphere

The standard VMware virtual switch has a number of simple capabilities that make network monitoring somewhat easier within virtual environments. There are other options for monitoring in VMware environments, but these are the simplest and most flexible with native VMware technology. The first, and by far the simplest, is enabling promiscuous mode on a vSwitch or port group. When promiscuous mode is enabled, an intrusion detection/prevention VM with two NICs can monitor the switch traffic on one NIC and have a monitoring NIC connected to a different vSwitch, as shown in Figure 4.6.

To enable promiscuous mode on a vSwitch or port group, follow these steps:

1. In vCenter, select Inventory, then Hosts And Clusters. Then choose a single ESX or ESXi host in the left-hand pane. For a direct connection, just highlight the host. Choose the Configuration tab in the right-hand pane, and then choose Networking.

2. For the virtual switch on which you'd like to set up promiscuous mode, click the Properties link to the right of the vSwitch.

FIGURE 4.6
Promiscuous
mode monitoring
architecture

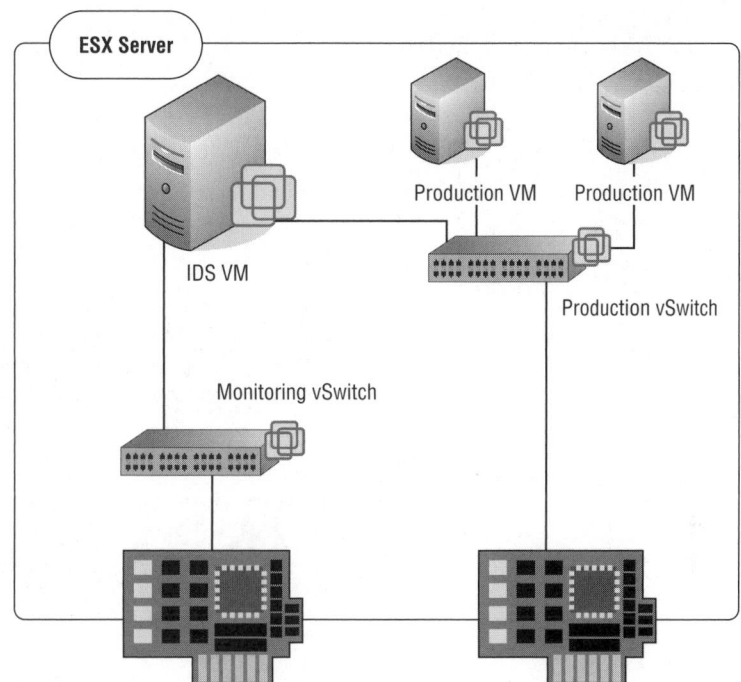

3. Double-click the vSwitch icon or a port group icon in the left-hand pane. Then choose the Security tab and set Promiscuous Mode to Accept, as shown in Figure 4.7.

FIGURE 4.7
Enabling promiscu-
ous mode

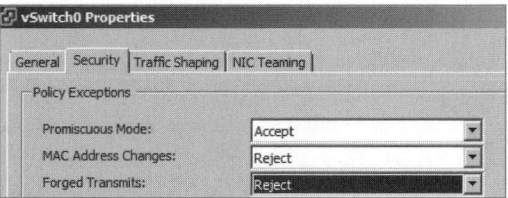

4. Enabling promiscuous mode on a port group can override the setting on the vSwitch, as well. Click OK twice to finish.

On vSphere 5 distributed vSwitches, you have some great new features that make enterprise-class monitoring possible. The first is port mirroring, commonly called SPAN on Cisco switches. Whether you use a Cisco Nexus 1000v or the built-in vSphere dvSwitch, you can now copy network traffic to existing IDS or other monitoring tools, making architecture and planning much simpler for network and security teams. This architecture (shown using the Nexus 1000v) is depicted in Figure 4.8.

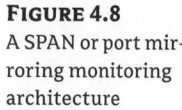

FIGURE 4.8
A SPAN or port mirroring monitoring architecture

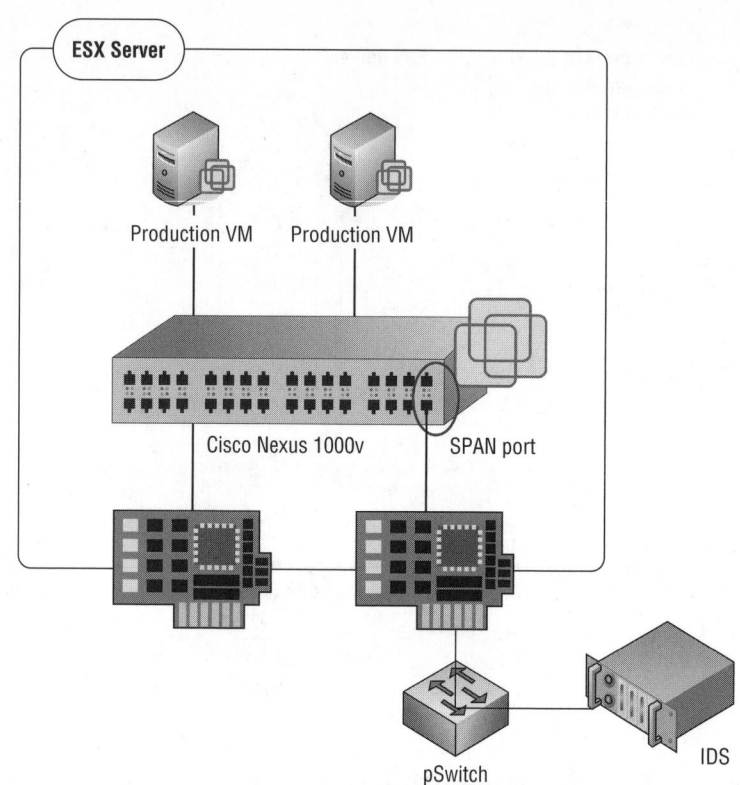

To enable port mirroring on the built-in dvSwitch, follow these steps:

1. First, decide what you want to mirror. This will be a port or ports on the dvSwitch, and you can see them by logging into vCenter, choosing Inventory and then Networking, and highlighting your dvSwitch in the left-hand pane. Select the Ports tab in the right-hand pane, and you can decide what to monitor, as shown in Figure 4.9.

FIGURE 4.9
dvSwitch ports

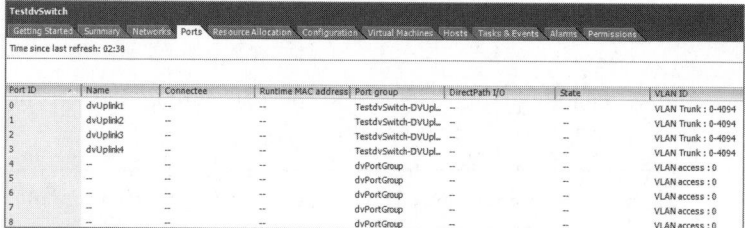

2. Now, right-click the dvSwitch and choose Edit Settings. Select the Port Mirroring tab on the top, then click Add.

3. Add a name and description for the mirroring session, such as IDS mirror or Troubleshooting mirror. You can also make the following settings:

Allow Normal IO On Destination Ports: If you want the destination port you define to handle normal traffic I/O as well as receiving mirror traffic, check this box.

Encapsulation VLAN: If you will be sending this mirrored traffic outside of the virtual environment, you can encapsulate the mirror traffic to another VLAN.

Mirrored Packet Length: If you need to change the size of the mirrored traffic packets, check this option and set the size of the fragments you would like.

4. Once you've configured these options, click Next. Configure the ports you want to mirror, as well as the direction of the traffic (Ingress, Egress, or both). This is shown in Figure 4.10.

FIGURE 4.10
Configuring mir-
rored ports

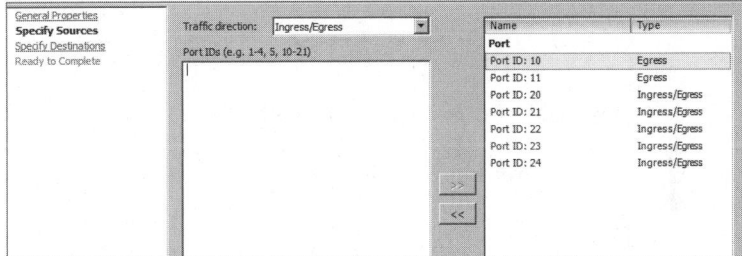

5. Once you've chosen ports and directions, click Next. Now you can choose your destina-tion. You've got two options: Ports and Uplinks. A port is simply another port on the dvSwitch, perhaps one hosting an IDS VM. An uplink is a physical adapter on the physi-cal ESXi host. Make your destination selection and then click Next. Check the box to enable the session (shown in Figure 4.11), and click Finish.

FIGURE 4.11
A configured port
mirroring session

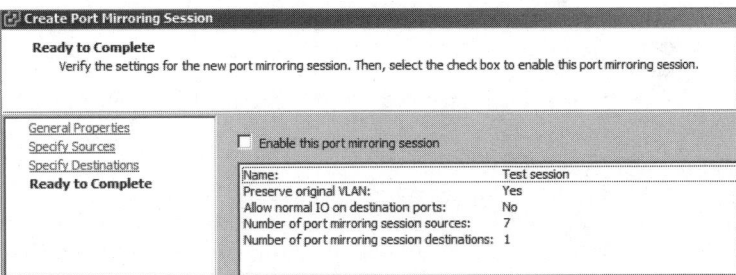

NetFlow is another type of monitoring that can be configured on VMware vSphere 5 distrib-uted virtual switches. NetFlow captures source and destination IP addresses, source and desti-nation TCP/UDP ports, switch port info, and IP Type of Service (ToS) data. Network teams use flow data to map out network and traffic behavior within network segments, and this is usually done by sending flow data to a separate flow collector.

To set up NetFlow on vSphere 5 dvSwitches, do the following:

1. Select the Inventory page, and then choose the Networking section in vCenter. Right-click your dvSwitch and choose Edit Settings. Select the NetFlow tab on the top. (See Figure 4.12.)

FIGURE 4.12
NetFlow
configuration

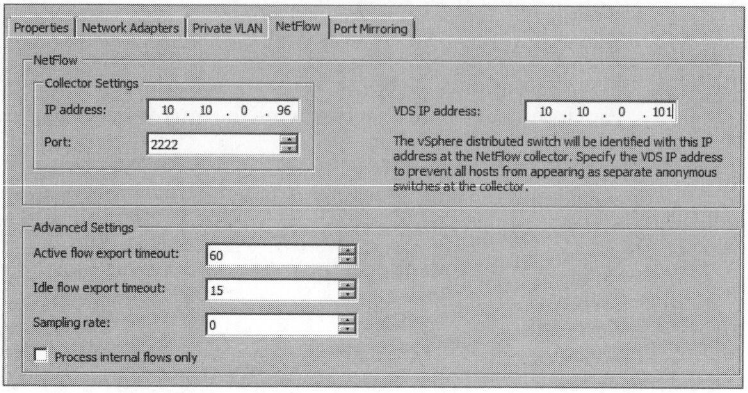

2. In the Netflow settings area, specify an IP address for the NetFlow collector and a port it will listen on. In the box labeled VDS IP Address, configure the IP address of the dvSwitch as the definitive source IP.

3. In the Advanced Settings area, if necessary, specify advanced settings for performance. If your network team has specific parameters in place for flow collectors, these settings may need to be configured for optimal performance. If you don't know what these settings should be, you should probably leave them as is:

   Active Flow Export Timeout: How long each flow is "recorded" before being exported to the collector

   Idle Flow Export Timeout: How long the switch "waits" before exporting an idle flow record

   Sampling Rate: How often the record is updated during its life span (e.g., every 2 seconds)

4. Check the box labeled Process Internal Flows Only to gather only internal (VM-to-VM) flows.

5. Click OK.

6. Next, enable NetFlow for individual dvPortGroups. Select a group in the left-hand pane, right-click, and choose Edit Settings. Click the Monitoring option on the left side, and then change the drop-down menu on the right to Enabled, as shown in Figure 4.13.

FIGURE 4.13
Enabling NetFlow
for dvPortGroups

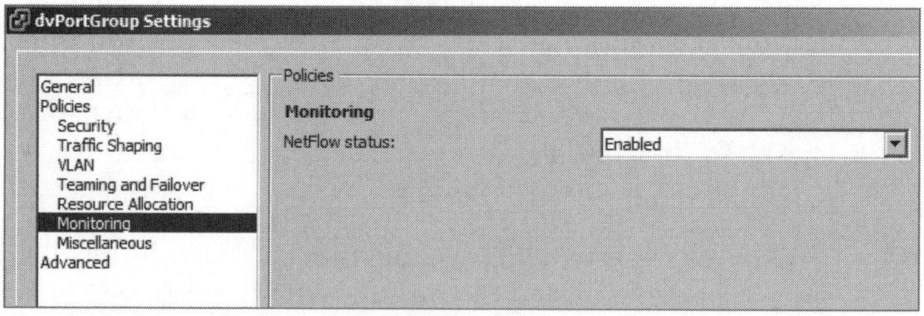

Network Operations in Microsoft Hyper-V

Server 2008 R2 Hyper-V environments, as I've already covered, do not offer much in the way of advanced networking capabilities. Simple load balancing is possible for VMs with Microsoft's Network Load Balancing (NLB) functionality, and there are some specific nuances to this that I'll cover. Hyper-V also offers some interesting network-optimization capabilities, although explicit Quality of Service (QoS) configuration is not really available in Hyper-V on Server 2008 R2.

NOTE Windows Server 2012 provides more granular control over QoS for network traffic.

Load Balancing in Hyper-V Virtual Environments

Windows Server 2008 supports NLB for virtual machines but not for Hyper-V hosts. NLB can help to manage the load between Windows VMs, although some specific configuration will be needed. First, you'll need to install NLB on the VMs you want to balance. You can do this by adding the NLB feature with Server Manager or using the following command:

```
servermanagercmd -install nlb
```

Once NLB is installed, configure the node as follows:

1. Run the NLB Manager by executing `nlbmgr` at the command line or by choosing it from the Administrative Tools menu.

2. In the NLB Manager window, select the Cluster menu and then choose New or Connect To Existing. The following steps assume a new cluster, but you can edit any settings for an existing one as well.

3. Choose a priority as well as dedicated IP addresses for the node.

4. Choose a dedicated IP address or addresses for the cluster node, and click Next.

5. Finalize the cluster parameters and choose a mode (Unicast, Multicast, or IGMP Multicast). Most of the time, you'll choose Unicast or Multicast. The Cluster Parameters settings are shown in Figure 4.14.

   Both Unicast and Multicast will work, but virtual environments are usually best served with Multicast where possible. There are a few reasons for this. First, the adapter for each cluster host keeps the original hardware unicast MAC address (as specified by the hardware manufacturer). Second, cluster adapters for all cluster hosts are assigned a multicast MAC address that is derived from the cluster's IP address. Finally, each cluster host retains a unique MAC address. Retaining this unique MAC address makes a difference because Unicast assigns the same MAC address to all cluster members. The MAC address is then modified when traffic is sent to an upstream switch.

6. Define specific port rules for the cluster. TCP and UDP traffic on various ports can be directed to cluster hosts equally or pointed to one host or another. When you're finished selecting these, click Finish.

7. Now repeat this process for any other VMs you want to be in the cluster.

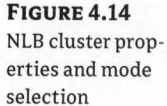

FIGURE 4.14
NLB cluster properties and mode selection

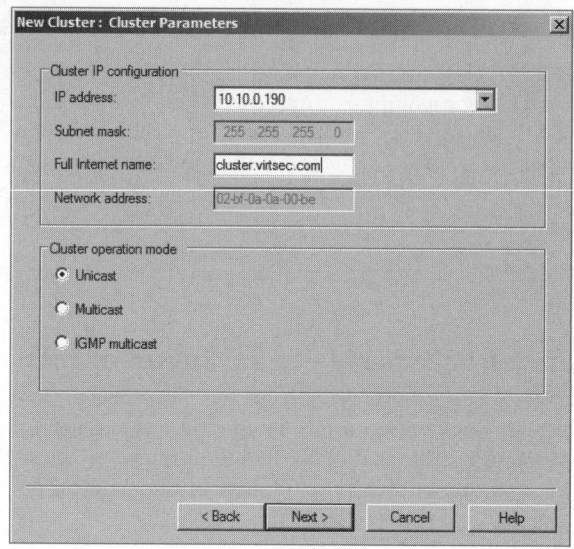

If you set up NLB to use unicast clustering, you'll need to enable MAC spoofing for the VM's adapter. MAC address spoofing is normally associated with Layer 2 man-in-the-middle attacks, but in the case of unicast NLB-enabled VMs, you'll need to enable it on VM adapters so that multiple MAC addresses can communicate through the virtual switch. Normally, a Hyper-V virtual switch will "learn" a single MAC address when a VM connects to it, and this assignment will remain static until the VM is disconnected. MAC address spoofing overrides this feature.

To enable MAC spoofing, first make sure the VM is turned off, and then follow these steps:

1. Open the virtual machine settings by right-clicking the VM in Hyper-V Manager or SCVMM and click Settings.

2. Select the network adapter where NLB is applied in the list of hardware in the left-hand pane.

3. In the right-hand pane, check the box labeled Enable Spoofing Of MAC Addresses. This is shown in Figure 4.15.

4. Click OK and then restart the VM.

Traffic Shaping and Network Performance in Hyper-V

A number of network-optimization features available on Windows Server 2008 R2 Hyper-V can be configured through SCVMM:

Virtual Machine Queue (VMQ) is a technology that allows packets to be routed directly from hardware NICs to VMs, somewhat "bypassing" the underlying OS (in this case, Windows Server 2008 R2 with Hyper-V). This can help to make network traffic flow more efficiently and improve speed.

FIGURE 4.15
Enable MAC spoofing for unicast NLB

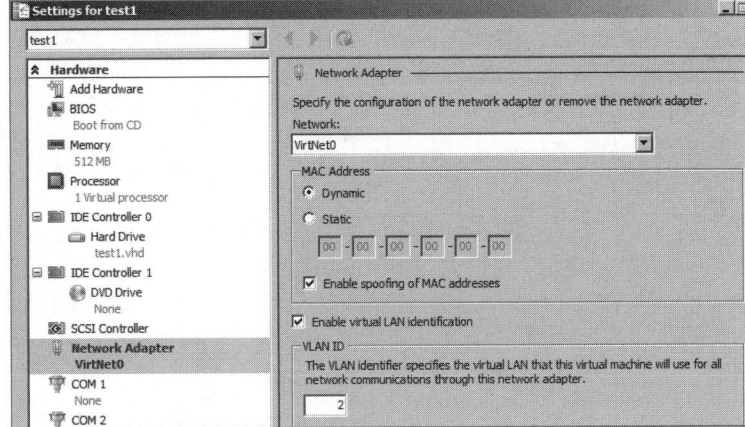

TCP Chimney (or TCP Chimney Offload) transfers TCP packet processing from the CPU to the physical hardware NIC, reducing load on the CPU and allowing it to provide more resources to application-layer processing.

Enabling TCP Chimney Offload requires two steps in Windows Server 2008:

1. At the Administrator command prompt, type the following to globally enable TCP Chimney Offload:

   ```
   netsh int tcp set global chimney=enabled
   ```

2. Open the Device Manager, right-click your NIC adapter, and select Properties. Select the Advanced tab, then look for your hardware manufacturer's version of TCP Offload. In the right-hand drop-down menu, select Rx &Tx Enabled. This is shown in Figure 4.16.

FIGURE 4.16
Enabling TCP Chimney Offload on the NIC

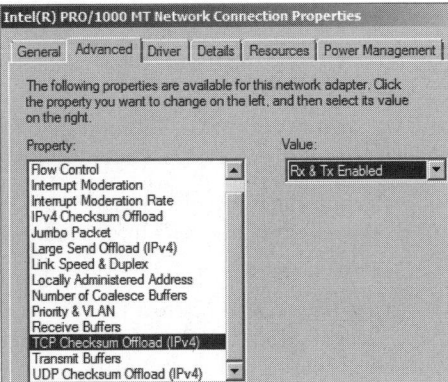

Both technologies require NICs that support them. If Windows Server 2008 R2 or Server 2012 has supported NICs installed, SCVMM will detect this on the host and allow VMs to take advantage of these features. Enabling this is simple! There is a single check box in the VM NIC Properties window labeled Enable Virtual Network Optimizations, as shown in Figure 4.17.

FIGURE 4.17
Enabling VM
network-optimiza-
tion capabilities

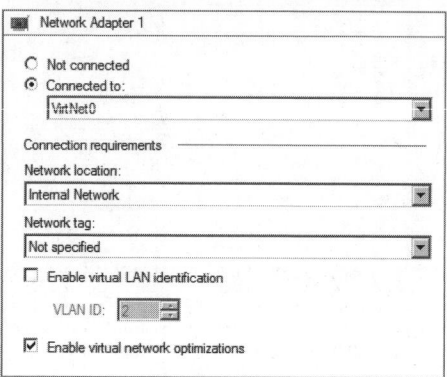

Creating a Sound Network Monitoring Strategy in Hyper-V

Unfortunately, Windows Server 2008 and Hyper-V do not allow for promiscuous mode monitoring of virtual machine traffic at the host level. You will need to enable Switched Port Analyzer (SPAN) ports on your physical switch or leverage network taps for monitoring traffic to and from Hyper-V hosts.

Fortunately, however, Windows Server 2012's version of Hyper-V does support simple network monitoring for virtual machines. This works a bit differently than it does for VMware. As mentioned in Chapter 3, "Designing Virtual Networks for Security," this feature is called port mirroring and is enabled on the virtual machine, not on the switch. In essence, what you're doing when you enable port mirroring is copying the traffic from one specific VM to a separate location that you specify. The key to successful port mirroring on Hyper-V is to understand that you can set up only one traffic monitoring endpoint, and it needs to be another VM on the same virtual switch.

To set up network monitoring, follow these steps:

1. Within Hyper-V Manager or SCVMM, highlight the VM you would like to protect, then right-click and select Properties.

2. In the left-hand pane, find the network adapter connected to the vSwitch that you'll be editing. Expand the network adapter's information, and then select the Advanced Features item.

3. You will see an option labeled Port Mirroring. This option has three possible configuration settings: None, Destination, and Source. This is shown in Figure 4.18. For the VM you want to monitor, set this to Source.

4. On a different VM on the switch, perform the same actions, but set the Port Mirroring option to Destination. You can now capture traffic on this destination VM using a sniffer or intrusion detection software.

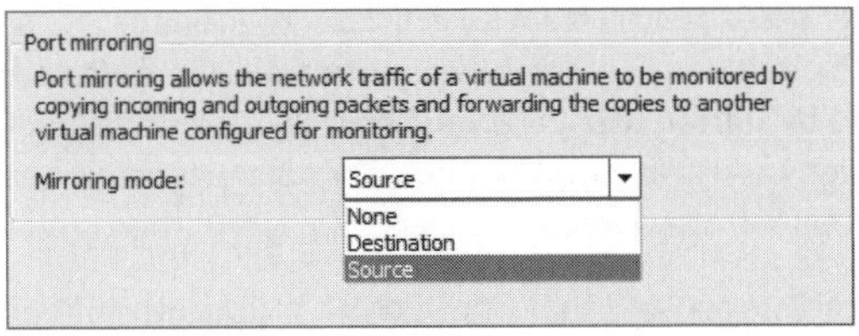

FIGURE 4.18
Hyper-V port
mirroring

Port mirroring

Port mirroring allows the network traffic of a virtual machine to be monitored by copying incoming and outgoing packets and forwarding the copies to another virtual machine configured for monitoring.

Mirroring mode: Source ▼
None
Destination
Source

Network Operations in Citrix XenServer

The default settings in XenServer leave something to be desired for configuring granular traffic shaping and availability options, although there are a number of basic capabilities offered. Most of these are concerned with creating redundancy between NICs by bonding them, and creating simple Quality of Service (QoS) bandwidth controls for the amount of traffic a virtual machine can generate on a XenServer host.

Load Balancing in XenServer Virtual Environments

To create a simple load balancing scenario particular to XenServer hosts and the VMs they are running, the platform supports two features: NIC bonding and High Availability (HA).

NIC bonding can be performed on three major NIC types: management NICs, VM production traffic NICs, and specialized NICs such as those allocated for iSCSI storage traffic. In this section, I'll focus on the first two cases because many organizations choose to implement multipathing for storage NIC redundancy and balancing.

Let's explore the differences between NIC bonding on management NICs and NIC bonding on production traffic NICs:

◆ For NIC bonding related to management traffic, XenServer really supports only failover scenarios—an active-passive configuration where one NIC is active and another is a standby in case of the first NIC experiencing failure. In other words, you can bond a management NIC to another nonmanagement NIC, and this will create a sound redundancy strategy but won't allow for true traffic balancing. One IP address is used for the bond, and this address is also used in the case that the second NIC becomes active due to failover.

◆ When VM production NICs are bonded, both failover and load balancing are supported. Both active-passive and active-active configurations are possible, with active-active providing the load balancing features. Active-active for VM traffic performs load balancing only in the sense that a single VM's traffic is sent across one physical NIC at a time, with other VMs also being sent to one NIC or another to keep the amount of traffic somewhat similar across the NICs in the bond. A single VM cannot send traffic through both bonded NICs simultaneously. For bonding between VM production NICS, each NIC maintains its own address because the bond is created at Layer 2 (the Data-Link layer).

WARNING When a failover scenario occurs between bonded NICs, gratuitous Address Resolution Protocol (ARP) packets are generated. If gratuitous ARP monitoring is in place on your network, you will likely be alerted when this happens. Also, be mindful of MAC address binding and additional security monitoring on physical switch ports when a binding failover occurs because you will see "new" traffic from a switch port.

It is highly recommended that bonded NICs for both management ports and VM production ports be distributed between multiple physical switches for improved redundancy. However, you will need to ensure that these switches are in a contiguous domain because MAC addresses for VMs will be changing back and forth between the physical devices regularly.

To create a NIC bond using the XenCenter interface, follow these steps:

1. Highlight the XenServer you want to create a bond on. Choose the Networking tab in the right-hand pane.

2. Click Add Network and then choose Bonded Network. Click Next.

3. On the next screen, choose the physical NICs you would like to be a part of the bond. You can also select Active-Active or Active-Passive, the maximum transmission unit (MTU), and whether new VMs are automatically added to this network, as shown in Figure 4.19.

4. Click Finish to complete this process.

FIGURE 4.19
Creating a NIC bond
in XenCenter

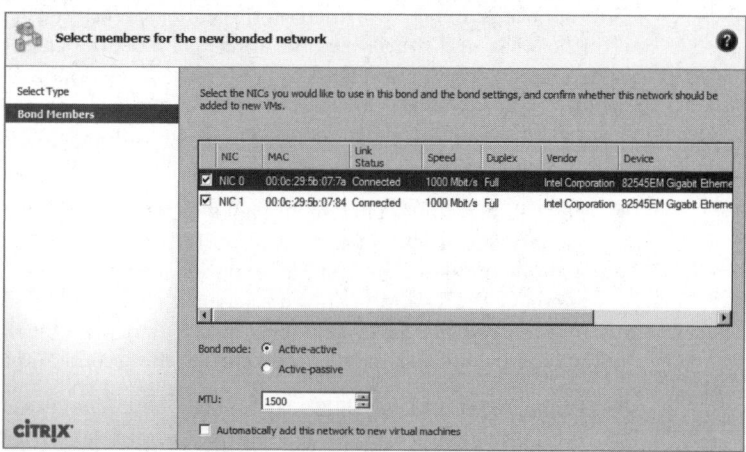

Creating a NIC bond at the command line is only slightly more work:

1. Log in to the command-line interface (CLI) at the direct console or using SSH.

2. Create a new network object for the bond as follows:
   ```
   xe network-create name-label=<bond UUID>
   ```

3. List the physical interfaces that you will use to create the bond:
   ```
   xe pif-list
   ```

You should see output like that in Figure 4.20.

FIGURE 4.20
Creating a NIC bond
at the CLI

```
[root@XenVoodoo /]# xe network-create name-label=bond0
6701fe0c-6d59-37b6-ca7b-0d11d84cab62
[root@XenVoodoo /]# xe pif-list
uuid ( RO)                      : 4062f23a-67e0-0d83-82b2-b922bdd4e48b
              device ( RO): eth0
   currently-attached ( RO): true
                VLAN ( RO): -1
          network-uuid ( RO): d04c24cd-0058-7805-9752-f789bc7c9348


uuid ( RO)                      : 89edb5c0-445f-f41a-7432-0d8efef8341e
              device ( RO): eth1
   currently-attached ( RO): true
                VLAN ( RO): -1
          network-uuid ( RO): 8e89efe3-99c5-011d-ea69-418d4b5f676a
```

4. Add NICs to the bond with the following command:

   `xe bond-create network-uuid=<bond UUID> pif-uuids=<NIC UUID 1>,<NIC UUID 2>`

   You can also add the following parameters to this command to modify it:

   `mode=active-backup` changes the bond from active-active (default) to active-passive.

   `mac=<MAC Address>` changes the default MAC address to one you specify.

Speaking of default MAC addresses, a bond's MAC is selected based on what NICs are in the bond itself. If a primary management interface is part of the bond, that MAC will become the bond MAC. If the primary management NIC is not in the bond, but a different management NIC is, that NIC's MAC will become the default. If no management interfaces are members of the bond, the bond will assume the MAC of the first named NIC.

When adding a NIC bond to a new resource pool, many of the steps are the same. First, you will need to determine which XenServer host in the pool will be the designated master. Now follow these steps after accessing the master host's command-line interface:

1. List the resource pools known to the host:

   `xe pool-list`

2. Note the pool you would like to assign the bond to. If you need to rename the default pool (nameless by default), you can do so with this command:

   `xe pool-param-set name-label=<"Pool Name"> uuid=<Pool UUID>`

3. Create a NIC bond as described earlier using the `xe bond-create` syntax.

4. Now join the master to the pool as follows:

   `xe pool-join master-address=<master UUID> master-username=root master-password=<password>`

5. If you already have an existing pool in place, you can replicate the bond to other pool members by running `service xapi restart` on each of them once the master is configured. This will restart the network service and all bond and VLAN information will be replicated to the hosts.

Traffic Shaping and Network Performance in XenServer

XenServer includes a very basic set of Quality of Service (QoS) configuration options. Really, the QoS on XenServer's default virtual switches allows rate limiting only on outbound traffic, that is, on the traffic *coming from* the VM. This can be done in a number of places, but perhaps the simplest way to set QoS is via the command line on XenServer:

1. First, log into the XenServer platform and access the command-line interface. Then, run the following command to list the VM virtual interfaces on the system:

   `xe vif-list`

2. Once you've identified the virtual interface to set the QoS on, run the following command to set QoS:

   `xe vif-param-set uuid=<vif_uuid> qos_algorithm_type=ratelimit`

3. Now set the rate with the last command:

   `xe vif-param-set uuid=<vif_uuid> qos_algorithm_params:kbps=100`

You can modify the kbps value to anything you'd like. This whole process is depicted in Figure 4.21.

FIGURE 4.21
Setting QoS on a
virtual interface

```
[root@XenVoodoo ~]# xe vif-list
uuid ( RO)            : d505398a-c038-37be-02eb-59281262730e
       vm-uuid ( RO): b3d8ee07-b589-d505-b416-32388f423ed6
        device ( RO): 0
   network-uuid ( RO): d04c24cd-0058-7805-9752-f789bc7c9348


[root@XenVoodoo ~]# xe vif-param-set uuid=d505398a-c038-37be-02eb-59281262730e qos_algorithm_type=ratelimit
[root@XenVoodoo ~]# xe vif-param-set uuid=d505398a-c038-37be-02eb-59281262730e qos_algorithm_params:kbps=1000
```

Creating a Sound Network Monitoring Strategy in XenServer

As discussed earlier in the chapter, enabling promiscuous mode on interfaces is the most prevalent way to start performing traffic monitoring and capture.

There are numerous options for setting up network monitoring on XenServer platforms, at both the physical NIC and virtual machine interfaces. In addition, organizations leveraging the Citrix virtual switch controller can enable remote Switched Port Analyzer (SPAN) capabilities, sending traffic from the virtual switch to a remotely situated monitoring device. We'll explore how to configure each of these options.

To set up physical NIC promiscuous mode on XenServer, the command is exactly the same as that on a Linux platform. Simply execute the following (this process is shown in Figure 4.22):

   `ifconfig <interface> promisc`

FIGURE 4.22
Promiscuous mode
on XenServer physi-
cal NIC

```
[root@XenVoodoo ~]# ifconfig eth0 promisc
[root@XenVoodoo ~]# ifconfig eth0
eth0      Link encap:Ethernet  HWaddr 00:0C:29:5B:07:7A
          UP BROADCAST RUNNING PROMISC MULTICAST  MTU:1500  Metric:1
          RX packets:811322 errors:0 dropped:0 overruns:0 frame:0
          TX packets:95217 errors:0 dropped:0 overruns:0 carrier:0
          collisions:0 txqueuelen:1000
          RX bytes:1114442163 (1.0 GiB)  TX bytes:9037815 (8.6 MiB)
```

To enable promiscuous mode on virtual machines, you'll have a bit more work to do. First, access the XenServer console interface, and then follow these steps:

1. List the physical interfaces known to the XenServer platform hosting the VM. You'll need to tell XenServer to recognize promiscuous mode on the NIC to which the virtual machine connects:

   `xe pif-list`

2. Once you've gotten the UUID of the interface, run this command to enable promiscuous mode on this interface:

   `xe pif-param-set uuid=<NIC UUID> other-config:promiscuous="true"`

3. To verify that the physical NIC has promiscuous mode enabled, run the following command:

   `xe pif-param-list uuid=<NIC UUID>`

4. Look for output at the end that resembles the following:

   `other-config (MRW): promiscuous: true`

   This process is shown in Figure 4.23.

FIGURE 4.23

Promiscuous Mode Parameters on a Physical NIC

```
[root@XenVoodoo ~]# xe pif-param-set uuid=943583cf-e3e8-8fc0-1192-df98e6d67233 other-config:promiscuous="true"
[root@XenVoodoo ~]# xe pif-param-list uuid=943583cf-e3e8-8fc0-1192-df98e6d67233
uuid ( RO)                        : 943583cf-e3e8-8fc0-1192-df98e6d67233
                   device ( RO): eth0
                      MAC ( RO): 00:0c:29:5b:07:7a
                 physical ( RO): true
        currently-attached ( RO): true
                      MTU ( RO): 1500
                     VLAN ( RO): -1
            bond-master-of ( RO):
             bond-slave-of ( RO): <not in database>
        tunnel-access-PIF-of ( RO):
     tunnel-transport-PIF-of ( RO):
               management ( RO): true
             network-uuid ( RO): b45fcec8-f07b-0590-50ef-e7a3c754f71b
       network-name-label ( RO): Pool-wide network associated with eth0
                host-uuid ( RO): 377eb25c-5e70-493f-b596-1dff37baa487
          host-name-label ( RO): XenVoodoo
      IP-configuration-mode ( RO): Static
                       IP ( RO): 10.10.0.199
                  netmask ( RO): 255.255.255.0
                  gateway ( RO): 10.10.0.1
                      DNS ( RO): 10.10.0.110
              io_read_kbs ( RO): 1.743
             io_write_kbs ( RO): 2.056
                  carrier ( RO): true
                vendor-id ( RO): 8086
              vendor-name ( RO): Intel Corporation
                device-id ( RO): 100f
              device-name ( RO): 82545EM Gigabit Ethernet Controller (Copper)
                    speed ( RO): 1000 Mbit/s
                   duplex ( RO): full
          disallow-unplug ( RW): false
             pci-bus-path ( RO): 0000:02:01.0
             other-config (MRW): promiscuous: true
```

5. Now, you'll need to place the VM's virtual interface (VIF) into promiscuous mode as well. First, list the interfaces with `xe vif-list` if there are a small number of VMs or the following for a larger number:

   `xe vif-list vm-name-label=<VM Name>`

6. Note the UUID value presented, and add promiscuous mode to the VIF:

   `xe vif-param-set uuid=<uuid_of_vif> other-config:promiscuous="true"`

7. To verify that the virtual NIC has promiscuous mode enabled, run the following command:

   `xe vif-param-list uuid=<VIF UUID>`

8. Look for output at the end that resembles the following:

```
other-config (MRW): promiscuous: true
```

9. The final step is to disconnect and reconnect the VIF on the VM. Do this with the following commands, keeping in mind that the VM will be offline momentarily:

```
xe vif-unplug uuid=<VIF UUID>
xe vif-plug uuid=<VIF UUID>
```

The final method for enabling monitoring capabilities on XenServer is via the SPAN (Remote SPAN, or RSPAN) functionality on the Open vSwitch Distributed Virtual Switch (DVS). This can be enabled in the console of the DVS Controller. Although this is somewhat outside the scope of this book, the process in a nutshell is as follows:

1. Much like port mirroring with the VMware vSphere 5 dvSwitch, you first need to determine the RSPAN VLAN you want to monitor. This should be the VLAN for any VIF on which you are enabling RSPAN.

2. Ensure that your target physical switches are configured to communicate on this same VLAN.

3. In the graphic interface for the vSwitch Controller, select the Visibility And Control section. Open the Status tab for a resource pool or server you wish to monitor.

4. Click the + sign in the RSPAN Target VLAN IDs section and add your monitoring VLAN for RSPAN.

5. Click Save Target VLAN Change.

6. Now you can select a node in the left-hand pane (resource tree) and highlight the Port Configuration tab in the right-hand pane. You can choose one of three options for RSPAN policies:

   Inherit RSPAN Policy From Parent (default): Applies the policy from the level above this node.

   Disable Inherited RSPAN Policy: Ignores policies that are set at higher levels, and essentially negates any RSPAN policies for VIFs at the current level.

   RSPAN Traffic On VLAN: You can select a target VLAN from a list as long as they are available per the policy applied at the existing node.

7. Click Save Port Configuration Changes to complete.

Chapter 5

Virtualization Management and Client Security

The management servers and clients connecting to virtual infrastructures can also be points of potential exposure. The security issues cover a wide spectrum—access to privileged accounts, excessive privileges and permissions, operating system hardening, network access controls, and issues with the management platforms and connectivity to them. Security best practices play a big role in locking down management platforms, and there are a few specific steps to keep in mind that go beyond the basics.

The good news is that by following some simple best practices related to database installation, local users, secure connectivity, and hardening and securing the OS, you can greatly improve the security of your virtualization infrastructure.

This chapter will describe the types of issues that may be present in the various vendors' components, and will outline both configuration options and architecture considerations that can be effectively used to create a more secure implementation. In addition, roles and privileges will be considered in depth, and a number of security considerations will be outlined for VMware, Microsoft, and Citrix platforms.

In this chapter, you will learn about the following topics:

- ◆ Securing the vCenter, SCVMM, and XenCenter virtualization management platforms

- ◆ Properly configuring database permissions for virtualization management platforms, where appropriate

- ◆ Configure logging for virtualization management platforms and clients

- ◆ Configuring user and group roles and permissions for virtualization management platforms

- ◆ Configuring encryption for client and management platform access to virtualization infrastructure

General Security Recommendations for Management Platforms

Not all virtualization deployments will have a dedicated management server, but most will. It is critical to understand that virtualization management servers are the primary control point for almost everything else in the virtual infrastructure, so protecting them is essential. If someone were to gain illicit access to these systems, they could potentially wreak havoc not just with that system but with any virtualization components, including the hypervisors and any VMs running on them. In addition, this could lead to unauthorized access to database instances, storage environments, and any manner of other sensitive areas that are connected to these systems.

The applications vCenter, XenCenter, and Microsoft System Center Virtual Machine Manager (SCVMM) are usually installed on Microsoft Windows 2003 or 2008 Server platforms today, with Microsoft Server 2012 likely to replace these in the near future. These platforms have had a significant number of security vulnerabilities over the years, so the first step in securing any management server installation is to properly lock down the underlying OS platform that hosts it.

SECURING THE UNDERLYING OS

This book won't focus on securing the basic underlying OS; there are plenty of resources available to harden and secure a Windows operating system. The following resources are among some of the best:

◆ Center for Internet Security (CIS) benchmarks download form:

https://benchmarks.cisecurity.org/en-us/?route=downloads.multiform

◆ Defense Information Systems Agency (DISA) Secure Technical Implementation Guides (STIGs):

http://iase.disa.mil/stigs/os/index.html

◆ Microsoft Hardening Guides for each platform (for example, Microsoft Windows Server 2008 Security Baseline) can be found at the TechNet Library:

http://technet.microsoft.com/en-us/

It's also imperative to implement sound patching and malware prevention technologies and processes. Despite the performance hit from running antivirus software, the last thing you need is your management server getting taken down by a worm. Consider installing a host-based intrusion detection or prevention system (HIDS/HIPS) as well as file integrity monitoring tools. Control access to the system with a local firewall, and be sure to place the system in a secure network subnet, which we covered in the network architecture sections in Chapter 3, "Designing Virtual Networks for Security."

Network Architecture for Virtualization Management Servers

Another major consideration for any management platform in a virtualization environment is the network design that affords you the most isolation and control over who can access what.

To begin with, the most ideal scenario is to have a dedicated physical network segment where all critical management functions are carried out. A simple representation of this type of architecture is shown in Figure 5.1.

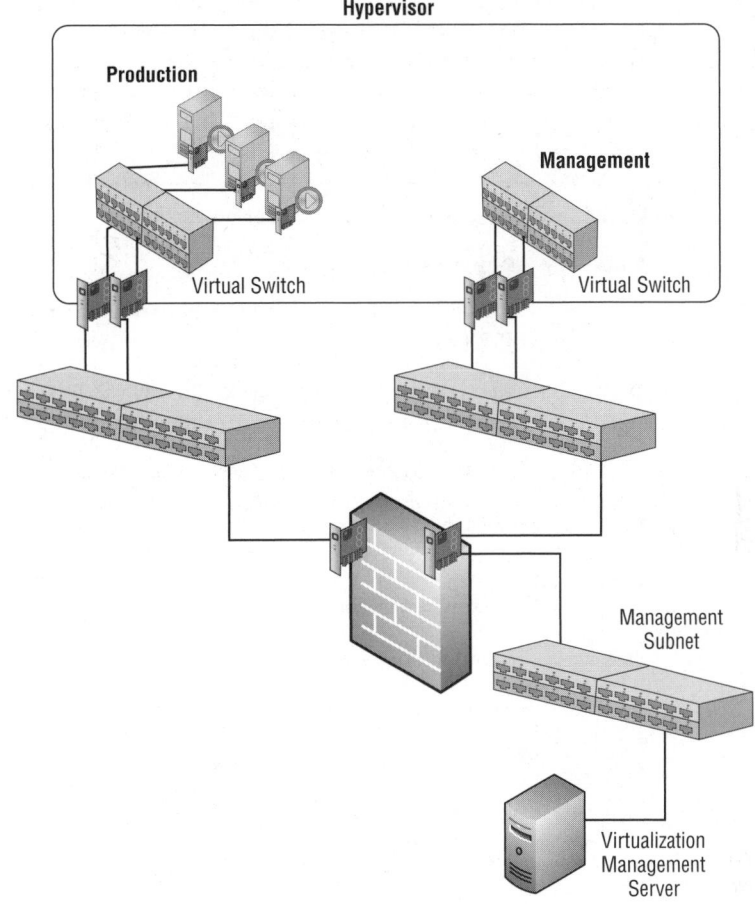

FIGURE 5.1
Separate management network

Setting up a separate management network is the ideal scenario, but at the very least, all management services should be on a separate virtual LAN (VLAN). This traffic is sensitive in nature, even encrypted, and should be protected from man-in-the-middle (MITM) and other attacks. By way of example, an exploit kit called Virtualization Assessment Toolkit (VASTO) integrates with the Metasploit Framework and includes several modules that can take advantage of management traffic. One in particular called VILurker is a MITM attack that points a VMware vSphere Client to a fake update package. This operates much like a number of traditional Metasploit MITM attacks but leverages the `clients.xml` file retrieved from an ESX host with a malicious URL for the client to retrieve updates from. From within a virtual environment, this attack can be easily as effective as other well-known MITM attacks; the only caveat is the pop-up error associated with a "bad" SSL certificate. Many users will ignore these, particularly because most VMware installations are still leveraging the original self-signed certificates in place originally. For this reason, it's important to keep this management traffic isolated.

To keep the traffic on a separate subnet or VLAN, it's important to open the proper firewall ports for traffic to and from the management servers. Table 5.1, Table 5.2, and Table 5.3 list the necessary ports for VMware vCenter, Citrix XenCenter, and Microsoft SCVMM respectively. Keep in mind that these are just the base ports needed for many implementations, and it's highly likely others will also be required (and some of these may not be needed, as well).

TABLE 5.1: Required vCenter server ports

PORT	DESCRIPTION
80	vCenter Server can use port 80 for direct connections, but connections will be redirected to TCP port 443.
389	Most vCenter Server instances are linked to Active Directory (AD), so this port is required for communication to and from AD or any other LDAP store.
443	All vSphere clients connect to vCenter on TCP port 443. SDK clients also use TCP port 443.
636	vCenter Server Linked Mode uses TCP port 636 for its local SSL connection.
902	vCenter uses both TCP and UDP port 902 to communicate with managed ESXi hosts and also receives heartbeat updates from them.
1433	Microsoft SQL Server traffic to and from the vCenter system.
8080	VMware VirtualCenter Management Web Services HTTP.
8443	VMware VirtualCenter Management Web Services HTTPS.
10080	vCenter Inventory Service HTTP connectivity.
10443	vCenter Inventory Service HTTPS connectivity.
10109	vCenter Inventory Service Database Service Management.
10111	vCenter Inventory Service Linked Mode Communication.
60099	Web Service change service notification port.

TABLE 5.2: Required XenCenter ports

PORTS (TCP)	DESCRIPTION
22	SSH communications to and from XenServer hosts.
389	Many XenCenter instances are linked to Active Directory, so this port is required for communication to and from AD or any other LDAP store.
443	XenCenter communicates with XenServer hosts on TCP port 443.

TABLE 5.2:   Required XenCenter ports   *(CONTINUED)*

PORTS (TCP)	DESCRIPTION
3389	RDP communications with Windows guests.
5900	Connectivity for VNC for Linux guests.

TABLE 5.3:   Required SCVMM ports

PORTS (TCP)	DESCRIPTION
22	SFTP communications to and from any managed VMware hosts.
80	WS-Management communications between VMM server and agents on Windows platforms.
135	DCOM communications with P2V source agents.
389	Many SCVMM instances are linked to Active Directory, so this port is required for communication to and from AD or any other LDAP store.
443	Many services to and from SCVMM use HTTPS on port 443, including VMM agent data transfer, VMware Web services, VMM's Self-Service portal, and others.
1433	Microsoft SQL Server traffic to and from the SCVMM system.
2179	VMConnect (RDP) to Hyper-V hosts.
3389	RDP communications with Windows VMs.
5900	VMRC connection to Virtual Server hosts.
8100	VMM Admin console and Self-Service portal traffic.

While patching, configuration management, and basic network access controls may not sound like a lot of security measures, they actually form the core of management platform hardening and protection. Aside from these basics, let's explore some specific controls and security measures that can be implemented on each of the three major vendors we've been covering.

VMware vCenter

VMware vCenter has the most flexible options available overall, but you've got security concerns before you're even finished installing the application! Unfortunately, there are a few concessions you make when installing the vCenter database. The database can be installed on the same system as vCenter or on a separate system or cluster entirely. The latter is strongly recommended in most cases because it provides more flexibility and avoids a single point of failure with a single system. The Database Options screen in the installation wizard is shown in Figure 5.2.

FIGURE 5.2
Installing the
vCenter database

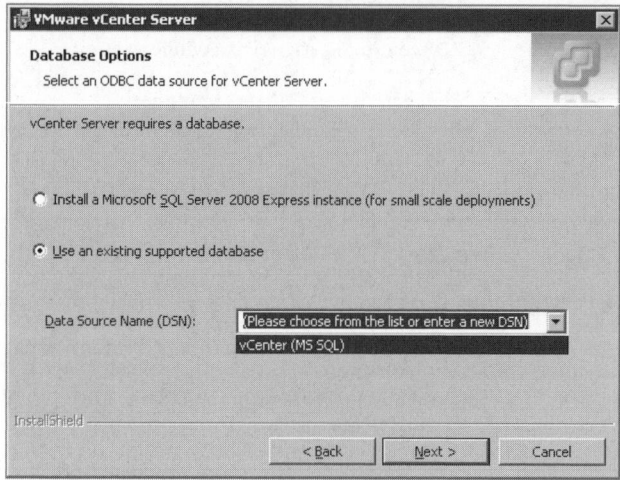

Security and operations teams should be aware of some of the caveats in installing the vCenter database. A stand-alone install of vCenter supports DB2, Oracle, and Microsoft SQL Server databases, and each has several basic considerations that must be evaluated. VMware's vCenter Server Appliance (a Linux-based virtual machine) supports only Oracle and DB2. Oracle installation and configuration is relatively basic but requires that the database user be assigned the CONNECT role and certain DBA role privileges, allowing extensive database access and control. SQL Server usually requires granting the db_owner role for installation of the database, although this role can be removed once the database is actually up and running.

As most organizations tend to use SQL Server, there are a few options to evaluate. The first is to assign the dbo schema and assign the db_owner role for the vCenter database installation, as mentioned earlier. Alternately, you can set the database permissions by creating specific database roles and the VMW schema for use with your new VCDB database. The basic steps to do so are as follows (after creating the VCDB database and assigning the VMW role to the user vpxuser):

1. Create a user role called VC_ADMIN_ROLE.

2. Grant the following privileges to this role:

   Schema permissions: ALTER, REFERENCES, INSERT

   Permissions: CREATE TABLE, CREATE PROCEDURES, VIEW

3. Create a VC_USER_ROLE user role.

4. Grant the following permissions to VC_USER_ROLE:

   Permissions: SELECT, INSERT, DELETE, UPDATE, EXECUTE

5. Grant both VC_USER_ROLE and VC_ADMIN_ROLE to the user vpxuser.

6. In the MSDB database, create a new vpxuser user.

7. In MSDB, create the VC_ADMIN_ROLE and assign these privileges:

    Grant EXECUTE for stored procedures sp_add_job, sp_delete_job, sp_add_jobstep, sp_update_job, sp_add_jobserver, sp_add_jobschedule, and sp_add_category.

8. Grant SELECT permissions for the MSDB tables syscategories, sysjobsteps, and sysjobs to "vpxuser".

9. In the MSDB database, grant VC_ADMIN_ROLE to vpxuser.

Now you can install vCenter Server, creating a new ODBC DSN to connect to the VCDB database with user vpxuser. When you're finished, remove the VC_ADMIN_ROLE from vpxuser.

vCenter Service Account

When installing vCenter, the setup asks you to designate a local user account to run the vCenter Server service under. The default option is to run vCenter as the local SYSTEM user on Windows platforms, which is a noninteractive account that has extensive privileges (shown in Figure 5.3).

FIGURE 5.3

Choosing a vCenter service account

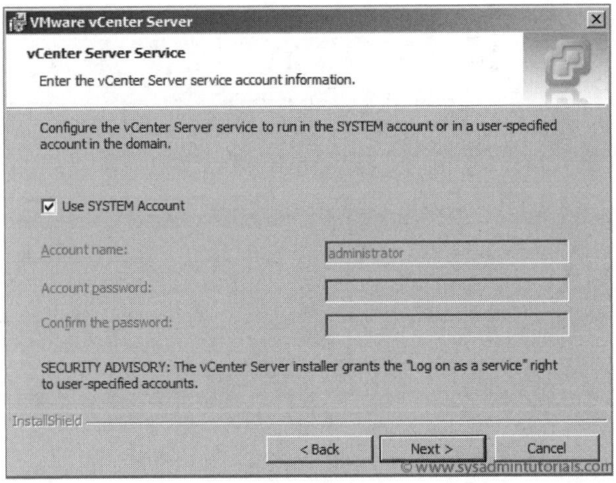

This is not ideal at all because vCenter will now have extensive privileges on the system that are not easily controlled through standard Windows-based security tools such as Group Policy and file permissions. There are two other options:

◆   Initiate the service as a local Administrator account (better than using the SYSTEM user, but still bad)

◆   Use a domain-level account with local privileges on the system (much better)

The local Administrator option is simple, and many organizations unwittingly choose this, not realizing how vulnerable this strategy is to configuration issues and potential attacks. The major issue stems from the fact that many local Admin accounts share the same password across server images and multiple administrators know the password. This can lead to exposure if one admin makes a mistake or deliberately decides to sabotage the organization for some reason.

Using a domain account with local privileges has a number of advantages. First, the account is centrally controlled and can be disabled in one place if the person leaves the organization for any reason. Second, there can be a more granular and limited assignment of privileges to the system overall in this case, whereas a local Administrator account tends to have complete ownership and control of the platform, which may not be desirable. Unless there are pressing reasons not to, I highly recommend using a domain-level account.

For the Linux-based vCenter appliance, you will need to access the appliance and manage it with the *root* account. The default credentials for this account are as follows:

Username: root

Password: vmware

As you can guess, this password should be changed immediately to something more complex that meets your organization's password policies. This can be done by clicking the Administration tab under the vCenter Server section and typing the current password, then the new one, as shown in Figure 5.4.

FIGURE 5.4
Changing the vCenter appliance admin password

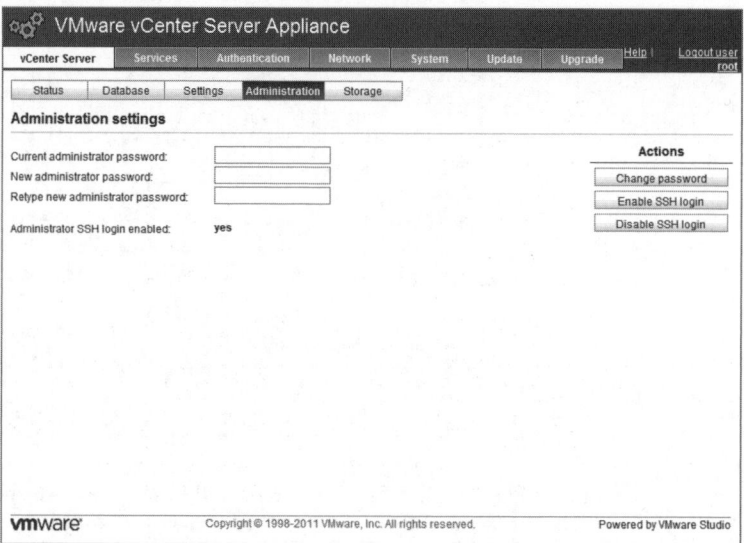

Secure Communications in vCenter

vCenter uses SSL/TLS for secure communications between the vSphere client and ESXi hosts. The digital certificates on both vCenter systems and ESXi hosts are self-signed certificates, and using self-signed certificates is widely regarded as a poor security practice. These certificates will function properly to establish SSL connectivity between vSphere clients and vCenter, as well as vCenter and ESXi hosts, but they will not provide the same level of security as certificates signed by root authorities. The self-signed certificates should ideally be replaced, if not with commercial certificates, then with certificates from a trusted certificate authority (CA) maintained by your organization.

VMware uses standard X.509 v3 certificates for SSL establishment. On ESX versions 3.*x* and vCenter 2.*x* and later, the private key is named `rui.key` and the certificate is named `rui.crt`. The default location for these files on vCenter running on Windows Server 2008 is:

```
C:\ProgramData\VMware\VMware VirtualCenter\SSL\
```

You can use OpenSSL to generate a certificate request (CSR) that can then be submitted to any CA to generate a base64-encoded `rui.crt` and `rui.key` pair. For Windows vCenter installs, you'll need to leverage OpenSSL again to generate one additional file: a PFX certificate file that contains both the private key and certificate in DER-encoded format. You can perform this task using the following command in OpenSSL for Windows:

```
openssl pkcs12 -export -in rui.crt -inkey rui.key -name rui -passout
pass:testpassword -out rui.pfx
```

NOTE As a word of caution, don't change the password because vCenter needs it to be **testpassword.**

To replace the certificates, follow these steps:

1. Disconnect all ESXi hosts being actively managed by the vCenter server: In the Inventory section of vCenter, select Hosts And Clusters, and then right-click each ESXi server and choose Disconnect.

NOTE If you are running vCenter in Linked mode, you do not need to disconnect all ESXi hosts on other Linked mode vCenter installs, only those directly managed by the one for which you're replacing certificates.

2. Close your connection to vCenter, and then use the Services console to stop the vCenter service on the Windows platform it's running on.

3. Copy the current `rui.crt`, `rui.key`, and `rui.pfx` files into a new folder (call it Backup or something similar). Now copy the new files into the SSL directory at `C:\ProgramData\VMware\VMware VirtualCenter\SSL\`.

4. Reset the vCenter database password, because the old one was tied to the original SSL certificate. Open a command prompt on the Windows platform and navigate to the `VMware\Infrastructure\VirtualCenter Server` directory, which is in `C:\Program Files` or `C:\Program Files (x86)`. Enter **vpxd.exe -p**.

   You'll be prompted to enter a new password for the database. Enter one and close the command prompt.

5. You can now restart the vCenter services, log back in to the vCenter server with the vSphere client (using the FQDN deployed with the new certificate), and reconnect all ESXi hosts.

For the Linux-based vCenter appliance, things are vastly simpler:

1. Make sure you have your new `rui.crt`, `rui.key`, and/or `rui.pfx` files as well as the public key PEM file.

2. Disconnect ESXi hosts being managed from the vCenter appliance. Log into the appliance using SSH as root.

3. Change into the certificate storage directory, /etc/vmware-vpx/ssl.

4. Move all the rui.* files into a new directory called backup:

```
mkdir backup
mv rui* backup
```

5. Now copy your new certificate files (rui.crt, rui.key, and/or rui.pfx) into the /etc/vmware-vpx/ssl directory using SCP or another secure file transfer protocol of your choice (SCP works well).

6. Restart the vCenter Server (VPXD) service:

```
service vmware-vpxd restart
```

7. Copy your PEM file to /etc/ssl/certs and run the following command:

```
c_rehash /etc/ssl/certs
```

vCenter Logging

vCenter produces a number of logs locally that virtualization and security teams should pay attention to. Important events to focus on include client and user access times and information, resource utilization alerts, creation or deletion of objects, and changes to roles and privileges. These logs are usually located in the following folders:

◆ vCenter on current Windows platforms: %ALLUSERSPROFILE%\VMware\VMware VirtualCenter\Logs\

◆ vCenter Linux Appliance: /var/log/vmware/vpx/ and /var/log/vmware/vami/

The following are common log names and content:

vpxd.log: The primary vCenter Server log file(s). These include all client and Web services connections, internal events, and communication with vCenter Server agents (vpxa) on managed ESX/ESXi hosts.

vpxd-profiler.log, profiler.log, and scoreboard.log: vCenter metrics.

cim-diag.log and vws.log: Common Information Model (CIM) monitoring logs.

drmdump\: VMware Distributed Resource Scheduler (DRS) events and actions.

All logs can be sent to a syslog or other centralized logging platform with an agent installed on Windows systems or natively on the Linux appliance.

To check the logs in the vCenter interface, browse to Home, then to Administration, then to System Logs to reach the screen shown in Figure 5.5. You can choose from a variety of logs, including the vCenter instance.

FIGURE 5.5
Viewing vCenter
log files

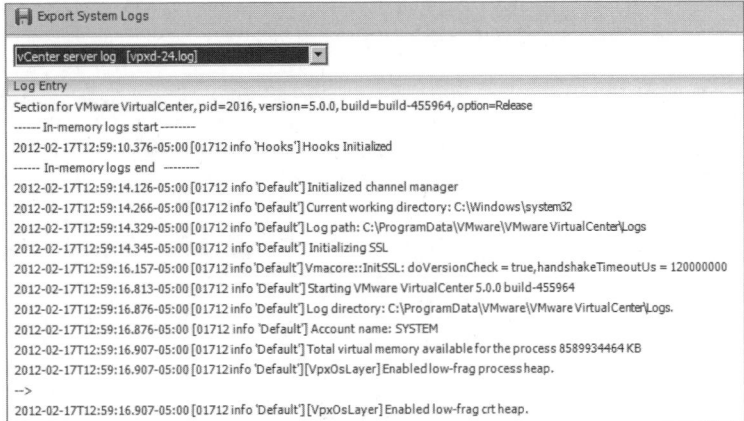

To set the level of logging verbosity, follow these steps:

1. Navigate to the top-level Administration menu item, and then select vCenter Server Settings. Choose Logging Options from the left-hand menu, and then choose from the drop-down menu as shown in Figure 5.6.

FIGURE 5.6
vCenter log settings

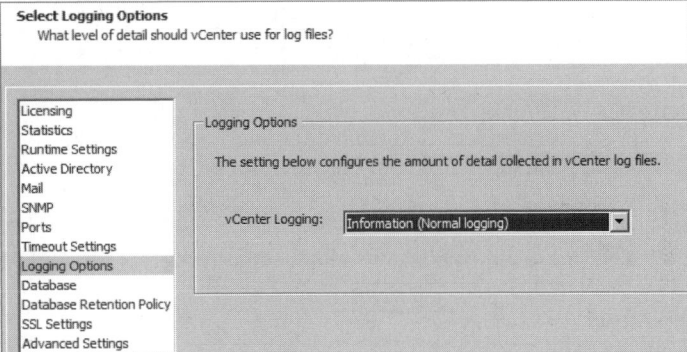

2. Choose from a range of options. None disables logging altogether and Trivia logs large amounts of information. The default setting is Normal, and this will be adequate for most organizations.

One final option for logging within vCenter is the full Log Export option. To export logs, follow these steps:

1. Choose the top-level Administration option, then select Export System Logs. You'll see a screen like that shown in Figure 5.7.

FIGURE 5.7
Exporting vCenter logs

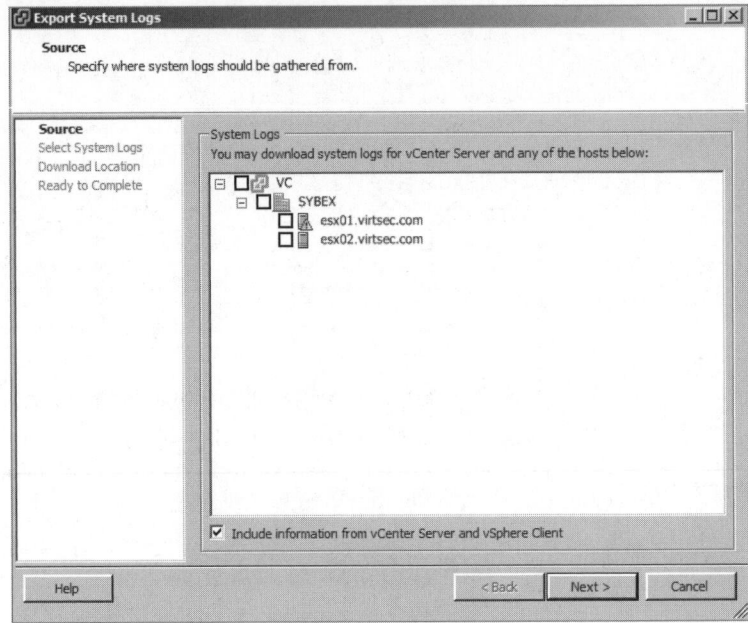

2. In this window, if you have a modern ESXi host, you can select vCenter logs as well as any managed ESX and ESXi host logs. Click Next.

   Older ESX hosts may not support individual log selection.

3. Choose the specific logs you want to collect, as shown in Figure 5.8.

FIGURE 5.8
Choosing specific system logs to export

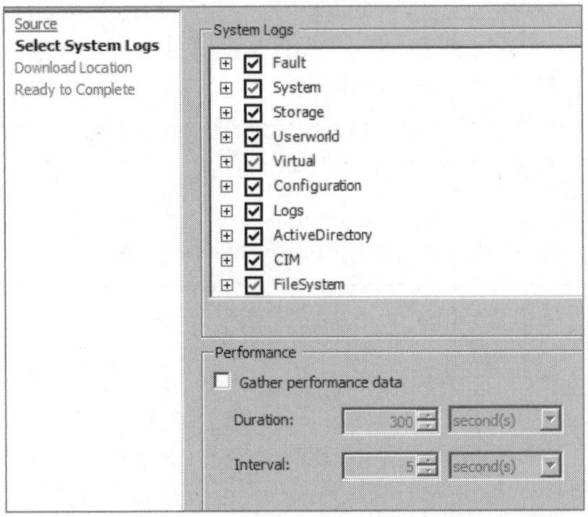

4. Click Next, and then select your download destination. Click Next again, and then finish the wizard.

Users, Groups, and Roles in vCenter

In addition to architecture design and critical operations, vCenter provides admins with granular control over vSphere roles and the privileges granted for each. This allows for very flexible role-based administration of the vSphere infrastructure as well as the ability to create roles for management and auditing teams to gain access to vCenter for very specific tasks.

The process is simple for Windows administrators used to Microsoft's nested AGULP (Account ➤ Global Group ➤ Universal Group ➤ Local Group ➤ Permissions) model. Users are created or pulled from an existing directory store and added to groups, and then these groups are assigned to resources with roles that exist within vCenter. These roles have privileges assigned to them.

Users must come from existing locations within the environment. vCenter will pull users from the domain the VC server is connected to as well as any local users and groups. When you're applying roles and groups to resources, vCenter will give you the ability to select groups and users from both the local system and the domain the VC server is a member of.

TIP Both local users and domain users can be added to resources with no problem, but this can get confusing, so it's best to allocate specific groups within the environment that are clearly labeled and easy to identify rather than using a mix-and-match approach. Using groups instead of stand-alone users is strongly recommended because this makes administration much easier over time as the environment grows in size and complexity.

vCenter ships with a number of built-in roles. Each of these roles has a long list of specific privileges associated with it but they are all built for specific purposes:

System roles: There are three built-in system roles that cannot be modified:

No Access: Used only to specifically block role inheritance.

Read-Only: Grants read-only access to resources in the vSphere inventory but no changes can be made.

Administrator: Grants full access to all privileges within vSphere for an object and corresponds to root-level accounts on each ESX/ESXi host with full privileges to all VMs on the host as well.

Datastore Consumer: A very simple role with only one explicit privilege, the ability to allocate space from a datastore.

Network Consumer: Much like the Datastore Consumer role, a simple role that grants permission to assign networks and nothing else.

Virtual Machine Power User: Allows users to manage existing virtual machines as well as take snapshots and schedule tasks specific to these virtual machines.

Virtual Machine User: Can interact with existing virtual machines and schedule tasks. No management of the virtual machines is permitted, nor is the ability to take snapshots of the VMs.

Resource Pool Administrator: Used to manage resource pools (pools of shared resources on clusters and/or individual ESX hosts; further discussed in Chapter 8, "Change and

Configuration Management," and Chapter 9, "Disaster Recovery and Business Continuity"). This role can dictate how the resource pool is set up and modified depending on available memory, disk space, and so on.

VMware Consolidate Backup User: Allows user to initiate the VMware Consolidated Backup (VCB) snapshot sequence. (VCB is a way to take snapshots of VMs, move them to a backup "proxy" server—in other words, an intermediate disk store—and then ultimately copy to tape. VCB is further discussed in Chapter 9).

NOTE Note that any assigned role is automatically granted read-only access as well.

Best practice for managing roles in vCenter is to create custom roles with the specific privileges that are needed to perform certain tasks. This requires an understanding of privileges and what they actually mean in terms of managing vSphere environments.

The three system roles cannot be modified, as mentioned earlier. However, they can be cloned, and the clones can be modified with no trouble at all. In fact, one of the best approaches to creating new roles is to clone an existing role that ships with vCenter and then modify the clone to meet the specific needs of the organization. The alternative is simply adding new roles and starting from scratch.

There are a number of privilege categories present within vCenter that allow very granular control of objects and functions. A brief description of each follows:

- Global: Manage vCenter tasks, licensing, and settings.

- Folder: Create, delete, rename, and move folder objects.

- Datacenter: Create, delete, rename, and move datacenter objects.

- Datastore: Manage datastores within vSphere.

- Network: Remove networks.

- Resource: Manage all aspects of resource pools.

- Alarms: Create, remove, and modify alarms.

- Tasks: Create or update tasks.

- Scheduled Task: Create, remove, run, or modify tasks.

- Sessions: Manage existing vCenter sessions.

- Performance: Modify performance measurement intervals.

- Permissions: Modify roles and permissions, reassign role permissions.

- Extension: Register, update, or unregister extensions to vCenter.

- Distributed Virtual Port Group: Create, delete, and modify distributed virtual port groups on dvSwitches.

- Distributed Virtual Switches: Create, delete, modify, and move dvSwitches; add and remove ESX/ESXi hosts; configure ports.

- Host Profile: Create, edit, delete, and view host profiles.

- Storage Views: Access storage views and modify server configurations.

- vApp: Control all aspects of vApps (creation, deletion, import/export, and modification); add VMs to a vApp; view OVF environments.

- VMware vCenter Update Manager: Manage system baselines/updates and VMware Update Manager service control.

- Host: Specific to ESX and ESXi hosts, with subcategories:

    - Inventory: Add, remove, rename, and modify hosts or clusters.

    - Configuration: All configuration options for ESX/ESXi hosts.

    - Local Operations: Create and delete VMs on a host, add hosts to VC, and manage user groups.

    - CIM: Establish remote connections to a Common Information Model (CIM) interface.

- Virtual Machine: Specific to VMs, with subcategories:

    - Inventory: Create, remove, and move VMs.

    - Interact: Power on/off, suspend, and reset VMs; configure CD and floppy devices, and so on.

    - Configuration: All VM configuration options, including modifying hardware settings, upgrading VMs, managing disks, and so on.

    - State: Manage all aspects of snapshots.

    - Provisioning: Manage VM customization, cloning, template creation and deployment, and disk and VM access control.

When assigning roles and privileges to vCenter objects, the process is very simple:

1. First, right-click the object in vCenter's Inventory screen where you want to apply roles and privileges. Select Add Permission. You'll see a window pop up like that shown in Figure 5.9.

2. Select the users and groups you want to add from either the local system or a known domain in the left-hand pane, and assign defined roles to each of them in the right-hand pane.

3. An additional item that is extremely important is the check box in the right-hand pane labeled Propagate To Child Objects. Checking this box will allow the selected users and groups and associated roles to apply to any child objects within the hierarchy object selected. It's checked by default, so leave it as is or uncheck as needed.

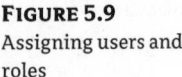

FIGURE 5.9

Assigning users and roles

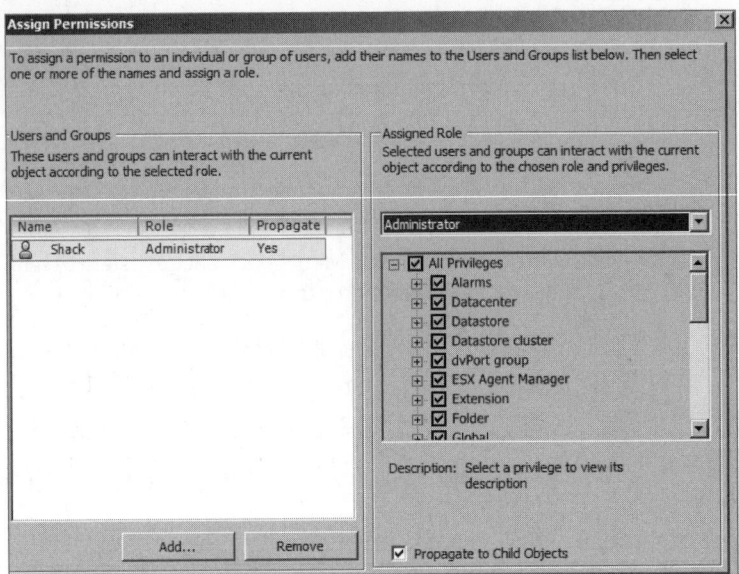

Roles assigned to users and groups, which are then allocated to specific resources within the vCenter architecture, are propagated by default to all child objects underneath higher-level objects. This can be blocked in one of two ways:

◆ The easiest way is simply to deselect the Propagate check box on an object's Permissions property screen or in the initial Role/Privilege allocation screen for the object.

◆ The other way is to apply the No Access role to users and groups on child objects. This will prevent any inheritance from higher-level objects and give the administrator more granular control over which users and groups can access particular resources.

There are several nuances to be aware of regarding role inheritance within vCenter:

◆ Any roles applied directly to an object will override those inherited from a higher-level object. For example, if Bob has administrative rights assigned to a Datacenter object but read-only rights assigned to a particular ESX host, the read-only rights will apply to that ESX host regardless of the inheritance.

◆ On the other hand, if two specific roles are assigned to the *same* object—most likely when two different groups are given access to an object and a user is a member of both groups—the role's privileges are combined. This means that, in essence, the *least restrictive* role will predominate for that particular object. In many cases, this can lead to unwanted privilege conflicts that must be remedied.

◆ When a user is *individually* granted access to an object (and assigned a role accordingly), that user's role will *override* any group roles that pertain to the user. For example, if Dave is granted individual administrator access to a cluster and also belongs to the Cluster Auditor group that has read-only access, the individual administrator access will override the read-only access.

TIP The complex interaction between user and group privileges is one major reason it is always recommended to use groups instead of individual users for assigning roles and privileges to resources. Maintaining group membership is usually easier than keeping track of all individual users that have access to resources, but keeping track of users in multiple groups can also be time consuming in large environments.

Another key point to mention is that the top-level object where a role is assigned will dictate what can be accessed and configured, so it's important to plan this carefully.

Role Creation Scenarios

Let's take a look at three simple role creation scenarios.

NETWORK ADMINISTRATOR

This role needs to access and manage vSwitches and networking components. The following actions will be needed:

1. Log into vCenter.

2. View ESXi hosts within datacenters, folders, and clusters.

3. Access the configuration area for ESXi hosts.

4. View and modify all aspects of vSwitches, port groups, and NICs.

To accomplish these tasks, two categories of privileges will be needed:

Host ➤ Configuration ➤ Network Configuration

Host ➤ Configuration ➤ Security Profile and Firewall

DEPLOY RESOURCE POOL TEMPLATES

A common role in many organizations is one that permits business unit operations teams to create new VMs based on a preexisting template. These VMs can be deployed into an existing resource pool, which would dictate how many resources were available and prevent a denial of service event. This differs from the existing Resource Pool Administrator role in vSphere in that many administrative privileges are disabled with this deployment role. The following privileges will be needed:

VM ➤ Inventory ➤ Create

VM ➤ Configuration ➤ Add New Disk

VM ➤ Provisioning ➤ Deploy Template

Resource ➤ Assign VM to Resource Pool

VM ➤ Interaction (all)

Now, users with this role can create a new VM and deploy it from a template, add a new virtual disk to the VM, assign the VM to a resource pool, and then interact with it fully. This role has no other privileges, so the user couldn't remove the VM or move it elsewhere.

AUDITOR

This role needs to be able to access vCenter and view all settings and architecture configuration. The auditor should never be able to change anything; any test of controls will be conducted with an administrator or other user.

To accomplish this, simply assign the auditor the built-in Read-Only role (or a renamed clone of this role) and allocate this role to the resources needed. Auditors can log in and look at all settings and users but won't be able to make any changes.

WARNING By default, the local administrator on the system has full Administrator access to vCenter! A better practice is to add a domain group to a local group on the system, then grant this local group Administrator privileges in vCenter. After testing this access, remove the local Administrator account from vCenter.

vSphere Client

Very little needs to be done to secure the vSphere Client other than limiting where it can be installed and what systems are used to access vCenter. If a single "jump box" or bastion host is used, from which all administrators connect, it's easier to maintain vSphere Client logs, which are usually stored on the local workstation in the following location:

```
C:\Documents and Settings\<username>\Local Settings\Application Data\VMware
```

Microsoft System Center Virtual Machine Manager

During the installation of SCVMM, there are a few things to plan for with regard to security. These include largely the same categories of controls we covered for vSphere vCenter, namely database security and local service accounts. When setting up the SQL Server database for SCVMM, there are several considerations:

◆ For remote instances of SQL Server, ensure that the account with which you run the SCVMM Setup Wizard and connect to the database is a member of the database server's sysadmin server role. Use the ALTER SERVER ROLE T-SQL command to add this user if needed.

◆ If the remote SQL Server system is not using the default local SYSTEM account and is running under a service account like Network Service or others, you'll need a local service principal name (SPN) for the SQL Server service. More information on creating an SPN is available in the article "How to troubleshoot the 'Cannot generate SSPI context' error message" from Microsoft:

http://support.microsoft.com/default.aspx?scid=kb;en-us;811889

◆ Enable SSL between the SCVMM server and SQL Server. This will be covered in the next section, "SCVMM Service Account."

◆ Create a dedicated service account for use with the SCVMM server, and make sure this is associated with the SQL Server system hosting the VMM database. This account will need to be a member of the db_owner role for the VMM database in order for it to function properly as well.

◆ Consider using a port other than the default SQL Server port (TCP 1433) to communicate to the remote SCVMM database installation.

SCVMM Service Account

When installing SCVMM, you'll be presented with the option to choose which local or domain account to run the SCVMM service with. Much as with vCenter, the standard user account for installation is the local SYSTEM account. It's highly recommended that you use a dedicated domain account with privileges on the system, and this is shown in Figure 5.10.

FIGURE 5.10
SCVMM service account specification

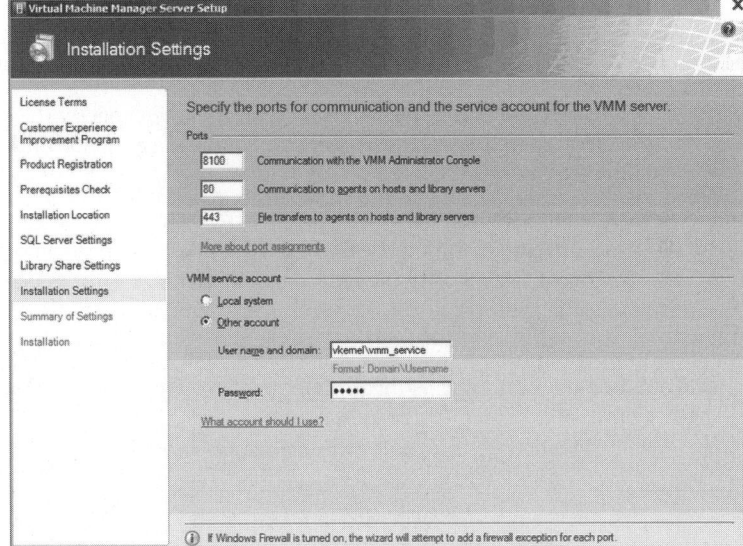

There are specific use cases in which you *must* use a domain account, and these are important to know:

◆ When you want to share ISO images between Hyper-V platforms.

◆ If you are using the Restricted Groups policy in a highly locked down Active Directory environment, the local SYSTEM account is removed from the local Administrators group, which will cause issues for SCVMM installation and operation.

◆ If there are unusual or disjointed DNS configurations with mismatched FQDNs in the environment, the use of a domain account is recommended, as well.

WARNING When you're installing the SCVMM service account, there's a "gotcha" consideration that's extremely important: You must use a different domain account than you use for other purposes. Create a domain account, or set of accounts, that is used for this and nothing else. The reason for this is straightforward: When a Hyper-V host is removed from SCVMM, the local SCVMM service account is removed from the Administrators group. If this account is being used for additional administrative purposes, operational issues could occur.

Secure Communications with SCVMM

SCVMM can leverage SSL communications with Hyper-V platforms, although the default communications mechanism uses the Background Intelligent Transfer Service (BITS) on port 443. To set up the most secure sessions between SCVMM and Hyper-V hosts, you'll need to set the Hyper-V platforms up as *perimeter hosts*. This is also the easiest way to enable and start using CA-generated SSL certificates for this communications channel. There are two major parts to this process. The first is to set up the SCVMM agent on the Hyper-V host and generate a security file. The second is to import this security file to SCVMM and connect the host.

The first process is to set up the Hyper-V agent:

1. Run the SCVMM `Setup.exe` process as Administrator.

2. Under Setup, click Local Agent, then click Next on the Welcome page.

3. Accept the license terms, click Next, and then specify the destination folder for installation. Click Next. Choose ports for communication (80 and 443 by default). In most cases, these can be left alone.

4. On the Security File Folder page, select "This host is on a perimeter network." Enter a shared secret (called the file encryption key) that will be used in the system's security file. Choose the security file location or leave the default in place. Check the "Use a CA signed certificate for encrypting communications with this host" option, and enter the thumbprint of the certificate. This screen is shown in Figure 5.11.

FIGURE 5.11
Securing the
Hyper-V Host agent

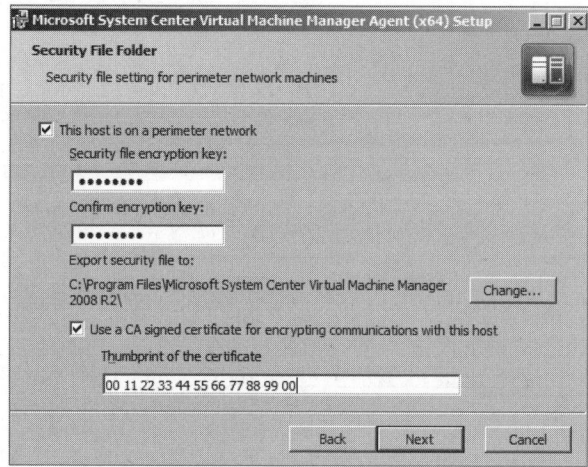

5. When finished, click Next.

6. Choose how the VMM management server will contact the host (by IP address or name), and then click Next.

7. Click Install to complete the installation.

Now copy the `SecurityFile.txt` file to a share reachable by SCVMM or to the SCVMM server itself. Then follow the next set of steps:

1. In the Actions pane within the SCVMM Administrator Console, click Add Hosts.

2. Select Windows Server-Based Host On A Perimeter Network. Click Next.

3. Enter the name or IP address of the host you want to add. Enter your shared secret encryption key, and then browse to the `SecurityFile.txt` file, as shown in Figure 5.12.

FIGURE 5.12
Security settings for the Hyper-V host

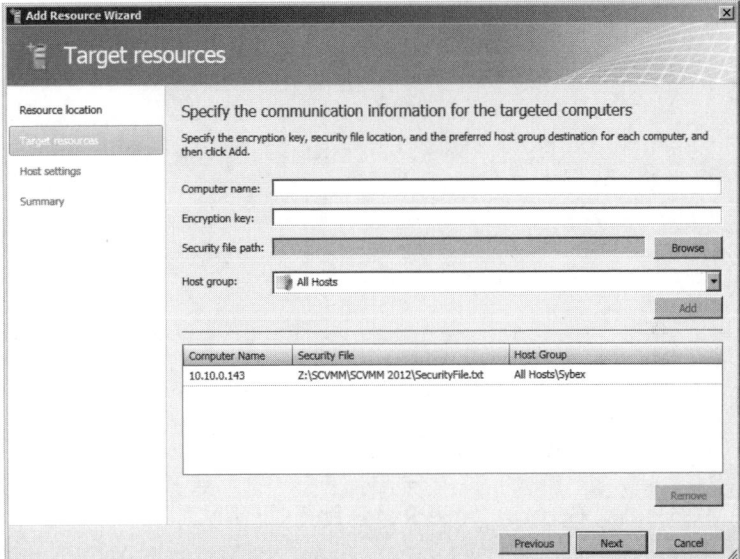

4. Select the Host group from the Host Group list and click Next.

5. Specify any virtual machine paths or leave the defaults in place; then click Next.

6. Review your settings, and then click Add Hosts.

You will now have secure Hyper-V to SCVMM communications in place with your own certificate files. You can also set up SSL from SCVMM to the SQL Server installation you have in place. More information on using SSL to connect to SQL Server can be found at "How to enable SSL encryption for an instance of SQL Server by using Microsoft Management Console" on Microsoft's site:

`http://support.microsoft.com/kb/316898/en-us`

SCVMM Logging

Unfortunately, all local logs for SCVMM are focused on installation and change tasks associated with the software and its components. These are located in the following directory:

`C:\ProgramData\VMMLogs\`

Quite a few operational logs are kept in the standard Windows Event Viewer for the system, though, and have their own category labeled VM Manager. This is shown in Figure 5.13.

FIGURE 5.13
SCVMM Event
Viewer logs

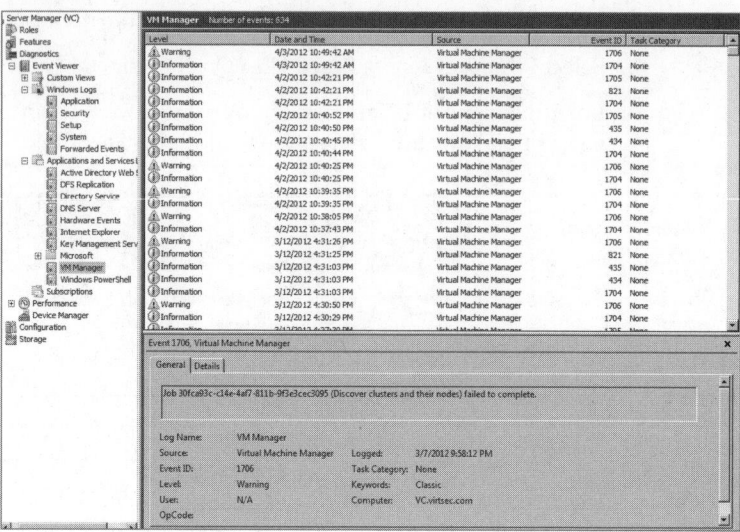

To integrate these into a centralized logging infrastructure, you'll need to install a syslog-compatible Windows agent such as Snare. More specifics on logs will be covered in Chapter 7, "Logging and Auditing."

Users, Groups, and Roles in SCVMM

We covered Hyper-V local roles using the Microsoft Authorization Manager in Chapter 2, "Securing Hypervisors." There are a few differences in the roles/privileges model for SCVMM, however. First, any host that is managed by SCVMM has its roles and privileges "overtaken" by the SCVMM privilege model. *Profiles* are sets of actions a role can take. The *scope* of the role defines the objects that can be affected by the role and profile, and the *membership list* defines who is a member of the role (usually taken from Active Directory, but may include local accounts as well). Roles fall into four categories (and have profiles with the same names):

Administrator: The Administrator role can perform all actions. Only one of these roles can exist on SCVMM installations.

Delegated Administrator: A delegated administrator can't modify SCVMM settings or add/remove members of the Administrator role but can access SCVMM as an administrator for defined objects and hosts. This is an ideal role for branch office or business unit administrators who need to maintain only a subset of the Hyper-V environment.

Read-Only Administrator: Read-only administrators are not able to modify any settings within SCVMM but can view profiles, status information, and object information within assigned host groups. This role is a good fit for auditors.

Self-Service User: Self-service users access the SCVMM Self-Service Web Portal to manage VMs defined within their scope. These roles encompass the actions users can perform on their specific VMs as well as any associated files like ISO images and templates. Quotas for VM deployment can be set as well.

To create a new role, assign profiles and users to it, and apply it to scopes of assets, follow these steps:

1. In the SCVMM 2012 console, select the Settings tab on the left side; then choose Security and click User Roles in the tree. Now click the Create User Role button on the top.

2. In the wizard that opens (shown in Figure 5.14), enter a role name and description (optional), and click Next. Now choose the type of role you would like to create (Delegated Administrator, Read-Only Administrator, or Self-Service User). Click Next.

FIGURE 5.14
Creating new
SCVMM roles

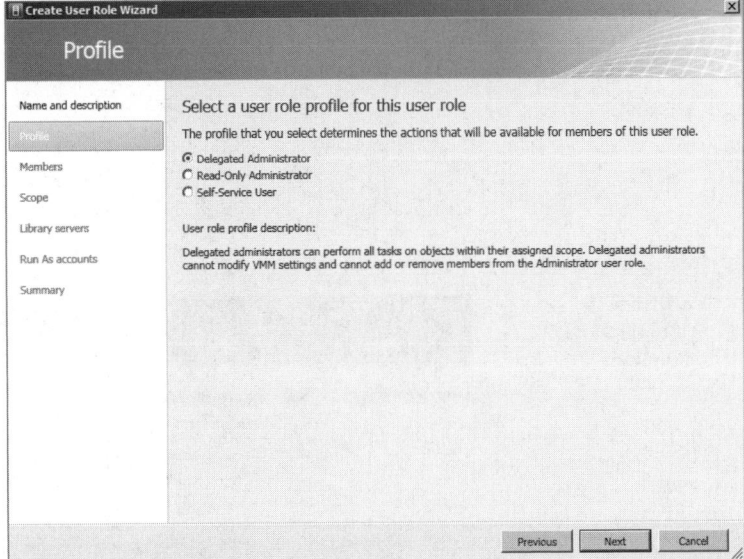

3. Now, choose users and/or groups to add to this role. Click Next when finished.

4. Choose the scope of the role (Figure 5.15). Click Next.

5. If you chose to create a Delegated Administrator or Read-Only Administrator role, you can then select specified library servers (specific catalogs of usable resources) and Run As accounts (if you prefer actions to be performed in a different user context), and then you're done. Review all the final details, and then click Finish.

    If you created a Self-Service User role, you've got two different steps. First, select the resources that this user or group can interact with within SCVMM. Then, select the specific actions you would like the user or group to be able to perform and choose those appropriate to the group, as shown in Figure 5.16. Click Next.

FIGURE 5.15
Choosing a role
scope

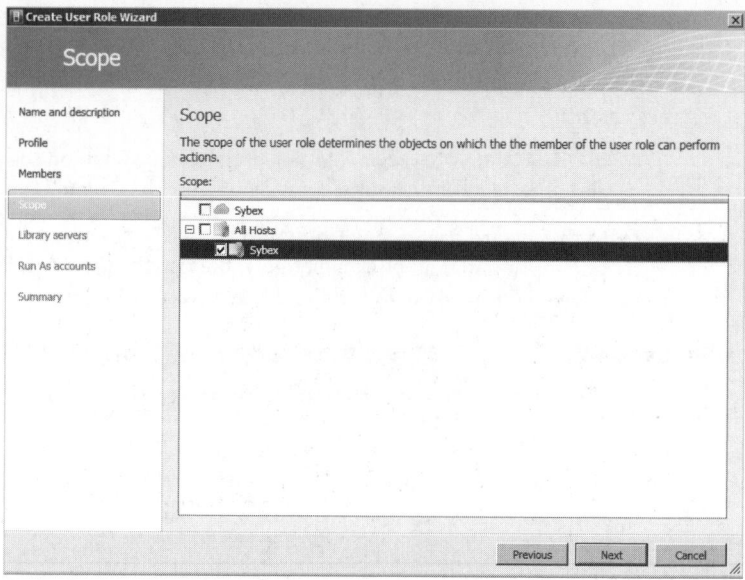

FIGURE 5.16
Self-Service User
role actions

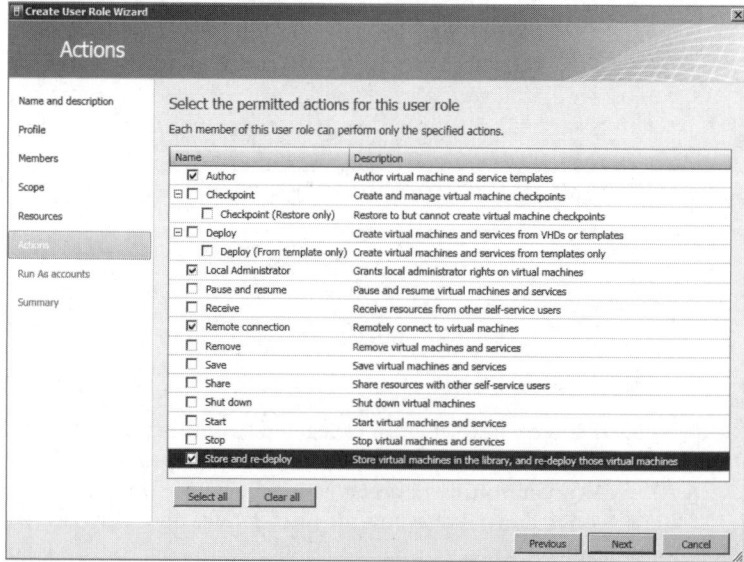

6. Now choose any Run As accounts you want user actions to be performed as. Once done, click Next.

7. Review your chosen options, and click Finish.

Keep in mind that in order to allow users to share or transfer ownership of a VM, you'll need to assign them both to a security group and then assign this group to the Self-Service User role you create.

Client Security

Most Windows environments leverage the Remote Desktop Protocol (RDP) for connectivity to SCVMM platforms, and Microsoft recommends running SCVMM's Administrative Console on the same platform where SCVMM is installed. Securing RDP is beyond the scope of this book, but Microsoft has a number of resources available on this topic.

Citrix XenCenter

XenCenter is a bit more simplistic than either vCenter or SCVMM and doesn't have the range of security considerations and controls that the others do. The first simple consideration for XenCenter is during installation. XenCenter's setup program asks whether XenCenter should be installed for all users or whether you want to choose the Just Me option. Even if you select Just Me, any user with privileges to the platform it's installed on can run it. Selecting Just Me is better than arbitrarily granting XenCenter access to everyone, though, so you should select it. Aside from this option, you have no additional configuration to do during installation of XenCenter.

Once XenCenter is up and running, you'll need to keep it updated, and you can do so automatically with a configuration option in the console. Open XenCenter, click the Tools menu at the top and select Options. The second item in the left-hand menu pane is Updates, and you can check for new XenCenter versions routinely, as shown in Figure 5.17.

FIGURE 5.17
XenCenter updates

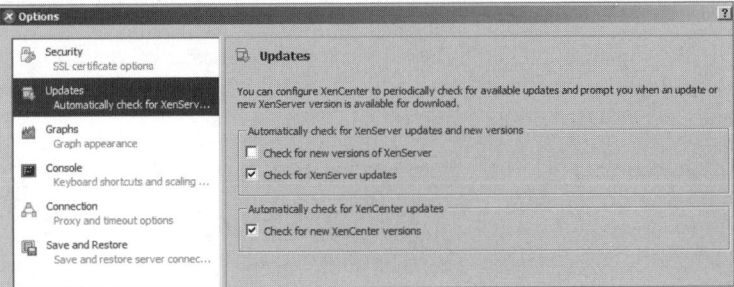

Secure Communication with XenCenter

XenCenter communicates with XenServer hosts using SSL, but the certificates are stored and managed on the individual hypervisor hosts, not on the XenCenter platform. The default certificates can and should be replaced with more secure ones generated by a trusted certificate authority (as discussed in Chapter 2). You can monitor any changes to these certificates by selecting the Tools menu item and then choosing Options. The first menu item on the left side, Security, allows you to monitor for new or changed host certificates and generate alerts. This screen is shown in Figure 5.18.

FIGURE 5.18
SSL alerting in
XenCenter

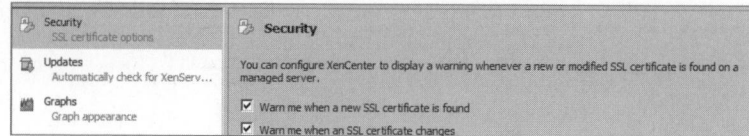

XenCenter also supports VNC-based communication for graphical console connectivity, which should be secured with a password if possible. This will depend on your VNC client in use, which may differ from one organization to the next.

Logging with XenCenter

XenCenter has a minimal set of logs that are available on Windows platforms. The good news is that these logs are useful in troubleshooting connectivity to XenServer hosts. The bad news is that almost no security information is present in the log files. Nonetheless, these logs may be useful. They are usually found in the following directory:

```
%userprofile%\AppData\Citrix\Roaming\XenCenter\logs\XenCenter.log
```

Two files are often present, `XenCenter.log` and `XenCenter Audit Trail.log`. Both contain various operational data.

Users, Groups, and Roles in XenCenter

XenCenter does not allow for dedicated user, group, and role creation within the application itself. All of these are handled at the local XenServer and pool level. For this reason, it's imperative to limit access to the host where XenCenter is running, using strict password policies and access controls, ideally employing multifactor authentication such as hardware token-based one-time passwords or client-side digital certificates.

In addition, XenCenter can maintain a master password for controlling all privileged connections to XenServer hosts, and this is an option presented when establishing host connections, as shown in Figure 5.19.

FIGURE 5.19
XenCenter master
password

> **Save and Restore Connection State**
>
> XenCenter can remember login credentials for your managed servers and use them to automatically restore the connection state of your servers when you start a session.
>
> ☑ Save and restore server connection state on startup
>
> **Master password**
>
> When set, the master password protects all your server login credentials. You will need to enter this password at the beginning of each session.
>
> ☐ Require a master password   Change Master Password...
>
> OK   Cancel

Chapter 6

Securing the Virtual Machine

For most organizations, the entire point of virtualizing is to create and maintain virtual machines that take the place of physical platforms in the datacenter. In many ways, these virtual machines (VMs) have the exact same behavior and security profile as their physical counterparts. However, there are some inherent changes in the risk profile of VMs versus physical systems due to the nature of VMs themselves — in essence, they're simply a collection of files that represent systems. Files can be corrupted, stolen, manipulated, intercepted, and parsed for sensitive data, unlike standard physical machine builds.

In addition, there are particular connectivity elements and configuration options that make VMs potentially more vulnerable to attacks. This chapter will explore some of the more prevalent security concerns related to VMs and also explore some specific threats and vulnerabilities related to VMs. We'll look at some of the security options available to administrators of VMware, Microsoft, and Citrix virtualization environments, too, and provide guidance on how to effectively lock down VMs to mitigate attacks.

In this chapter, you will learn about the following topics:

◆ The types of threats that face virtual machines, and how they differ from traditional system and application attacks

◆ The vulnerabilities virtual machines are susceptible to, and some research that explores new ways to compromise virtual machines

◆ The types of files that make up virtual machines, and what function they serve

◆ How to secure virtual machines against various attacks

Virtual Machine Threats and Vulnerabilities

There are quite a few different types of virtual machine security issues on which administrators and security professionals should be focused. In general, these fall into several major categories:

Attacks against the VM operating system and applications   The first category of threats is the set of traditional remote or local exploits affecting operating systems and applications. These are no different than those affecting traditional platforms, and they can be largely mitigated by proper configuration management and patching processes. All virtual machines should be locked down properly using guidance from operating system and application vendors, the Center for Internet Security (CIS), and other sources.

Virtual machine theft   Another potential category of virtual machine security concerns is virtual machine theft. Given that virtual machines are simply a collection of files, a user with physical access to a datastore where VMs are maintained, or a local hypervisor, could potentially copy all the files of the VM to local media and remove them. This was easily possible in an older version of VMware Virtual Infrastructure, covered in the next section, "Virtual Machine Security Research."

◆ Attacks from one VM to another: This is not a new attack vector, per se, but fast-spreading malware and disruptive attacks could easily be somewhat more effective due to the "proximity" that virtual machines may share with one another in a cluster or locally hosted environment. Additionally, attackers could leverage VM escape types of attacks (covered in Chapter 1, "Fundamentals of Virtualization Security") to exploit one system and then attack others by way of the hypervisor platform.

◆ Code/file injection flaws: As VMs are simply a collection of files, the addition or modification of configuration and other VM-specific data in these files could cause a variety of conditions, ranging from system exploits to DoS scenarios.

◆ Denial of service (DoS): DoS attacks can happen to any system or application, and many classic attacks have been noted in the past. These range from remote network DoS attacks using large numbers of packets or malformed packets to local DoS attacks that consume resources or cause the system to crash. A new type of DoS attack is now possible due to the resource sharing between VMs. If several VMs (or even one) start consuming too many physical resources like RAM, disk space, or network throughput, others may suffer as a result. This is an entirely new DoS variant that relies on multiple systems sharing resources, which is almost always the case for VMs.

"Information leakage" attacks Although this class of attacks has less immediate impact than some others, the reality is that much information can often be gleaned from VMs that could then lead to more effective attacks later. VMs running in a cloud environment are particularly susceptible to these attacks, and several security researchers have uncovered disturbing side effects of running VMs in cloud environments (covered in the next section).

These are just a few of the various attacks that could befall virtual machines in typical internal or public cloud environments. A white paper published by IBM's X-Force in 2010 does an excellent job of laying out, at a high level, the types of VM-focused attack scenarios and considerations that operations and security teams need to understand. In addition to those already mentioned, the paper describes the various security issues your organization could face if an attacker successfully compromised an administrative VM. Many of these issues echo those we covered in Chapter 5, "Virtualization Management and Client Security," but the IBM team also mentions DoS attacks against the administrative VM, privilege escalation, and authentication bypass.

The paper can be found here:

```
http://blogs.iss.net/archive/papers/VirtualizationSecurity.pdf
```

Virtual Machine Security Research

In the following sections, I'll cover three interesting research projects that represent significant VM-focused attacks (as opposed to attack scenarios against the virtualization environment as a whole). These VM attacks can also be used in more complex attack scenarios, and this is an area of security research that is evolving at a rapid pace.

NOTE *Securing the Virtual Environment: How to Defend the Enterprise Against Attack* by Davi Ottenheimer and Matthew Wallace (Wiley, 2012) is an excellent book that discusses a variety of virtualization security research, ranging widely across practical and theoretical security scenarios. For more information, see www.wiley.com/WileyCDA/WileyTitle/productCd-1118155483.html.

Stealing Guests

The first project is the result of research done by Justin Morehouse and Tony Flick and presented at the ShmooCon conference in 2010. The title of their conference talk was "Stealing Guests…the VMware Way." They described a way to locate and remotely download VM guest files from ESX and ESXi servers.

By default, all VMware hypervisor platforms offer some management Web services on ports TCP 8307/8308 (VMware Server) or TCP 80/443 (ESX and ESXi). Vulnerable versions of these platforms allowed an attacker to easily enumerate the host's virtual machine inventory and then actually traverse the hypervisor file system to access the VM's configuration file(s). The main VMware VM configuration file (covered shortly) could be parsed to locate the virtual disk and other files, and all of these could be downloaded ("stolen") by the attacker remotely. Morehouse and Flick released a Perl script called GuestStealer that could automate the process.

VMware issued a patch for this security flaw in late 2009 after working with Morehouse and Flick to identify and resolve the issue, so the attack now works against only certain older versions of VMware's Virtual Infrastructure 3.*x* product line. However, the attack is ingenious and simple.

Since the publication of this research, this attack and others are included in a set of modules for the popular Metasploit Framework, an attack toolkit used by security professionals and attackers alike. Called the Virtualization Assessment Toolkit (VASTO), these modules helped automate this and other virtualization-specific attacks. VASTO was written by Claudio Criscione and a team of contributors, and can be found at http://vasto.nibblesec.org.

The original presentation by Morehouse and Flick can be found here:

www.fyrmassociates.com/pdfs/Stealing_Guests_The_VMware_Way-ShmooCon2010.pdf

A search engine will find you the presentation in additional formats.

Cloud VM Reconnaissance

In a 2009 paper, four researchers at the University of California, San Diego, and Massachusetts Institute of Technology determined that there were significant risks to VMs running in public cloud environments. The risks stemmed from the multitenant nature of virtualization-based cloud environments. One major revelation this team exposed for the first time was the general lack of trust in cloud environments; in other words, how can you determine who your "neighbors" are on a shared virtualization platform in a cloud provider environment? Criminals and other malicious attackers can provision VMs just as you do, and this can potentially have negative consequences.

The first step in the attack is to place a malicious VM into a cloud provider environment in such a way as to maximize the likelihood that the VM will reside on the same physical server as a target. The research team determined that they could first perform "cloud cartography" — determine IP address and round-trip time values that could fairly accurately pinpoint where specific systems were located in the Amazon EC2 cloud. They also developed a strategy both for determining the likelihood of "co-residency" with an attacker VM and for a brute force strategy for placing their malicious VMs on the target physical hosts in the cloud.

Once this was accomplished, the researchers were able to perform side channel attacks against the target VMs on the same physical hypervisors. This means that they were able to surreptitiously monitor and assess target VMs through channels never intended for this purpose. The researchers were able to monitor the target VM cache usage and traffic quantity and patterns and then build on this information to measure the timing of keystrokes on the target VM, allowing them to plan for password guessing and other attacks.

The original paper, *Hey, You, Get Off of My Cloud: Exploring Information Leakage in Third-Party Compute Clouds* by Thomas Ristenpart, Eran Tromer, Hovav Shacham, and Stefan Savage, can be found here:

```
http://www.cs.cornell.edu/courses/cs6460/2011sp/papers/cloudsec-ccs09.pdf
```

Another presentation at DefCon 17 in 2009 from the research team at security consultancy Sensepost touched on a handful of similar issues. The presentation slides for "Clobbering the Cloud!" by Nicholas Arvanitis, Marco Slaviero, and Haroon Meer can be found here:

```
http://defcon.org/images/defcon-17/dc-17-presentations/defcon-17-sensepost-
clobbering_the_cloud.pdf
```

Virtual Disk Manipulation

In May 2012, a group of researchers at German security firm ERNW discovered that they could purposefully manipulate VMware VM virtual disk files to access and interact with files on the underlying hypervisor platform. By mounting virtual "disks" that actually referenced underlying VMware ESXi v5 file structures, the researchers demonstrated that any VM user could access sensitive areas of the hypervisor platform. The primary revelation of this attack is that virtualization vendors may have flawed trust models in place between components in the virtual infrastructure. If the hypervisor implicitly trusts any access from certain VM files and components, then attackers can leverage these to access data and applications they shouldn't be able to get to.

This attack has immense potential to cause harm in a cloud-based multitenant environment. A VM owner could purposefully deploy a modified virtual disk file that allows them to peruse the mounted disks known to the hypervisor. These will invariably contain other customers' data, leading to a significant breach of confidentiality and integrity at the very least.

The original post by the team at ERNW is titled "VMDK Has Left the Building — Some Nasty Attacks Against VMware vSphere 5 Based Cloud Infrastructures" and can be found on the Insinuator blog here:

```
www.insinuator.net/2012/05/vmdk-has-left-the-building/
```

Virtual Machine Encryption

This section was written in conjunction with this book's technical editor, Steve Pate, who has particular expertise in virtual machine encryption.

Because a virtual machine consists of a set of files, machine theft has now become much easier. People will notice you walking out of the building with a server but not with a USB stick containing a set of VM files. Furthermore, stealing a virtual machine can be achieved with relative ease by simply snapshotting the VM and copying the snapshotted files. All of this can be done without taking the virtual machine offline.

Fortunately, there are options available for encrypting all or parts of a virtual machine, whether the VM runs in a datacenter/private cloud or within an instrumented or un-instrumented public cloud. There are several layers in the virtualization stack where you can deploy encryption. Each option has pros and cons, especially when you consider management of encryption keys.

In June 2011, the Payment Card Industry (PCI) Security Standards Council released version 2.0 of its *PCI DSS Virtualization Guidelines*, an information supplement to version 2.0 of the Payment Card Industry Data Security Standard (PCI DSS). This new supplement walks through a whole list of new vulnerabilities that virtualization brings, including the exposure of credit card and other sensitive information in snapshot files as well as in dormant VMs. In the latter case, VM backups can exist for years and can be easily spun up because the operating system, applications, and application data are all held in the same VM backup image. For this reason, just encrypting at the OS and/or application layer may not be enough any longer.

NOTE The PCI DSS Virtualization Guidelines can be found here: www.pcisecuritystandards
.org/documents/Virtualization_InfoSupp_v2.pdf.

The following are potential places that virtual machines and data can be encrypted in a virtualized environment:

◆ Within the virtual machine itself. In this case, files other than those stored in VMDKs cannot be protected.

◆ Within the hypervisor. At the time of writing, none of the hypervisor vendors provide encryption solutions for server virtualization environments.

◆ On a network-attached storage (NAS) filer. In this case, it is most likely that all portions of the VM are encrypted, and if NFS is the protocol between the filer and the hypervisor, selected parts of the VM could be encrypted.

◆ Within the storage area network (SAN) fabric. Because this is block-level storage, all portions of the VM would be encrypted, and it is not possible to distinguish between one VM and another.

◆ Within the storage devices themselves. This is usually accomplished by means of full disk encryption (FDE).

◆ In backups / Disaster Recovery (DR). Note that backups can be taken at any layer in the stack.

Figure 6.1 shows the encryption options.

All of these choices offer some level of protection for VMs, but some options are rather static in nature and don't reflect the increasing use of virtual machines as mobile containers for workflow. For example, if a virtual machine migrates from a private cloud to a public cloud, switch-level encryption or full disk encryption becomes useless because you don't migrate your switches or disks to a public cloud along with the VM!

To solve these issues, we need a flexible storage model that encompasses strong encryption and policy-driven key management capabilities (to mitigate the complexities found around key management). Furthermore, as the *PCI DSS Virtualization Guidelines* specifies, we need strong separation of duties to allow different workloads with different privilege levels, or virtual machines from different customers, to share the same infrastructure.

FIGURE 6.1
VM encryption
options

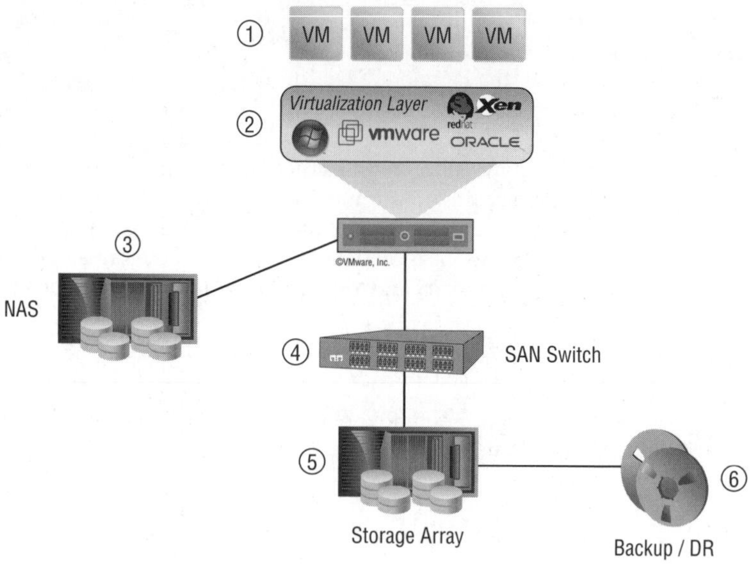

ENCRYPTION UNDER THE HYPERVISOR

Figure 6.2 shows how VMs can be encrypted underneath the hypervisor. By using standard protocols such as NFS or iSCSI, the encryption is independent of the hypervisor platform. That means hypervisor features such as vMotion and Live Migration continue to work unchanged. As VMs are copied into an encrypted datastore, they will be encrypted according to the encryption policy that is put in place.

FIGURE 6.2
Encryption
"underneath" the
hypervisor

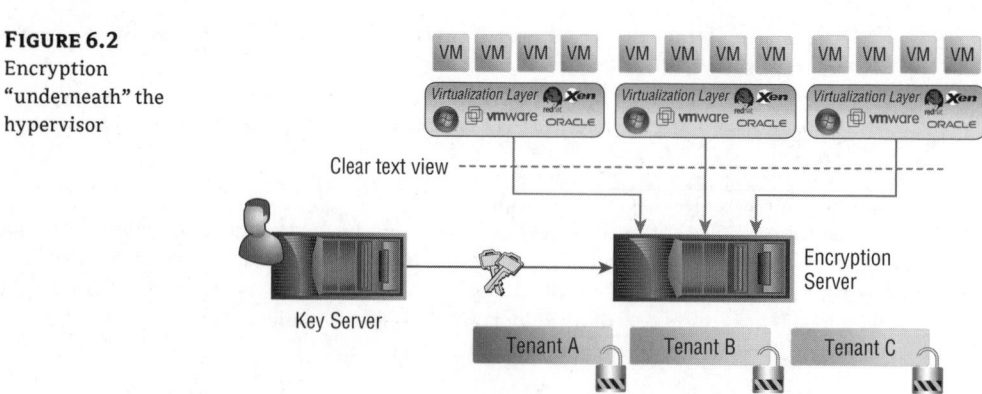

A great benefit with this approach is that no modifications are needed to the virtual machines themselves. Regardless of operating system or applications, the data is encrypted at rest. For large organizations that may have many thousands of applications modifying each and every VM, attempting to secure the VM directly is certainly problematic and therefore this approach works well.

The key server could reside anywhere:

◆ In the customer's datacenter

◆ At the provider site where the VMs reside

◆ At a third-party site that only hosts key services

The one drawback with this encryption approach is that the VM administrator sees a clear text view of the VMs as they are read from storage and through the hypervisor. This is not a problem in all environments, however. If backups are taken at the hypervisor layer, encryption may already take place within the backup app, and therefore, cleartext data at this layer may be beneficial for use with other operational applications or processes. Even so, there are many organizations that are concerned about exposing data to VM administrators.

Another disadvantage with this approach is that service providers will need to deploy the technology in their infrastructure. Some providers will work with you to customize your environment, while others, such as Amazon AWS, allow you to encrypt only within the VM itself.

It is important to note that encryption at rest solves only part of the data security problem. The backup images generated must also be secure so that as the VMs are moved to backups/archives, between datacenters for replication purposes, or to wherever else they are copied, they remain secure at all times.

ENCRYPTION WITHIN THE VM

Figure 6.3 presents another model. In this model, for all devices encrypted, there is an encrypted path from the VM's operating system through the hypervisor and down to the storage layer. This prevents VM administrators from being able to view sensitive data that resides within the VM. In this environment, as with the previous one described, the key server could reside anywhere.

FIGURE 6.3
Encryption within the VM

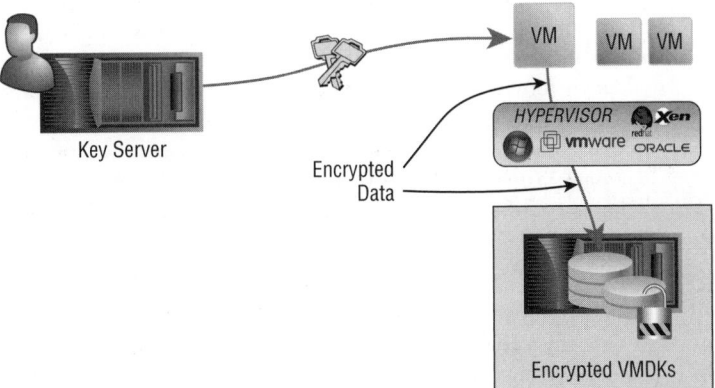

Key Server

Encrypted Data

Encrypted VMDKs

ENCRYPTION OF VM IMAGES AND APPLICATION DATA

Another model combines encryption at the VM and storage layers. This combined option is superior because there's an encrypted path for sensitive data all the way from the VM through the hypervisor. This prevents the VM administrator from seeing cleartext data. In addition, the snapshot, suspend, log, and other important VM files can be encrypted too, because the encryption "container" encompasses all VM files. If a snapshot is taken, the contents are also encrypted. Most virtualization platforms give you the flexibility to split VM files and place them on different datastores, allowing for more flexibility in encryption deployment and implementation. This option is shown in Figure 6.4.

FIGURE 6.4
Encryption of both
VM images and
application data

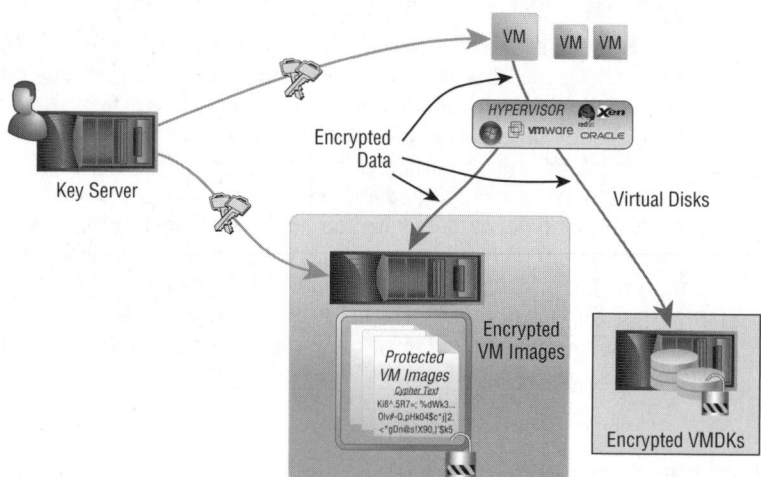

KEY MANAGEMENT CHALLENGES

In the preface to the second edition of his book *Applied Cryptography* (Wiley, 1996), Bruce Schneier is quoted as saying "Key management is the hardest part of cryptography and often the Achilles' heel of an otherwise secure system." Encryption systems are typically hard to crack and certainly beyond the capabilities of most individuals. However, unless a good key management solution is put in place, keys can be easily exposed or lost.

As we move toward hybrid cloud models where organizations have VMs and data in multiple locations, the need for encryption as a means to protect sensitive data beyond the traditional security boundary is becoming more mainstream. The focus from security teams then typically becomes, Who owns the keys and where should they be held?

Figure 6.5 shows three possible options for key management that we will see being deployed over the next several years.

The three key management options are as follows:

The cloud service provider owns the keys as well as the VMs. Providers can certainly provide this capability, and for many, the fact that their data is encrypted and they do not have to manage keys themselves is seen as a big plus. However, if authorities were to seize systems containing your VMs/data, they would likely have access to the keys as well.

The customer owns the keys in its own datacenter. There are many organizations for which this is an absolute must. In particular, some large organizations are distrustful of service provider staff that they have no control over and will not relinquish control of key services.

Third-party key services host the keys. Some of the cloud service providers don't want to host keys, and there are many places where organizations require encryption but do not wish to host the keys themselves. This model certainly will be interesting for smaller organizations that want to use the public cloud but do not wish to have the responsibility for managing keys on site.

The discussion around where to host keys is becoming increasingly popular, particularly as we see the balance of production servers in the public cloud moving passed the 50 percent mark and as more and more sensitive data migrates into public cloud environments.

FIGURE 6.5
VM encryption
key management
options

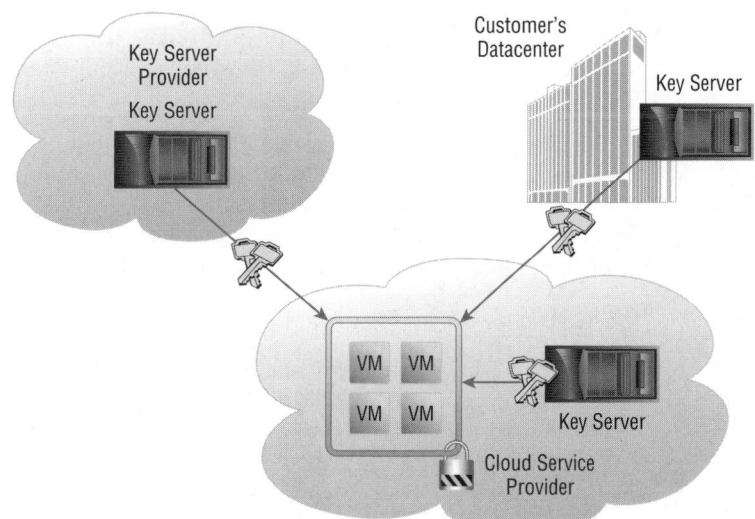

Locking Down VMware VMs

Now that you know some of the potential attacks, let's turn our attention to how you can lock down virtual machines using the native tools from the vendors.

VMware virtual machines have a different format than Microsoft and Citrix virtual machines. The VMware format leverages a text configuration file that is separate from the virtual disk file, virtual memory files, and others. To understand how to lock down VMware VMs, you must know a little about these files.

Let's say that you create a virtual machine named SQL01. The following files would be created:

♦ SQL01.vmx: The VMX file is the VMware configuration file that defines all your VM's virtual hardware. This file is unique in the sense that it is completely independent and the other files aren't affected when you make changes to it. For this reason, the VMware VMX file is incredibly simple to manually edit, allowing for more flexible configuration of virtual machines. You need to protect this file because it contains a lot of detail about the VM, and any changes to this file could dramatically affect the VM's functions and settings.

◆ SQL01.vmdk: VMDK files represent a VM's virtual disk configuration. This file is also essentially a text file. It describes the types of disks in use and specific file system information and points to the actual file system disk images in use by the VM. If an attacker gained access to this file, they could easily learn where the VM disk file itself is located as well as details about its configuration.

◆ SQL01-flat.vmdk: This file represents the actual VM disk, with all space allocated to it. Multiple *-flat.vmdk files can be in use for a given VM, depending on how the disk is created and the file system in use. This file contains the VM's actual data and should be protected accordingly, just like a real disk.

◆ SQL01.nvram: NVRAM files are the VM's BIOS. This file is re-created every time the VM starts and is based on the well-known Phoenix BIOS platform.

◆ SQL01.log or vmware.log: This file is your VM's current log, and there can be multiple log files for a given VM. As they reach a specific size, they are usually rotated. The names of older logs will include a dash following the word *vmware* and then a number. Higher numbers indicate older logs, thus vmware-2.log is older than vmware-1.log. Log files may contain a variety of sensitive and important information, and could even be used to recreate a corrupt VMX or VMDK file in extreme circumstances.

There are a number of additional files that you may have, depending on the state of the VM:

◆ SQL01.vmxf: In VMware Workstation, you can designate multiple VMs as a "team" to be controlled together. If a VM has been a part of a team, it will have a VMXF file that acts as a supplemental text-based configuration file, much like the standard VMX file. Enterprise VMs running on ESX or ESXi can still have VMXF files associated with them, but it will largely be for backward compatibility.

◆ SQL01.vmem: The *.vmem file is a backup of the VM's swap, or paging, file and is usually created only if a VM is running or if it has crashed. Each VM on an ESX server gets its own swap file, which is created when the VM is powered on. The purpose of the swap file is to store memory pages when the VM's designated RAM is overcommitted. This file is not necessary (it's a convenience feature) and can be disabled. It may contain sensitive data stored in the VM's memory.

◆ SQL01.vswp: The VSWP file is your VM's paging file on older ESX platforms. This file format is largely deprecated today. This file, if it exists, also may contain sensitive memory data.

◆ SQL01.vmsd: Snapshots of virtual machines can be taken at a certain point in time, and the virtual machines can be restored from these snapshots later. The VMSD file contains metadata about the VM and will be created only once snapshots are actually taken.

◆ `SQL01.vmsn`: The VMSN file is the snapshot state file, and it may be large or small depending on whether you include the VM's memory in the snapshot. Each snapshot will have an associated VMSN file that corresponds to it. Much like the VSWP and VMEM files, the VMSN file can contain sensitive data stored in the VM's memory when a snapshot is taken and should be protected carefully.

◆ `SQL01-delta.vmdk`: The DELTA file contains all changes to the VM disk once a snapshot is taken. This file will disappear once a snapshot is actually applied.

◆ `SQL01.vmss`: VMSS files store memory data about a VM that has been temporarily suspended. Once the VM is started again, this file disappears. This is another file that contains memory data and thus should be protected if it exists.

A representation of a VMware virtual machine files and functions is shown in Figure 6.6.

FIGURE 6.6
A VMware virtual machine image

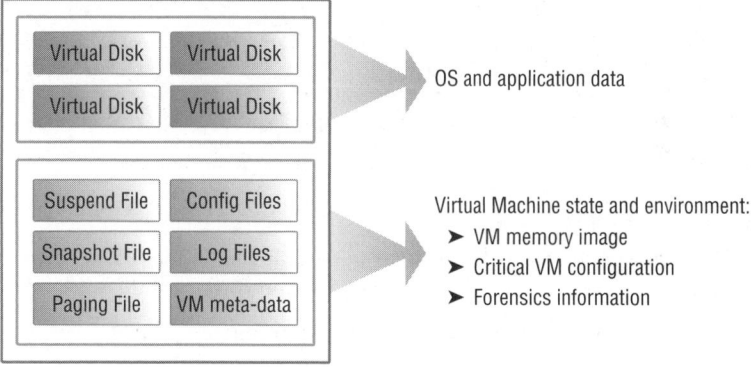

Virtual Machine Image

All major configuration changes that you'll want to make for locking down VMware VMs will be made in the VM's associated VMX file. There are two ways to edit these files.

The first method is to simply open the file in any text editor like WordPad or Notepad and then add or modify entries in the file.

The second method is to use vCenter. Follow these steps:

1. Log into vCenter, right-click a VM, and select Edit Settings.

2. Choose the Options tab, highlight General under the Advanced list, and click the Configuration Parameters button in the right pane. The resulting screen is shown in Figure 6.7.

3. To add an entry in the configuration file, click the Add Row button on the lower right, and then enter the name and value for the configuration entry.

NOTE Unfortunately, entries can only be added this way, not deleted, so you'll still need to manually edit the VMX file to remove configuration entries entirely.

FIGURE 6.7
VMware VM
Configuration
Parameters screen
in vCenter

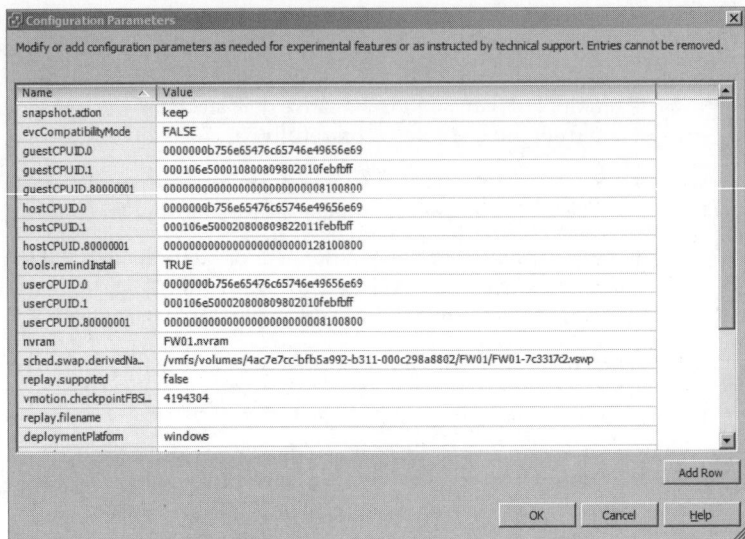

VMware Tools

One decision most administrators will need to make is regarding the installation of VMware Tools. The Tools package is a stand-alone binary that enables quite a few features:

◆ Installation of enhanced SCSI drivers

◆ Improved mouse and graphics performance

◆ Installation of a simple VM heartbeat service, which is helpful for monitoring

◆ Improved memory management and paging handling

◆ Ability to enable the "freezing" of the VM for snapshots and backups, known as *quiescing*

◆ Ability to enable time synchronization between the VM and underlying host

As far as security controls related to VMware Tools goes, there's really only one setting that administrators should worry about, and that one deals with the automatic installation of Tools. Many administrators automatically install Tools in all VMs to quickly enable needed features, but this can cause the VM to reboot. Aside from causing availability issues by restarting, a VM could potentially be reconfigured at reboot time, which is a security issue. To prevent automatic installation from happening, enter the following parameter in the VMX file:

```
isolation.tools.autoInstall.disable="TRUE"
```

This setting, once included in a VM's configuration file, will prevent Tools from being installed automatically.

Copy/Paste Operations and HGFS

VMware virtual machines have a number of controls that can be configured to permit or disallow data being placed on a virtual "clipboard" to pass between the virtualization host and VM guests. These features are primarily intended for use with consumer products like VMware Workstation or VMware Fusion. Explicitly disabling the features is considered a security best practice and should be done for all VMs in an enterprise setting. You can think of this as "covering your bases" in case a VM is moved to a laptop or desktop for testing or other operations. By explicitly limiting the functionality, you can ensure that no security issues arise regardless of where the VM is being hosted and run. The following settings should be in place within the VMX file for all VMs:

```
isolation.tools.copy.disable="TRUE"
isolation.tools.dnd.disable="TRUE"
isolation.tools.setGUIOptions.enable="FALSE"
isolation.tools.paste.disable="TRUE"
```

Another setting that administrators will want to consider configuring is that of the Host Guest File System (HGFS). This is a hypervisor component that allows installation of Tools and other virtualization applications and upgrades into the VM automatically. Any automatic installation tools or mechanisms can lead to unpredictable behavior, loss of availability, or other problems, so it's a good idea to disable this capability. To do so, include the following line in the VMX file:

```
isolation.tools.hgfsServerSet.disable="TRUE"
```

Virtual Machine Disk Security

There are a number of controls administrators can configure related to virtual machine disk files. While most of these are focused on performance and disk specifications, several are related to security and operational integrity. The following settings should be in place to better protect VM disks from user interaction concerns:

```
isolation.tools.diskShrink.disable="TRUE"
isolation.tools.diskWiper.disable="TRUE"
```

These settings prevent VM users from reclaiming unused space in virtual disk files. Reclaiming unused space is discouraged in most environments because it can seriously affect performance while the disk is being "shrunk," leading to local denial of service (DoS) scenarios.

One other setting that administrators should pay attention to is the type of disk itself. VMware disks can be either persistent or nonpersistent. Persistent disks are like traditional hard drives, retaining data and settings when powered off or rebooted. Nonpersistent disks are essentially ephemeral and are wiped clean when rebooted. On nonpersistent disks, attackers can eradicate all evidence of their activities, so nonpersistent disks should be used only in specific situations where they fulfill a business need (for example, at kiosks in airports or retail establishments).

To disallow the use of nonpersistent disks, make sure the following $scsiX:Y.mode$ settings are *not* present in the VMX file:

```
scsiX:Y.mode=
scsiX:Y.mode="independent nonpersistent"
```

VM Logging

Setting some general parameters around what types of logs VMs generate, how large log files can grow, and how often they're rotated can be good for both security and operational effectiveness. The first reason is simple — you really don't want to log information that isn't useful or necessary! In many cases, VMs can generate a lot of extraneous log data that isn't very useful. I recommend starting out logging everything (or close to it) and then removing log types you don't want or need. You should also rotate logs and limit their size to preserve disk space and keep your storage environment (and logging platforms) free from old logs and other "clutter" that just doesn't need to hang around forever.

From a security perspective, it's also a good practice to limit logging because a vast amount of sensitive and useful information about VM configuration and operations will reside in log files. Keeping only what you need for operations, security, and compliance is a simple way to limit information an attacker could discover in the event of a compromise.

First, you can disable virtual machine logging entirely by setting the following parameter in the VMX file:

```
logging="FALSE"
```

Many administrators won't want to disable logging entirely, but there are additional options to configure. First, administrators can set the number of VM logs that are retained. VMware recommends setting this to 10, but you can choose anything that works well for your organization:

```
log.keepOld="10"
```

You'll also want to specify the size to which each log file can grow. There are many recommendations from both VMware and others regarding the most appropriate size, but my recommendation is 100 KB. If you are very limited on space, or prefer to rotate logs often, then a smaller size may suit you. On the flip side, having larger log files allows you to maintain more data in one place and reduces the need to rotate the log files frequently. However, larger log files can take longer to parse and evaluate, which may bog down any log management or analytics tools you're using. 100 KB is usually adequate for a single log file and can be set with the following configuration entry (the number is in bytes):

```
log.rotateSize="100000"
```

While not strictly a logging concern, a similar setting relates to "informational" messages that a VM can place into the VMX file itself. These messages are not a security concern, but they can clog up a VMX file and larger VMX files take longer to load. They can also clutter a datastore if left unchecked. It's best to limit them to 1 MB or less, or even disable them entirely if you can. Many organizations need these messages because they relate to VM data displayed in the vSphere Client, but you could potentially disable them for test lab systems or in highly secure environments where security is valued more than operational needs. By default, a VM can place up to 1 MB of this content into a VMX file, and VMware recommends setting this explicitly to ensure that the VMX file can never grow larger. Use the following statement:

```
tools.setInfo.sizeLimit="1048576"
```

Device Connectivity

Virtual machine configuration files contain all the VM's information about connected devices. For most enterprises, there is really no need for VMs to have serial and parallel ports or floppy drives, and limiting the kinds of input and connectivity a VM has can improve security. To disable devices in a virtual machine, the following device statements must be set to FALSE or should not exist at all:

```
floppyX.present="FALSE"
ideX:Y.present="FALSE"
parallelX.present="FALSE"
serialX.present="FALSE"
usbX.present="FALSE"
```

Replace the X and Y variables with numbers, starting at 0 in many cases.

There are two other settings that also relate to VM device connectivity but pertain to the users of the virtual machines. By default, most users of virtual machines, even those that are not administrators, can modify devices like DVD drives, network cards, and others. This could lead to security issues if a VM user modifies settings that cause availability failures or mount a new drive to copy and remove data from the environment. To prevent VM users from connecting devices or editing them in any way, include the following statements:

```
isolation.device.connectable.disable="TRUE"
isolation.device.edit.disable="TRUE"
```

Guest and Host Communications

There are a few settings that administrators can configure to properly lock down some of the communications between the hypervisor host and VMs as well as between VMs:

Virtual Machine Communications Interface   It's a good idea to disable the ability for VMs to communicate using the Virtual Machine Communications Interface (VMCI). This is a socket interface and accompanying application programming interface (API) that allows certain applications to interface and communicate with other VMs in a more efficient manner. Unfortunately, the VMCI can also allow VMs to determine how many other VMs are present and may also expose vulnerable applications.

To disable this communication channel, include the following line in a VMs configuration:

```
vmci0.unrestricted="FALSE"
```

WARNING   Because the VMCI is often used for legitimate applications, it is highly advised that you test this setting before implementation!

Remote console sessions   Many administrators use remote console sessions to connect to VMs and administer them. By default, however, this console session is visible to other users of the VM, and a non-administrator may be able to leverage this "session snooping" capability to see what commands administrators are running. Connections through a jump box, or proxy, can also stay active if the administrator loses connectivity to that system during a session, which can cause later connectivity issues or security exposure.

A reasonable security measure is to limit the number of users who can concurrently view a session. Set the following configuration entry to 1, or 2 at the most:

```
RemoteDisplay.maxConnections="1"
```

VMware Tools   Another source of significant data exposure is VMware Tools. With Tools installed, VMs might be able to enumerate significant data about the hypervisor host, potentially providing valuable information to an attacker within a VM. This setting, which enables hypervisor configuration settings to be passed to VMs, is disabled by default (set to "FALSE"). Ensure that it's set to "FALSE" in the configuration file unless you need the VM to monitor the host for specific reasons:

```
tools.guestlib.enableHostInfo="FALSE"
```

VM Self-Awareness   A similar setting relates to a VM monitoring its virtual environment. It's often known as the VM Self-Awareness setting because it allows a VM's operating system to recognize that it's a virtual machines rather than a physical system. Disabling this monitoring will completely isolate the VM's guest operating system from the underlying host:

```
isolation.monitor.control.disable="TRUE"
```

WARNING   You should test this setting explicitly before implementing.

Controlling API Access to VMs

There are a number of APIs available to VMware VMs that allow the VMs to be recognized, monitored, controlled, and changed. Anytime APIs like these are exposed, VMs and applications could potentially leverage them to change settings, monitor data, and engage in other activities. This could lead to a security problem (either intentional or accidental) if left unchecked, ranging from network disruption to file corruption and illicit traffic monitoring. If these APIs are not in use (and you should test very carefully to ensure that they're not), you can disable them with the following set of configuration controls.

This setting disables the VIX API (used to interact with and control VMs) so it can't send data from VMs to the underlying host:

```
isolation.tools.vixMessage.disable="TRUE"
```

The dvfilter API allows VMs to monitor other VMs' network traffic. This should not be allowed by default, so you should simply look for the presence of the setting *ethernetX* .*filterY*.name="*Filter Name*", where X and Y are the numbers of the VM's defined NICs and DV filter, respectively, and *Filter Name* is a specific name allocated to the filter established. The best solution is to remove the setting entirely, if possible, and the setting should not exist by default.

The VMsafe API set is integral to many virtual monitoring and security solutions from both VMware and partners. If you are not using any products or services that require the VMsafe APIs, you should disable them entirely and purposefully with the following configuration setting:

```
vmsafe.enable="FALSE"
```

You can look for these additional VMsafe settings:

```
vmsafe.agentAddress=
vmsafe.agentPort=
```

Both of these should exist only if VMsafe is in place and required, and they should have settings specific to the solution(s) you're using. If VMsafe isn't required, remove the settings altogether for the most secure posture.

Unexposed Features

VMware VMs are intended to run unchanged on any of their hypervisors, ranging from enterprise hypervisors like ESX and ESXi to local products like Workstation and Fusion. There are a number of features in the Workstation and Fusion products that could potentially expose VMs if enabled in enterprise settings, and VMware recommends that security-conscious enterprises disable them purposefully. Table 6.1 lists the settings that can be configured, but they aren't discussed in any depth here.

TABLE 6.1:   VMware recommended security settings

SETTING	ACTION	SECURITY CONCERN
`isolation.tools.ghi .autologon.disable="TRUE"`	Disallows automatic logon for Workstation and Fusion VMs through VMware Tools.	Automatic logon can give unauthorized people access to the system.
`isolation.bios.bbs .disable="TRUE"`	Disables VMware Tools BIOS interaction on Workstation and Fusion.	BIOS settings should be protected from interaction and tampering because this could interfere with the host operation.
`isolation.tools.getCreds .disable="TRUE"`	Prevents Workstation and Fusion VMs from accessing host credentials via VMware Tools.	Access to host credentials could expose them to attackers.
`isolation.tools.ghi .launchmenu.change="TRUE"`	Limits certain Guest Host Interaction features on Workstation and Fusion.	Guest Host Interaction (GHI) features could allow data leakage or corruption scenarios to occur.
`isolation.tools .memSchedFakeSampleStats .disable="TRUE"`	Disables certain VMware Tools memory interactions on the host.	Memory interaction is potentially dangerous because VMs and the host could potentially expose sensitive data in memory to one another.
`isolation.tools.ghi .protocolhandler .info.disable="TRUE"`	Limits certain Guest Host Interaction features on Workstation and Fusion.	Guest Host Interaction (GHI) features could allow data leakage or corruption scenarios to occur.
`isolation.ghi.host .shellAction .disable="TRUE"`	Limits certain Guest Host Interaction features on Workstation and Fusion.	Guest Host Interaction (GHI) features could allow data leakage or corruption scenarios to occur.
`isolation.tools .dispTopoRequest .disable="TRUE"`	Prevents VMware Tools from accessing the host's disk topology.	Limiting VMware Tools access to host disks can prevent accidental disk enumeration or changes to the disk topology.

TABLE 6.1:   VMware recommended security settings *(continued)*

SETTING	ACTION	SECURITY CONCERN
isolation.tools .trashFolderState .disable="TRUE"	Prevents VMware Tools from accessing the Recycle Bin or Trash folder on the host.	Sensitive data that has been deleted could potentially be available on the host in the Trash or Recycle Bin containers.
isolation.tools.ghi .trayicon.disable="TRUE"	Limits certain Guest Host Interaction features on Workstation and Fusion.	Guest Host Interaction (GHI) features could allow data leakage or corruption scenarios to occur.
isolation.tools.unity .disable="TRUE"	Disables the Unity capability and its features on Workstation and Fusion.	The Unity features allow VMs to be integrated with the host OS, and numerous data and memory stores are intermingled and potentially exposed.
isolation.tools .unityInterlockOperation .disable="TRUE"	Disables the Unity capability and its features on Workstation and Fusion.	The Unity features allow VMs to be integrated with the host OS, and numerous data and memory stores are intermingled and potentially exposed.
isolation.tools.unity .push.update .disable="TRUE"	Disables the Unity capability and its features on Workstation and Fusion.	The Unity features allow VMs to be integrated with the host OS, and numerous data and memory stores are intermingled and potentially exposed.
isolation.tools.unity .taskbar.disable="TRUE"	Disables the Unity capability and its features on Workstation and Fusion.	The Unity features allow VMs to be integrated with the host OS, and numerous data and memory stores are intermingled and potentially exposed.
isolation.tools .unityActive .disable="TRUE"	Disables the Unity capability and its features on Workstation and Fusion.	The Unity features allow VMs to be integrated with the host OS, and numerous data and memory stores are intermingled and potentially exposed.
isolation.tools.unity .windowContents .disable="TRUE"	Disables the Unity capability and its features on Workstation and Fusion.	The Unity features allow VMs to be integrated with the host OS, and numerous data and memory stores are intermingled and potentially exposed.

TABLE 6.1: VMware recommended security settings *(continued)*

SETTING	ACTION	SECURITY CONCERN

`isolation.tools`
`.vmxDnDVersionGet`
`.disable="TRUE"`
	Disables certain drag-and-drop capabilities on Workstation and Fusion.	Drag-and-drop features allow data transfer between VMs and the host, which should be limited as much as possible.

`isolation.tools`
`.guestDnDVersionSet`
`.disable="TRUE"`
	Disables certain drag-and-drop capabilities on Workstation and Fusion.	Drag-and-drop features allow data transfer between VMs and the host, which should be limited as much as possible.

For more information, consider checking the latest VMware security guidance:

`http://communities.vmware.com/community/vmtn/server/security`

Locking Down Microsoft VMs

Microsoft virtual machines use the Virtual Hard Drive (VHD) format. A typical Microsoft VM might consist of the following file types:

◆ VHD files are the primary disk files associated with a Hyper-V VM.

◆ VHDX files are the new Hyper-V hard disk format in Windows Server 2012. This format has improved capacity (up to 64 TB), better storage for VM metadata, and many other features that are primarily focused on performance improvements.

◆ AVHD files are present only when snapshots have been taken of the Hyper-V VM. These are the "delta" or "difference" files that represent what has changed since the snapshot was taken.

◆ The VSV file is a VM's saved state information, particularly related to devices associated with the VM.

◆ The `*.bin` file is the contents of a running VM's memory when you take a snapshot.

◆ The XML file associated with a Hyper-V VM is named after the VM's unique globally unique identifier (GUID) and contains all the fundamental VM configuration details.

By default, Hyper-V VM files can be found in two locations:

`%programdata%\Microsoft\Windows\Hyper-V\`: This folder contains all the configuration files and associated state files for each VM.

`%users%\Public\Public Documents\Hyper-V\Virtual hard disks`: This folder contains the VM hard drives.

Unfortunately, Microsoft's format doesn't give you the ability to simply edit the configuration file as VMware does. Although the XML file for a given VM can be easily opened and manipulated with a text editor or other parsing/editing tool, there are no simple ways to manually add security-specific settings. With the latest version of Hyper-V, administrators have more flexibility in configuring and managing VMs with PowerShell (covered in Chapter 10, "Scripting Tips and Tricks for Automation"), but even this doesn't allow for the same degree of security granularity as VMware. Another issue is the lack of documentation from Microsoft regarding the XML file and how to add security configuration entries. The company has emphasized the use of the VM Properties screen or PowerShell to perform all configuration of VMs within Hyper-V and continues to do so with the 2012 release.

There are a number of general security practices that you can implement for Hyper-V VMs, however.

First, as always, lock down the guest operating system and application footprint as tightly as possible.

Second, install the VM integration services (or Virtual Guest Services in SCVMM) for enhanced control and performance in your Hyper-V environment. Much like VMware Tools, this independent package allows VMs to have tighter integration with the hypervisor. Installing this package in SCVMM is incredibly simple. To enable and configure integration services, perform the following actions:

1. Highlight a VM in the SCVMM console, and then click the button labeled Install Virtual Guest Services in the top bar (this is shown in Figure 6.8).

FIGURE 6.8
Installing guest services in SCVMM

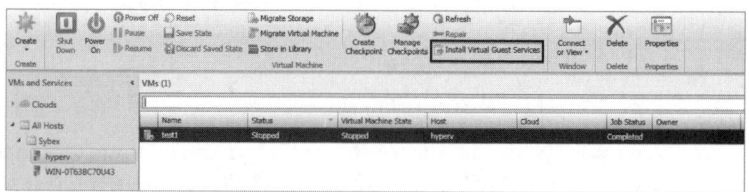

You can also right-click the VM and choose Install Virtual Guest Services from this menu.

2. To install the integration services in Hyper-V Manager, right-click a VM and select Connect. In the Virtual Machine Connection window that opens, select the Action menu along the top, and then choose Insert Integration Services Setup Disk.

3. For some OS versions, the installation will start automatically. For others, you'll need to log in to the VM and then navigate to the DVD drive that has been mounted with the VM Services virtual disk. Click this to start the program.

4. You can control what integration services are available within the VM by right-clicking the VM and choosing Properties in SCVMM or Settings in Hyper-V Manager. Highlight the Hardware Configuration menu item in SCVMM (it will already be open in Hyper-V Manager), and then scroll down to the Advanced category. Highlight the Integration Services item. You'll see a screen like that in Figure 6.9.

5. You can select a variety of options available for VM management and control, including OS shutdown, time synchronization, heartbeat services for availability between the VM and OS, and backup capabilities via a volume snapshot on the VM. The data exchange

service allows for streamlined communications for numerous virtualization services between Hyper-V and the VM. Click OK when finished.

The only other general recommendation is to carefully look at the options selected for hardware components such as COM ports, floppy drives, IDE and SCSI devices, NICs, and others to ensure that nothing is connected when it shouldn't be.

To improve security for Hyper-V VMs overall, you might consider implementing auditing and access control lists on the two folders mentioned earlier, at least for those VMs known to the Hyper-V server. Follow a least-privilege model for all Hyper-V services and needed administrators, and block all other access. You can enable auditing for object access and generate Windows event logs, too, which may improve your VM audit trail for the hypervisor host.

FIGURE 6.9
Integration services configuration

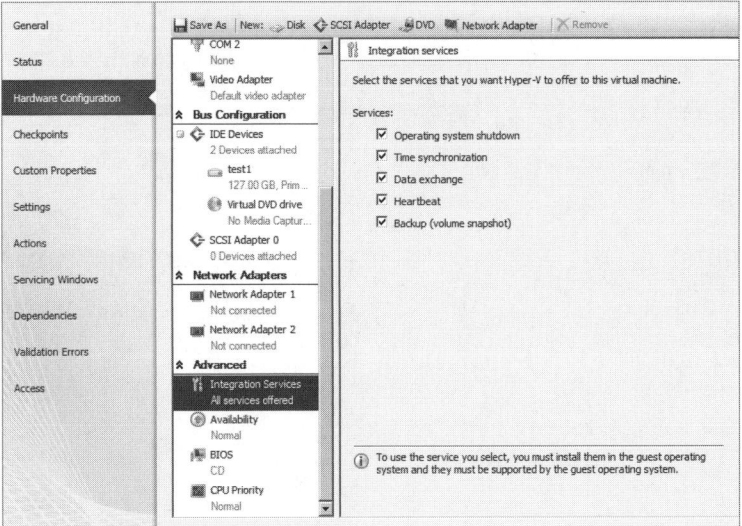

Locking Down XenServer VMs

XenServer is a bit different than Hyper-V and vSphere in the sense that it can natively accommodate typical virtual machines (called hardware virtual machines, or HVMs, in Xen parlance) as well as paravirtualized VMs (which have a much deeper integration with and dependence on the XenServer hypervisor component, the Dom0 virtual machine). Paravirtualized VMs are not covered here.

Citrix XenServer also uses the VHD format for all VMs stored on defined storage repositories (SRs), which are typically remote file systems on a SAN or NAS. For virtual machines on local storage, XenServer natively leverages the Linux Volume Manager (LVM) format to store virtual machines, and identifying individual files corresponding to VMs is next to impossible. You can view the known logical volumes for a given XenServer system with the `lvdisplay` command.

VM configuration settings on a local LVM are stored in a file called `/var/xapi/state.db`. This is an XML representation of the types of configuration files discussed in the previous section on

Hyper-V, "Locking Down Microsoft VMs," with some XenServer-specific information included, and all of it in one place. Citrix recommends against directly editing this file, and this is probably a good suggestion because corrupting the file or making unusual changes could render the VMs inoperable or unstable.

Most XenServer VM modification should be done through XenCenter. The first step for most XenServer VMs, as with Microsoft or VMware technology, is installing a set of drivers and utilities that make the VMs much more functional and improve performance. With XenServer, this package is called XenServer Tools. To install this package, simply highlight a VM in XenCenter, then select the VM menu at the top of the screen. In this menu, select Install XenServer Tools as shown in Figure 6.10.

Editing VM properties in XenCenter is easily accomplished. Right-click a VM and select Properties. You'll see a screen that lists the various configuration options on a standard VM, including general properties (name, description, etc.), CPU and boot options, startup information, alert settings, and others, as shown in Figure 6.11.

FIGURE 6.10
Installing
XenServer Tools

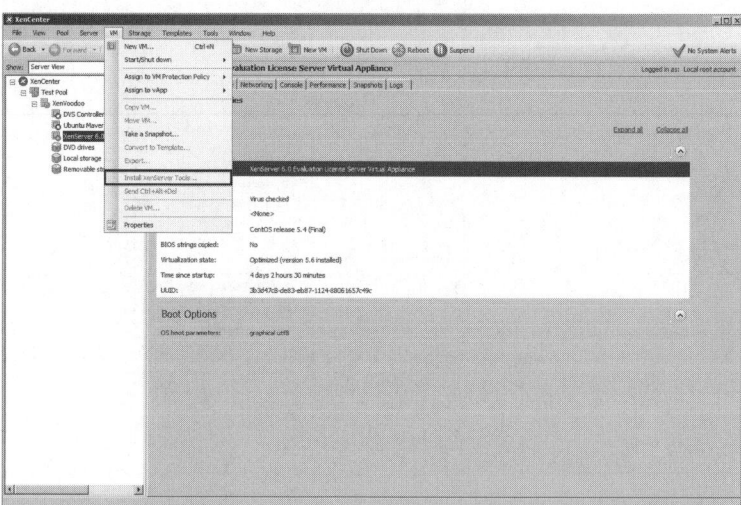

As with Hyper-V, the best practices for managing a XenServer VM's configuration are to carefully review and audit the settings you can access and manage in XenCenter. There are other ways to monitor and in some cases change a VM's configuration parameters. To list a VM's configuration parameters at the command line, follow these steps:

1. Log in to your XenServer console. At the command line, execute the following command to list the UUID values for each VM:

   ```
   xe vm-list
   ```

2. Once you have the UUID for the VM you want to evaluate, run the following command:

   ```
   xe vm-param-list uuid=<your VM UUID>
   ```

3. You will see a list of configuration parameters like that shown in Figure 6.12.

FIGURE 6.11
VM configuration options in XenCenter

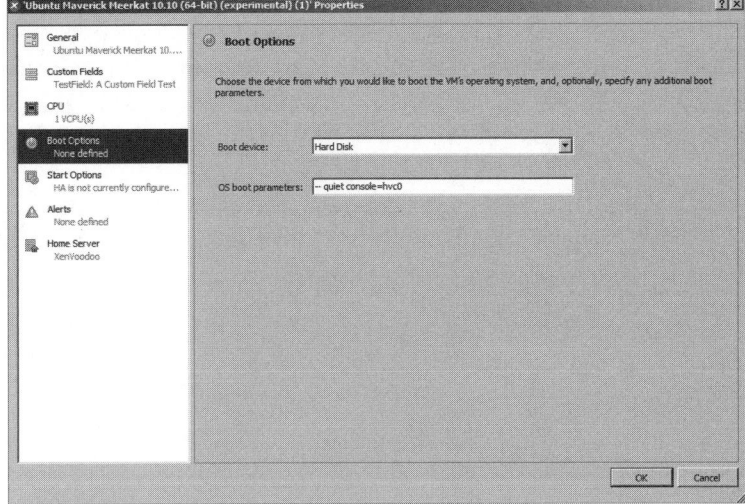

FIGURE 6.12
VM configuration parameters using the `xe` command

```
[root@XenVoodoo ~]# xe vm-param-list uuid=fb69a48e-4fe3-4f23-9ef0-149b9cb8db9d
uuid ( RO)                        : fb69a48e-4fe3-4f23-9ef0-149b9cb8db9d
                 name-label ( RW): Ubuntu Maverick Meerkat 10.10 (64-bit) (experimental) (1)
          name-description ( RW):
              user-version ( RW): 1
             is-a-template ( RW): false
             is-a-snapshot ( RO): false
               snapshot-of ( RO): <not in database>
                 snapshots ( RO): 0c2329ce-8ded-eb3b-15ab-1181d572c7bd
             snapshot-time ( RO): 19700101T00:00:00Z
             snapshot-info ( RO):
                    parent ( RO): 0c2329ce-8ded-eb3b-15ab-1181d572c7bd
                  children ( RO):
          is-control-domain ( RO): false
               power-state ( RO): halted
             memory-actual ( RO): 0
             memory-target ( RO): 0
           memory-overhead ( RO): 4194304
         memory-static-max ( RW): 268435456
        memory-dynamic-max ( RW): 268435456
        memory-dynamic-min ( RW): 268435456
         memory-static-min ( RW): 134217728
           suspend-VDI-uuid ( RW): <not in database>
            suspend-SR-uuid ( RW): d8d57eb3-acaf-9de3-2968-442f74451104
              VCPUs-params (MRW):
                 VCPUs-max ( RW): 1
           VCPUs-at-startup ( RW): 1
      actions-after-shutdown ( RW): Destroy
        actions-after-reboot ( RW): Restart
         actions-after-crash ( RW): Restart
              console-uuids (SRO):
                  platform (MRW): nx: false; acpi: true; apic: true; pae: true; viridian: true
```

There are several different types of options, distinguished by label:

◆ RO (Read-only): Cannot be configured manually

◆ RW (Read-write): Can be changed

◆ M (Map): Contains multiple key:value pairs

◆ S (Set): Contains a list of configuration options

4. While none of these parameters just covered are strictly security specific, there are some that pertain to devices and memory management. To configure writeable parameters, use the various subcommands available with the `xe vm-param-set` command. The syntax is as follows:

```
xe vm-param-set <param name>=<value>
xe vm-param-set <param name>:<list of params>
```

The *Citrix XenServer 6.0 Administrator's Guide* is an excellent reference to the various parameters available with the xe command-line tools. It is available at citrix.com here:

```
http://support.citrix.com/servlet/KbServlet/download/28751-102-673823/XenServer-
6.0.0-reference.pdf
```

Chapter 7

Logging and Auditing

Virtualization administrators need to ensure that logs are being generated by both virtual machines and the virtualization infrastructure components. This chapter will outline some best practices you can follow to make sure you're getting the right log information for troubleshooting and security, the logs are managed as effectively as possible, and logs are available for audit and security purposes when needed.

In this chapter you'll learn about the following topics:

- Important logs for security and compliance on VMware, Microsoft, and Citrix infrastructures

- Logging options for major virtualization components

- What to look for in the logs you collect

- Integrating virtualization logging into your existing log management infrastructure

- Best practices for effective log management

Why Logging and Auditing Is Critical

What are logs exactly, and why are they so important? Logs are records of activities happening on information systems or network segments. Here are some of the many reasons they're important:

Optimizing system and network performance Operational teams often use log data for assessing the health of their systems, networks, and applications. Logs can tell operations teams a lot about how well systems are running and can also reveal specific errors and problems in both technology implementation and processes. Organizations that seek to fine-tune their IT infrastructure can benefit from log analysis.

Recording the actions of users Logs are the primary source of monitoring user activities in many enterprises. Usually, logs of user activities focus on when a user logged on or off a system or application and also reveal specific activities users performed while logged on.

Identifying security incidents, policy violations, fraudulent activities, and operational problems Often, log entries can act as the initial impetus into information security incident response efforts. Unusual user activities, strange system or application behavior, or specialized security events from monitoring systems can all serve as indicators that policies have been violated, malicious programs are afoot, or just that "something isn't right."

Performing audits and forensic analyses   Many audits can make use of log data to show that something actually happened when you said it did. For example, if a batch job is scheduled to run at a certain time every day or you applied a specific patch to a system, there's likely a log entry that can verify that this happened. Internal audit teams can make good use of detailed logs. Similarly, forensic analysts can use logs to verify or correlate forensic data with times/dates of occurrence in some cases.

Supporting internal investigations   Internal investigators who are putting together cases for Human Resources or criminal prosecution will likely look to log data for evidence of activities and to help build a timeline.

Establishing baselines   Developing operational and security baselines is a sound practice for understanding your environment. Usually, this requires longer-term log collection efforts, but it can help to drive business and IT decisions. For example, certain logs can tell you how your customers and partners are making use of specific systems and applications, and you can then tailor your operational controls and processes to better meet their needs.

Identifying operational trends and long-term problems   Once baselines are in place, true data-mining tools and programs can help organizations to glean more insight into IT and business trends in their log data. Sometimes these trends can help to ferret out the root cause of long-term problems as well. For example, consistent failures in patch application may illustrate a problem with an organization's change management program or process, and this may only become obvious over a longer period of log retention and analysis.

Regulatory concerns and compliance   Compliance is a fact of life these days. Several compliance regulations require that organizations collect and retain logs. For example, the Payment Card Industry Data Security Standard (PCI DSS) version 2.0 includes an entire section pertaining to logs. Requirement 10 (track and monitor all access to network resources and cardholder data) explicitly describes the types of audit trail data organizations need to collect and retain, how to protect this data, how long to keep it, and how often to review it. This is only one example; most compliance mandates now include some reference to logging and log management.

With the important role virtualization infrastructure plays in our datacenter environments today, the need for logs on most, if not all, the components in this infrastructure should be obvious. What are the various VM users doing? What actions are storage and network administrators performing within the virtual management console? What kinds of error messages are we getting related to the unusual performance hiccups we're experiencing? How can we show the auditors that we're carefully monitoring and managing the environment? The answers to these questions and more can be had with a proper virtualization logging strategy and implementation.

Unfortunately, not all virtualization platforms make logging simple and painless. Next, we'll take a look at the different logging options for VMware, Microsoft, and Citrix virtualization platforms.

Virtualization Logs and Auditing Options

Before delving into any of the major virtualization platforms and their logging options, it's important to mention logging formats and standards.

Syslog

By far the most prevalent logging standard in use today is *syslog* and its variants. Syslog logging has been a staple of most Unix-based operating systems for many years. Syslog log messages are broken into three sections. The first is the *header* of the log; it includes the date and time of the log generation as well as the name of the system that generated the log entry. The second part of the log identifies which process or application generated the log entry. The final part of the log entry is the actual log information itself.

A simple set of syslog entries is shown here:

```
Apr  7 21:09:25 XenVoodoo sshd[11385]: Accepted password for root from 10.10.0.1
port 53244 ssh2
Apr  7 21:09:25 XenVoodoo sshd[11385]: pam_unix(sshd:session): session opened for
user root by (uid=0)
```

We can see that both of these entries were generated on April 7 on the system named XenVoodoo. The sshd program generated the logs, and the user root successfully logged in using the SSH remote access protocol (one entry shows root's password being accepted, followed by another entry indicating that a session was established).

NOTE   Logging in as root over SSH is a poor security practice incidentally!

Syslog configuration is broken down into two major considerations that are represented in the configuration file for the service (often /etc/syslog/syslog.conf or /etc/syslog.conf on Unix platforms).

The *facility* defines the general category of the message itself. These can represent different aspects of the OS itself or (more likely) the types of applications and services you want to focus on. Table 7.1 includes examples of facility values.

TABLE 7.1:   Facility values in syslog

VALUE	CATEGORY	NAME
0	Kernel messages	kern
1	User-level messages	user (the default)
2	Mail system	mail
3	System daemons	daemon
4	Security/authorization messages	auth
5	Internal syslogd	syslog
6	Line printer subsystem	lpr
7	Network news subsystem	news

The *severity* dictates what level of "seriousness" you want to receive in your logging messages. For each type of message, you dictate a severity level, and everything at that level and above will be logged (although the numbers are lower). Table 7.2 lists the severity levels.

TABLE 7.2: Severity levels in syslog

LEVEL	MEANING	LABEL APPEARING IN LOG
0 Emergency	System is unusable	emerg
1 Alert	Action must be taken immediately	alert
2 Critical	Critical conditions	crit
3 Error	Error conditions	error
4 Warning	Warning conditions	warn
5 Notice	Normal but significant condition	notice
6 Informational	Informational messages	info
7 Debug	Debug-level messages	debug

VMware ESX and ESXi and XenServer use some form of syslog that adheres to this standard configuration.

There are several distinct benefits to using syslog as the hypervisor logging format. First, it's well known and understood, which makes it easy to start leveraging by anyone who has used it before. Second, it's flexible, allowing admins to get the log data they want and need without too much work. Third, it integrates with most major log management platforms or can be used in a stand-alone fashion with remote logging collectors (covered later).

A newer variety of syslog is syslog-NG, which supports reliable TCP-based transport, encryption with TLS, database logging support, message filtering and flow control, and many other features. Syslog-NG is widely considered to be the better logging protocol, but support by virtualization vendors is somewhat sporadic. The latest versions of VMware ESXi support some of the syslog-NG features.

Windows Event Log

Microsoft Windows uses a different logging format called the Windows event log. The Windows log events are broken down into several major categories. Every Windows system has the following log types:

Application logs are events logged by applications running on the Windows system.

Security logs contain records of user and service logon attempts and any events related to resource utilization, such as creating, opening, or deleting files or other objects. This event category can be customized and configured.

System logs contain events related to system components, such as driver failures and hardware problems.

Windows domain controllers have at least two extra log categories:

File Replication Service logs contain Windows File Replication Service events.

DNS server logs are used to store DNS events like zone transfers.

Security and operations teams have struggled with the Windows event log format for many years because it is not natively compatible with syslog and uses proprietary event identification and description information. But there are ways to get Windows events into a syslog format and forwarded to a central server, all involving a third-party agent. Several well-known tools for accomplishing this are listed here, and there are many more free and commercial solutions available:

◆ The Splunk Universal Forwarder: www.splunk.com/download/universalforwarder

◆ Datagram SyslogAgent: www.syslogserver.com/syslogagent.html

◆ Snare Agent for Windows: www.intersectalliance.com/projects/SnareWindows/

◆ OSSEC Windows agent: www.ossec.net

The Windows Audit Policy, a Group Policy category, controls most Windows logging. The settings in this configuration area dictate what gets recorded in event logs. Options include successful events, failures, and nothing at all (which is all too common as a default setting, unfortunately).

Hyper-V has quite a few specific types of event log entries, many of which can be easily configured.

VMware vSphere ESX Logging

There's a fair amount of variation in how VMware platforms and components log events and information. For instance, there are significant differences between ESX and ESXi hypervisors, and there are more subtle differences between ESXi 4.*x* and 5.*x*.

For organizations that are still using any version of ESX, there's some good news! ESX, with its Linux-like Service Console, uses a common variant of syslog for all hypervisor logging. This means that administrators familiar with syslog on Unix platforms will easily recognize the configuration options available to them within the Service Console. For ESX systems, the following logs are the most important to monitor:

/var/log/messages: The majority of the Service Console logs are stored in this file, which represents "standard" syslog events. This is by far the most important log file to monitor and maintain on ESX platforms because much of the most valuable hypervisor-related information you're interested in will be here.

/var/log/secure: Critical daemons and processes in the Service Console will store authentication details in this file.

/var/log/vmkernel: The main VMkernel log file contains quite a bit of important data about the operation of the hypervisor kernel itself as well as interaction with VMs.

/var/log/vmkwarning: VM-related warnings or problems may be logged here.

/var/log/vmksummary.txt: This log file contains details about uptime and availability statistics on the ESX system.

/var/log/vmware/vpx/vpxa.log: This log file is the vCenter agent log, and connectivity and operations events are stored here.

/var/log/vmware/webAccess: If ESX Web Access is enabled, this set of logs records all events related to access through the browser.

/var/log/vmware/hostd.log: The ESX hostd process is a critical one, and this log file stores information about hostd incoming connections and authentication requests from the vSphere Client and vCenter.

/<VM Path>/vmware.log: Individual VM guest logs that contain useful information about VM-host interactions, resource issues, and other details are stored in this file.

All of these logs should be monitored and maintained, and you can easily configure the logs you want, with more or less detail, by editing the /etc/syslog.conf file. By default, this file should already be configured to gather the most important logs. On an ESX 4.0 system, the default /etc/syslog.conf file contains the information in Listing 7.1.

LISTING 7.1:   Default/recommended settings for the ESX 4.0 /etc/syslog.conf file

```
# Log all kernel messages to the console.
# Logging much else clutters up the screen.
#kern.*                                    /dev/console
# Log anything (except mail) of level info or higher.
# Don't log private authentication, cron, or vmkernel  messages!
*.info;mail.none;authpriv.none;cron.none;local6.none;local5.none
/var/log/messages
# The authpriv file has restricted access.
authpriv.*                                 /var/log/secure
# Log all the mail messages in one place.
mail.*                                     /var/log/maillog
# Log cron stuff
cron.*                                     /var/log/cron
# Everybody gets emergency messages
*.emerg                                            *
# Save news errors of level crit and higher in a special file.
uucp,news.crit                             /var/log/spooler
# Mostly unused facility
local7.*                                   /var/log/messages
#send all local6.info messages to special summary log only.
local6.info;local6.!notice         /var/log/vmksummary
#send all vmkernel .warning messages to warnings logs.
local6.warning                    /var/log/vmkwarning
#send all local6.notice and higher  messages to vmkernel log.
local6.notice                              /var/log/vmkernel
#send all userworld proxy messages to proxy log
local5.*                          /var/log/vmkproxy
```

These settings work well for most organizations, and I recommend leaving them as is unless you need more details or different log data.

You'll also want to make sure the logs are being rotated. Rotating log files is important for two reasons. First, conserving space on the ESX host is always a good idea, and log files can quickly grow, depending on which logs you're talking about. Second, orderly rotation makes log maintenance and review much simpler, which is good for overall security and operational health.

Fortunately, VMware ESX systems have the standard Linux *logrotate* daemon installed, and you can easily configure this to meet your operational needs.

Logrotate is controlled with two types of files. The first, /etc/logrotate.conf, is the default configuration. By default, logs are rotated weekly. However, most of the specific log files have their own rotation configuration in the /etc/logrotate.d/ directory that supersedes these default settings. In most cases, ESX log files are kept for 36 months, which may be far too long! I recommend checking all the files in /etc/logrotate.d and change the "rotate 36" value to something smaller like "rotate 12," which then causes the files to rotate monthly for 12 months. You may want to change the "monthly" value to "weekly" and modify the "rotate 36" value to something even smaller if you're sending all your logs to a remote storage location (which you should).

We'll set up ESX for remote logging in "Enabling Remote Logging on VMware vSphere" later in this chapter.

VMware vSphere ESXi Logging

Table 7.3 lists the logs you should pay attention to on ESXi systems.

TABLE 7.3:   Important logs on ESXi systems

LOG NAME	WHAT IT STORES
/var/log/auth.log	ESXi Shell authentication success and failure events
/var/log/dhclient.log	All activities related to address leases (if DHCP is in use on the ESXi system)
/var/log/esxupdate.log	Events related to ESXi patches and updates
/var/log/hostd.log	Host management service logs, similar to the same file on ESX
/var/log/shell.log	What activities have been performed in the ESXi Shell
/var/log/sysboot.log	VMkernel startup and module information
/var/log/syslog.log	Equivalent of the "messages" file on ESX; records a variety of important events
/var/log/usb.log	USB-related connections and interaction with VMs
/var/log/vobd.log	VMkernel Observation events, many of which are very important

TABLE 7.3:   Important logs on ESXi systems *(continued)*

LOG NAME	WHAT IT STORES
/var/log/vmkernel.log	Core VMkernel logs related to hardware interaction and VM activities
/var/log/vmkwarning.log	VMkernel warning and alert logs stored in this file
/var/log/vmksummary.log	Details about uptime and availability statistics on the ESXi system
/var/log/vpxa.log	vCenter agent log; stores connectivity and operations events
/var/log/fdm.log	vSphere high availability logs

ESXi logging is done a bit differently than traditional Unix-based syslog logging. The first thing you need to do on ESXi systems is ensure that logs are being stored in a persistent manner. Since the ESXi file system is largely ephemeral (it is wiped after every reboot), the traditional location of log files (/var/log/) will be cleared on reboot. The new location for logs since ESXi 4.1 is /scratch/log/, which will survive a reboot. This should be the default setting, but it pays to double-check!

You'll also want to configure the default log rotation, which is another "global" log setting for ESXi. There are several ways to set these. The first is via the /etc/vmsyslog.conf file, which contains all global logging settings for ESXi. The default file on ESXi 5.*x* contains the following configuration settings:

```
[DEFAULT]
size = 1024
logdir_unique = false
loghost = <none>
rotate = 8
logdir = <none>
[vmsyslog]
rotate = 8
logdir = /scratch/log
size = 1024
```

SETTING UP PERSISTENT LOGGING

There are two ways to modify the /etc/vmsyslog.conf file: using the vi editor or through the vSphere Client or vCenter.

To modify the file using vi, follow these steps:

1. Open /etc/vmsyslog.conf using the vi editor and change the settings as recommended here:

   ◆ The default size is 1024 KB, or roughly 1 MB. This is adequate for most organizations, but you can increase it to 2048 if this works better for your organization.

   ◆ The default rotation schedule (rotate) is 8, but I recommend changing this to 10. This setting dictates how many individual log files are archived before new ones will overwrite and replace old files.

   ◆ Ensure that logdir is set to /scratch/log instead of /var/log.

2. Save the file and exit.

To modify this file through the vSphere Client or vCenter, do the following:

1. Connect to the ESXi host or vCenter with the vSphere Client.

2. Navigate to Inventory, then Hosts And Clusters. Highlight the ESXi host in the left-hand pane.

3. On the right side, click the Configuration tab, and then choose Advanced Settings under the Software category.

4. You should see a menu item in the tree labeled Syslog. For ESXi 5.*x* systems, a submenu underneath should exist called Global. Highlight this menu item on the tree.

5. You can now configure the following entries on the right side:

Syslog.global.defaultRotate: Set to 10.

Syslog.global.defaultSize: Set to 1024 or 2048.

Syslog.global.logDir: Make sure it is set to `/scratch/log`

Syslog.global.logDirUnique: Check this box to create a new log directory based on the ESXi hostname under `/scratch/log`.

NOTE You also need to set remote log collectors in Syslog.global.logHost. This is covered in the next set of steps.

6. You should have settings like those shown in Figure 7.1 when finished. Click OK.

FIGURE 7.1
ESXi logging settings

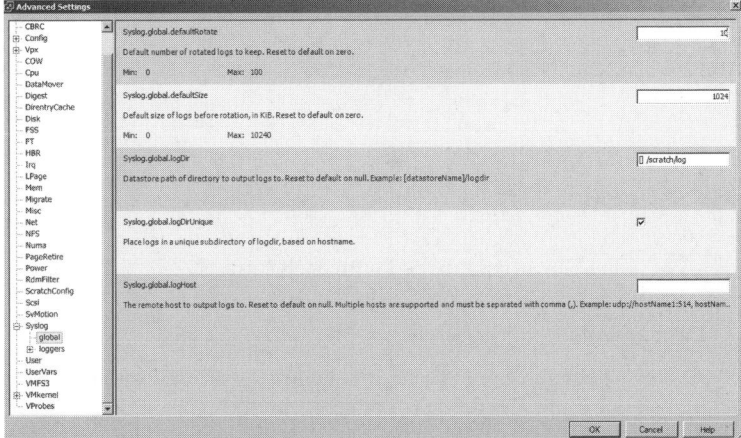

SETTING UP LOG SIZE AND ROTATION SCHEDULE

The second step to configure logging is to set the specific log size and rotation schedules for individual log entries. Each log type has its own size (1024 by default) and rotation schedule (8 by default). You should change these to match your operational policies. My recommendation is to change the size to 2048 and the rotation to 10.

These changes can be done by editing the individual log configuration files that reside in /etc/vmsyslog.conf.d/, which have the same settings as the /etc/vmsyslog.conf, discussed earlier in this section.

You can also easily change these in the GUI as follows:

1. Connect to the ESXi host or vCenter with the vSphere Client.

2. Navigate to Inventory, then Hosts And Clusters. Highlight the ESXi host in the left-hand pane.

3. On the right side, click the Configuration tab, and then choose Advanced Settings under the Software category.

4. You should see a menu item in the tree labeled Syslog. For ESXi 5.x systems, a submenu underneath should exist called Global. Highlight this menu item on the tree.

5. There is a submenu under Syslog labeled Loggers. Under this submenu, there are names of individual log files, and you can configure each one of these by highlighting it and entering values on the right side. This is shown for the auth log in Figure 7.2.

FIGURE 7.2
Configuring log
rotation settings

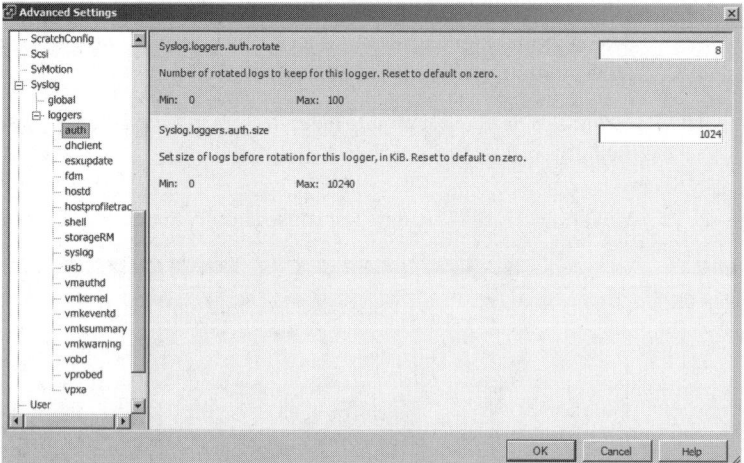

6. Click OK when finished with each setting.

Configuring Logging with the esxcli Commands

Now that you've seen the manual editing and GUI methods to configure logging, let's take a look at one more. On ESXi 5.x systems, you have a flexible set of command-line options that can be used to configure both default logging options and log-specific options. To use the esxcli commands, follow these steps:

1. Log into the ESXi system via the local console or via SSH.

2. Get the defaults you have in place currently with this command:

```
esxcli system syslog config get
```

3. You can now set the defaults for log rotation. To set up the same defaults discussed in the previous two sections, use the following options:

```
esxcli system syslog config set
--default-rotate=10
--default-size=2048
--logdir=/scratch/log
```

4. To set a specific log type's configuration, use the following example as a guide. This example sets the individual fdm log size to 2048 KB and configures it to rotate 10 times:

```
esxcli system syslog config logger set --id=fdm --rotate=10 --size=2048
```

You'll also want to gather vCenter logs (discussed in Chapter 5, "Virtualization Management and Client Security.") vSphere Client logs can be collected from the local workstation where they're generated. They are usually stored in the following directory:

```
C:\Documents and Settings\<username>\Local Settings\Application Data\VMware
```

Microsoft Hyper-V and SCVMM Logging

Microsoft Hyper-V has a number of logs that can be configured. Follow these steps to access them:

1. On a specific Hyper-V machine, open the Event Viewer.

On Windows 2008 Server, this can be opened by clicking Start, then Administrative Tools, then Event Viewer.

On Windows Server 2012, you can open the Event Viewer by selecting the Server Manager icon, clicking the Tools menu item on the top right, and then selecting Event Viewer.

2. To locate the Hyper-V logs, select Applications And Services, then Microsoft, and then Windows. If you scroll down, you should see a number of categories of logs.

Some of the logs are present only in Windows 2008, while others are present in 2012. For more information, see Table 7.4.

TABLE 7.4: Microsoft Hyper-V log categories

LOG NAME	WHAT IT STORES
Hyper-V-Config	Anything related to virtual machine configuration files. This is where you'll likely troubleshoot any VM issues, such as missing or corrupt VM files.
Hyper-V-High-Availability	Hyper-V actions and/or changes (if you have Hyper-V clustering enabled).
Hyper-V-Hypervisor	Hypervisor-specific information, including hypervisor operations failures.

TABLE 7.4: Microsoft Hyper-V log categories *(continued)*

LOG NAME	WHAT IT STORES
Hyper-V-Image-Management-Service (or Hyper-V-vhdsvc); Hyper-V-VMMS (Windows Server 2012)	Virtual hard disk (VHD) operations involving creating, editing, or converting VHDs. On Server 2012, these events will be covered in the Operational subcategory.
Hyper-V-Integration	Integration Services event information (installation success/failure, upgrades, operations issues).
Hyper-V-Network (Windows 2008); Hyper-V-VMMS/Networking (Windows Server 2012)	Creation, deletion, and configuration of virtual networks. Virtual NIC information is not included here because there are separate categories for these.
Hyper-V-SynthFC	Virtual Fibre Channel adapter events
Hyper-V-SynthNic	Virtual NIC events, including configuration issues or NIC failures. When a VM with virtual NICs starts up, a lot of log entries will usually be generated.
Hyper-V-SynthStor	Virtual storage operations events. Unlike the Image Management Service logs, these pertain to interaction with and use of VHDs by the VMs themselves, not administrative tasks.
Hyper-V-VID	Non-Uniform Memory Access (NUMA) memory scheduling (when enabled on the Hyper-V hardware).
Hyper-V-VMMS	The primary section most admins will want to focus on when concerned with Hyper-V operations and security. Contains multiple subcategories. Covered in more detail later in this section.
Hyper-V-Worker	Worker processes that coordinate and maintain VM operations.

A screen shot of these categories within the Event Viewer console is shown in Figure 7.3. The majority of Hyper-V logs administrators will be interested in will reside in the Hyper-V-VMMS category. Under this category, there will be several subcategories as follows:

Admin The majority of the logs you will want to examine reside here. These logs, usually the most valuable, contain all administrative activities that have occurred within the Hyper-V realm, particularly those related to operations processes running under the

SYSTEM or other local privileged account. This category exists on both Hyper-V 2008 and Hyper-V 2012.

FIGURE 7.3
Hyper-V event cat-
egories in the Event
Viewer

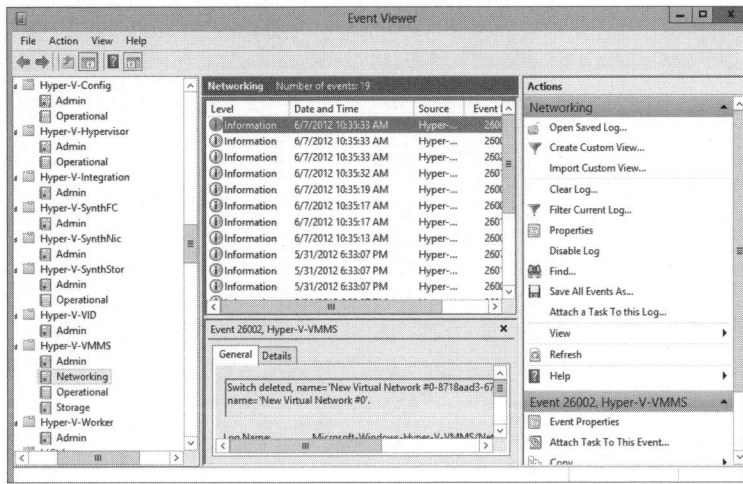

Networking On Windows Server 2012, logs related to virtual network activities and operations can be found in this section. All virtual switch creation, deletion, and modification should be logged here, making this a very important log file to monitor.

Operational On Windows Server 2012, all activities related to virtual disks—creating, deleting, modifying, converting, and so on—are stored here. Again, this is critical information for administrators to keep up with, so this is a very important event area to monitor.

Storage All storage connectivity and creation of storage objects for use within Hyper-V can be found in this section. Especially for organizations heavily using SAN and NAS resources, all activities related to storage use and connectivity with Hyper-V systems will be found here.

Organizations using System Center Virtual Machine Manager will also want to monitor logs. With SCVMM, Microsoft has created a new category of events, called VM Manager, under the Applications and Service Logs category. All SCVMM logs can be found in this category, logs that record actions ranging from VM changes to virtual network changes. SCVMM systems record all access to the SCVMM console, as well as SCVMM connections to Hyper-V systems, in the Security event category. An example of a connection event from SCVMM to a managed Hyper-V host is shown in Figure 7.4.

To monitor Windows logs, you have two primary options. The first is using the Event Viewer console itself. Within Event Viewer, perform the following actions:

1. Highlight the event category you are interested in perusing, such as Hyper-V-VMMS/ Admin. In the right-hand pane, you should see a variety of events, as shown in Figure 7.5.

FIGURE 7.4
SCVMM security
event for connec-
tion to Hyper-V host

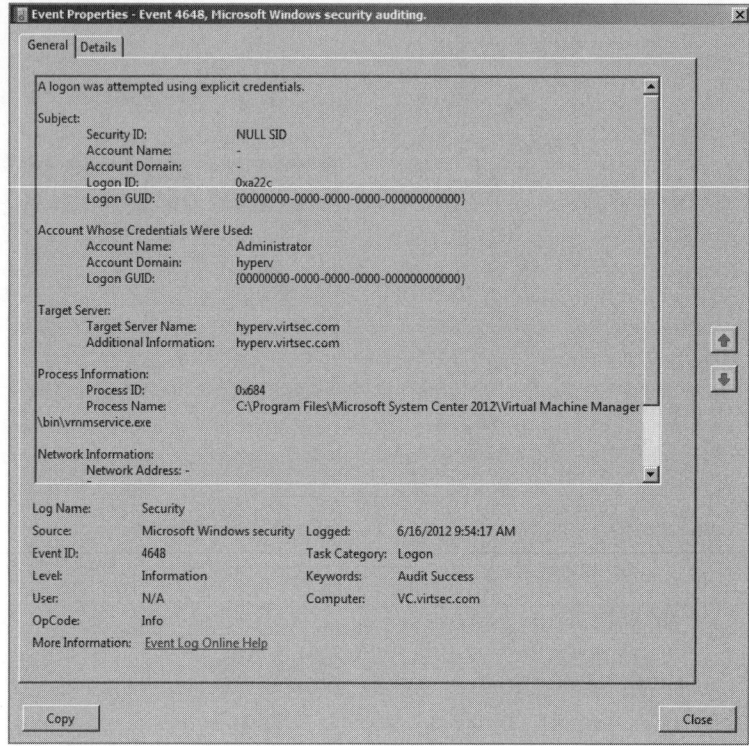

FIGURE 7.5
Hyper-V events

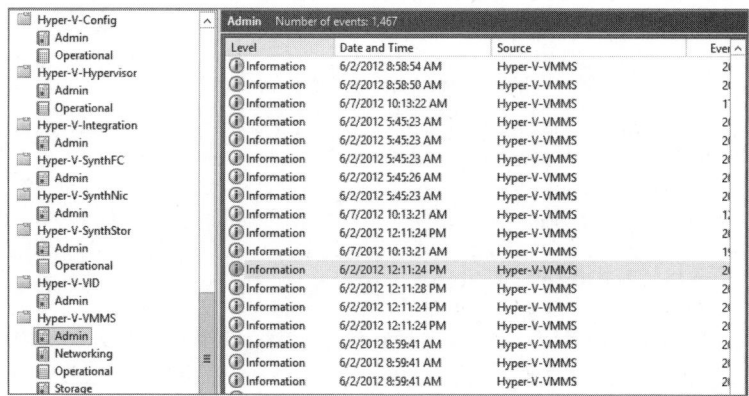

You can simply highlight each event or double-click it to open a new window with more information.

2. For categories with a large number of events, you can also select the button on the right side labeled Filter Current Log. This opens a new window, shown in Figure 7.6.

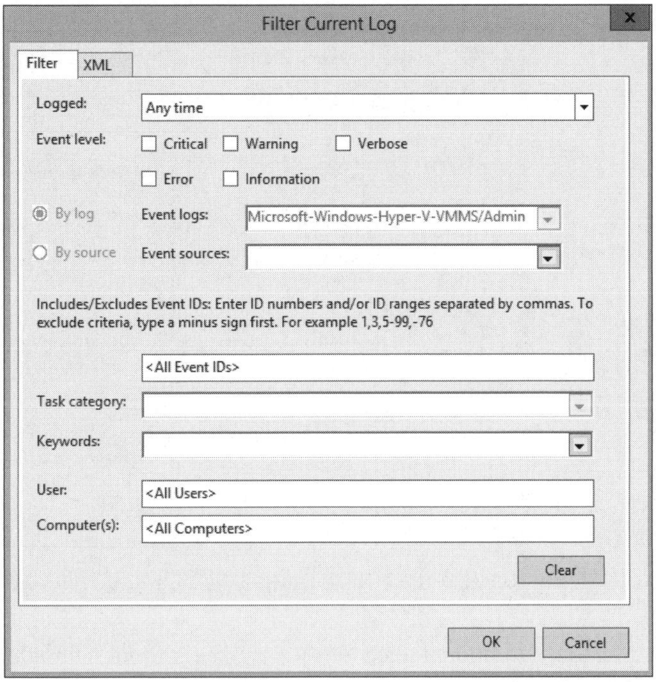

FIGURE 7.6
Event filtering in
Event Viewer

3. Here, you can select different event severity levels, specific event ID numbers to search for, keywords, users, and computers. Choose the specific criteria you are interested in, and then click OK.

You can use Event Viewer to create a custom event view:

1. To create a new view specifically for all Hyper-V events, select the Create Custom View button on the right side. The Create Custom View window will open.

2. Choose the time category you would like (Any Time is the default) as well as severity levels you are interested in.

3. Select events from specific log types or event sources.

The simplest way to get all Hyper-V logs is to select By Log, expand Microsoft and then Windows, and then select all the Hyper-V categories, as shown in Figure 7.7.

4. Make any additional selections you'd like for users, computers, keywords, and so on, then click OK.

You will likely be warned that views with large numbers of categories together may have performance issues.

5. Choose a name for the view and click OK, and it will be created in the Event Viewer console (under Custom Views by default).

Another option is to export events for analysis in another format. The easiest way to do this is to select an event category, right-click, and choose Save All Events As. You can choose to save the file in EVTX, XML, TXT, or CSV format for later analysis. If you've created a custom view, select it, then click the menu option in the right-hand pane labeled Save All Events In Custom View As. You will be presented with the same options to export all events.

You can also use the command line to search for specific log entries with the `wevtutil` tool. To get started using this utility, perform the following steps:

1. At the command line (likely PowerShell for newer versions of Windows Server), take a look at the different Hyper-V event categories with the following command:

```
wevtutil el | find "Hyper-V"
```

This will list all the Hyper-V event categories that you can then reference.

2. To query events within one of these categories, use this example as a guide. (This example searches the Hyper-V-VMMS-Admin category for the keyword "failed"):

```
wevtutil qe microsoft-windows-hyper-v-vmms-admin /f:text | find /i "failed"
```

3. You can easily modify this search to look for whatever you need. The /f:text flag outputs the results in text format, and the /i flag with find makes the search not case sensitive. You can script this easily to output results into a file.

NOTE In Chapter 10, "Scripting Tips and Tricks for Automation," we'll look at some simple PowerShell examples to parse log information.

As a final configuration option to note, you can configure each specific logging subsection by right-clicking it and selecting Properties. You'll see the log file path on the local system, and you'll have several simple options to choose from. The options are as follows:

1. Ensure that logging is enabled by checking the check box labeled Enable Logging.

2. Choose the maximum log size in KB. The default for most logs is 1028 KB. I recommend doubling this to 2048 KB in most cases, unless you're extraordinarily short on local storage space.

3. Choose what to do once the maximum log size is reached.

The options are to overwrite events (the default), archive the log, or manually clear the log. I recommend archiving if possible. You should also send the logs to a remote log host, which we'll cover shortly in the section "Integrating with Existing Logging Platforms."

A completed Hyper-V log configuration that matches these specifications is shown in Figure 7.8.

FIGURE 7.8
Modified
configuration for
Hyper-V logging

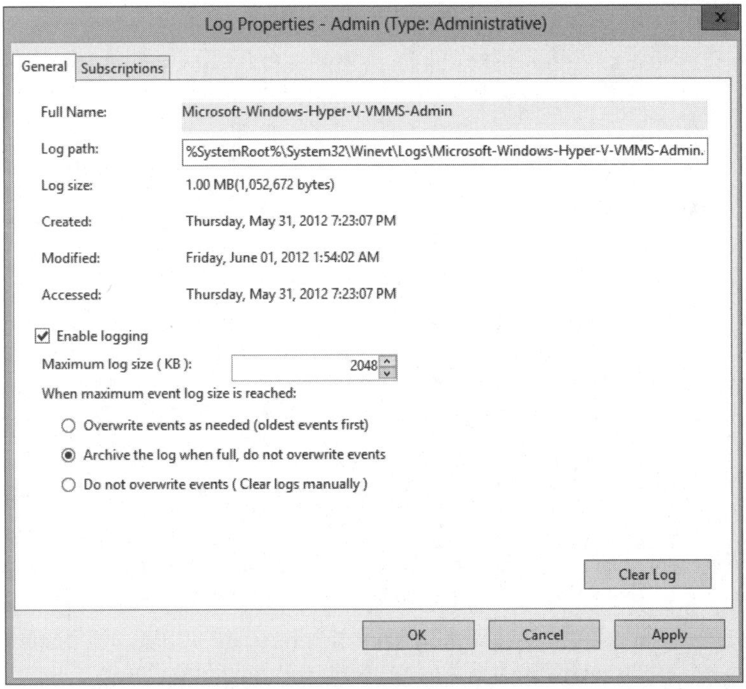

Citrix XenServer and XenCenter Logging

Citrix XenServer and XenCenter have a fairly straightforward set of logs that you can monitor, because they are largely built on syslog.

LOGS TO MONITOR

The following are logs that you should monitor carefully:

/etc/xensource-inventory: This log file contains information about the server hardware and configuration, software versions, and install date.

/var/log/audit.log: This file contains very detailed information related to interaction with RBAC roles, as discussed in Chapter 2, "Securing Hypervisors." There are specific Xen commands available to assess this log's data, discussed later in this section.

/var/log/cron: This file logs all scheduled tasks that are run as cron jobs on the local XenServer machine. This file is important for several reasons. First, it will help troubleshoot operational processes that have been included as scheduled jobs. Second, attackers commonly leverage scheduled jobs to create persistent back doors or malicious processes of their own, and administrators should ensure that there is nothing running on the system that they aren't aware of.

/var/log/daemon: This file contains log data pertaining to daemons running on the XenServer host, some of which may be of interest in both operational and security analysis processes. Although most of this data will be purely operational in nature, it should be included in your list of standard XenServer logs to assess.

/var/log/dmesg: More of a traditional Linux log, the dmesg log contains boot data and potentially valuable error information.

/var/log/installer/*: All the log files in this directory are useful for seeing what occurred during system installation. Grab them after installation; then archive and store securely.

/var/log/maillog: XenServer systems can leverage SMTP for sending alerts, which is attractive for some organizations. If you send alerts this way, this log will likely contain useful information about what mail messages were sent and when.

/var/log/messages: This is the main log file for all XenServer systems and contains the majority of logs you'll be interested in from both a security and operational perspective. Virtual switch information, all system configuration steps, processes starting and stopping, and more are stored here, making this an invaluable file to keep up with.

/var/log/secure: All connections to the XenServer system are logged in this file, ranging from XenCenter management connections to SSH connections for administration.

/var/log/SMlog: XenServer storage mounts, connections, and health checks are all logged in this file, as well as file locks during certain operations. This file will primarily be useful during troubleshooting operations for administrators having issues with storage connections.

/var/log/squeezed.log: This file primarily records information about memory reservations and transfers as well as any changes to memory allocation for the XenServer host.

/var/log/user.log: This log may contain commands run and configuration settings changed on the XenServer host. Much of what's here will likely be redundant with other log files.

/var/log/v6d.log: This file may contain information about XenServer licensing.

/var/log/xensource.log: This is another critical log for XenServer because it contains a huge array of information about processes and drivers loaded and other information about the day-to-day operation of the host. This is also the primary log file for all access to and interaction with the Xen API (xapi).

/var/log/xenstored.log: This file contains detailed information related to the function and operation of the XenServer's xenstore space, used for configuration and status information.

/var/log/xenstored-access.log: This file contains detailed read and write information about data access on defined Xen storage devices.

/var/log/xha: If High Availability services are enabled, this log file will contain operating information and error data about them.

/var/xen/domain-builder-ng.log: This file stores details about resource allocation and configuration, device changes, and interaction with storage. This file is primarily concerned with domain creation and interaction on the XenServer platform and is not particularly useful for security.

CONFIGURING LOGGING ON XENSERVER

To configure logging on XenServer platforms, you have a few options. The first, and likely the simplest, is to use the xe command. To configure XenServer logging using xe, do the following:

1. Log into the XenServer console using SSH or via XenCenter.

2. At the command line, enter a command using the following syntax:

   ```
   xe log-set-output level=<level> output=<output-type>
   ```

   For the level option, you can enter one of several severity levels: debug, info, warning, or error (which log progressively less information). Setting the level to debug will provide you with an enormous level of detail, but much of it is likely unnecessary. I recommend setting the level to info or warning and then gauging how much information you receive.

   For the output option, you can select one of the following:

   ◆ file will send all XenServer logs to a file that you specify, which may be adequate for small organizations or test scenarios.

   ◆ nil doesn't record logs at all.

   ◆ syslog sends all important XenServer messages to the native Unix syslog daemon. This is the best option for most organizations.

To configure the types of logging you would like to record, XenServer has two locations you should pay attention to: /etc/syslog/conf and /etc/xensource/log.conf:

`/etc/syslog/conf` The typical Syslog configuration file can be found at `/etc/syslog.conf`. Configuring log entries in this file follows standard syslog configuration practices, and the only default entry that is specific to Xen is the XAPI RBAC audit access logs stored in `/var/log/audit.log`.

`/etc/xensource/log.conf` In this file, a number of specific event types are sent to `nil`, `syslog`, or `file` output (these align to the `xe log-set-output` options mentioned earlier). You should monitor this file carefully for any changes, and configure it if necessary. The default options are usually adequate for most organizations.

XenServer also has the ability to leverage the logrotate daemon. There are two specific configuration areas to note. First, the general `/etc/logrotate.conf` file has the overall log rotation information most administrators will be interested in. By default, logs are rotated 20 times and rotated daily. This is usually fine for most organizations. Specific log rotation activities can be found in `/etc/logrotate.d/`, where you can specify postrotation actions for any of the specific logs on XenServer. Again, the defaults are largely fine for most organizations, but pay close attention to the `audit`, `syslog`, and `xapi` configuration entries.

There are a variety of auditing capabilities present on XenServer platforms, some common to Unix platforms and others particular to XenServer. If you peruse the `/var/log` directory, you'll notice the `btmp` and `wtmp` binary files. These files are used to log failed login attempts and successful user login sessions, respectively. To access the data from these files, you can use the `w`, `who`, and `last` commands for active or recent sessions and the `lastb` command for failed logins. There's a freely available tool for parsing and analyzing XenServer logs as well, called the XenServer Auditing Tool. This is a part of the XenServer Resource Kit, and is available from Citrix here:

`http://community.citrix.com/cdn/xs/XenServer+Resource+Kit`

The RBAC audit logs on XenServer will focus on several specific types of information related to logged-on user activities:

- The Subject ID and username associated with related sessions
- Authorization failures associated with user activities
- "Success" messages related to activities and error codes for operations failures

To get an export of audit log records, run the following command:

`xe audit-log-get filename=<file to save to>`

For even more specific or granular results, this command can also take a time stamp value as the starting point for the log entries to export. For example, if a forensic or other security investigation is initiated, you may need audit entries from only a certain date and time. To include these, use the following syntax:

`xe audit-log-get since=2012-06-19T16:44Z filename=<file to save to>`

This will generate an export file of all audit data since June 19, 2012 at 4:44 p.m. You can also be more granular, drilling down to the millisecond. This will generate an audit trail from June 19, 2012 at 4:44:21 p.m. at the 139th millisecond:

`xe audit-log-get since=2012-06-19T16:44:21.139Z filename=<file to save to>`

One last option for generating bulk log data (primarily for troubleshooting and operations, particularly when generating data to send to Citrix support teams) is the `xen-bugtool` command. Running this will prompt you for a vast array of files and information to include in an export file that's intended to be shared with vendors and internal support staff.

You may also want to enable the Xenstored logs for all operations related to the Xenstore daemon, which can produce a staggering volume of log information. To do this, edit the `/etc/xen-source/xenstored.conf` file. You'll see the following lines (notice they are all commented out):

```
# Xenstored logs
# xenstored-log-file = /var/log/xenstored.log
# xenstored-log-level = null
# xenstored-log-nb-files = 10
```

These three settings enable Xenstored logs, set the minimum level of logging (discussed earlier), and set the number of files to maintain, respectively. These logs can contain a wealth of data related to the XenServer system configuration and operation and should be enabled if possible. Just keep in mind that you may end up with a lot of logs and a slight performance hit.

XenCenter logs should also be monitored and maintained. For XenCenter installations on Windows platforms, you can easily locate the logs by clicking the Help menu item within XenCenter (on the top menu bar) and then selecting View Application Log Files. This should open the log location in Windows Explorer. For most organizations, these will be found in the following location:

```
%userprofile%\AppData\Roaming\Citrix\XenCenter\logs\
```

The two files you should usually focus on are:

`XenCenter.log`: This is the general log file for XenCenter and contains the majority of the log data you'll be interested in. Most information around operational events and errors will be found here.

`XenCenter Audit Trail.log`: Some user-specific interactions are recorded in this file as well, so you should include it in your log monitoring efforts as well.

Integrating with Existing Logging Platforms

To integrate any of the major virtualization vendors' logging components with an existing log collection/monitoring infrastructure, you'll need to enable remote logging on both hypervisor platforms and management systems. In some cases, this is simple. In others, it requires a bit more work.

Enabling Remote Logging on VMware vSphere

To enable remote logging on ESX systems, you will need to modify the `/etc/syslog.conf` file to send messages to a remote system. Doing this is simple:

1. Log into the ESX platform using the console or SSH.

2. Using the Vi editor, open the `/etc/syslog.conf` file mentioned earlier.

3. For any entries in the file that you would like to send to a remote log host, create a duplicate line that changes the filename (such as `/var/log/messages`) to the name of a remote

host or an IP address preceded by the @ symbol. For example, take the following log configuration entry:

```
local6.warning                          /var/log/vmkwarning
```

To send these same entries to the remote log collector at 10.10.0.99, you would add the following line:

```
local6.warning                          @10.10.0.99
```

To send everything to a remote log host, you could add a line like the following (any-where in the file):

```
*.*                        @10.10.0.99
```

4. Save the file by pressing Escape, typing **:wq!**, and pressing Enter.

To send logs to a remote log host on ESXi, you have several easy options In ESXi 5.*x*, you can now send a syslog message using TCP or UDP, or even SSL-based logging (TCPS) if your log collector supports it. The ability to send logs to multiple hosts is a new feature too. So in addi-tion to specifying the remote log host(s), you'll need to include the protocol and possibly also the remote ports that are listening.

One way to enable this is via the GUI:

1. Connect to the ESXi host or vCenter with the vSphere Client.

2. Navigate to Inventory, then Hosts And Clusters. Highlight the ESXi host in the left-hand pane.

3. On the right side, click the Configuration tab, and then choose Advanced Settings under the Software category.

4. You should see a menu item in the tree labeled Syslog. For ESXi 5.*x* systems, a submenu underneath should exist called Global. Highlight this menu item on the tree. You will see an option labeled Syslog.global.logHost.

5. In the field to the right of this option, enter remote log hosts in the following format:

   udp://loghost:514 or udp://loghost

   tcp://loghost:1514 or tcp://loghost

   ssl://loghost:1514 or ssl://loghost

   Specifying ports is not required, but is a good idea. You can list several hosts separated by commas.

6. Click OK when finished.

When finished, you should have entries like the one in Figure 7.9.

FIGURE 7.9
Remote Log Hosts
for ESXi

| Syslog.global.logHost | udp://10.10.0.99:514 |

The remote host to output logs to. Reset to default on null. Multiple hosts are supported and must be separated with comma (,). Ex...

Another way to enable remote logging is at the command line of ESXi. You can use the `esxcli` commands to specify remote log hosts as follows:

1. Log into the ESXi host at the DCUI or using SSH.

2. At the command line, enter the following:

```
esxcli system syslog config set --loghost <host1,host2...>
```

The names of the log hosts will have the same format as those mentioned previously in the vSphere GUI: `udp://loghost:514` or `udp://loghost`, and so on.

For example, to send logs both via UDP to 10.10.0.99 and via SSL to 10.10.0.100, you would enter the following command:

```
esxcli system syslog config set --loghost
udp://10.10.0.99:514,ssl://10.10.0.100:1514
```

A third way to enable remote logging on ESXi systems is with the vCLI. On your vSphere Management Appliance (vMA) or vCLI management system, run the following command for ESXi 4.*x* systems:

```
vicfg-syslog --server <ESXi name/IP> --username root
 --password <password> --setserver <log host>
 --port <log host listening port>
```

For ESXi 5.*x* systems, use the following command (you will need a vCenter instance running):

```
esxcli --server=<vCenter name/IP> --vihost <ESXi name/IP>
username=<vCenter Admin User> system syslog config set
 --loghost=<log host>
```

VMware vSphere now offers a built-in syslog collector service that can be used to send all virtualization logs to either a vCenter host or another system where you can install this service. Installation of this service is out of the scope of this book, but it's discussed in Scott Lowe's book, *Mastering VMware vSphere 5* (Sybex, 2011):

```
http://www.wiley.com/WileyCDA/WileyTitle/productCd-0470890800,
miniSiteCd-SYBEX.html
```

Enabling Remote Logging on Microsoft Hyper-V

For Microsoft Hyper-V, you've got two options for enabling remote log messages from SCVMM and Hyper-V servers. The first is a native Microsoft option that has become more popular since Windows 2008 Server and leverages the Windows Event Collector Service. This is known as the Event Subscription capability of Microsoft's Event Viewer console and acts as a centralized log collector.

To enable the Event Subscription capabilities, perform the following steps:

1. On all Hyper-V systems or SCVMM systems from which you want to collect logs, run the following command to enable Windows Remote Management capabilities that allow the central log collector(s) to connect and gather data:

```
winrm quickconfig
```

2. On the central log collector, open the Event Viewer as an administrator (Start, then Administrative Tools, then Event Viewer).

3. Right-click Subscriptions in the console tree, and then select Create Subscription in the menu that appears.

4. In the window that appears, enter a name and description for your subscription, and specify the destination log category where collected events will be stored. By default, subscription events are stored in the Forwarded Events section under Windows Logs in the main Event Viewer tree.

5. You will see two options for Subscription Type And Source Computers. Select the Collector Initiated option (the default), and then click Select Computers. Click Add Domain Computers and select the Hyper-V and/or SCVMM systems from which you want to collect events. Click OK twice once you've selected these systems.

6. Click Select Events to display the Query Filter window. Choose the event severity and types you want to collect. Click OK when finished. A completed Subscription screen is shown in Figure 7.10.

FIGURE 7.10

A Windows Hyper-V event subscription

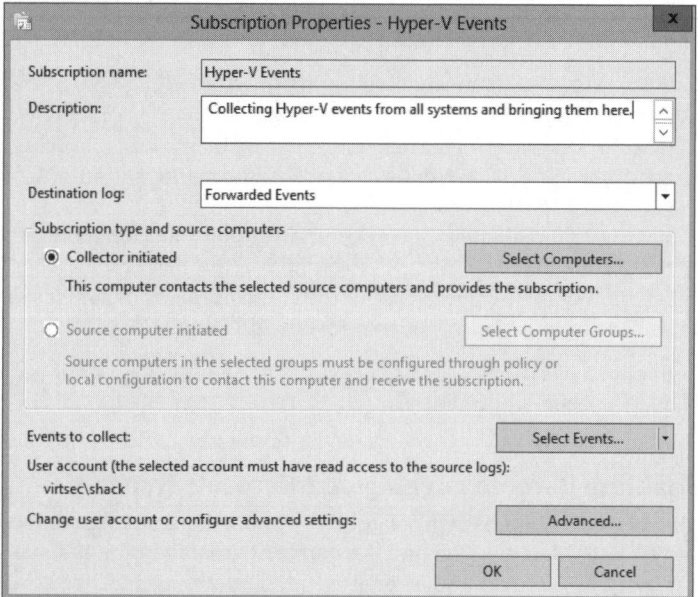

7. A final set of options can be configured by clicking the Advanced button. Here, you can set a different log collection user account and choose the transport priority and method (HTTP or HTTPS) that will be used for the subscription. Set these options if desired, and then click OK.

8. Click OK to finish.

You should now have a subscription listed for your Hyper-V systems with a status of Active. The second option for Microsoft systems is to use a third-party log collection agent that can monitor event logs, translate them to syslog or another format, and then send them to a central collector. There are many options available, both open source and commercial, such as the following solutions:

Splunk: Both free and commercial solutions for log monitoring, management, and analysis:

`www.splunk.com`

Snare: Formerly an open-source project, Snare now has commercial options as well for log monitoring and transfer with syslog compatibility:

`www.intersectalliance.com/projects/BackLogNT/`

Kiwi Syslog: Now owned by Solarwinds, Kiwi Syslog is one of the most well-known Windows logging and event management toolkits available:

`www.kiwisyslog.com`

Enabling Remote Logging for XenServer

Even though XenServer has "normal" syslog capabilities, the preferred method for enabling remote log generation and transport is through XenServer-specific commands. There are two ways to enable remote logging on XenServer platforms. The first is via XenCenter and is incredibly simple:

1. Log into XenCenter. Right-click a XenServer host and choose Properties.

2. Click the Log Destination option on the left-hand menu. By default, this should be set to Local.

3. In the right-hand pane, the Local option will be selected if you've never configured this. The only other menu selection is Remote. Click that now, and then enter a remote logging server that will listen for and collect logs from the XenServer host. You can use the hostname or IP address, and this is shown in Figure 7-11.

FIGURE 7.11
Configuring a
remote log server in
XenCenter

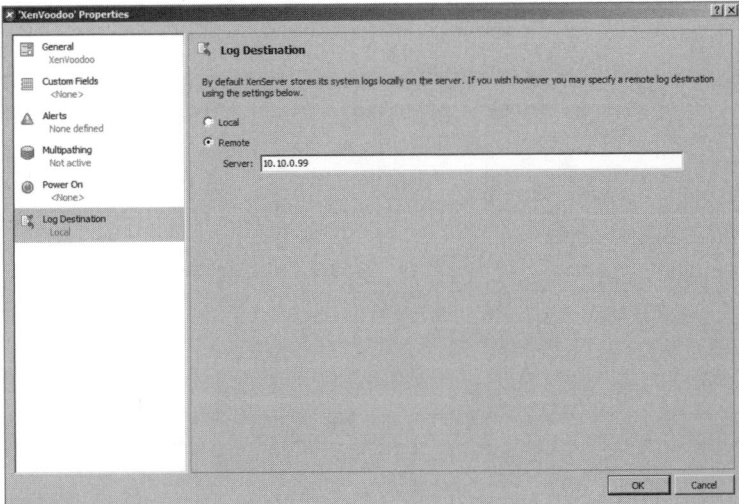

4. When finished, click OK.

To accomplish the same thing using the command line, you can use custom parameters with the xe command. First, log into your XenServer host with the local console, XenCenter console, or via SSH. Now, follow these steps:

1. First, set the `syslog_destination` parameter for the remote system where you want the logs to be sent with the following command:

```
xe host-param-set uuid=<XenServer UUID> logging:syslog_destination=<remote
logging host or IP>
```

Remember that you can get your XenServer host's UUID with the following command:

```
xe host-list
```

2. To accept and set this syslog change, run the following command:

```
xe host-syslog-reconfigure uuid=<XenServer UUID>
```

That's all there is to it! You should now have syslog events being sent to a remote log host.

Effective Log Management

There are quite a few considerations when it comes to effective log management, and there are entire books written on this subject alone. Here, we'll consider some of the high points you should take into account when planning your log management strategy, especially as the volume of logs increases with the addition of virtual infrastructure.

The first thing most operations teams will need to look at is the overall scope of log management. There are a few categories of log management tools that most organizations will want to consider:

Log management platforms   Solutions in this category include sophisticated parsing engines, log "search engines," and data storage and archival. These systems usually consist of management consoles, log collectors where many logs from disparate systems are sent, and possibly additional storage or analysis components.

Log rotation and conversion tools   These single-function tools ease administrative tasks.

Single-host tools   Host-based intrusion detection systems and file integrity monitors may fall into this category.

Security information and event management (SIEM) tools   SIEM platforms will include log analysis and correlation capabilities and will be much more flexible and robust. They're also much more complex to set up and maintain.

For any of these different types of log analysis products and solutions, organizations will need to evaluate the following criteria:

Real-time or batch: Are logs continually processed, or are they processed in a batch job (on a schedule)?

Storage capacity: Does the log management toolkit integrate with existing storage infrastructure like your SAN or NAS, or is specialized storage necessary?

Architecture (multitier or stand-alone): How many different levels of collectors and analysis tools does the log management tool offer or require? For large organizations, a more flexible architecture model may be ideal.

Integration with other applications and management components: If you already have a SIEM in place, for example, can you integrate new logging components into that readily? Can you export data to an existing management dashboard?

Ease of configuration and ongoing maintenance: Some log management tools are much more work to configure and manage than others.

Footprint (appliance or software): Some organizations prefer a hardsare-based solution, while others prefer software implementations on existing hardware or virtual systems.

Failover and redundancy: Log management is rapidly becoming a critical element of both operations and security teams. As a core infrastructure component, log management tools should have redundancy and failover capabilities to prevent any downtime or loss of important information.

The next key aspect of log management is defining your log management requirements. These will include the following:

Types of log generation: Most organizations will generate a significant quantity of log data from systems, applications, services, and security and network components and devices. Most virtualization infrastructure log data conforms to syslog or Windows Event Viewer formats and can be parsed and managed fairly easily.

Quantity of log data produced: Organizations will need to consider how much log data they'll generate, both for transport planning (how much traffic is generated) and log storage and analysis.

Accessibility of logs: Can the logs be automatically sent to a central location? For large, distributed organizations, planning to get all logs to one or more central collectors can be an architecture project itself.

Additional factors to consider will include cost, data classification and sensitivity, and operational overhead. In general, any hypervisor logs and audit trail information related to virtualization administration should be considered highly sensitive and important data. Other logs from virtual machines and additional components will vary in criticality from one organization to the next.

One final note regarding any log management environment: You need to protect the logs! Once logs have been transmitted to a central collector and stored, you need to ensure that they're not being tampered with. The easiest way to do this is via some type of file integrity monitoring, often performed with cryptographic hashing tools and algorithms. Most commercial log management solutions have some of these capabilities built in, but you can easily build your own as well. Another option for your most sensitive log data is encryption.

As an example of best practice recommendations regarding secure log management, consider the following information from the National Institute of Standards and Technology (NIST) in Table 7.5.

TABLE 7.5: NIST logging recommendations

CATEGORY	LOW-IMPACT SYSTEMS	MODERATE-IMPACT SYSTEMS	HIGH-IMPACT SYSTEMS
How long to retain log data	1 to 2 weeks	1 to 3 months	3 to 12 months
How often to rotate logs	Optional (if performed, at least every week or every 25 MB)	Every 6 to 24 hours, or every 2 to 5 MB	Every 15 to 60 minutes, or every 0.5 to 1.0 MB
How frequently the system should transfer log data to the log management infrastructure (if required)	Every 3 to 24 hours	Every 15 to 60 minutes	At least every 5 minutes
How often log data needs to be analyzed locally (through automated or manual means)	Every 1 to 7 days	Every 12 to 24 hours	At least 6 times a day
Whether log file integrity checking needs to be performed for rotated logs	Optional	Yes	Yes
Whether rotated logs need to be encrypted	Optional	Optional	Yes
Whether log data transfers to the log management infrastructure need to be encrypted or performed on a separate logging network	Optional	Yes, if feasible	Yes

These are many more recommendations on log management available in "NIST Special Publication 800-92", and I encourage you to read this as an excellent starting guide to log management best practices:

`http://csrc.nist.gov/publications/nistpubs/800-92/SP800-92.pdf`

Chapter 8

Change and Configuration Management

With proper oversight, virtualization can significantly enhance change and configuration management practices through simplified template creation and management, but this usually requires some changes to existing processes as well as new methods of doing things.

In this chapter, you will learn about the following topics:

- ◆ The fundamental concepts of change and configuration management, and how they relate to virtualization

- ◆ Integrating virtualization into existing workflows

- ◆ Assessing and creating new processes for change and configuration management

- ◆ Creating VM templates in VMware, Microsoft, and Citrix virtualization platforms

Change and Configuration Management Overview

There is a well-known concept in the field of epidemiology called "shift and drift." The concept relates specifically to the mutation and spread of viruses or other types of infectious diseases. "Shift" occurs when a virus can spread from one species to another. "Drift" describes the process of gradual transformation and mutation that helps viruses survive antibiotics and natural antigens. Change within IT organizations can behave in much the same way.

Some changes can have a persistent and varying effect on systems and applications. For example, an application or operating platform configuration change could lead to a modified file or directory, which then leads to exposure and/or corruption of a different file, and so on. In such cases, a system or application can "drift" out of a set configuration standard into a new one before administrators know what has actually happened or what the root cause of the issues are. Another situation involves the "downstream impact" of changes made to one system that "shift" and affect other systems and applications in other areas. An example of this would be a network device configuration change that modifies traffic flow into or out of particular network segments, causing applications to fail.

These kinds of changes, particularly those that go unnoticed and unchecked for a long time, can lead to problems with an organization's security and compliance posture. These changes can open critical security weaknesses in systems and applications, affect other systems in a dynamic fashion, and generally lead to additional security problems like data exposure, accidental or malicious attacks and compromise, and increased risk overall.

WHAT IS ITIL?

The Information Technology Infrastructure Library, or ITIL, is mentioned several times in this chapter. What is it, and why is it relevant to the topics of change and configuration management? ITIL is a collection of IT service management standards and practices that seek to establish a minimum standard of processes and controls in areas like change management, configuration management, and incident management. The ITIL framework, now in its third edition, defines five major categories: service strategy, service design, service transition, service operation, and continual service improvement. Change and configuration management are two disciplines that fall under the service transition category and are often the two areas with which organizations start an ITIL implementation.

While ITIL isn't perfect (and in fact has several common criticisms), it's widely considered the de facto standard for IT services management, and many large organizations are adopting some or all of its key tenets. For this reason, it makes sense to align with ITIL for fundamental change and configuration management discussion points and concepts.

Change Management for Security

So what are change management and configuration management, exactly? Using the definitions from the *ITIL Glossary of Terms, Definitions and Acronyms V3*, change management is "the [p]rocess responsible for controlling the Lifecycle of all Changes. The primary objective of Change Management is to enable beneficial Changes to be made, with minimum disruption to IT Services." Configuration management, on the other hand, is defined as "the [p]rocess responsible for maintaining information about Configuration Items required to deliver an IT Service, including their Relationships. This information is managed throughout the Lifecycle of the CI [Configuration Item]. Configuration Management is part of an overall Service Asset and Configuration Management Process."

INFORMATION ABOUT ITIL

For more information on the IT Service Management (ITIL) definitions of change management, configuration management, and other related terms, see:

www.best-management-practice.com/gempdf/ITIL_Glossary_V3_1_24.pdf

The security team's challenge is to integrate itself into existing IT change management processes to gain increased visibility and awareness of what is happening in the IT environment. Organizations should include security to help evaluate requested and planned system changes and advise business management of associated risks. Getting a seat at the table is becoming easier because organizations are starting to understand the risks some IT changes could introduce.

A typical change management program often comprises the following five high-level steps:

1. **Request and Approval**: Changes are requested via some type of system (manual or automated), and the requests are validated and approved or denied. Security's role would be to authenticate change requestors and establish audit trails for the requests.

2. **Planning and Testing**: Changes are planned and assessed in a lab or sample population. Security's role is to determine the risks associated with the change, ensure that back-out plans are defined and adhere to policies, and assess control risks once changes are tested.

3. **Scheduling and Communication**: Changes are scheduled and all stakeholders are notified. Security needs to be aware of changes taking place.

4. **Implementation**: Changes are implemented, and security should be on call or available, particularly for high-risk changes with significant potential impacts.

5. **Documentation and Follow-up**: The loop is closed on the changes by final documentation sign-off and agreement that all went as planned. Security should be involved in signing off on the change implementation.

Security should be involved in every step of the change management process and understand what systems are impacted, how they may be impacted, and how best to minimize the immediate and "downstream" risks to IT assets. In a perfect world, IT security and audit would know what state every asset was in, what changes were occurring and planned, and what the impacts would be on security and compliance posture. However, it's *not* a perfect world for one major reason: lack of visibility. Before covering this, let's examine the infrastructure components commonly encountered as well as the compliance and policy framework within which these components operate.

The Change Ecosystem

In most IT environments, there are four major areas that typically contain the majority of security- and compliance-related controls maintained by security and operations teams:

Physical host operating systems   The bulk of most IT infrastructures is physical servers and workstations. The operating system that runs on these physical systems has a number of distinct controls, including access controls, OS tuning parameters, and file-level controls for data storage.

Virtual operating platforms and guest operating systems   As more organizations realize the cost savings and operational benefits of virtualizing systems, more and more virtual technology will be deployed. In addition to containing traditional operating system controls, these systems contain their own platform-specific code and virtual network infrastructure that must have controls applied.

Applications and databases   Applications and databases have their own specific sets of controls to maintain and monitor. Web servers have access controls and file and directory permissions as well as customized database calls and scripts, while databases have controls for data presentation and retention as well as stored procedures and other database-implementation-specific aspects.

Network devices and infrastructure   Network devices such as routers, switches, and firewalls all have specific controls that apply to segmentation of network traffic, inspection of traffic, and encryption of traffic.

These four categories frequently overlap. Applications run on both physical and virtual servers, or a virtual server is the backup for a physical server. Network devices route traffic and provide access controls to both physical and virtual hosts, running a number of different applications. An application on a virtual host may store sensitive data on a single-purpose physical server elsewhere. As the IT environment becomes more complex with the addition of new technologies, often provisioned and maintained by different teams with different business and operating agendas, the ability to maintain a satisfactory compliance posture becomes more and more difficult. A simple representation of how these overlap, with compliance overlaid, is shown in Figure 8.1.

FIGURE 8.1
IT infrastructure
components and
change overlap

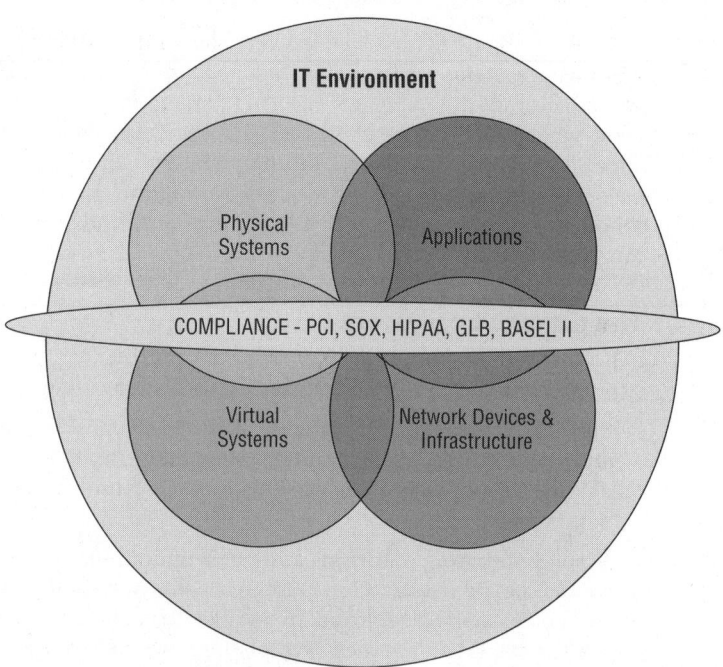

For each of these four categories of infrastructure elements, there are controls that can be applied to implement a specific security or compliance goal. The sum of these controls constitutes a security or compliance posture, which operates within the framework of internal policies and external regulations and mandates. This is demonstrated in Figure 8.2.

Internal policies are also applicable for any and all of these levels. The entire IT ecosystem then interoperates with controls and a defined security posture in place, shown in Figure 8.3.

FIGURE 8.2
Relationship between controls, configuration, and posture

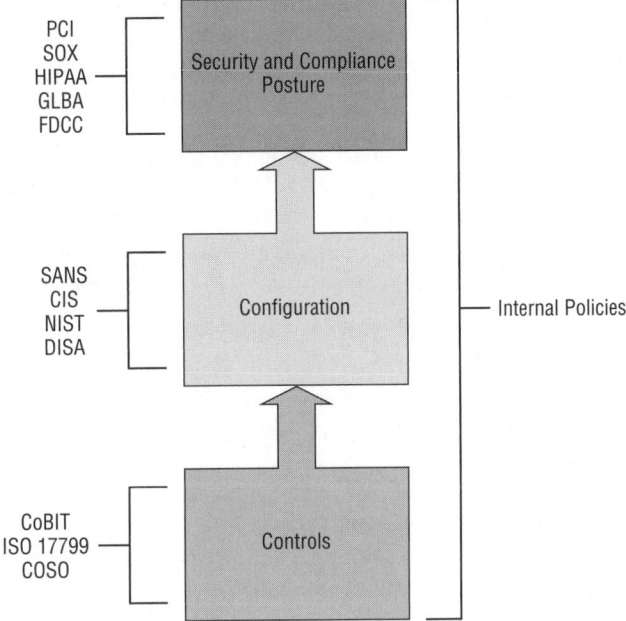

FIGURE 8.3
Interrelation between components and controls

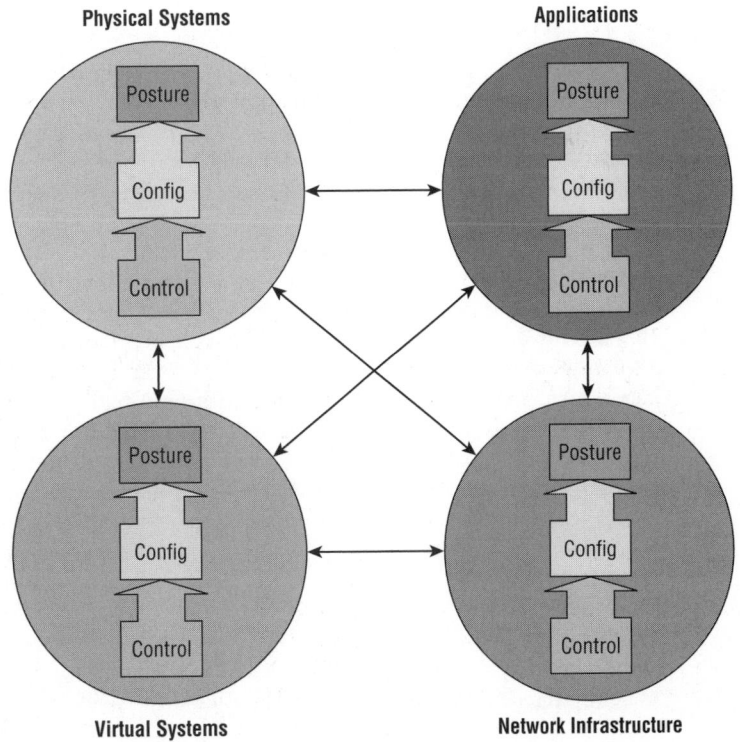

Within most IT environments, there are innumerable ways that system interactions can occur. Changes to a virtualization host platform may affect the virtual guest systems that run on it, leading to modifications in operating system parameters, all ultimately causing the system to no longer conform to the CIS Windows 2008 benchmark that serves as the corporate configuration standard. Because the auditing program has been built on this standard, this change could lead to a failed audit or compliance violation.

The primary culprit behind changes that "get out of hand" is a lack of visibility in most organizations. This lack of visibility can take a number of forms:

Network visibility   Different subnets are segregated in such a way that certain systems cannot be identified from other parts of the network.

Application visibility   Ports and services may be unavailable to certain networks, groups, or individuals.

Configuration visibility   Certain groups and individuals may not have the access rights to determine a system or application's configuration options.

Communication issues   Certain groups may intentionally or accidentally withhold information from other teams, which leads to a lack of visibility. Without the proper visibility, many teams will not be up-to-date on what systems are deployed, what state those systems are in, and how these changes and discrepancies may affect other parts of the organization. With the growth in virtualization technology, this visibility issue can get even worse.

How Virtualization Impacts Change and Configuration Management

With many organizations today implementing server virtualization technologies, the opportunities for misconfigured systems and applications is rising exponentially. Virtual sprawl, or the rapid proliferation of virtual machines (VMs), is becoming more common, which can lead to virtual systems that are not patched regularly. Virtual systems that are used for testing are common too, and these often have configurations that do not meet an organization's standards and policies.

Here's a simple example to illustrate this point. VirtSec Inc.'s system administrators are tasked with developing and maintaining a number of virtual hosts running on VMware ESXi. The goal is to replace the company's physical web servers running Microsoft IIS with virtual machines on the ESXi hosts as a cost-savings project. This is easily accomplished using VMware's technology, and over the course of several months, the team virtualized the web server farm and created 30 virtual machines running IIS to replace the physical systems.

Unfortunately, the VirtSec virtual switches are not properly configured in promiscuous mode or using SPAN capabilities (discussed in Chapter 4, "Advanced Virtual Network Operations") to support the security team's intrusion detection systems, and traffic between the new virtual machines is not observed and monitored. One of the VMs is compromised by an attacker, who then is able to access the other IIS systems without triggering any alarms. This leads to a significant loss of sensitive customer data over a period of several months.

Another example of physical and virtual system changes leading to additional problems would be the configuration of certain ESXi hosts as cluster members supporting VMware's vMotion technology for redundancy and backup. This technology allows a running virtual machine to be migrated from one ESXi host to another very easily. In this scenario, the virtualization team configures several ESXi hosts to support vMotion, not thinking about the compliance posture of certain VMs that need to be contained to locked-down ESXi hosts. If one of the VMs containing sensitive data is accidentally migrated to a noncompliant ESXi host, the entire organization's compliance posture is in jeopardy.

Best Practices for Virtualization Configuration Management

Configuration management can be defined in a number of ways, but a fairly common implementation cycle is shown in Figure 8.4.

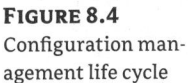

FIGURE 8.4
Configuration management life cycle

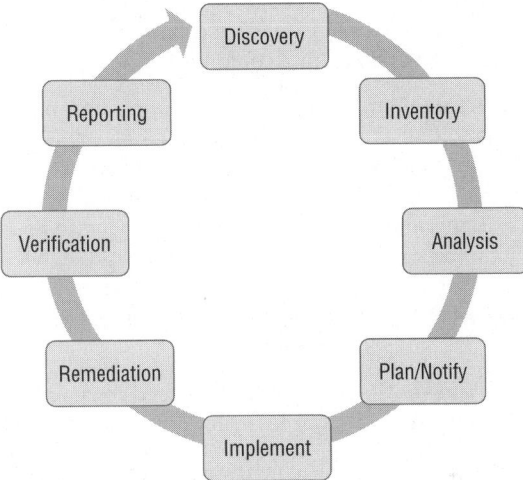

These phases are described in the following list, with a focus on virtualization technologies:

1. **Discovery**: The configuration management process begins with discovery of all virtual infrastructure components, including hypervisor hosts, virtual machines, storage, and management application components. Discovery is a key foundational step for the rest of the configuration management process because it identifies the scope of what needs to be evaluated.

2. **Inventory**: After the discovery is complete, an accurate and up-to-date inventory of the infrastructure should be in place. There are numerous ways to develop and maintain inventory of virtual infrastructure components. Some organizations will leverage management tools like vCenter, XenCenter, and SCVMM. Others will perform more traditional discovery and inventory management techniques that leverage tools like network scanners and spreadsheets. More advanced organizations will have a configuration management database (CMDB) that conforms to ITIL and other standards and can be leveraged for inventory maintenance as well.

3. **Analysis**: After the inventorying process is completed, analysis of what configuration changes are warranted needs to occur. The analysis phase determines whether the current state of the infrastructure meets (or will meet) organizational metrics for operations,

security, and compliance. The analysis phase also determines what necessary approved changes might need to happen and what their potential impact might be. For virtual environments, these will likely be focused on configuration changes and patches for management components, virtual networks, storage, hypervisors, and virtual machines. Impact analysis can be very challenging in virtual environments because virtual components tend to have numerous interrelationships between physical and virtual networks, storage, and other parts of the environment.

4. **Plan/Notify**: Once the analysis phase is complete, the planning and notification phase will focus on developing work plans for virtual systems and network components that will have changes applied to them. Contingency plans should be included in case the changes have an unexpected impact on the organization. During this phase, a request for change (RFC) will be filed and maintenance windows should be scheduled. Developing an adequate back-out plan is paramount for virtual infrastructure due to the number of related systems that could be affected.

5. **Implement**: Notification to all applicable parties occurs once the RFCs are approved, and then changes to the virtual infrastructure will happen in the implementation and remediation phases. Leveraging test labs or less-essential machines first is highly recommended. This way, changes can be implemented and actual impact (or a close approximation) can be assessed before moving on to production systems. Virtualization may offer some significant advantages in this phase because templates (discussed in the next section, "Cloning and Templates for Improved Configuration Management") can be used to test change impact and orchestration tools can do most of the heavy lifting for rolling out the changes themselves.

6. **Remediation**: If any changes need to be remediated or adjusted, this can be done simultaneously with implementation or immediately after.

7. **Verification**: In the verification and reporting phases, a postmortem on the requested change takes place. The main objective in the verification phase is to validate that the approved changes occurred on the approved targets. All changes need to be reconciled with a change management or ticketing system. Documentation is needed to verify that the requested change occurred and also that nonapproved changes did not occur. The key to a successful verification phase for virtualization configuration and change management is to ensure that change tickets (created within traditional change management systems) are customized to include all necessary categories and specific details about the virtual environment. There will be more on this shortly.

CHANGE MANAGEMENT SOFTWARE EXAMPLES

Two traditional change management systems are BMC Software's BMC Remedy IT Service Management Suite and HP IT Change Management Suite:

www.bmc.com/products/product-listing/it-service-management-suite.html

www8.hp.com/us/en/software-solutions/software.html?compURI=1175646

8. **Reporting**: The final step of the configuration management process, the reporting phase, consists of documentation that's generated for disaster recovery and audit purposes. Documentation should be published for management review and to provide "lessons learned" information for the next round of configuration management.

Several components need to be accommodated for virtualization configuration management:

◆ Hypervisor hosts

◆ Virtual networks

◆ Storage connections

◆ Management platforms

◆ Virtual machines

Provisioning and controlling the configuration of hypervisors and virtual machines is arguably the most vital aspect to successful virtualization configuration management. The key to this, in turn, is the use of templates. Let's cover template creation and best practices for each of the major platforms.

Cloning and Templates for Improved Configuration Management

What, exactly, are templates? For virtual machines, a template is a copy of the virtual machine in a format that is not bootable or editable. It is intended to serve as a "gold image" that can be modified only by first deliberately converting the template to a VM. This is a safety feature! This means that administrators cannot accidentally or inadvertently make a change to a template without planning it beforehand.

Although you will want to maintain configuration consistency for virtual networks and storage, there is no simple way to do this with templates as you can with VMs. Using distributed virtual switches in vSphere or the Open vSwitch controller for Citrix can simplify the management of a consistent virtual switch definition for those platforms, but the best configuration management guidance here is to use scripting techniques (covered in Chapter 10, "Scripting Tips and Tricks for Automation") that can pull configuration data about the switches on a regular basis and then maintain this information in a central repository.

The first type of template that you will want to define is a standard build for hypervisor platforms. Unfortunately, the only vendor that supports a hypervisor template and management/ monitoring capability for it at the moment is VMware, with its Host Profiles capability. This is covered in detail in Chapter 2, "Securing Hypervisors," and we won't revisit this feature here.

The other major template type is for VMs, and all the major vendors support this readily. Let's dig into how to create templates for VMware, Microsoft, and Citrix environments. Before doing so, it's worth mentioning that VMs you use to create templates should be in as pristine a state as possible!

WARNING   If you have any existing malware or security issues present in a running VM, a template generated from it will have the same issues! This is a surefire way to rapidly manifest security issues in your environment!

One last configuration management feature that all major virtualization platforms include is *snapshots*. A snapshot essentially captures a "point in time" for the entire virtual machine, including memory, VM settings, and the contents of the virtual disk.

Snapshots can be used as a poor man's backup solution, because you can use the functionality to take regular snapshots over time and can revert to any of the specific points at which a snapshot was taken. They can also be used for effective configuration and change management testing because snapshots can be required before making changes, and the rollback/contingency plan can include restoring a snapshot in test or production environments.

Running with snapshots can have a performance impact, therefore, snapshots should be used only for change and configuration testing or as a short-term backup strategy (covered in Chapter 9, "Disaster Recovery and Business Continuity").

Creating and Managing VMware vSphere VM Templates and Snapshots

You'll need an existing virtual machine from which to create a template for a virtual machine. Installation of an operating system and creation of a virtual machine is beyond the scope of this book. An excellent reference that outlines this process in detail is *Mastering VMware vSphere 5* by Scott Lowe (Sybex, 2011).

WORKING WITH TEMPLATES IN VMWARE VSPHERE

To create a template, follow these steps:

1. Right-click a VM in the Inventory view in either Hosts And Clusters or VMs And Templates. Select the Template menu option.

2. Choose one of the following options:

   ◆ Convert to Template will convert the existing VM to a template, which renders it unbootable. This option is available only if the VM is not running and will generate a template without any additional selections.

   ◆ Clone to Template starts the Clone Virtual Machine To Template Wizard. Follow the rest of these steps if you choose this option.

3. Name the template and choose where it will reside (which datacenter). Click Next.

4. Choose which cluster or hypervisor host you want to store the template on, and then click Next.

5. Choose a datastore and a virtual disk format. This is actually an important decision! The following options are available:

   Same Format As Source   Use the existing virtual disk format from the VM you are cloning to a template.

   Lazy Zeroed Thick   This is the default Virtual Machine Disk (VMDK) type. This disk type allocates all needed space up front and writes random data over any accessed areas the first time a VM tries to access them. This disk type strikes a good balance between performance, efficiency, and security.

Eager Zeroed Thick This disk type is similar to the Lazy Zeroed Thick disk type, but it overwrites all disk space with zeros upon initial creation.

Thin Thin VMDK files are both allocated and zeroed at the time of access, which is very efficient but also consumes more resources in real time. This is the default disk type for VMDKs created on NFS volumes as well as VMDKs created in VMware Workstation.

The options are shown in Figure 8.5.

FIGURE 8.5
Choosing a datastore and virtual disk format

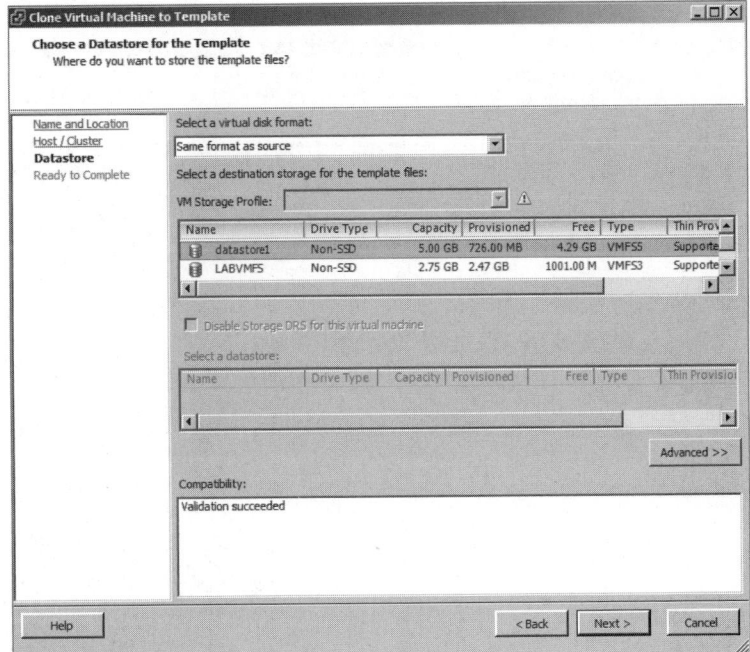

6. Click Next. Make sure everything looks okay, and then click Finish.

Once you have a template created, you have a nonbootable system that cannot be changed until it has been converted to a VM first. To accomplish this, right-click the template, and select Convert To A Virtual Machine. This will change the template back to a VM, and you can then make any changes needed (patch application, configuration changes). Once the VM has been modified, you can convert the VM back into a template.

The other powerful option you have with a VM template is to deploy new VMs directly from the template:

1. Right-click the VM and select Deploy Virtual Machine From This Template, which will open the Deploy Template Wizard.

2. Choose a name and datacenter where the VM will reside. Click Next.

3. Choose a cluster or host. Click Next.

4. Choose a datastore and virtual disk type, and click Next.

5. Decide whether to customize the VM before deployment. Your options are as follows (shown in Figure 8.6):

  ◆ Do Not Customize (skips customization right now)

  ◆ Customize Using The Customization Wizard

  ◆ Customize Using An Existing Customization Specification

FIGURE 8.6
VM customization from a template

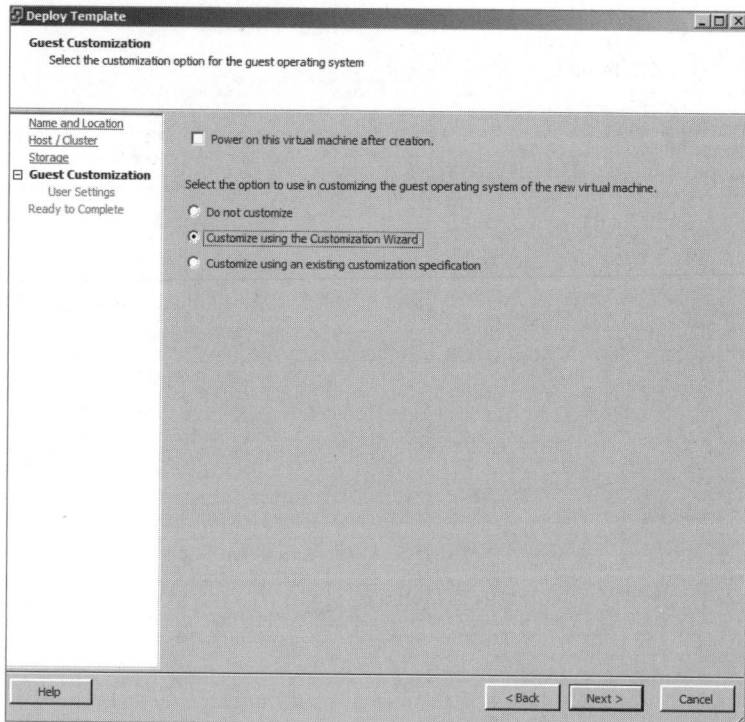

NOTE To customize a VM deployed from a template, VMware will leverage open-source tools for Linux VMs or the sysprep tools from Microsoft. You'll have to install the sysprep tools on your vCenter server beforehand, however. This is also covered in great detail in Scott Lowe's book mentioned earlier, *Mastering VMware vSphere 5*.

6. If you choose to customize a Linux VM with the wizard, you'll see the screen in Figure 8.7. (Windows is somewhat different and is not covered here.) Follow steps 7 through 10.

7. Choose a name and/or domain name and click Next. Choose a time zone and click Next, and then choose virtual network settings. You can select "typical" settings that mimic the

template or enter DHCP or manual addressing, gateways, subnet masks, and so on. When finished, click Next.

FIGURE 8.7

Customizing a Linux VM

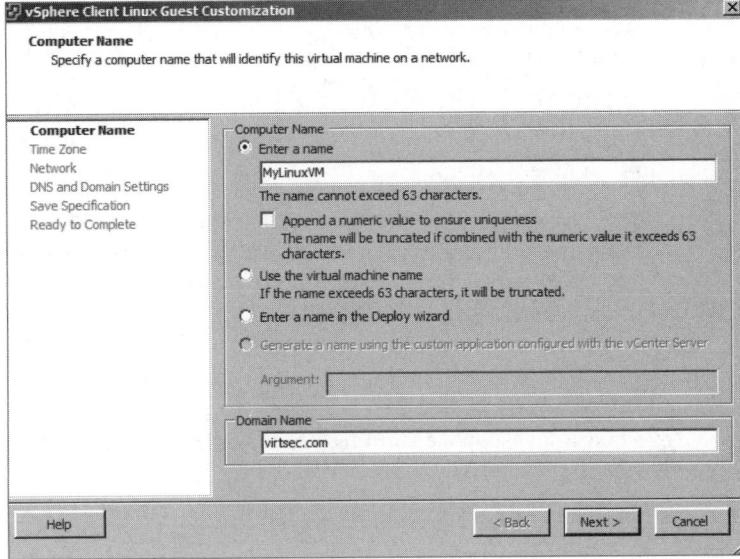

8. On the next screen, choose up to three DNS servers as well as domains to query, as shown in Figure 8.8. Then click Next.

FIGURE 8.8

DNS and domain settings for a template VM deployment

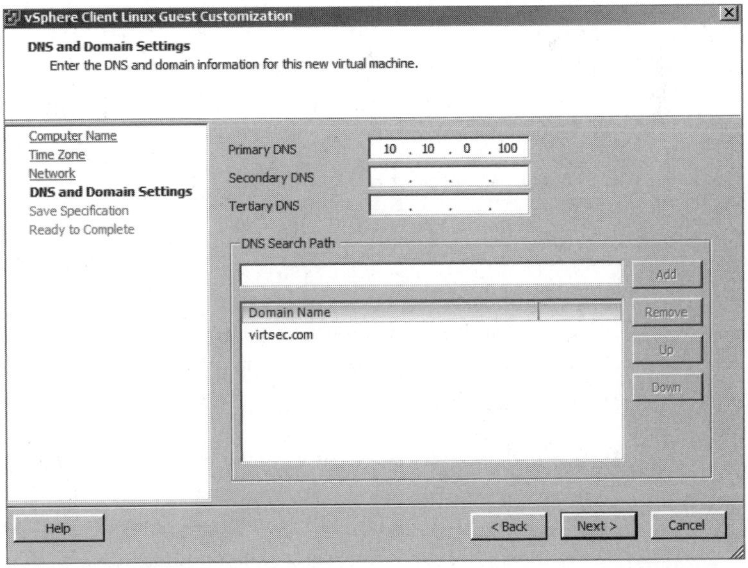

9. You can optionally save this configuration for later VM deployments. If you choose to, provide a name and optional description for the configuration, and then click Next. Ensure that all of your settings are okay and click Finish.

10. You'll be back at the original Deploy Template Wizard. If everything looks okay here, click Finish.

You've now got a new VM running that was created from a template! This is an excellent way to quickly deploy consistent VMs that meet patching and configuration policies and standards in your organization.

TIP You can also deploy VMs from Open Virtualization Format (OVF) templates by selecting the vCenter File menu option and then choosing Deploy OVF Template. This is a format defined by the Distributed Management Task Force (DMTF), and more information can be found here: http://dmtf.org/standards/ovf.

Working with Snapshots in VMware vSphere

To take a snapshot of a running VM in vSphere, right-click the VM and select the Snapshot menu. From here, you have several options:

◆ Take Snapshot: Take a new snapshot of the VM.

◆ Revert To Current Snapshot: Revert to the last snapshot taken; this is a reasonable option for reverting from a change that went awry.

◆ Snapshot Manager: View and manage the existing snapshots for a VM.

◆ Consolidate: Combine VM snapshots in a single image where reasonable (only recommended if storage space for snapshots is becoming an issue).

To create a new snapshot, follow these steps:

1. Right-click a VM in any Inventory screen in vCenter or from the main console in the vSphere Client and select the Snapshot menu. Then click Take Snapshot.

2. Provide a snapshot name and description. You can also choose from two more options.

◆ Snapshot The Virtual Machine's Memory is a good idea if you have ample storage space and want to preserve the contents of memory on the running VM.

◆ Quiesce Guest File System reduces the risk of file corruption during snapshot operations by placing all files into a static state (in other words, freezing any changes during the snapshot operation).

This screen is shown in Figure 8.9.

3. Click OK when finished, and a snapshot will be created.

Creating and Managing Microsoft Hyper-V VM Templates and Snapshots

Before creating a Hyper-V template, you should know that there is no option to generate a template from the VM and preserve the original VM, as you can with VMware. For this reason, you're advised to first create a clone of the VM from which you want to generate a template and then create a template. To do this, right-click a VM in SCVMM, choose Create, and then choose Clone. Follow the wizard to create the clone, and then follow these steps to generate a template:

FIGURE 8.9

Creating a VMware
VM snapshot

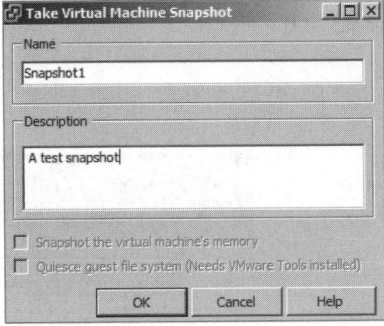

1. Right-click a VM and choose Create. Then choose Create VM Template. You'll be prompted to continue because template creation destroys the original VM. Choose Yes.

2. In the Create VM Template Wizard, enter a VM template name and (optional) description, and then click Next.

3. You can now customize all the hardware for the VM or choose an existing hardware profile, as shown in Figure 8.10. Make your selections and click Next.

FIGURE 8.10

Hyper-V template
customization

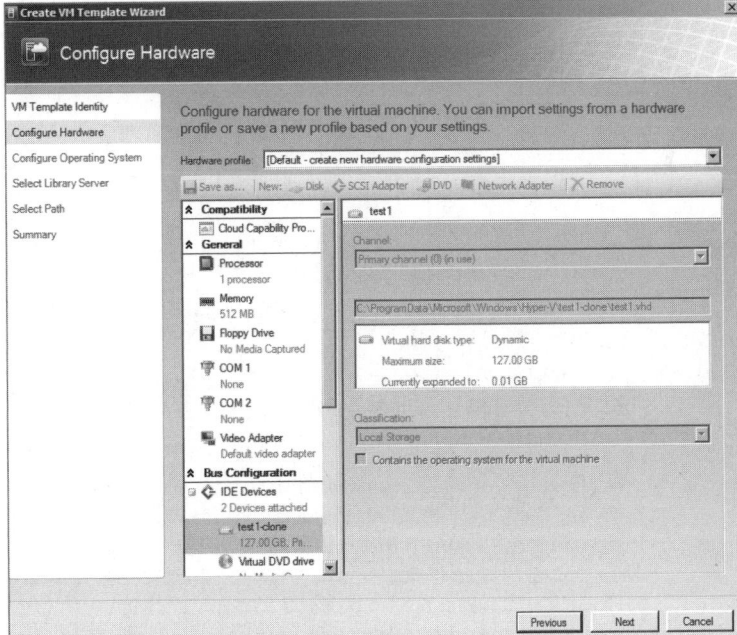

4. Now you can customize the OS if it's a Windows VM and even select roles such as Hyper-V for the new template.

WARNING This differs vastly from Host Profiles in the sense that there's no simple way to compare and assess the hypervisor configuration attributes, so be forewarned!

This set of configuration options is shown in Figure 8.11. Click Next to continue.

FIGURE 8.11
Template OS customization

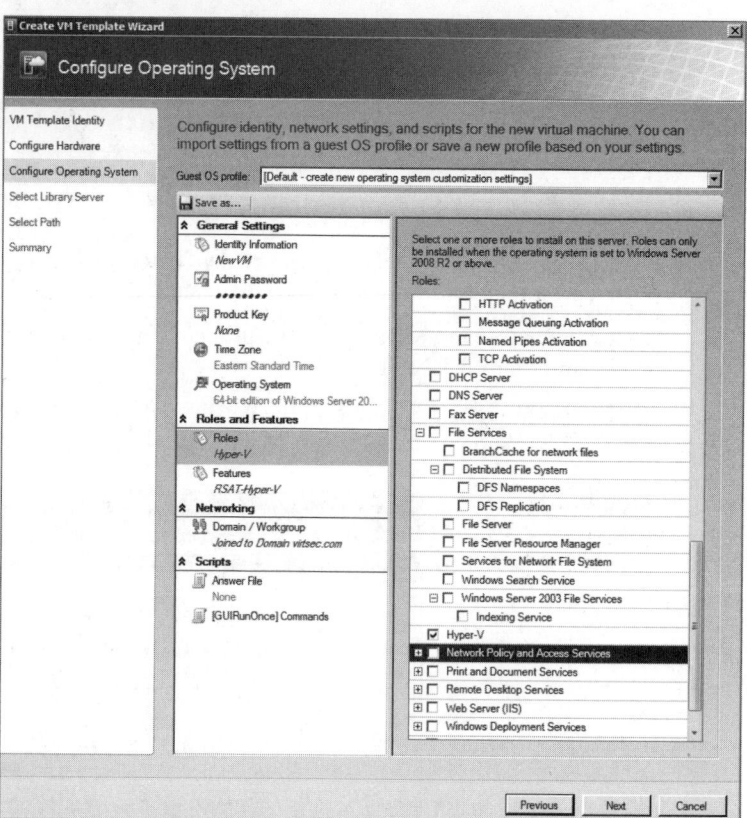

5. Choose a library server, click Next, and finally choose a VM path (for all VMs deployed from the template) in the chosen library. When finished, click Next.

6. Review your selections, and then choose Create. Within the SCVMM console, you should see the template being created. Windows templates that you customize will be generated using the sysprep tool, as shown in Figure 8.12.

These templates can now be used to deploy VMs very simply, much like vSphere VMs.

To create a snapshot with Microsoft Hyper-V, you have two options: Hyper-V Manager and SCVMM 2012.

FIGURE 8.12
Template creation
with sysprep

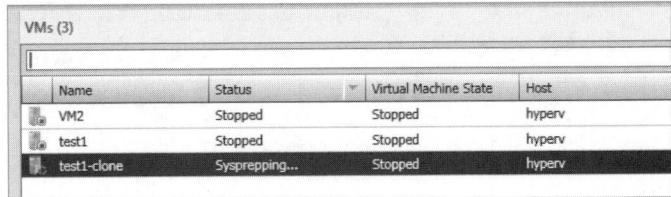

To create a snapshot using the local Hyper-V Manager, right-click a VM in Hyper-V Manager's window and select Snapshot. This will automatically create a snapshot, which will appear in the Snapshots section in the Virtual Machines pane, as shown in Figure 8.13.

FIGURE 8.13
Snapshots on
Hyper-V

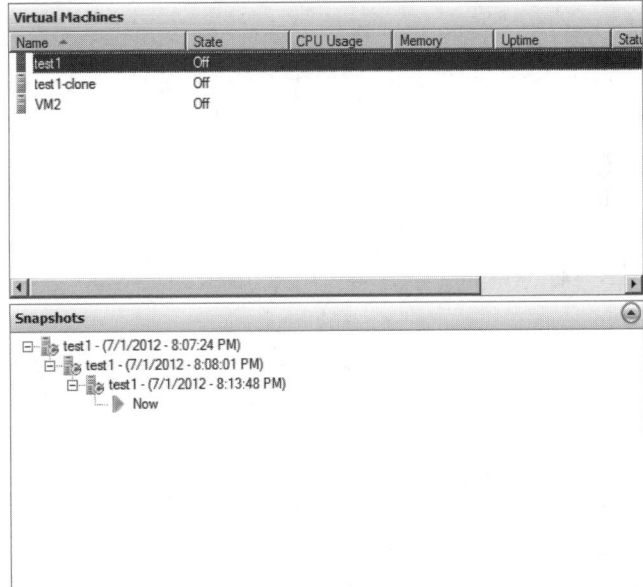

To change the settings of a snapshot in the Hyper-V Manager, right-click the snapshot and select Settings. You can use the same menu to delete the snapshot or its entire subtree.

Snapshots in SCVMM 2012 are called checkpoints. To create a checkpoint in SCVMM, right-click a VM in the Virtual Machine pane and choose the Create Checkpoint option. You will be prompted to enter a name and description for the checkpoint. Click OK when finished.

To manage checkpoints, follow these steps:

1. Right-click a VM and select Manage Checkpoints. A list of checkpoints appears, as shown in Figure 8.14.

2. Select a checkpoint and click the Properties button on the right side. A new window appears.

3. To change the checkpoint's name and description, click the General tab and make the changes you want. To manage particular attributes of the checkpoint, click the Hardware Configuration tab (shown in Figure 8.15).

FIGURE 8.14
SCVMM checkpoint management

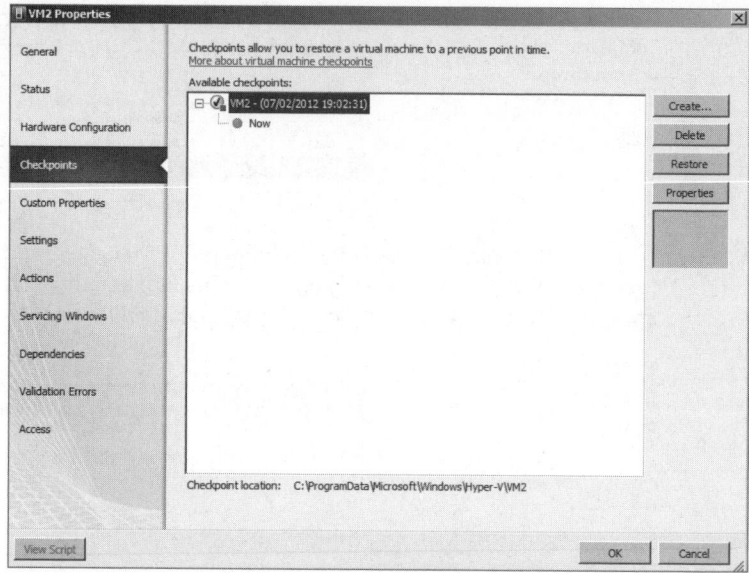

4. When finished making changes, click OK.

FIGURE 8.15
Checkpoint hardware configuration

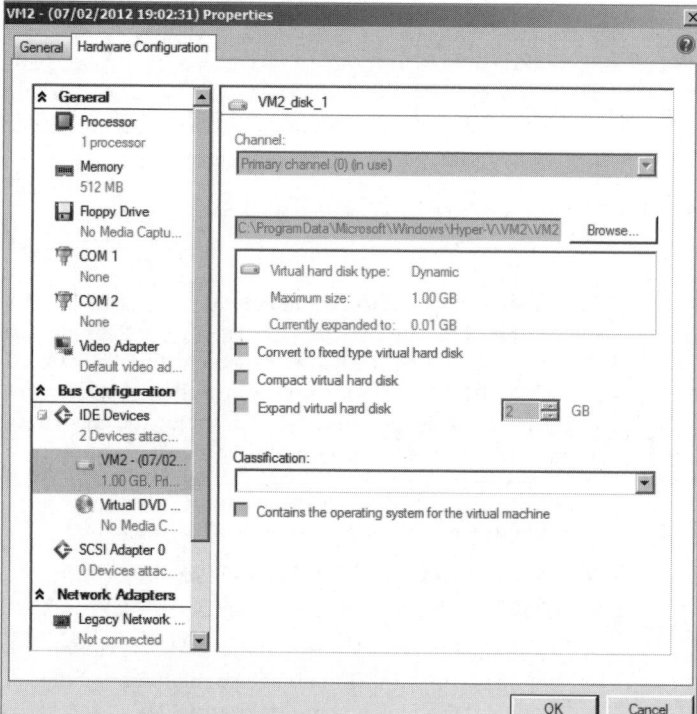

Creating and Managing Citrix XenServer VM Templates and Snapshots

To create a template in XenCenter, you'll need to convert a VM into a template, rendering the original VM unusable as a VM at that point (much like Microsoft environments). So you'll want to create a clone of the VM before creating a template. The process to clone a VM is simple. Right-click the VM in XenCenter, choose Copy VM, and then name the new VM.

You can also select a fast clone or full copy operation. The Fast Clone option just uses the existing disk and replicates the other VM files with a new disk on the storage medium. The Full Copy selection will create true duplicate copies of the VM files, which is preferred.

When you have a copy VM, follow these steps to convert it to a template:

1. Right-click the VM and select Convert To Template. You'll be prompted to make sure you are willing to do this. Select Convert.

2. The VM will be converted, and then will show up in XenCenter with a blue square icon. Right-click this icon to deploy VMs from it.

Just as with the VMware and Microsoft templates, you can generate VMs at will from this template. To deploy VMs from this template, follow these steps:

1. Right-click the template and select New VM Wizard. You'll then be asked to select a template. Choose the one you've created (this is a somewhat redundant step). This is shown in Figure 8.16. Click Next.

FIGURE 8.16
VM creation from a template

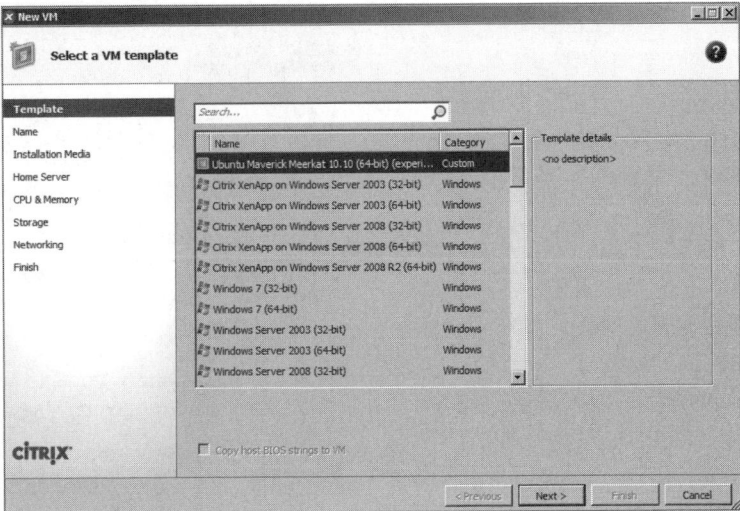

2. Provide a name and description for the VM, and then click Next.

3. Choose any OS installation media and the media's location (DVD drive or other storage area), and then click Next.

4. Choose a home server (preferred XenServer host) or not. Click Next.

5. Specify the number of virtual CPUs (vCPUs) and memory the VM should have, and then click Next.

6. Choose the storage location for the new VM's files and click Next, and then select any networking options you want. Click Next again and then Finish when done.

TIP   An alternative method of creating an exact replica of this template is to right-click it and select Quick Create. This will create a new VM in one step, as long as there are no errors or storage shortages for the files.

To patch or change the template significantly, you'll need to generate a VM, then convert a clone of it (or the new VM itself) to a new template.

Creating snapshots with XenServer is a breeze. Within XenCenter, follow these steps:

1. Right-click a VM and select Take A Snapshot.

2. Enter a name and description for the snapshot. Choose whether to take a snapshot of just the VM disk (and also quiescing the disk if it's a Windows VM) or of both the disk and memory. These options are shown in Figure 8.17.

FIGURE 8.17
Taking a XenServer
VM snapshot

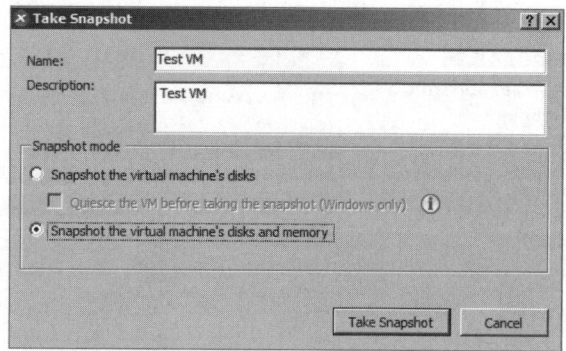

3. Once you have a snapshot or set of snapshots, you can see them in the Snapshots pane on XenCenter's right-hand side when you highlight a VM, as shown in Figure 8.18.

4. If you highlight the snapshot and then select the Actions menu, you can choose to generate a new VM from the snapshot, save the snapshot as a new template, or export the snapshot to a file. This file is stored in XVA format, which is the XenServer virtual appliance format, based on OVF.

FIGURE 8.18
Viewing XenServer
snapshots

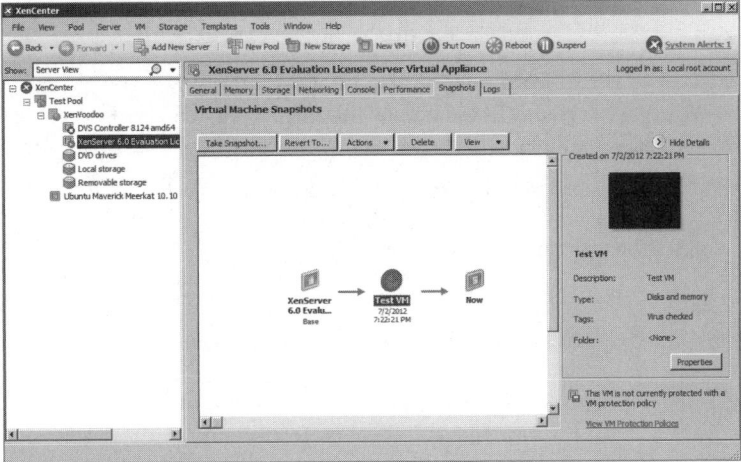

Integrating Virtualization into Change and Management

With the ever-changing environment and complexity of virtualization, effective change management can become more difficult. With virtualization technology, IT can create a virtual machine within a matter of minutes. In self-provisioning scenarios, which are common in private cloud implementations, the end users are able to self-provision a virtual machine, which could easily create a headache for administrators and security teams if not monitored and managed effectively. In either case, because VMs can be quickly and easily deployed, as well as moved or suspended, the organization can quickly lose track of how many VMs are in use, how many application licenses are being used, and which configuration images they came from.

As an example of a virtualization-specific change scenario, when trying to predict change impact, virtualization requires more in-depth analysis of technology in use due to the interactions between those technologies (as discussed earlier in the chapter in the section "Change and Configuration Management Overview"). The following questions are among those operations teams might need to ask:

- What is the supporting infrastructure for the IT service in use within the virtual environment?

- How can the organization restore services after a change was made in a virtual environment? Can snapshots be reverted? Which VMs need to be restored?

- What hypervisor host, VM, storage, and networking are needed to support critical applications such as customer relationship management (CRM) solutions, middleware, and financials?

♦ How will a VM migration or patching cycle affect the organization's service delivery and compliance posture?

♦ Since networking and storage are managed by groups that are different from those in charge of the virtual infrastructure, who is responsible for approving the change and implementing the change, because it impacts all of these?

To properly ensure that virtualization is integrated into change management tickets, you should create new categories or configuration item listings in your change ticketing solution for the following, at a minimum:

♦ For virtualization hypervisor platforms and management tools:

  ♦ Updates/upgrades to OS, application, database or hardware

  ♦ Addition/modification of objects

  ♦ New/modified users, groups, and roles

♦ For VMs:

  ♦ Deployment/modification/deletion of VM

  ♦ Change in life cycle stage

  ♦ Movement of VM to new host

♦ For virtual networks:

  ♦ Adding/deleting/modifying virtual switches

  ♦ Modifying VLANs, trunks, and so on

  ♦ Network properties (for example, promiscuous mode)

♦ For VM templates:

  ♦ Generation of a new template from a VM

  ♦ Conversion or cloning to a VM for changes

  ♦ Reconversion of a VM back to a template after changes

This is a reasonable starting point, but you'll likely want to add your own varieties to these.

Additional Solutions and Tools

This chapter serves as a brief overview of how virtualization infrastructure ties into configuration and change management processes you have in place. To that end, I've really only illustrated some of the native capabilities and tools that the leading vendors have in place, but many organizations will need more robust capabilities than these can provide. There are a few tools available that may be useful.

VMware has steadily increased its configuration management capabilities since 2009, when it acquired the assets of a company called Configuresoft that was first purchased by its parent company, EMC. (Full disclosure: I was the chief security officer (CSO) at Configuresoft when it was acquired.) Configuresoft had a number of powerful configuration tools specifically focused on the virtual environment, and these have now been integrated and enhanced in the form of VMware vCenter Configuration Manager. This product, depending on the licensing model you choose, can help to configure and manage both ESXi and VM images, with extensive compliance and reporting capabilities as well. More on this product can be found here:

`www.vmware.com/products/configuration-manager/overview.html`

For Microsoft environments, organizations will likely want to take a look at Microsoft System Center 2012 Configuration Manager (SCCM), perhaps in conjunction with System Center Virtual Machine Manager. While SCCM is a bit more focused on OS and application controls, virtual machine images can be assessed and managed as well. More information is available at Microsoft's site:

`www.microsoft.com/en-us/server-cloud/system-center/configuration-manager-2012.aspx`

Chapter 9

Disaster Recovery and Business Continuity

Virtualization can play a big role in disaster recovery (DR) and business continuity planning (BCP) operations. There are several aspects to this. First, you have tools and controls available within the virtual infrastructure to allow High Availability and continuity to occur. This includes clustering, resource pooling, and various features provided by hypervisor manufacturers. The second major aspect to availability and DR/BCP involves leveraging virtualization explicitly for this purpose; in other words, changing your continuity strategy to include virtualization, and there are advantages to doing this (as well as new challenges).

This chapter will delve into some of the ways that virtualization administrators can make their virtual environments more durable and available and also takes a look at some of the ways virtualization plays into the larger scheme of DR and BCP.

In this chapter, you will learn about the following topics:

◆ The fundamentals of disaster recovery and business continuity

◆ High Availability features with VMware vSphere, Microsoft Hyper-V, and Citrix XenServer

◆ Ways that virtualization can lead to new DR/BCP strategies, with considerations for networking and datacenter operations

Disaster Recovery and Business Continuity Today

The goal of disaster recovery (DR) and business continuity planning (BCP) is to be prepared for a variety of disruptive events and have a set of controls and procedures in place to recover an organization to a point of full or reduced capacity. This will generally involve multiple recovery plans. For instance, you will have different plans and actions defined for a lengthy power outage, an earthquake, and a pandemic.

What does this have to do with virtualization? First of all, if you have service-level agreements (SLAs) with your user or customer community (particularly in the case of a private cloud), you've made a commitment to have a disaster recovery plan so that even in the event of a disaster you can meet your service objectives.

NOTE   SLAs are formal or informal definitions of a level of service, often focused around uptime and availability. They can also focus on security processes like incident response and incident notification.

Second, the hardware abstraction associated with virtualization can make recovery easier, and the complexity in recovery processes related to matching hardware in primary and secondary sites can be simplified in some cases with a properly designed virtual environment.

The tools for creating VM checkpoints and snapshots, and performing replication and image backups, are built into virtualization platforms and toolkits. Many commercial products are available to provide additional capabilities. Replication products and free scripts for replication are readily available and often integrate with storage platforms.

Today, most businesses will engage in planning exercises and processes that lay out what types of DR/BCP strategies they want to adhere to. The first thing organizations will need to do is identify business and technical services, data, systems, and applications that are essential to the operation of the business. There can be a temptation to include "everything," but this isn't usually realistic unless you're a smaller organization with fewer assets. Then, the following metrics will need to be defined:

- Maximum tolerable outage (MTO): How long can services remain offline before business continuity fails?

- Recovery time objective (RTO): How soon must systems and services be recovered?

- Recovery point objective (RPO): At what point is data too old to recover gracefully?

- Work recovery time (WRT): How long will it take to get things running smoothly again once initial recovery is underway and critical systems are operational?

Once these metrics are in place, your organization will need to define how long you are capable of maintaining the organization in a limited capacity while leveraging DR systems and resources. Business priorities should be taken into account first, which will require discussions with business leaders and allocation of budget. Then, of course, you'll need to pick a DR site.

NOTE   A DR site is a facility that hosts backup and redundant systems in the case of an emergency. Many organizations leverage DR site companies that run entire DR-focused datacenters for multiple clients. Some organizations build a dedicated facility of their own for this purpose, but that is expensive.

As this is not intended to be a general treatise on DR/BCP, I won't cover more on DR sites here, but if you're looking into traditional DR providers like Sungard, you'll likely find that they support or plan to support full virtual machine backup and DR strategies with varying degrees of flexibility.

There are many sources of guidance for developing DR metrics and planning strategies, and a great starting place for those who would like to join a DR-focused online community is www.drplanning.org/portal/.

Shared Storage and Replication

Since virtualization technologies almost always make use of large-scale shared storage environments, most organizations will seek to perform some sort of storage area network (SAN) replication between the primary datacenter and a backup location, using either native storage tools or virtualization-compatible tools. There are several options for doing this:

SAN replication   Native SAN replication tools and software are available from most leading storage vendors. For example, EMC offers several solutions:

- MirrorView replicates SAN data across IP and Fibre Channel networks.

- ◆ Replication Manager can perform data discovery and device management and provide centralized control over the entire SAN replication process for DR scenarios.

- ◆ SAN Copy specifically allows data replication between EMC storage devices.

Netapp, another leading storage provider, offers SnapMirror Data Replication solutions for DR data migration between sites.

These are just examples, but if you can accommodate the networking architecture that allows high-speed data replication of this nature, most organizations will find SAN replication to be the best option. Understand, however, that this is also likely to be an *expensive* option due to the networking you'll need to provision and the new equipment and software needed.

Native virtualization replication options   If SAN replication is not an option due to architecture or bandwidth constraints, replication applications for the native hypervisor platforms are commonly employed. For VMware, most of these tools use the native Changed Block Tracking (CBT) feature in VMware vSphere (available in ESX4 and later). When CBT is enabled, virtual machines are able to monitor and track disk sectors that are changed and in use. Veeam and Quest Software make separate applications that leverage this feature, and Arkeia Software makes the same kind of app for Microsoft Hyper-V. VMware's Site Recovery Manager (SRM) product is also commonly leveraged for managing the DR processes and functions within the VMware infrastructure, and includes WAN-based replication as well. PHD Virtual Backup and Replication provides these capabilities for Citrix XenServer.

Tape backup and restore   Although decidedly less sophisticated than the previous two options, tape and disk backups are sufficient for some organizations' DR procedures using offsite storage facilities.

In addition to the replication tools for data, the replication path between datacenters needs to be evaluated for cost, flexibility, and speeds. There are a number of options for data replication paths. Paths for replication may include dark fiber or existing WAN connectivity with or without VPN tunnels. Dark fiber is a dedicated fiber link that can be used when needed and is much faster than most other options. Dark fiber is fairly expensive, however, and many organizations may look for cheaper options like traditional Multiprotocol Label Switching (MPLS) or dedicated leased circuits.

Replication schedules need to be determined. This is much easier with dedicated dark fiber connectivity because you can test anytime and always have your own dedicated connection but it can be managed with traditional rate-limiting tools and techniques for traditional WAN connectivity too. Common tools like Quality of Service (QoS) can help shape traffic for replication, allowing for easier scheduling, and built-in tools from storage hardware providers like Dell EqualLogic can allow for hardware-based data flow control. The key is to ensure that round-trip replication falls within the DR metrics determined during the planning phases.

Regardless of your replication strategy, you need to think about the security of your data traffic. This is less of an issue if you own the fiber connection, but it warrants consideration in all scenarios, particularly those involving WAN connectivity using VPN or other conduits. For DR plans leveraging tapes and disks, you'll need to evaluate the security at your offsite provider, if you use one. You'll also want to determine how restoration and backup scenarios factor into your recovery metrics. For example, tapes tend to be slower from both a replication and process standpoint. Will tapes be able to restore your data quickly enough?

Organizations that intend to include virtualization in their DR strategies will also need to evaluate network architecture options for the path between datacenters. In particular, there is a lot of interest in extending Layer 2 over the WAN, which allows for operations like vMotion and dynamic migration of VMs without the need for new Layer 3 addressing or access control modifications. There are lots of options emerging to support this kind of connectivity, although not all are inexpensive and some are proprietary. If dark fiber is connected, organizations can extend existing network VLANs to the backup datacenter and minimize the amount of configuration needed on both sides.

Over a typical Layer 3 WAN, there are a few tunneling protocols such as Layer 2 Tunneling Protocol version 3 (L2TPv3) to extend VLANs between datacenters. For organizations leveraging MPLS, protocols such as Ethernet over MPLS (EoMPLS) or Virtual Private VLAN Service (VPLS) can help in the design and implementation. There are also several proprietary Layer 2 over Layer 3 protocols emerging. One of the most talked about is Cisco's Overlay Transport Virtualization (OTV), which supports much higher throughput and efficiency than L2TPv3 and other protocols but requires high-end Cisco gear like Nexus 7000 platforms on both sides.

Regardless of what connectivity method you employ, you need to thoroughly plan routing and access control provisioning for this kind of data transfer and then test extensively. In addition, when setting up WAN VM replication, keep in mind that initial replication can take a long time (sometimes days or weeks). Performing the initial replication in the same physical location (before moving to a DR site) can help speed up the process, or you can use some sort of portable media.

Once the initial VM is replicated, ongoing VM replication times will vary between 5 and 15 minutes depending on size and activity of the virtualization platform. Your organization should also have a detection and response plan for handling problems with the replication process. If the replication services fail, or some other errors occur, alerts should be generated and response efforts undertaken as soon as possible. Replication logging is also critical. Logs of replication failures or other issues should be monitored and alerts sent immediately, if possible.

Virtualization Redundancy and Fault Tolerance for DR/BCP

All of the major virtualization providers offer several key functions that that can greatly facilitate backups, continuity, and even DR plans. I've mentioned several tools like VMware Site Recovery Manager, but they won't be covered in detail here — we're sticking to the fundamental platforms and infrastructure. All of the platforms covered in this book, however, have several core availability features:

- ◆ Host clustering: Hypervisors need to be placed into highly available and scalable configurations in order to balance resources and maintain continuity of virtualization services.

- ◆ Resource pools: Virtual machines hosted on hypervisor platforms will need to draw from a pool of defined resources, including memory and CPU.

- ◆ High Availability and Fault Tolerance: All the platforms have some variety of High Availability features to allow VMs and/or hosts to be redundant and available.

Clustering

Setting up clusters is one of the most fundamental aspects of administering a virtual datacenter. In essence, a cluster allows you to have a failover and load balancing setup for your virtual environment so that no single hypervisor host bears too much of the burden of operational overhead. Setting up resource pools and more advanced availability features also require the use of clusters, making this a mandatory configuration step in your availability strategy. There are many nuances to clusters, depending on the platform involved, and I'll focus on the core techniques you need to know to set up an available infrastructure.

CLUSTERING WITH VMWARE VSPHERE

To set up a cluster with VMware vSphere, you'll need to have a working installation of vCenter set up. Log into your vCenter console using the vSphere Client, and then follow these steps:

1. Navigate to the Inventory, Hosts And Clusters screen in the vCenter console. Right-click an existing datacenter and select New Cluster. This opens the New Cluster Wizard (see Figure 9.1).

FIGURE 9.1

Creating a new vSphere cluster

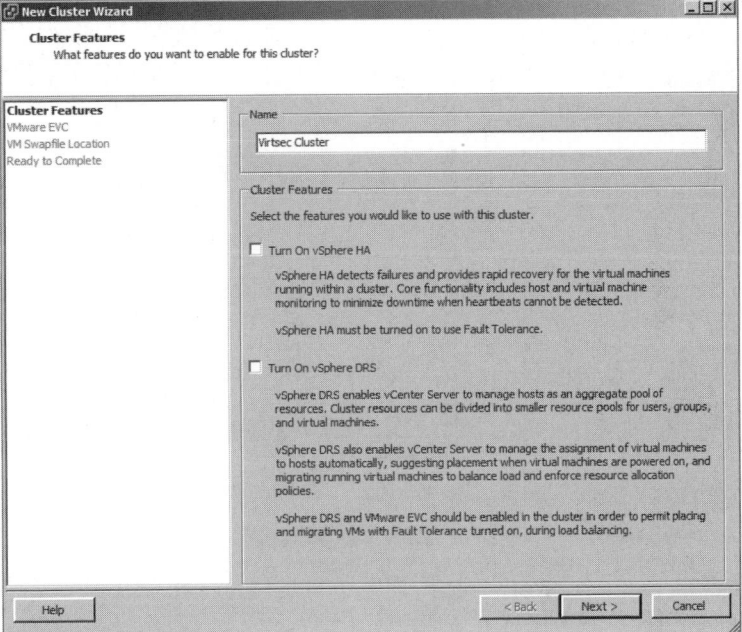

You'll also have options to turn on vSphere HA and vSphere DRS, which will be covered in the section "Resource Pools with VMware vSphere" later in this chapter.

2. Click Next, and then choose an option for Enhanced vMotion Compatibility (EVC). This feature attempts to set configuration controls around hypervisor host chipset compatibility to maximize the likelihood of successful virtual operations like vMotion, where VM memory is dynamically migrated between cluster members. You can select between three options. The first, Disabled, is self-explanatory. If you want to enable EVC, select the option for your chip vendor (AMD or Intel). Once you select one of these options, you can choose a specific type of AMD or Intel chip that you have standardized on (standardizing on a specific chip will allow for more compatible operations). This is shown in Figure 9.2.

3. Click Next, and then choose whether to store each VM's swapfile with the other VM files or in a separate location on a datastore. I recommend keeping the swapfile with the VM unless you have specific business or architecture reasons not to; this simplifies management of all the VM's related files because they're in one place. This is shown in Figure 9.3.

4. Click Next, review your options, and then click Finish.

FIGURE 9.2
Setting up vSphere
EVC

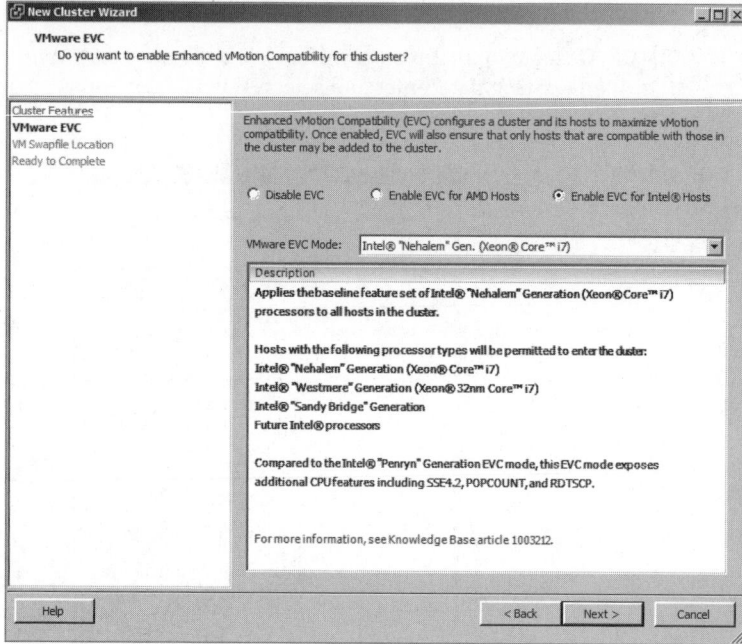

FIGURE 9.3
Choosing the swap-
file location

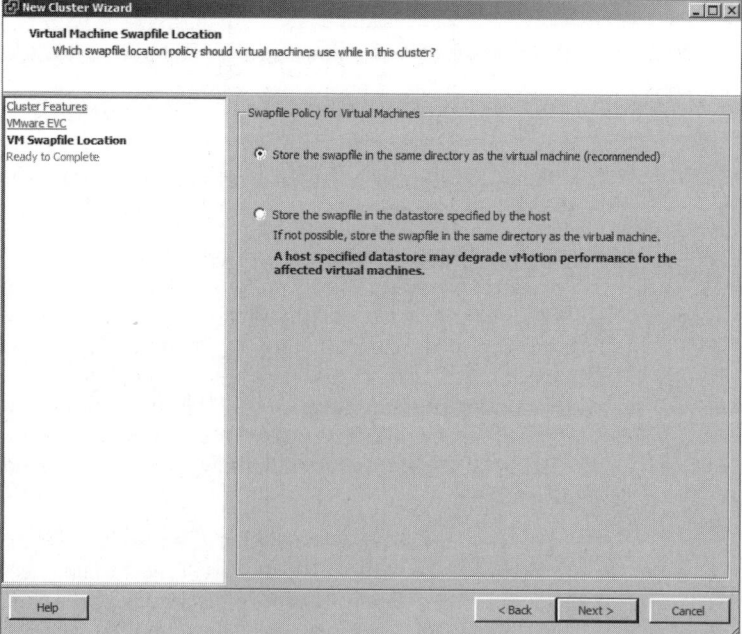

To add hosts to a cluster, you can either drag-and-drop existing hosts into the cluster object in the vCenter screen or right-click the cluster and choose Add Host. An example of a simple cluster with hosts added is shown in Figure 9.4.

FIGURE 9.4
A Simple vSphere cluster

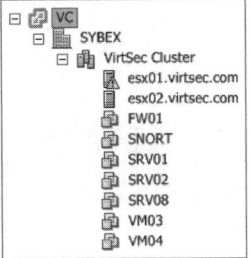

At any time, you can right-click a cluster object and select Edit Settings to add DRS or HA capabilities, which we'll do shortly.

CLUSTERING WITH MICROSOFT HYPER-V

In this section, we'll walk through creating a cluster within System Center Virtual Machine Manager 2012. Follow these steps:

1. Select the Fabric tab on the left-hand menu bar.

2. Click the Create button in the top menu bar, and choose Hyper-V Cluster from the drop-down menu that appears.

3. You'll now be presented with the Create Cluster Wizard. On this first screen, you can enter the name of the cluster and credentials for adding Hyper-V hosts to the cluster, as shown in Figure 9.5.

FIGURE 9.5
SCVMM Create Cluster Wizard

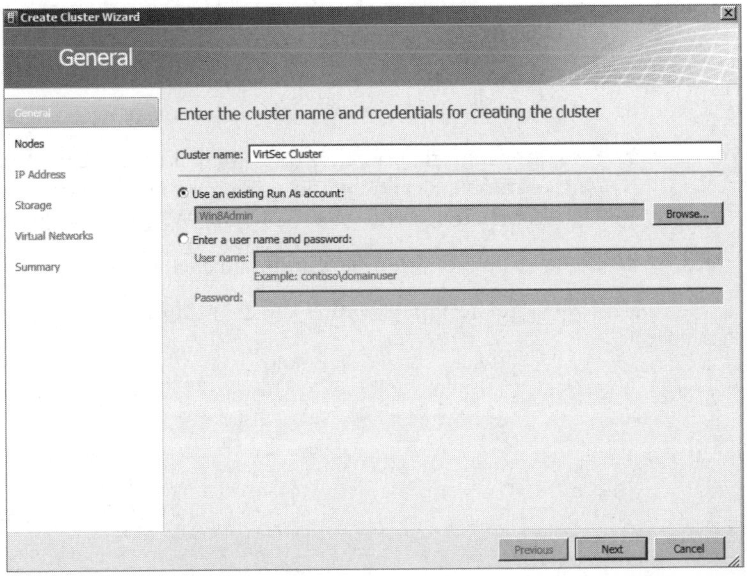

4. Click Next, and choose the host group you want to place the cluster in as well as any available hosts within the host group. At the bottom of the screen, there is an option labeled Skip Cluster Validation Tests. This bypasses all the standard validation checks that Microsoft performs when adding hosts to a cluster and should be left unchecked in most cases. If you have other configuration management tools for assessing the state of cluster hosts, not selecting this check box may be a reasonable option to save time and processing overhead. This screen is shown in Figure 9.6.

FIGURE 9.6

Adding hosts to a Hyper-V cluster

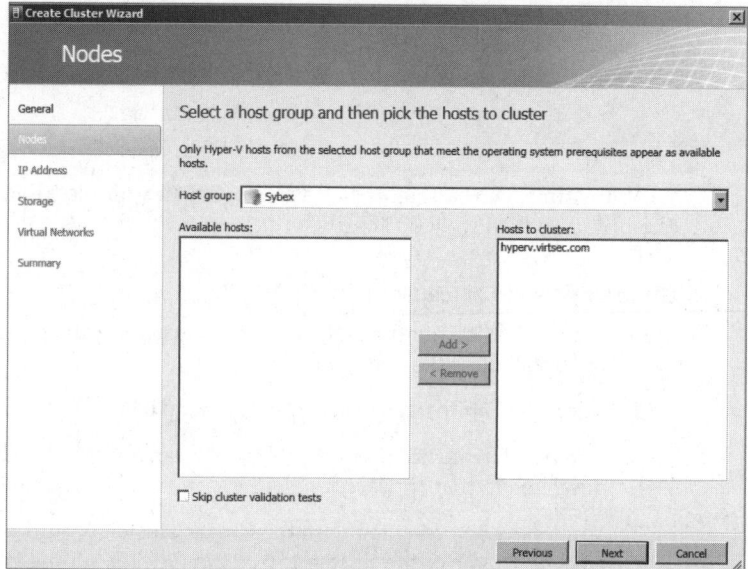

5. Click Next. You'll now be prompted to enter a cluster IP address (or addresses). This allows the cluster to be specifically contacted using this virtual address, as shown in Figure 9.7. Click Next.

6. Select any disks that you would like to cluster. Click Next.

7. Select any logical networks you want to add for generating new external networks for the cluster (these logical networks will create new external networks to allow physical network connectivity to cluster members). When finished, click Next.

8. Review your configuration, and then click Finish.

Now we've got a simple Hyper-V cluster set up.

FIGURE 9.7
Adding a cluster IP address or address pool

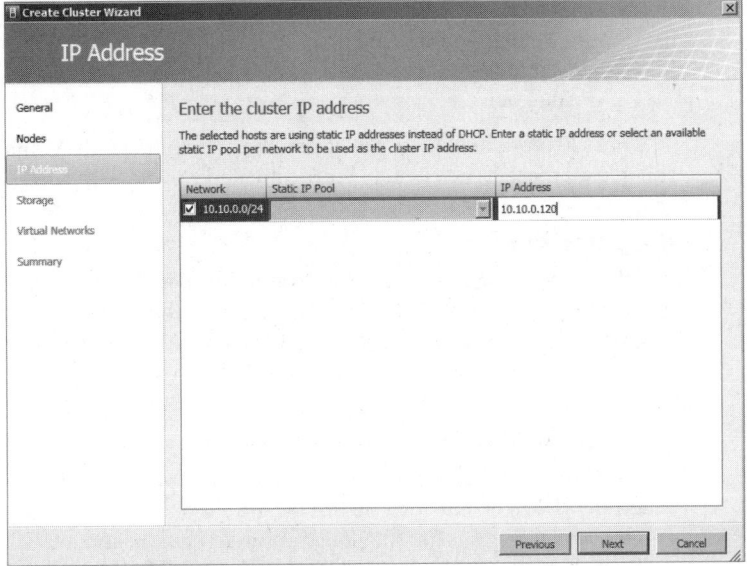

CLUSTERING WITH CITRIX XENSERVER

Setting up a XenServer cluster in XenCenter is a simple task, much like the operations with vSphere and SCVMM. A cluster configuration in XenCenter is essentially another option associated with a defined pool, so that's where you'll need to start. Open XenCenter, and then follow these steps:

1. Click the Pool menu at the top and select New Pool. You'll be presented with the Create New Pool dialog box, shown in Figure 9.8.

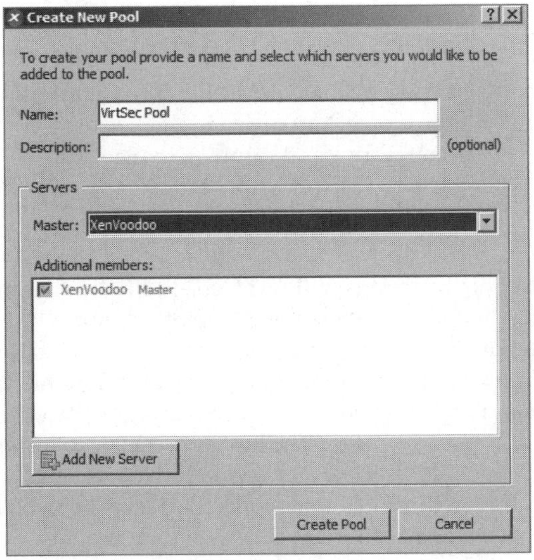

FIGURE 9.8
Creating a new XenServer pool

2. Enter a name and description (optional) for the pool, and choose a master XenServer. This is extremely important because the master will then set the configuration for the pool (although you can change this later). Add any additional XenServer hosts, and then click Create Pool.

That's it! Now, of course, you'll need to add some High Availability policies and other features to all these basic clusters you've created.

Resource Pools

Another core concept for virtualization redundancy and availability is resource pools. Resource pools allow multiple VMs to share resources with defined rules on how they can access and leverage RAM, CPU, and other virtualized physical resources. Ensuring that resource pools are properly set up and administered is a major factor in successful virtualization management.

RESOURCE POOLS WITH VMWARE VSPHERE

To create resource pools with VMware vSphere, you'll need to enable the Distributed Resource Scheduler (DRS) on clusters. Before taking a look at resource pools, let's look at the configuration options for DRS and what they mean from a security and availability perspective.

To enable DRS, right-click a cluster and choose Edit Settings. Then follow these steps:

1. On the initial screen labeled Cluster Features, check the Turn On vSphere DRS check box. When you do this, a number of other options become available under the vSphere DRS heading. Click vSphere DRS in the left-hand tree menu.

2. This initial screen asks you to select the DRS automation level. You can choose from the following options:

   ◆ Manual: All VM dynamic operations must be set in motion manually by an administrator.

   ◆ Partially Automated: VMs will be automatically hosted on hypervisor platforms based on VMware's analysis of resource balancing, and any further dynamic operations will need to be performed manually.

   ◆ Fully Automated: VMs will be dynamically migrated where VMware thinks it's appropriate. You can tune this setting with the slider, choosing a range between Conservative and Aggressive. The more aggressive, the more resource churn your cluster will experience because VMware will move VMs when even a slight improvement is possible. This screen is shown in Figure 9.9.

Most organizations will want to select Fully Automated with a medium level of migration threshold. The Fully Automated option allows VMware to dynamically manage the migration process, helping to automate your virtualization and private cloud environment and remove the need for manual involvement and human error. As mentioned, a medium level of migration threshold is usually a reasonable balance between resource consumption and too much resource churn. The best approach is to test this in a lab and see what is most appropriate, or start with a very conservative level and then gradually increase until you reach a migration threshold that works for you. When you have selected your options, click OK to move to the next option, DRS Groups Manager.

3. By defining virtual machine groups (groups of VMs you want to categorize together) and host groups (hypervisor platforms in the cluster that you want to categorize together), you can more easily set up resource-based rules about how they interact and tie those rules into rules for DRS dynamic operations. Create any groups you would like, and add VMs and hosts, respectively. This is shown in Figure 9.10.

FIGURE 9.9
DRS Automation Level settings

FIGURE 9.10
DRS groups

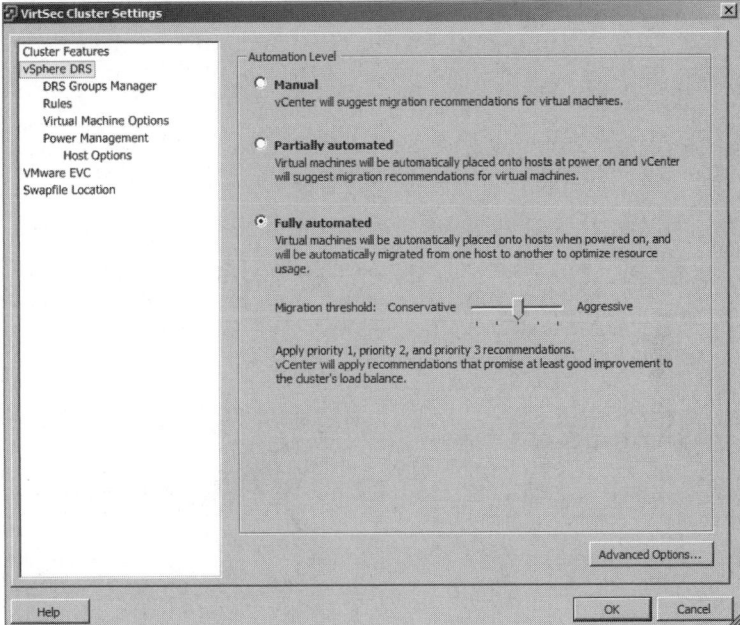

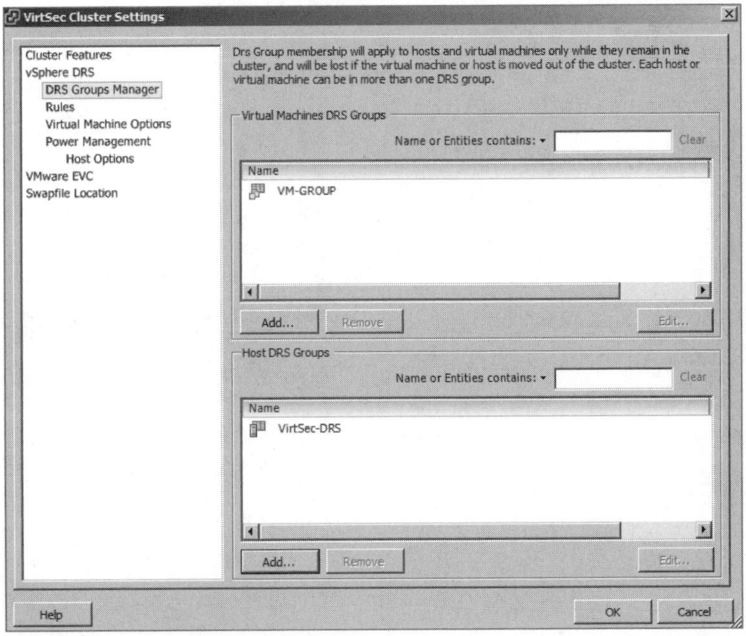

4. Move to the next section, Rules. Click the Add button to add a new DRS rule. In a new screen, add a rule by giving it a name and type. In the Type field, choose one of the following options:

    ◆ Keep Virtual Machines Together: Groups VMs and makes sure they stay together during dynamic operations

    ◆ Separate Virtual Machines: Keeps VMs away from one another (for example, if they are of different data classification or sensitivity levels).

    ◆ Virtual Machines To Hosts: Binds a VM to a hypervisor platform.

5. Create any rules you would like, such as the one shown in Figure 9.11, where VMs with a similar data sensitivity level are grouped together.

6. When finished, click OK.

7. Next is Virtual Machine Options. Choose specific VMs based on strings in their names, and then select automation levels for them: Fully Automated, Partially Automated, Manual, Default, or Disabled. See Figure 9.12.

FIGURE 9.11
Creating a DRS rule

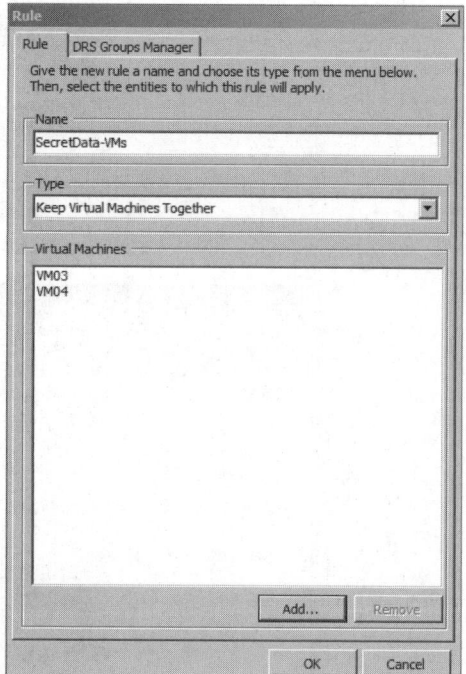

FIGURE 9.12
Virtual machine
automation level
options in DRS

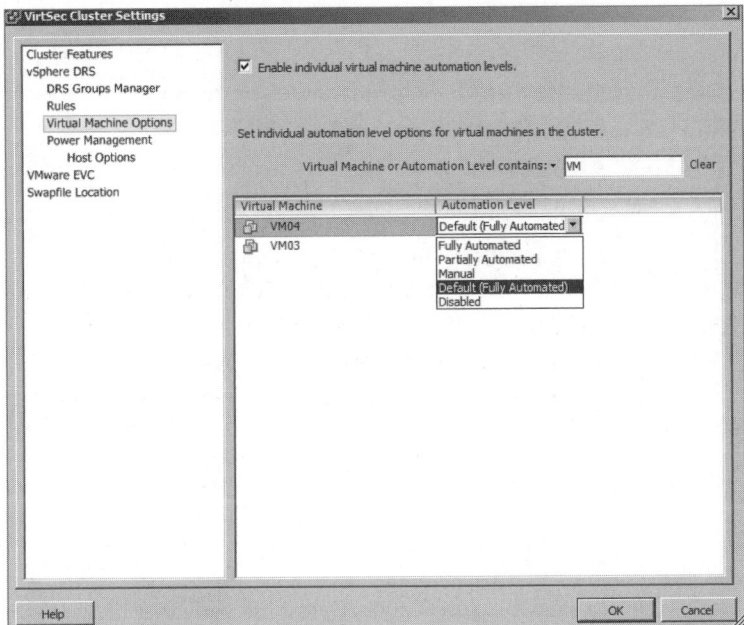

8. The next option is Power Management, which allows you to configure a vSphere feature called Distributed Power Management, or DPM. Choose from the following (these options are shown in Figure 9.13):

FIGURE 9.13
Power Management
options

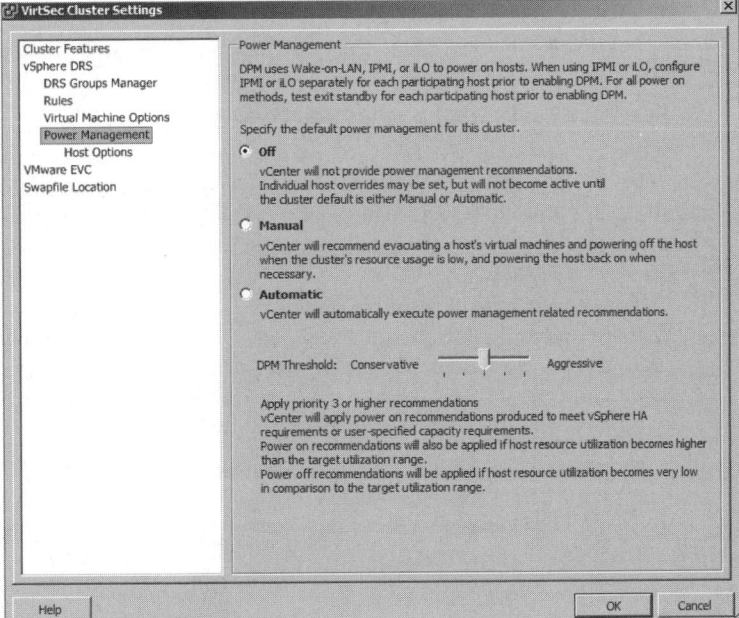

- Off: vCenter won't advise you regarding power conditions or manage power in the cluster.

- Manual: vSphere will advise you when you may want to shut down a cluster host and move VMs to other hosts to save power.

- Automatic: Allow vSphere to manage power to the cluster.

9. Click the final DRS-related option, Host Options.

10. Much like the Virtual Machine Options settings, where individual VM automation levels could be configured (in step 7), this allows you to configure individual DPM options for hypervisor hosts. Make your selections and click OK.

Now that you have DRS and/or DPM options in place, you can configure resource pools. This is actually fairly simple. Right-click your cluster, select New Resource Pool, and then configure the following options:

- Name

- Shares: Maximum amount of resources that a single VM can take in the pool.

- Reservation: Individual amount reserved for the pool.

- Expandable Reservation: Determines whether the pool can take CPU or memory from its parent.

- Limit: Upper limit for CPU or memory allocation for the pool. Many organizations set this to Unlimited, which allows the pool to allocate as many resources as it possibly can. Be careful though! This can overtax the pool's resources, causing unwanted migration activity and availability failures if not monitored.

These options are shown in Figure 9.14.

Now you can add VMs to the pool and they'll be governed by the defined policies.

RESOURCE POOLS WITH MICROSOFT HYPER-V

With SCVMM 2012 and Hyper-V, you can create three distinct types of resource pools as part of a cloud/virtualization fabric. We've already created a simple cluster with Hyper-V hosts, which allows for hosts to be grouped together. They can also be grouped simply in host groups, which don't provide clustering capabilities, but Hyper-V hosts are placed in a pool, or container, that groups like systems.

The second type of resource pool with SCVMM is the network pool. You can create two types of network pools: IP address pools and MAC address pools. These are used to create a redundant and available virtual network with Hyper-V and can also be used as simple virtual load balancers.

To create a virtual IP address pool, follow these steps:

1. On the Fabric tab, click the Create button on the top menu and select IP Pool.

2. You'll see the Create Static IP Address Pool Wizard. Enter the pool name and optional description, and then select the defined logical network where the pool should be created, as shown in Figure 9.15. Click Next.

FIGURE 9.14

A new resource pool

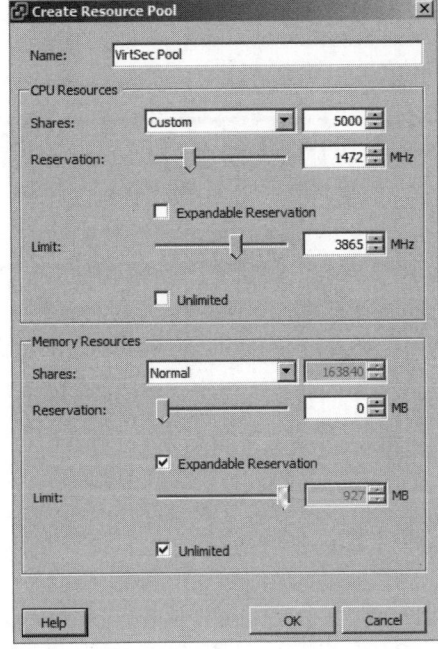

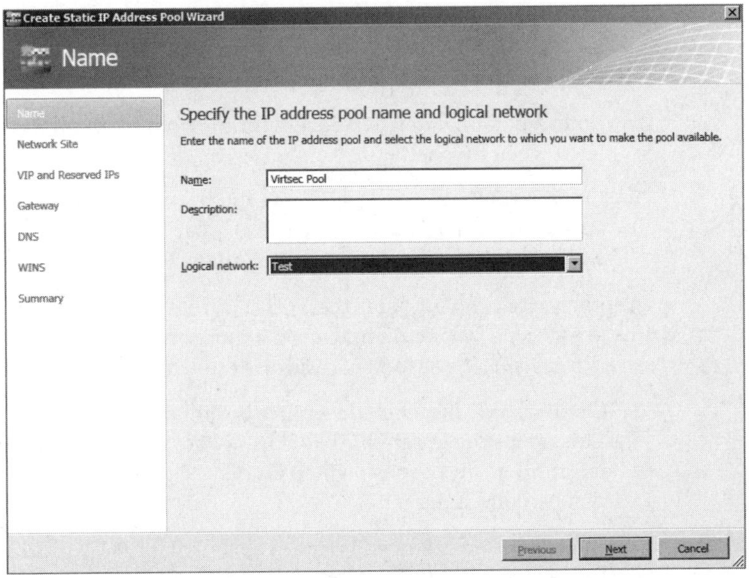

FIGURE 9.15

Creating a static IP
address pool

3. Select a network site to use with the pool. This is a logical network you've created that has a subnet associated with it already. You can also create a new site on this screen, shown in Figure 9.16.

FIGURE 9.16
Allocating a network site

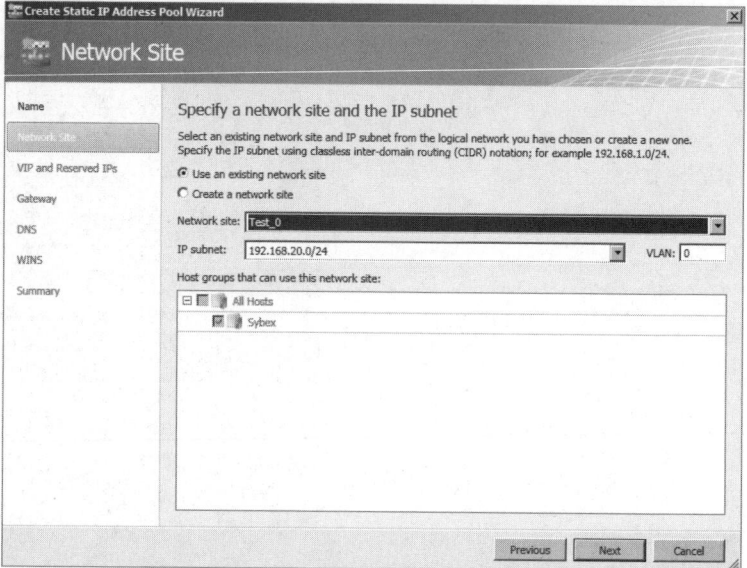

4. Choose the network IP range to be managed in this pool. You can also enter IP addresses to be used as virtual IPs (VIPs) by load balancers, and reserved IPs that aren't allocated in the pool, as shown in Figure 9.17. Click Next.

5. Enter a default gateway address for the pool (you can have multiple addresses). Click Next when finished.

6. Enter DNS servers that will serve the IP pool as well as any automatic DNS suffixes to append to searches. Click Next, and enter any WINS servers you may want to include as well. Click Next and then Finish if all details are correct.

Another networking pool is the MAC address pool. Organizations who need to rotate MAC addresses for load balancing may need a more automated and highly available way to manage these addresses. To create a MAC address pool, do the following:

1. On the Fabric tab, click the Create button on the top menu and select Create MAC Pool. This opens the Create MAC Address Pool Wizard. Enter a pool name and optional description, and choose which Hyper-V host groups can take advantage of the pool. This is shown in Figure 9.18.

2. Click Next, and then enter a range of available MAC addresses. Click Next when finished. Review your settings and click Finish.

Within SCVMM 2012, you can also create load balancers. These are associated with specific providers' add-ons that enable this functionality within Hyper-V environments. By default, Microsoft's Network Load Balancing (NLB) is installed and enabled. (Details on creating load balancers is outside the scope of this book.)

The last type of pool you can create within SCVMM is a storage pool. These are added by clicking the Add Resources button on the top menu bar and choosing Storage Devices. You'll walk through the wizard to add storage devices, finally choosing a new or existing storage pool in which to add the resource. These pools can then be used by clusters you've already set up.

FIGURE 9.17
IP ranges to allocate

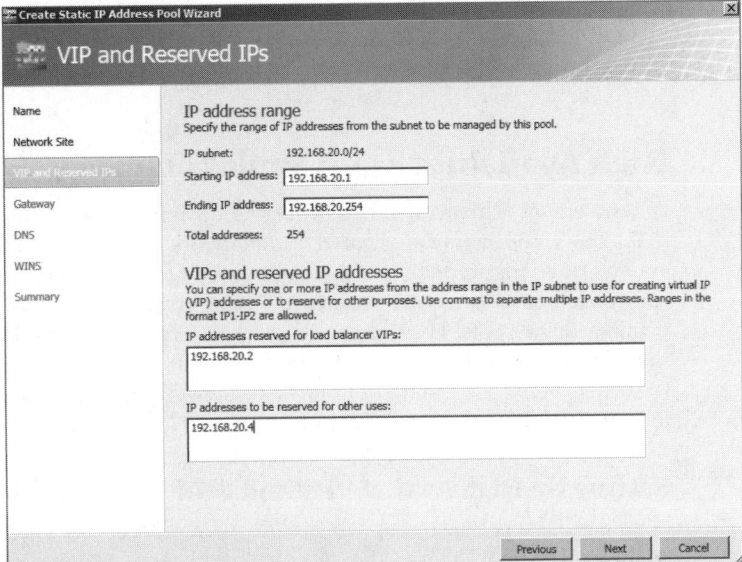

FIGURE 9.18
MAC address pool creation

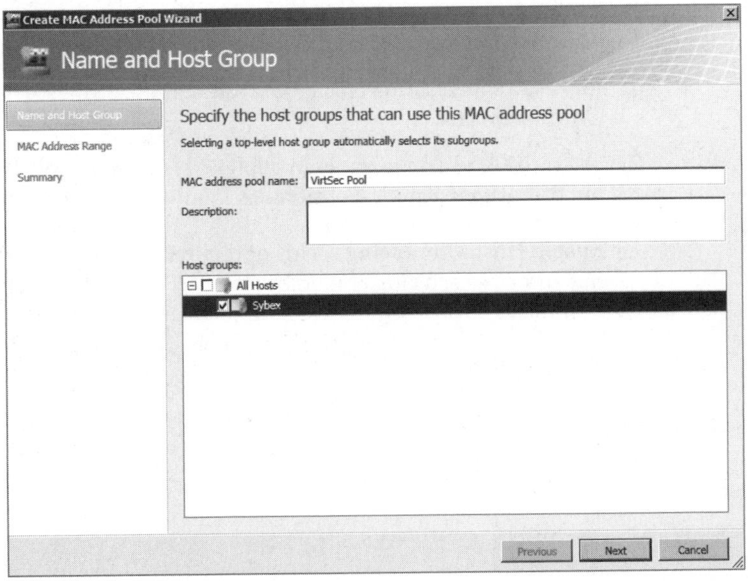

RESOURCE POOLS WITH CITRIX XENSERVER

We've already set up resource pools with XenCenter (see "Clustering with Citrix XenServer" earlier in this chapter), but you can also leverage an additional product from Citrix called Workload Balancer (WLB) to further configure and maintain specific attributes of how the pool functions. This is somewhat outside the scope of this book, however. More information on WLB can be found in the manual *Citrix XenServer Workload Balancing 6.0 Administrator's Guide,* available here:

```
http://support.citrix.com/servlet/KbServlet/download/28741-102-664453/XenServer-
6.0.0-wlb-userguide.pdf
```

High Availability and Fault Tolerance

A key element of an availability strategy for infrastructure components is High Availability (HA). HA is commonly associated with network devices like firewalls, routers, and load balancers. In HA configurations, one device is designated as the primary system, and the other is a fully redundant device with exactly the same configuration that can take over processing if the primary device fails. The same concept applies in many ways for virtual infrastructure, where multiple hypervisors can be set up to host virtual machines, one of which is the primary and the others being redundant or failover systems. Fault Tolerance is a VMware-specific concept (at least in title) that provides a different style of availability and redundancy for VMs.

Setting Up High Availability and Fault Tolerance in VMware vSphere

High Availability within vSphere 5 really means "recovery and restart" for VMs. If a hypervisor host with HA enabled goes down, VMs will be recovered and restarted on another HA-enabled host. One ESXi host is dedicated as the master server, and it maintains heartbeats with the slave servers in the cluster as well as caching cluster configuration information and reporting to vCenter on the cluster and HA status (among other things).

To enable HA services within a vSphere cluster, follow these steps:

1. Right-click an existing cluster and select Edit Settings. Then check the box labeled Turn On vSphere HA.

2. Select the left-hand menu item vSphere HA. On the resulting screen, you have several important configuration options, as follows:

   Enable Host Monitoring   This option will create a "heartbeat" service between hosts that informs each cluster member if a network or local service interruption makes the host unavailable. I strongly recommend checking this box unless you are using other network monitoring or load balancing tools that check for heartbeats or continually monitor all cluster members.

   Admission Control   Enabling Admission Control will prevent a dynamically migrated VM from powering on when its presence on a host will cause resource consumption issues. I recommend enabling Admission Control in any HA-enabled cluster.

Admission Control Policy   If Admission Control is enabled, then you can choose which type of policy will govern its behavior. You can specify a maximum number of host failures to tolerate, a "backup" CPU percentage to retain (in other words, when this percentage is remaining, Admission Control kicks in), or specific failover hosts for VMs to migrate to.

These options are depicted in Figure 9.19.

FIGURE 9.19
Setting up host monitoring and Admission Control

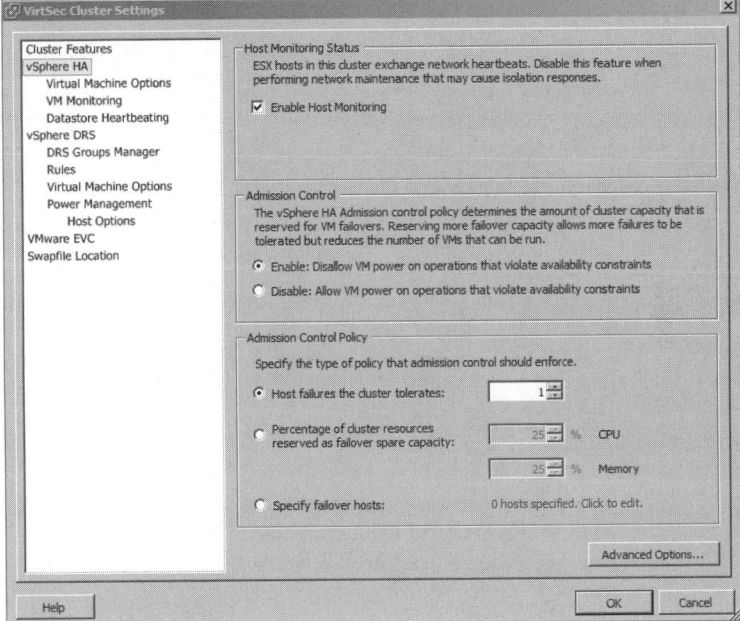

3. The next HA options are in the menu category labeled Virtual Machine Options. Here you have two options for each VM, or at a global level for all VMs in the cluster (individual VM settings override the global cluster settings):

VM Restart Priority   Specify the order in which you want VMs to start back up when a host fails. The global setting will set the default; then individual VMs can be configured for higher or lower than this threshold.

Host Isolation Response   If a hypervisor loses its console connectivity but is still running, this setting will dictate how it manages any VMs it's hosting. You can choose to leave them powered on, to power them off (a hard shutdown), or to shut them down (shut down the OS first, then power off). I recommend leaving them powered on if possible or performing a graceful OS shutdown to minimize corruption or data loss. This is slower than a hard shutdown, however, and may cause performance problems.

These options are shown in Figure 9.20.

FIGURE 9.20
Setting up VM
behavior defaults

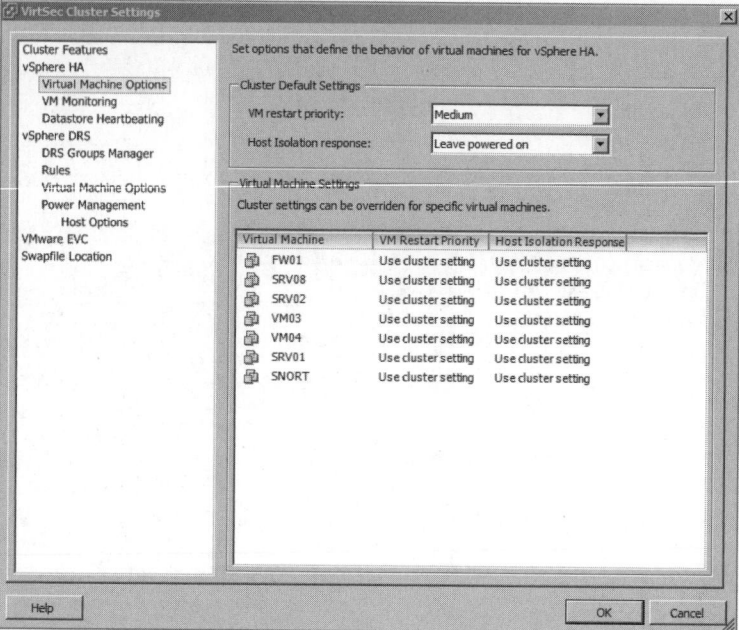

4. The next HA configuration area is VM Monitoring. Here, you can enable or disable VM heartbeat monitoring using VMware Tools integration. I recommend enabling this for both VMs and applications. You can configure the monitoring sensitivity for the cluster as well. The settings are Low (120 seconds), Medium 60 seconds), and High (30 seconds), or you can configure a custom setting by specifying the following:

- Failure Interval: Number of seconds after a heartbeat is missed that a VM failure is declared.

- Minimum Uptime: Time in seconds that a VM must be started before failure interval checking begins.

- Maximum Per-VM Resets: Number of times the VM can be reset once a failure is detected.

- Maximum Resets Time Window: Number of hours in which the maximum resets setting is enforced.

These settings are shown in Figure 9.21.

5. The final menu option for HA is Datastore Heartbeating. Here you can choose to maintain heartbeats on defined datastore objects in vCenter when vCenter's management network has failed. You can choose to monitor any cluster datastore, preferred datastores, or any datastores with your preferences included (the recommended setting). These options are shown in Figure 9.22.

6. When finished, click OK to save your changes.

FIGURE 9.21
Setting up VM
Monitoring

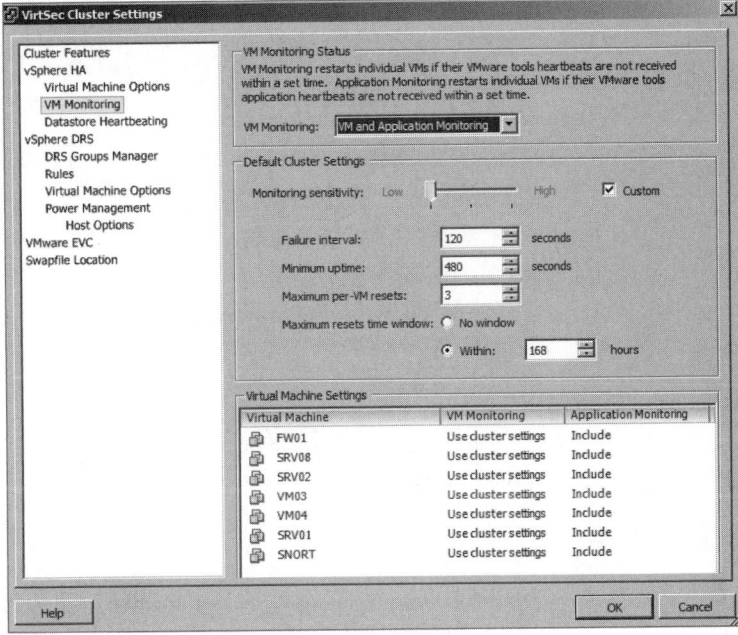

FIGURE 9.22
Setting up Datas-
tore Heartbeating

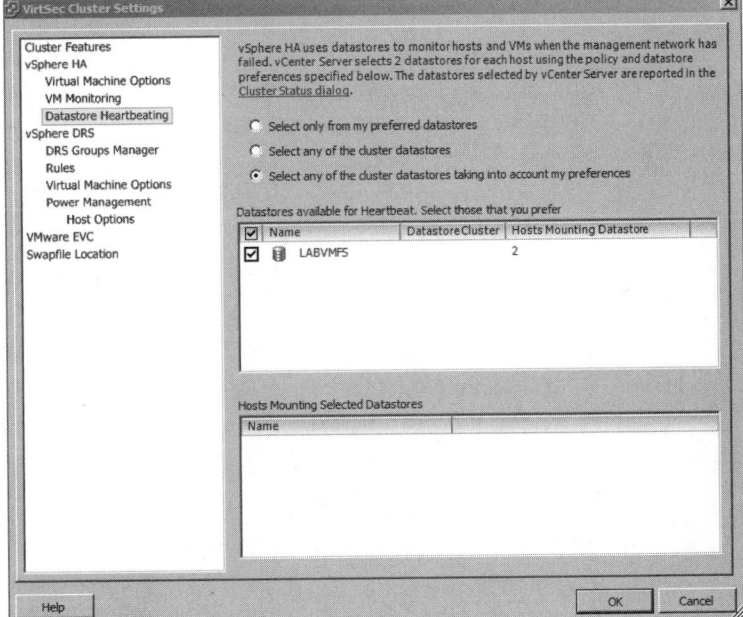

Fault Tolerance (FT) is another key availability feature on vSphere platforms today. Fault Tolerance is born of the original VMware Workstation record/replay functions. In essence, FT creates a replica of a VM and keeps it in "lockstep" with the original. If the original VM has issues, FT immediately transfers its functions to the replica, which has been keeping up with all critical functions of the original in near real time.

A number of prerequisites must be met before FT can be enabled and used in a DRS and HA-enabled cluster (note that the prerequisites aren't limited to the ones listed here):

- ◆ Enabling host certificate checking
- ◆ Enabling HA on the cluster where VMs are located
- ◆ Setting up virtual NICs with FT logging enabled on each ESX/ESXi host
- ◆ Providing FT-compatible CPUs

In addition, FT-enabled VMs must be devoid of snapshots, which can be a real challenge for some organizations

There are other requirements, and readers are encouraged to consult the latest VMware documentation.

To enable FT on a VM, simply right-click the VM and select Fault Tolerance, and then click Turn On Fault Tolerance. You'll get a warning message, and if you accept, the VM will be prepped and then enabled for FT. Once FT is enabled, you'll see that the VM's icon has changed to a small cluster of squares and FT features and status are shown on the VM's Summary tab, as shown in Figure 9.23.

FIGURE 9.23

Fault Tolerance enabled on a VM

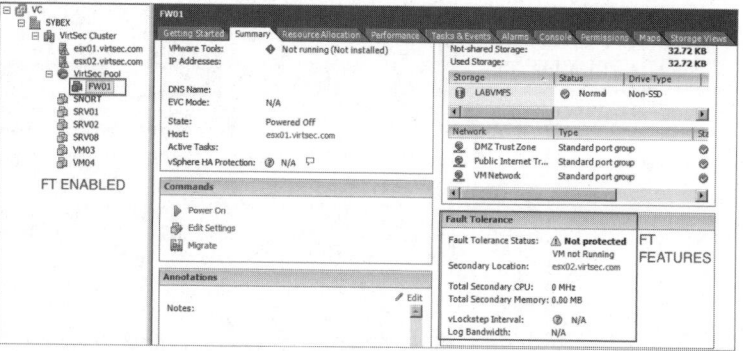

Setting Up High Availability and Fault Tolerance in Microsoft Hyper-V

The simplest High Availability features in SCVMM 2012 and Hyper-V are configured from within the host groups containing clusters and Hyper-V servers. Follow these steps:

1. Right-click a host group and select Properties.

2. Select the General option on the left side, and enter the name and a description of the host group.

3. Select Placement Rules and specify which VMs should be placed on which hosts. The default option is to use the built-in Microsoft Host Group allocation. To create custom rules, uncheck this option, click Add, and in the Create Custom Requirement dialog box, choose a custom property title as well as a requirement setting for the host group, as shown in Figure 9.24.

FIGURE 9.24
Creating a custom
SCVMM placement
rule

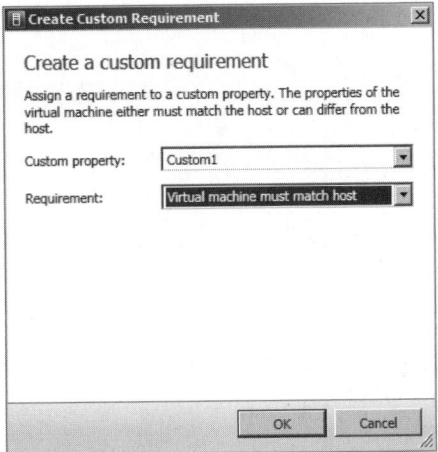

4. Choose whether the VM should, should not, must, or must not match the host; then click OK.

NOTE In general, the default settings should work for most cases, but if you have nested host groups with several layers of system and data classification or sensitivity, you will likely want to separate VMs from particular Hyper-V cluster members.

5. Select Host Reserves. Specify the minimum values the host must keep in reserve. If the reserve is not available, the VM will not start. You can set reserves related to CPU, memory, disk I/O, disk space, and network I/O, as shown in Figure 9.25.

TIP I recommend leaving the CPU threshold at a minimum of 10 percent, (preferably 15 percent) and memory at 10 percent of your total for the cluster and/or host group. The other setting will depend entirely on the needs of your organization.

6. Select Dynamic Optimization. Much like some of VMware's HA options, Dynamic Optimization allows you to control how often migration of the VM across Hyper-V hosts will occur. Settings range from Low (little to no dynamic migration for performance and resource consumption improvements) to High (much more frequent migration to better allocate and balance resources in the group). You can also select the levels of CPU, memory, and disk and network I/O at which hosts will be considered for migration of VMs. These settings are shown in Figure 9.26.

FIGURE 9.25
Specifying SCVMM
host reserves

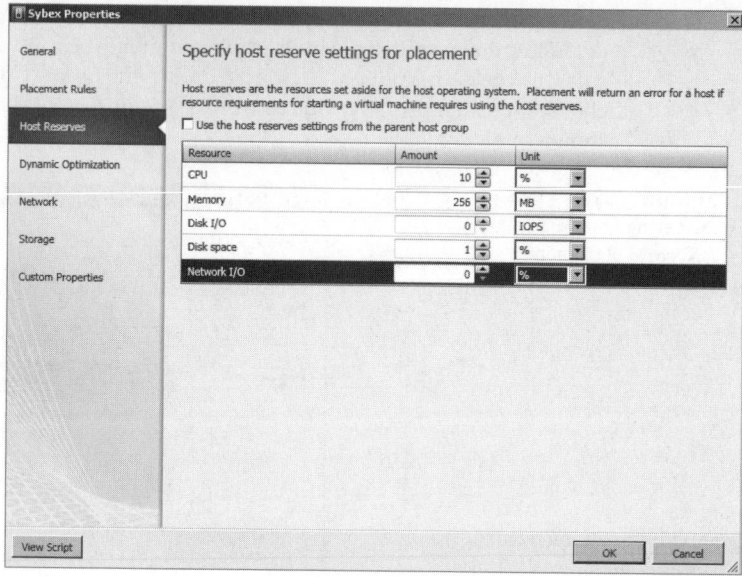

FIGURE 9.26
Dynamic optimiza-
tion options

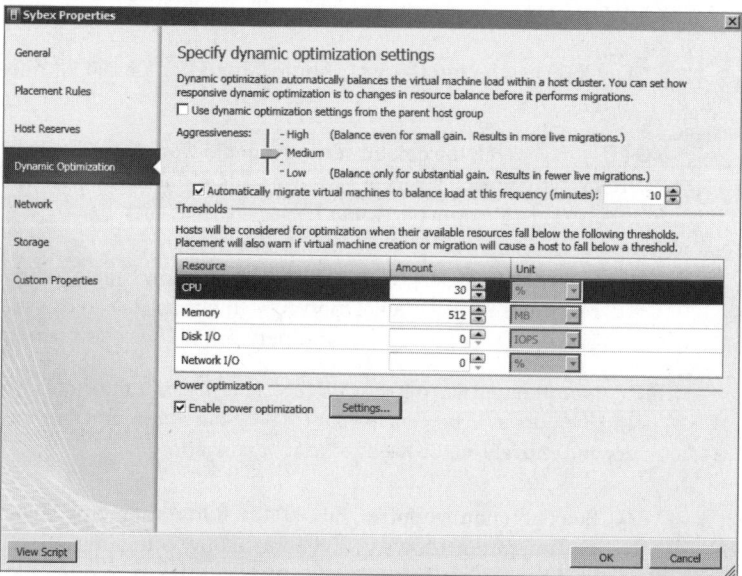

7. On this same screen, choose whether to check the Enable Power Optimization check box at the bottom. Click the Settings button next to the check box to see the options for fine-tuning and scheduling power optimization (see Figure 9.27).

FIGURE 9.27

Power optimization
in SCVMM

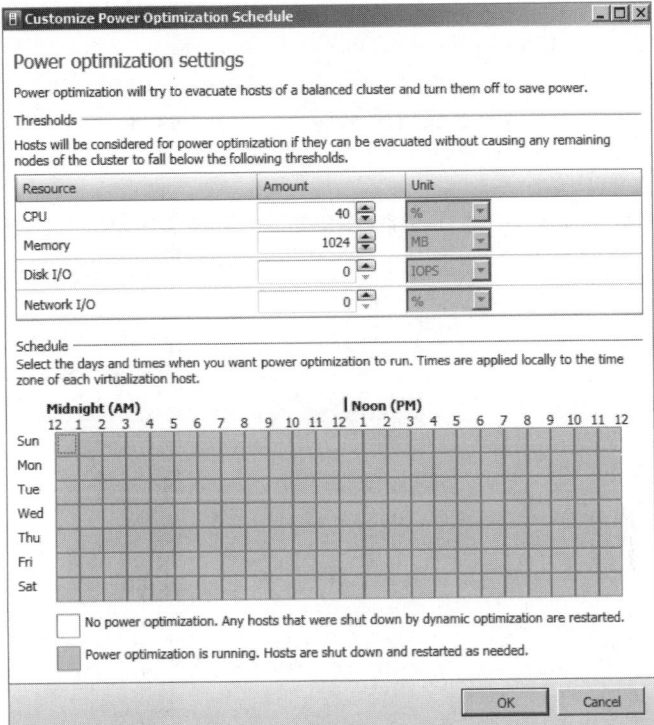

8. Select thresholds at which Hyper-V hosts will be considered for power optimization operations. In essence, high power consumption will trigger dynamic VM migration, much like some of the other HA features of SCVMM.

TIP My recommendation for most enterprises is to turn off power optimization during peak utilization periods to avoid unnecessary thrash. Peak periods depend on your business model and usage scenarios.

9. Back on the main screen, select Network and specify IP pools, MAC pools, logical networks, and virtual load balancers to the host group or cluster. These should align with the proper network segmentation scenarios you have in place (Figure 9.28).

10. Select Storage and allocate specific storage pools or logical units of defined storage for use by the hosts and VMs.

Setting Up High Availability and Fault Tolerance in Citrix XenServer

Using XenCenter, you can configure HA policies for your XenServer systems and also perform critical DR operations directly from the console. To configure XenServer HA, follow these steps once you're logged into XenCenter:

1. Select your cluster/pool within XenCenter, and then choose the HA tab on the right side. Click the button labeled Configure HA.

2. The heartbeat SR is the remote storage repository where VMs are stored. Select this SR, which must be available to all pool members, as shown in Figure 9.29. Then click Next.

FIGURE 9.28
Network resource allocation in SCVMM

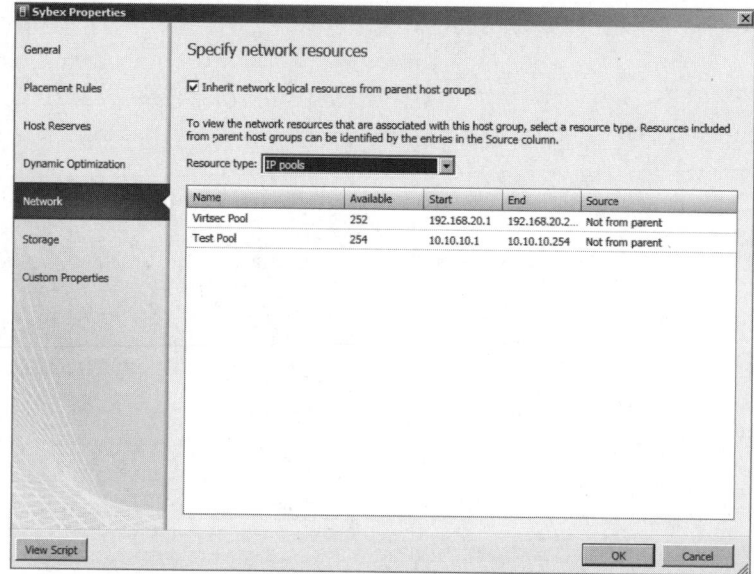

FIGURE 9.29
Selecting a XenServer heartbeat SR

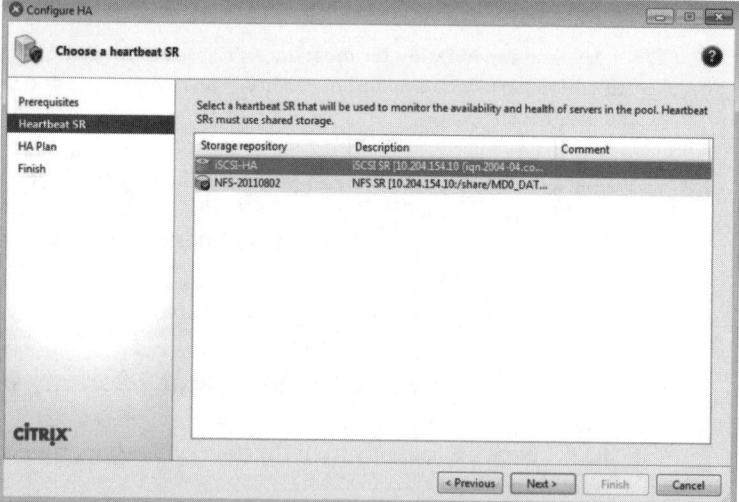

3. Configure the HA plan. In this screen, you select a number of attributes related to how VMs in the pool will restart in the case of host failure. The following can be set on this screen:

◆ HA Restart Priority: Options are Restart, Restart If Possible, and Do Not Restart. Machines labeled Restart will be given the highest priority.

◆ Restart Order: Starting with zero (0) as the highest priority, VMs will be started in the order you specify.

◆ Attempt To Start Next VM After: This is the number of seconds to wait before trying to start a new VM in the recovery efforts.

◆ Server Failure Limit: This is the maximum number of hosts that can fail in the pool as part of the HA plan before VMs no longer have actual High Availability; in other words, they'll fail if enough resources aren't available. This number needs to be higher than zero (0). XenCenter determines the optimal maximum for the HA plan when you initiate HA on the pool initially. You can then modify the recommended settings.

◆ VMs marked as Yes in the Agile column can be migrated dynamically, while those that have a No setting are essentially tied to one specific hypervisor. These options are shown in Figure 9.30.

FIGURE 9.30
XenServer Pool HA
Plan

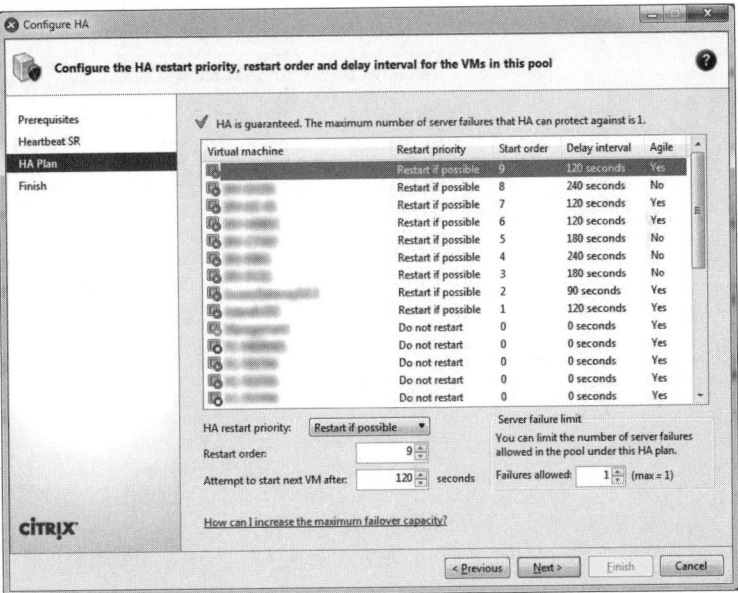

XenCenter can also be used to create and initiate simple DR replication and recovery scenarios for shared storage data. This is a simple way to perform DR operations and can be partially automated ahead of time by mirroring SRs and establishing replication schedules as covered in the earlier part of the chapter. Follow these steps to initiate DR processes for a pool:

1. Right-click the pool, select Disaster Recovery, and then select Disaster Recovery Wizard.

2. Select one of the three DR options as prompted:

   ◆ Failover: Migrate VMs and vApps to a failover DR location.

   ◆ Failback: The reverse of failing over, which means migrating VMs and vApps from the failover location back to the original location.

   ◆ Test Failover: Fail over but do not start any VMs or vApps, thus avoiding disruption.

   This is shown in Figure 9.31.

FIGURE 9.31
XenCenter Disaster
Recovery Wizard

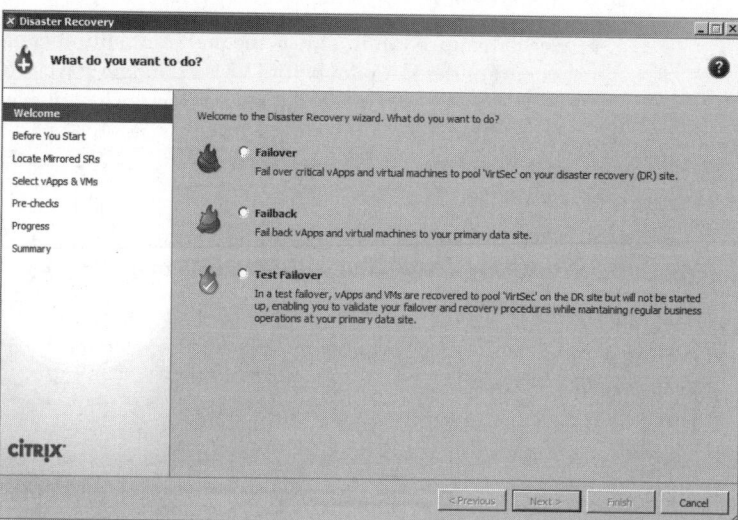

3. Walk through the wizard, selecting the storage repositories you have mirrored and the VMs and vApps you want to move. Then XenCenter will perform several checks to ensure that the operation will function properly.

Chapter 10

Scripting Tips and Tricks for Automation

There are lots of different types of scripting. Some scripting languages are more robust, like Perl, Python, and Ruby, and are used to create entire software suites, add-ons, and more. Others are primarily for automation of tasks, such as those used for Windows and Linux shell scripting. Then there are purpose-built scripting platforms that perform particular functions for vendor products, such as the VMware vSphere CLI. There are many ways scripts can make virtualization administrators lives much simpler in general.

This chapter will outline scripting tools that can be used with VMware, Microsoft, and Citrix platforms to accomplish specific operations and security-focused goals. I won't attempt to cover even a fraction of all the possible scripting scenarios administrators and operations professionals will encounter; instead I'll focus on key script types and goals that most teams will find beneficial in performing security-related tasks.

In this chapter, you will learn about the following topics:

◆ Fundamentals of scripting and why it's important

◆ Different scripting options for virtualization operations teams

◆ VMware scripting options and key examples

◆ Microsoft scripting options and key examples

◆ Citrix scripting and key examples

◆ Other types of scripting to consider

Why Scripting Is Essential for Admins

Most administrators perform the same types of actions over and over again, perhaps with some basic variations. On other occasions, admins and operations teams need to generate reports from data or gather data to then analyze with other tools. The question is, What's the best way to perform these actions? Many platforms and systems today have a graphical user interface (GUI), where admins can easily find what they're looking for (sometimes) and perform specific actions by clicking and entering text. For occasional tasks, this may work just fine. However, there are plenty of times you'll want more repeatable (and likely faster) ways to get information or perform actions. In these cases, you'll need to look for options at the command line where possible.

Once you find them, you may want to make them repeatable and schedulable. Anything you have to click doesn't really meet those criteria, but scripting commands and functions can help you get there.

SCRIPTING TYPES FOR VIRTUALIZATION ADMINS

There are a plethora of different scripting types for the major virtualization platforms today.

VMware has the most options available: PowerShell scripting with the PowerCLI, vSphere Command Line Interface (vCLI), shell scripting on ESX, and even native interpreters for Perl and Python on hypervisor platforms. More information on VMware scripting can be found here:

```
www.vmware.com/products/vsphere/esxi-and-esx/scripting.html
```

For Microsoft platforms, PowerShell is the scripting language of choice. Microsoft hypervisors can have any number of interpreters installed, allowing Perl, Python, and even Ruby to be used for interaction with the platform, although these aren't necessarily the best options for most tasks. A great page with information about Hyper-V scripting can be found on the Microsoft TechNet site:

```
http://social.technet.microsoft.com/wiki/contents/articles/176.hyper-v-
scripts.aspx
```

Shell scripting is the primary automation method for Citrix XenServer systems.

You have more options than those listed here! VMware generally supports the most options natively, although scripting interpreters for Python, Perl, and other languages could easily be installed on Hyper-V. TCL scripting can be used on VMware's older ESX platform, although this isn't supported on ESXi.

VMware Scripting: Power CLI and vCLI

VMware has a number of options for scripting security-related tasks and operations, some of which depend on the versions of hypervisors and products you're using. For the most recent versions of vSphere 5, most administrators seem to have settled on two options: a set of PowerShell extensions and scripts known as the PowerCLI and a more pared-down set of remote commands written in Perl called the vSphere CLI, or vCLI. In the following sections, I'll cover some of the fundamentals of both and provide some examples of security-related actions you'll likely want to perform with these tools.

Scripting with PowerCLI

The VMware PowerCLI can be downloaded from VMware's site at the following URL:

```
vmware.com/go/powercli
```

For this book, I used version 5.0.1 and tested against a vSphere 5 installation. As a sound starting point, readers should consider looking to automate all elements of the latest VMware hardening guide. The *vSphere 5.0 Hardening Guide* is available here:

http://communities.vmware.com/docs/DOC-19605

This new guide lays out the following categories of security controls. Most organizations will need to consider all of these controls for their virtual infrastructure:

◆ Virtual Machines

◆ Hypervisors (ESXi, in this case)

◆ Virtual Networks

◆ vCenter Management Servers

For each of these categories, there are specific recommended controls along with descriptions and methods for both assessment and remediation. This guide also lists key scripting commands to help with automation! In this discussion, we'll borrow some of those recommendations and leverage them.

Configuring VMs with PowerCLI

First, let's take a look at how we can secure virtual machines with PowerCLI commands. Keep in mind that the PowerCLI is only available for Windows with PowerShell enabled. Each of the VM configuration settings consists of a parameter and a value listed in the VMware configuration file (the VMX file discussed earlier in Chapter 6, "Securing the Virtual Machine"). For example, to disable the automatic installation of VMware Tools in a virtual machine, you could enter the following in its VMX file:

isolation.tools.autoInstall.disable=TRUE

VMware employees and virtualization gurus William Lam and Alan Renouf have put together a set of PowerCLI scripts that can be used to automate the assessment and remediation of most of these settings in the VMX file of any VM. This script creates a new PowerCLI function called Set-VMAdvancedConfiguration. The entire script is called "Retrieve and Set VM Advanced Configuration (VMX) settings" and can be found at this VMware web page:

http://communities.vmware.com/docs/DOC-18653

To execute the function and modify VMX settings, you have a few options. You can change a specific setting on an individual VM or a specific setting on all VMs known to the ESXi or vCenter server. Or you can add all your settings into a CSV file and make all the configuration changes to one or more VMs at the same time.

Follow these steps to get started:

1. Connect to a specific ESXi or vCenter server with the following command:

Connect-VIServer <server name or IP>

When connecting for the first time, you'll likely be prompted for a username and password, as shown in Figure 10.1.

FIGURE 10.1
Authentication
prompt for
PowerCLI
connection

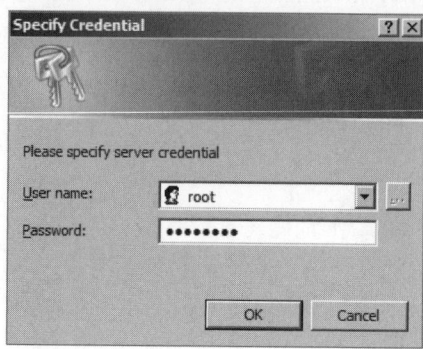

2. Once you're successfully connected, enumerate all VMs known to the platform by running the following command:

Get-VM

You should see a screen similar to that shown in Figure 10.2 (your VMs will vary, of course).

FIGURE 10.2
Listing known VMs

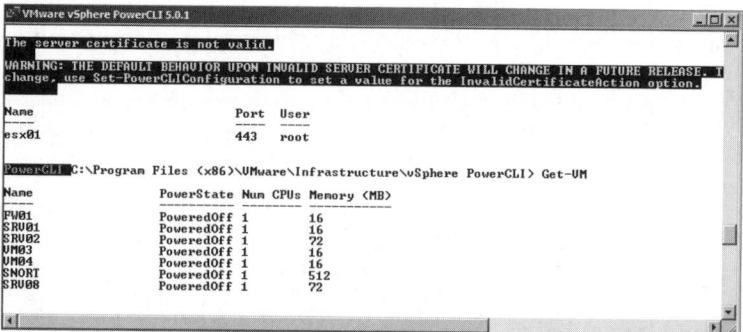

NOTE You'll note that the output in Figure 10.2 shows a certificate warning, which is expected. On the hypervisor being queried, the certificate in place is still the default, self-signed certificate, which I explained how to replace in Chapter 2, "Securing Hypervisors."

3. Perform configuration checks and remediation actions using the PowerCLI scripts mentioned previously.

For example, if you want to set the AutoInstall configuration item noted earlier, you could execute the following command to add it to all VMs listed in Figure 10.2:

```
Get-VM | Set-VMAdvancedConfiguration -key
"isolation.tools.autoInstall.disable" -value $true
```

The output of this command is shown in Figure 10.3.

FIGURE 10.3

Configuring all known VMs with PowerCLI

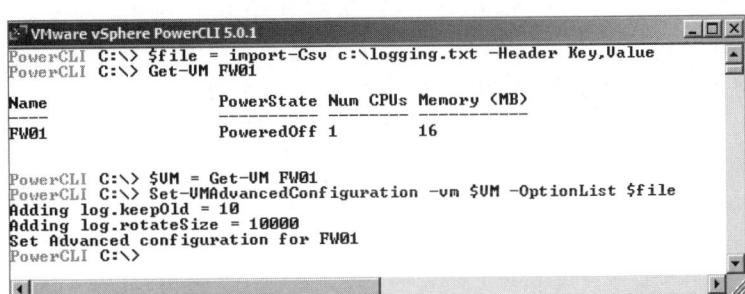

To make this process even more efficient, the configuration values can be added to a text file where the parameters and values are separated by commas. The following example sets a log rotation schedule for VMs of 10 individual log files, with rotation occurring when logs reach 10 KB in size:

```
log.keepOld,10
log.rotateSize,10000
```

These settings are placed in exactly this format into a file called `logging.txt`.

Once you've created the log file, you'll need to import it. Choose a VM to configure, and to configure these settings in one step, execute the following commands:

```
$file = import-Csv <file> -Header Key,Value
$VM = Get-VM <VM name>
Set-VMAdvancedConfiguration -vm $VM -OptionList $file
```

This can be seen executing with our `logging.txt` file for the VM FW01 in Figure 10.4.

FIGURE 10.4

Configuring multiple settings simultaneously

```
VMware vSphere PowerCLI 5.0.1                                    _ □ X

PowerCLI C:\> $file = import-Csv c:\logging.txt -Header Key,Value
PowerCLI C:\> Get-UM FW01

Name                       PowerState Num CPUs Memory (MB)
----                       ---------- -------- -----------
FW01                       PoweredOff 1        16

PowerCLI C:\> $UM = Get-UM FW01
PowerCLI C:\> Set-UMAdvancedConfiguration -vm $UM -OptionList $file
Adding log.keepOld = 10
Adding log.rotateSize = 10000
Set Advanced configuration for FW01
PowerCLI C:\>
```

More information on these scripts and techniques can be found in the VMware article "Automate the Hardening of Your Virtual Machine VMX Configurations" penned by William Lam and available here:

```
http://blogs.vmware.com/vsphere/2012/06/automate-the-hardening-of-your-
virtual-machine-vmx-configurations.html
```

Configuring VMs with vCLI

The second option for configuring VMs is the vSphere CLI, which can run from any system with Perl installed and enabled (although you'll need to check version compatibility). Many fantastic audit scripts can be built using nothing but the vCLI, and following are several examples to illustrate this. The good news is that many of the same commands have the exact same structure with variations of the `vmware-cmd` command. For all the examples, the following syntax is included:

```
/vmfs/volumes/[DATASTORE]/[VM]/[VM].vmx
```

Replace the [DATASTORE] value with the actual mounted datastore on the ESXi host, and the [VM] values with the name of the VM you are interrogating. Here are some examples:

◆ To check that the VMware Tools package is not installed automatically, run the following command:

```
vmware-cmd --server <server> --username <user> --password <password> /vmfs/
volumes/[DATASTORE]/[VM]/[VM].vmx getguestinfo isolation.tools.autoInstall
.disable
```

◆ To change the preceding setting to true, change the `getguestinfo` parameter to `setguestinfo` with the value following the parameter, as shown:

```
vmware-cmd --server <server> --username <user> --password <password> /vmfs/
volumes/[DATASTORE]/[VM]/[VM].vmx setguestinfo isolation.tools.autoInstall
.disable TRUE
```

◆ To set the number of log files that will be maintained for the VM to 10, execute the following:

```
vmware-cmd --server <server> --username <user> --password <password> /vmfs/
volumes/[DATASTORE]/[VM]/[VM].vmx setguestinfo log.keepOld 10
```

◆ Similarly, execute the following command to modify the size each log file can reach before rotation occurs to 10 KB:

```
vmware-cmd --server <server> --username <user> --password <password> /vmfs/
volumes/[DATASTORE]/[VM]/[VM].vmx setguestinfo log.rotateSize 10000
```

Another tactic that you can use with VMs and the vCLI is to download the actual VMX files associated with VMs and then parse them for specific string values associated with hardware and other settings. For example, to determine if the VM has any attached USB drives, run the following commands.

First, download the VM's VMX with the `vifs` command:

```
vifs --server <server> --username <user> --password <password>
-g "[DATASTORE] [VM]/[VM].vmx" VM.vmx
```

You should now have the VMX file in the same directory where you ran the vCLI command. Now, use the `grep` command to look for USB references (you'll need a separate Windows binary or a Unix system with `grep` to run this):

```
grep -i "^usb[0-9]*.present" [VMX]
```

You should see some output like the following (output may vary):
```
usb.present = "FALSE"
```

Configuring VMware ESXi with PowerCLI

The second major virtualization component that you'll want to lock down is the hypervisor itself. There are quite a few settings listed in the VMware hardening guide (discussed in

"Scripting With PowerCLI," earlier in this chapter), and over half can be audited and configured using PowerCLI. Several examples follow.

Configuring Remote Logging Servers

One standard security practice is to configure remote logging servers to which ESXi platforms can send all logging events for aggregation, correlation, and analysis. To check the current remote logging settings, execute the following:

```
Get-VMHost | Select Name, @{N="Syslog.global.logHost";E={$_ | Get-
VMHostAdvancedConfiguration Syslog.global.logHost | Select -ExpandProperty
Values}}
```

To set a value for the remote logging host, execute the following:

```
Get-VMHost | Foreach { Set-VMHostAdvancedConfiguration -VMHost $_ -Name Syslog.
global.logHost -Value "LOG HOST NAME/IP" }
```

Substitute LOG HOST NAME/IP with your system name or IP. In Figure 10.5, you can see that the ESX01 ESXi system has no remote log host initially. I then added the log host at IP address 192.168.206.204 and checked to see that the setting was in place, which it was.

FIGURE 10.5
Auditing and configuring remote log hosts

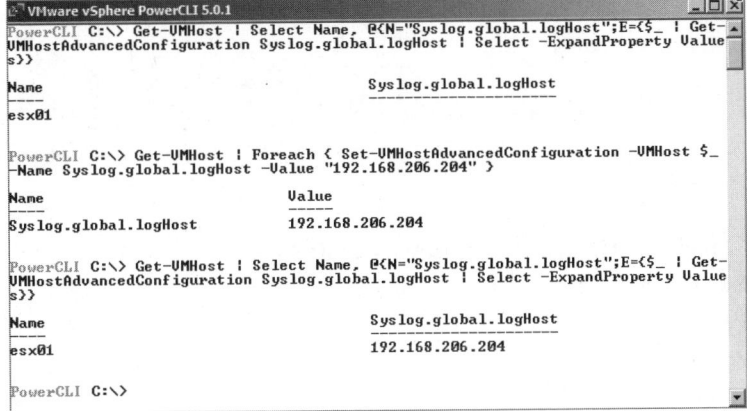

Establishing NTP Sources

Another common configuration option necessary for operations and security is to establish Network Time Protocol (NTP) time sources. In this example, I am using real NTP servers at ntp.org, but you should substitute those that work best for your organization. NTP servers can be added for all ESXi hosts with the following commands:

```
$NTPServers = "pool.ntp.org", "pool2.ntp.org"
Get-VMHost | Add-VmHostNtpServer $NTPServers
```

This will return a simple response affirming the added NTP IP addresses, as shown in Figure 10.6.

FIGURE 10.6

Adding NTP serv-
ers to an ESXi
configuration

FIGURE 10.6

Adding NTP serv-
ers to an ESXi
configuration

You can then use vCenter to confirm the addition of the NTP servers (see Figure 10.7). You can find this setting by highlighting your ESXi server in the Inventory, Hosts And Clusters view, selecting the Configuration tab in the right-hand pane and selecting the Time Configuration menu option on the left. Click Properties in the right-hand pane, then choose NTP Settings.

FIGURE 10.7

NTP server configu-
ration in vCenter

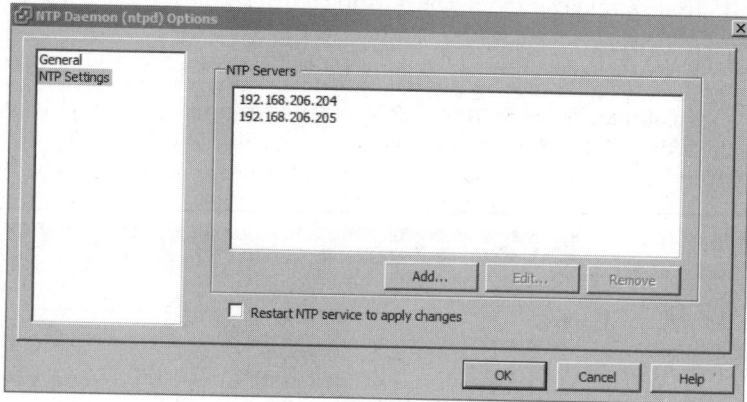

ENABLING AD AUTHENTICATION ON ESXi SERVERS

A sound security practice within an enterprise environment is to enable Active Directory authentication on ESXi servers. To see the current status of ESXi systems, run the following:

```
Get-VMHost | Get-VMHostAuthentication | Select VmHost, Domain,
DomainMembershipStatus
```

If the host is not yet a part of the domain, you can then add it with the following command:

```
Get-VMHost <hostname> | Get-VMHostAuthentication | Set-VMHostAuthentication
 -Domain <domain name> -User Administrator -Password <password> -JoinDomain
```

This will join your server to the domain and allow AD authentication.

CHECKING LOCKDOWN MODE

One final example of ESXi security that admins will want to check for is the presence of lockdown mode (discussed in Chapter 2). To determine if lockdown mode is enabled, run the following:

```
Get-VMHost | Select Name,@{N="Lockdown";E={$_.Extensiondata.Config.adminDisabled}}
```

You should get a listing of known ESXi hosts and a note as to whether lockdown is enabled or not. If Lockdown Mode is not enabled, you can enable it through the Direct Console User Interface (DCUI) or using vCenter.

Configuring VMware ESXi with the vCLI

There are quite a few more options to both assess and configure ESXi hosts using the vCLI. Many of the commands are separate scripts, making it simple to configure systems and include the commands in scripts.

TIP The vCLI scripts are all written in Perl, so they can be run from any system that has a Perl interpreter installed, including the vSphere Management Appliance (vMA).

Configuring NTP

To assess and configure NTP servers for an ESXi system, you can leverage the `vicfg-ntp` script as follows:

◆ To list the current NTP configuration:

```
vicfg-ntp --server <server> --username <user> --list
```

◆ To add a new NTP server's IP address:

```
vicfg-ntp --server <server> --username <user> --add <IP>
```

This is shown in Figure 10.8.

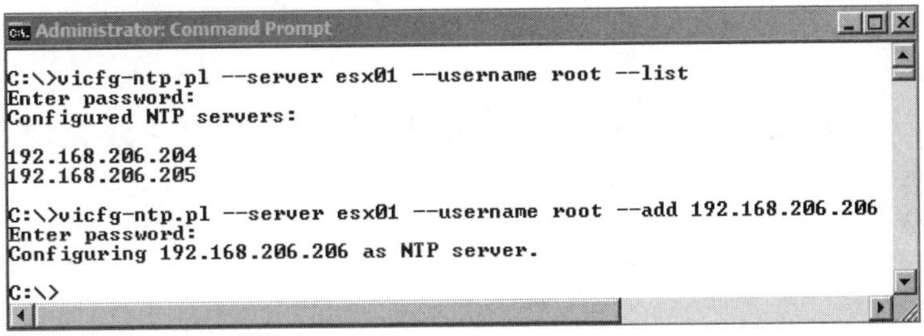

FIGURE 10.8
Auditing and configuring ESXi NTP options

```
C:\>vicfg-ntp.pl --server esx01 --username root --list
Enter password:
Configured NTP servers:

192.168.206.204
192.168.206.205

C:\>vicfg-ntp.pl --server esx01 --username root --add 192.168.206.206
Enter password:
Configuring 192.168.206.206 as NTP server.

C:\>
```

Configuring Logging

To determine what logging settings the ESXi system has in place, the multipurpose vCLI `esxcli` command can be run. You'll notice that the syntax and options for this command closely mimic the commands listed in Chapter 2 at the ESXi Shell's command line:

◆ To list the current logging settings, execute the following command syntax:

```
esxcli --server <server> --username <user> system syslog config get
```

◆ To add a new remote log host, use the following command syntax:

```
esxcli --server <server> --username <user> system syslog config set --loghost
<log host IP1,log host IP2, …>
```

This is shown in Figure 10.9.

FIGURE 10.9
Auditing and
configuring ESX
remote logging

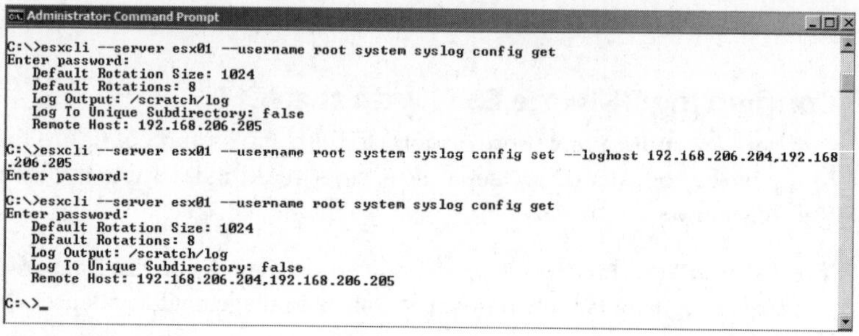

CONFIGURING DOMAINS

To determine what domain an ESXi server is part of, or whether it is joined to a domain for authentication, execute the following:

```
vicfg-authconfig --server <server> --username <user> --authscheme AD
--currentdomain
```

To add the ESXi server to a domain for authentication, run the following:

```
vicfg-authconfig --server <server> --username <user> --adusername <AD admin user>
--adpassword <AD admin password> --authscheme AD --joindomain <domain>
```

NOTE There is no simple way to leverage the vCLI for enabling or auditing lockdown mode, unfortunately.

Configuring VMware Virtual Networks with PowerCLI

There are many options available for assessing and configuring virtual networks with PowerCLI.

ASSESSING VIRTUAL SWITCHES

PowerCLI makes it easy to get information about virtual switches:

◆ To get a general description of the known virtual switches (standard), along with their VLAN IDs, run the following command:

```
Get-VirtualPortGroup -Standard | Select virtualSwitch, Name, VlanID
```

The output of this command is shown in Figure 10.10.

◆ To see a list of all standard and distributed vSwitches, along with total and available ports, use the similar Get-VirtualSwitch command.

The output of this command is shown in Figure 10.11.

FIGURE 10.10
Standard vSwitches
and VLANs

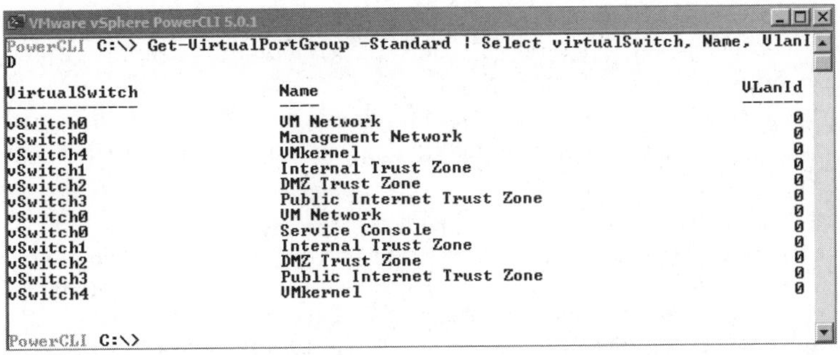

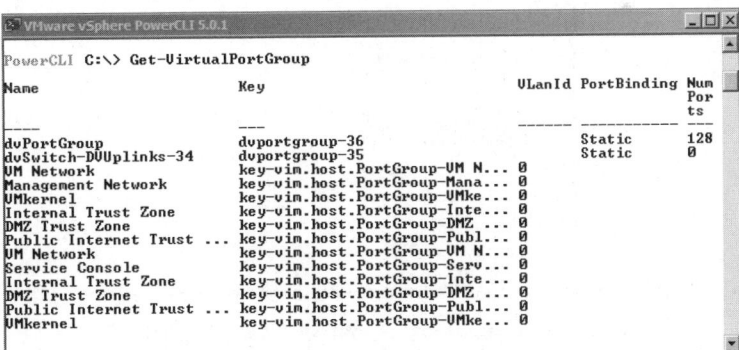

FIGURE 10.11
Full listing of all
vSwitches

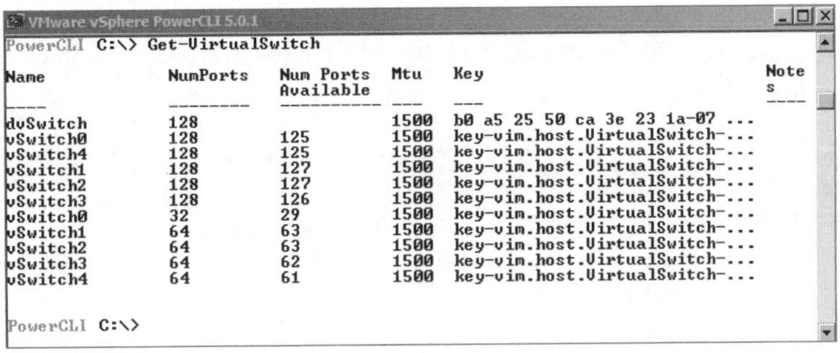

FIGURE 10.12
Listing of all virtual
port groups

To get a list of virtual port groups for both standard and distributed vSwitches, use the Get-VirtualPortGroup command.

The output of this command is shown in Figure 10.12.

CHECKING SECURITY POLICIES

You can use PowerCLI to check for the various security policies you may have in place on VMware virtual switches (Promiscuous Mode, Forged Transmits, and MAC Changes), which we covered in Chapter 3, "Designing Virtual Networks for Security," and Chapter 4, "Advanced Virtual Network Operations." The syntax is a bit more complex than some of our earlier script examples, though!

To check these settings on standard switches, enter the following into the PowerCLI prompt (please note the back-facing tick marks, usually found on the key next to the "1" on most keyboards):

```
Get-VirtualSwitch -Standard | Select VMHost, Name, `
 @{N="MacChanges";E={if ($_.ExtensionData.Spec.Policy.Security.MacChanges) {
"Accept" } Else { "Reject"} }}, `
 @{N="PromiscuousMode";E={if ($_.ExtensionData.Spec.Policy.Security.
PromiscuousMode) { "Accept" } Else { "Reject"} }}, `
 @{N="ForgedTransmits";E={if ($_.ExtensionData.Spec.Policy.Security.
ForgedTransmits) { "Accept" } Else { "Reject"} }}
```

Running this command, and the output from it, will yield results similar to those shown in Figure 10.13.

FIGURE 10.13
Standard vSwitch security policies

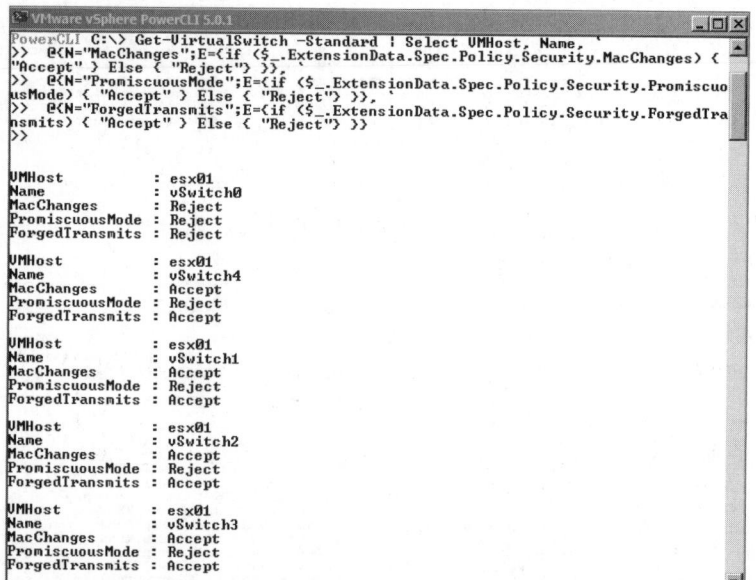

You can get the same information for dvSwitch port groups with the following command:

```
Get-VirtualPortGroup -Distributed | Select Name, `
 @{N="MacChanges";E={if
($_.ExtensionData.Config.DefaultPortConfig.SecurityPolicy.MacChanges.Value) {
"Accept" } Else { "Reject"} }}, `
 @{N="PromiscuousMode";E={if
($_.ExtensionData.Config.DefaultPortConfig.SecurityPolicy.AllowPromiscuous.Value)
{ "Accept" } Else { "Reject"} }}, `
```

```
@{N="ForgedTransmits";E={if ($_.ExtensionData.Config.DefaultPortConfig.
SecurityPolicy.ForgedTransmits.Value)
{ "Accept" } Else { "Reject"} }}
```

The output is shown in Figure 10.14.

FIGURE 10.14
dvSwitch port
group security
settings

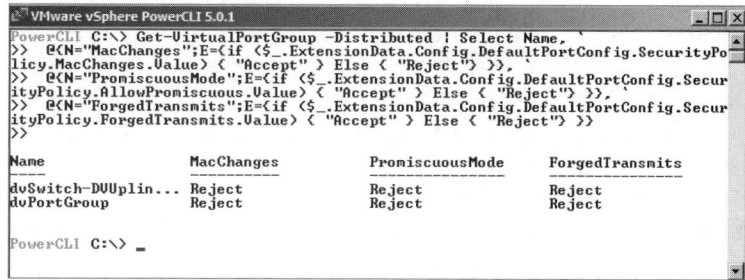

Configuring VMware Virtual Networks with the vCLI

The vCLI, in some ways, allows for more remediation activities and configuration on virtual switches than PowerCLI. The commands are also much simpler, making scripting a bit simpler and scripts easier to maintain. This really illustrates why there is no "one way" to do things in virtual environments — having a variety of tools at your disposal will help you get the job done more easily and effectively than relying solely on one language or toolkit.

Let's look at a few simple vCLI examples of assessing and configuring virtual switches, starting with a simple listing of vSwitches. This next example will query a hypervisor and list all known vSwitches along with their defined port groups and VLANs:

```
esxcli --server <server> --username <user> network vswitch standard portgroup list
```

The output of this command is shown in Figure 10.15.

FIGURE 10.15
Listing vSwitches
with port groups
and VLANs

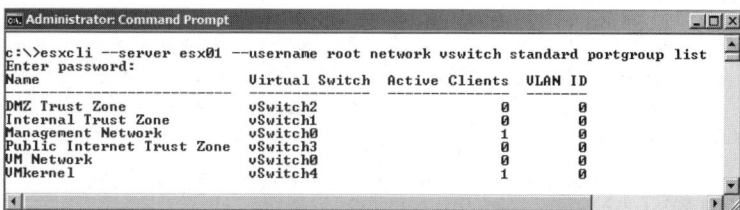

To get more detailed information about the standard vSwitches, run the following command:

```
esxcli --server <server> --username <user> network vswitch standard list
```

The output of this command is shown in Figure 10.16.

FIGURE 10.16
List of standard
vSwitches with
details

To acquire details of a vSwitch's security policy settings, you can use the following command:

```
esxcli --server <server> --username <user> network vswitch standard policy
security get -v <vSwitch>
```

An example of the output of this command is shown here:

```
Allow Promiscuous: false
Allow MAC Address Change: true
Allow Forged Transmits: true   [
```

NOTE   The vCLI doesn't afford as much access to and control over distributed vSwitches, unfortunately.

Configuring VMware vCenter with PowerCLI

There aren't too many configuration aspects of vCenter on Windows that can be checked with PowerCLI, but I will describe a few. We won't look at scripting vCenter configuration and assessment with the vCLI because most of the scripts are not really built to do this. Leveraging standard Windows scripting techniques and tools is a more realistic and effective approach for that. Following are some examples of common configuration tasks you may need to perform.

◆   To see what patches are installed on the vCenter server:

```
Get-WmiObject -ComputerName $DefaultVIServer Win32_QuickFixEngineering | select
Description, Hotfixid
```

The output of this command is shown in Figure 10.17.

FIGURE 10.17
vCenter patches

- To show the vCenter OS level and service pack:

```
Get-WmiObject Win32_OperatingSystem -computer $DefaultVIServer | select CSName,
Caption, CSDVersion
```

- To check the existing roles within vCenter, use `Get-VIRole`. The output of this command will show all roles defined on the vCenter server and should clarify which are system roles, meaning they are defined by VMware in a default install and can be modified only by cloning them and changing them afterward. See Figure 10.18 for an example.

FIGURE 10.18

vCenter roles

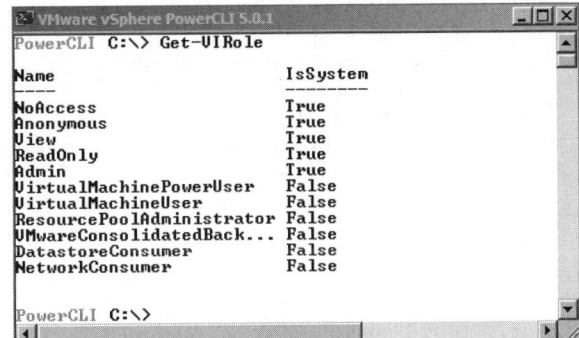

One additional check you can perform on vCenter systems is whether the SSL certificate in place for accessing vCenter's web interface (primarily the Managed Object Browser, Datastore Browser, or vSphere Web Client) is self-signed. Before doing so, you'll need to add a new function into PowerCLI. This function enables cryptographic checks and capabilities you'll need to query X.509 format certificates and their attributes, and you can simply paste it into a PowerShell browser and then press Enter twice to add and enable it. (See Listing 10.1. This script is also available on the book's web page at www.sybex.com/go/virtualizationsecurity.)

LISTING 10.1: Test-WebServerSSL function

```
function Test-WebServerSSL {
# Function original location: http://en-us.sysadmins.lv/Lists/Posts/Post.
aspx?List=332991f0-bfed-4143-9eea-f521167d287c&ID=60
[CmdletBinding()]
    param(
        [Parameter(Mandatory = $true, ValueFromPipeline = $true, Position = 0)]
        [string]$URL,
        [Parameter(Position = 1)]
        [ValidateRange(1,65535)]
        [int]$Port = 443,
        [Parameter(Position = 2)]
        [Net.WebProxy]$Proxy,
        [Parameter(Position = 3)]
        [int]$Timeout = 15000,
        [switch]$UseUserContext
    )
Add-Type @"
using System;
using System.Net;
```

```
using System.Security.Cryptography.X509Certificates;
namespace PKI {
    namespace Web {
        public class WebSSL {
            public Uri OriginalURi;
            public Uri ReturnedURi;
            public X509Certificate2 Certificate;
            //public X500DistinguishedName Issuer;
            //public X500DistinguishedName Subject;
            public string Issuer;
            public string Subject;
            public string[] SubjectAlternativeNames;
            public bool CertificateIsValid;
            //public X509ChainStatus[] ErrorInformation;
            public string[] ErrorInformation;
            public HttpWebResponse Response;
        }
    }
}
"@
    $ConnectString = "https://$url`:$port"
    $WebRequest = [Net.WebRequest]::Create($ConnectString)
    $WebRequest.Proxy = $Proxy
    $WebRequest.Credentials = $null
    $WebRequest.Timeout = $Timeout
    $WebRequest.AllowAutoRedirect = $true
    [Net.ServicePointManager]::ServerCertificateValidationCallback = {$true}
    try {$Response = $WebRequest.GetResponse()}
    catch {}
    if ($WebRequest.ServicePoint.Certificate -ne $null) {
        $Cert = [Security.Cryptography.X509Certificates.
X509Certificate2]$WebRequest.ServicePoint.Certificate.Handle
        try {$SAN = ($Cert.Extensions | Where-Object {$_.Oid.Value -eq
"2.5.29.17"}).Format(0) -split ", "}
        catch {$SAN = $null}
        $chain = New-Object Security.Cryptography.X509Certificates.X509Chain
-ArgumentList (!$UseUserContext)
        [void]$chain.ChainPolicy.ApplicationPolicy.Add("1.3.6.1.5.5.7.3.1")
        $Status = $chain.Build($Cert)
        New-Object PKI.Web.WebSSL -Property @{
            OriginalUri = $ConnectString;
            ReturnedUri = $Response.ResponseUri;
            Certificate = $WebRequest.ServicePoint.Certificate;
            Issuer = $WebRequest.ServicePoint.Certificate.Issuer;
            Subject = $WebRequest.ServicePoint.Certificate.Subject;
            SubjectAlternativeNames = $SAN;
            CertificateIsValid = $Status;
            Response = $Response;
            ErrorInformation = $chain.ChainStatus | ForEach-Object {$_.Status}
        }
        $chain.Reset()
        [Net.ServicePointManager]::ServerCertificateValidationCallback = $null
    } else {
```

```
        Write-Error $Error[0]
    }
}
```

Once this function is added, run the following command:

```
Test-WebServerSSL -URL $DefaultVIServer | Select OriginalURi, CertificateIsValid,
Issuer
```

The output of this command is shown in Figure 10.19.

FIGURE 10.19

SSL validation on
vCenter server

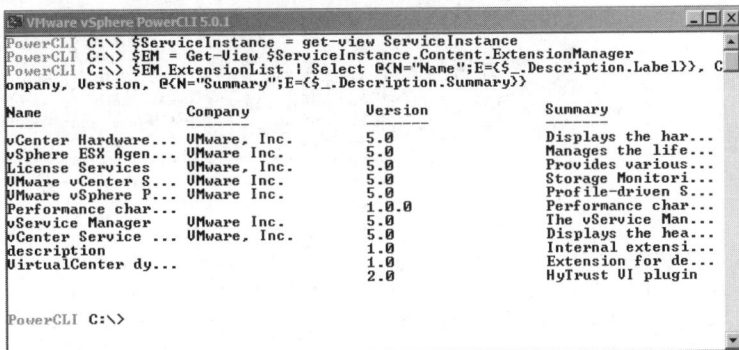

Finally, you can validate the vSphere Client plug-ins installed (which relate to vCenter). The series of commands you'll run to accomplish this are as follows:

```
$ServiceInstance = get-view ServiceInstance
$EM = Get-View $ServiceInstance.Content.ExtensionManager
$EM.ExtensionList | Select @{N="Name";E={$_.Description.Label}}, Company, Version,
@{N="Summary";E={$_.Description.Summary}}
```

The output of these commands should look something like the output shown in Figure 10.20.

FIGURE 10.20

vSphere Client
plug-ins

Microsoft Scripting for Hyper-V: PowerShell

For managing and assessing Microsoft Hyper-V systems, PowerShell is really the way to go. The best way to get started with Hyper-V PowerShell scripting is to download the PowerShell Management Library for Hyper-V, available here:

```
http://pshyperv.codeplex.com/
```

While there are numerous functions available within this library, most are entirely operational in nature; in other words, there aren't a lot of security-specific functions available. Let's explore a few of the functions you will likely want to make use of.

Getting Information about VMs

Getting a reasonable inventory of VMs known to the Hyper-V platform is critical and should be done on a regular basis. To pull this inventory from the Hyper-V platform, you can execute the get-vmsummary command. This will produce a fairly detailed list of information about the hypervisor and its VMs, as shown in Figure 10.21.

FIGURE 10.21

VM inventory on Hyper-V

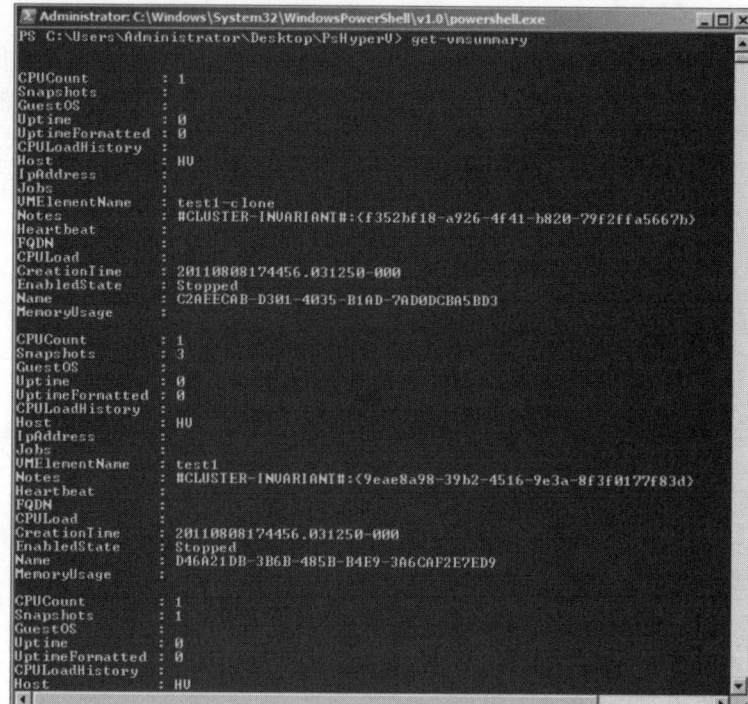

A similar function that may provide additional details is Get-VMState.

Another useful function for availability analysis is to query the hypervisor and determine how much memory is allocated to the system as well as how much memory the VM can potentially leverage. The function that provides this information is Get-VMmemory, and its output is shown in Figure 10.22.

FIGURE 10.22

VM memory configuration

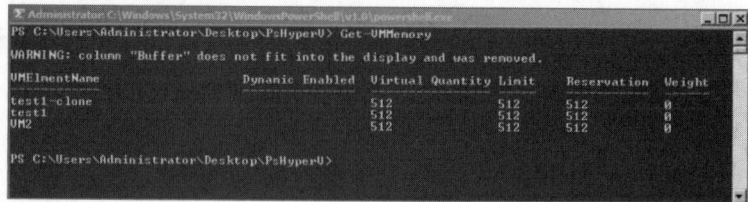

Getting Information about the Virtual Network

There are quite a few useful functions that pertain to virtual network configurations and settings.

Two functions that are useful allow for virtual NIC and switch assessment. The first is Get-VMNIC, and its output includes the VM that uses a certain NIC, the virtual switch it's attached to, VLAN info, and MAC addresses, as shown in Figure 10.23.

FIGURE 10.23

Virtual NIC and switch information on Hyper-V

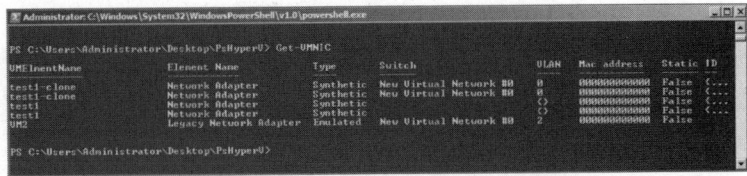

To simply view the virtual switches known to the Hyper-V host, along with the number of possible addresses it can manage, use the Get-VMswitch command, as shown in Figure 10.24.

FIGURE 10.24

List of Hyper-V virtual switches

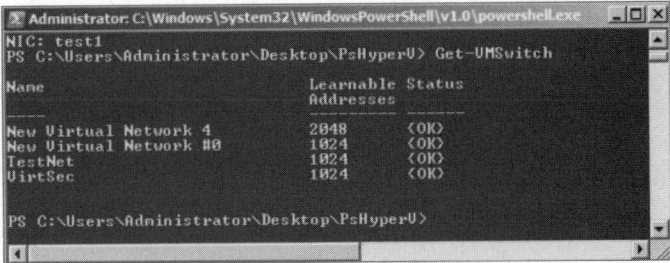

Assessing Other Aspects of the Virtual Environment

Another assessment function that is incredibly useful in evaluating the virtual environment is Get-VMdisk, which provides an enormous amount of detail about the VM disks in use on the Hyper-V platform, including SAN location, local disk information, and more:

- ◆ VM element name
- ◆ VM globally unique identifier (GUID)
- ◆ Controller name
- ◆ Controller instance ID
- ◆ Controller ID
- ◆ Drive name
- ◆ Drive instance ID
- ◆ Drive logical unit number (LUN)

♦ Disk path

♦ Disk image

♦ Disk name

♦ Disk instance ID

An example of Get-VMdisk output is shown in Figure 10.25.

FIGURE 10.25
List of VM disk information

One final assessment script that many admins will find useful for regular audits is Get-VMSnapshotTree, which allows you to query the Hyper-V host for a VM's known snapshots, as shown in Figure 10.26.

FIGURE 10.26
VM snapshots

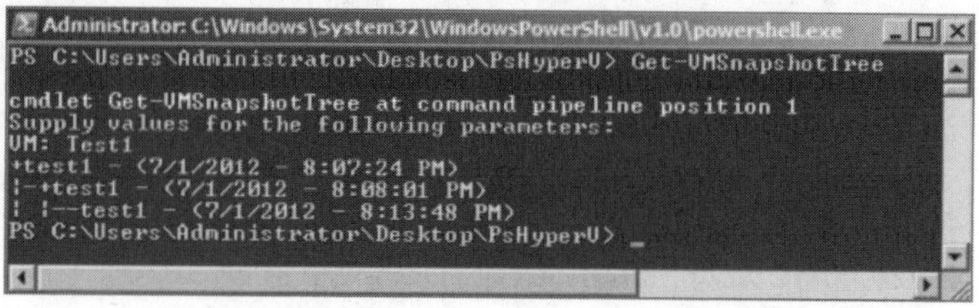

There are many more specific scripts and functions written for managing and configuring Hyper-V and especially VMs. A great list of these can be found at the Hyper-V: Scripts Microsoft site:

```
http://social.technet.microsoft.com/wiki/contents/articles/176.hyper-v-
scripts.aspx
```

Citrix Scripting: Shell Scripts

For scripting on Citrix XenServer, you'll likely find shell scripts to be the most useful and practical approach, although there are numerous efforts underway to leverage PowerShell and other languages as well. Here, I'll list a few simple examples that may be of use.

Scripting within the XenServer shell makes life simpler in many ways because you can leverage all the native commands described in Chapter 2 and others. For example, a simple script to shut down VMs rapidly (for maintenance or other operational reasons) could be as basic as this:

```
#!/bin/bash
xe vm-shutdown vm=VM1
xe vm-shutdown vm=VM2
xe vm-shutdown vm=VM3
```

You could make this more elegant by calling `xe vm-list` first and then feeding this into the shutdown functions within a loop.

Another common function in an assessment might be checking VM virtual network adapters using `vm-vif-list` or the XenServer networks using `xe network-list`.

Tobias Frigger at Citrix posted a great example of a shell script that could be used to list VMs and their MAC addresses in a CSV file for use with other operations programs. The script uses native XenServer command sets and parses output from them, dumping them into a file. For example, the following line sets up a loop that iterates through VM UUID values:

```
for vmuuid in `xe vm-list | awk -F': ' '/^uuid/ {print $2}'` ;
```

The following then grabs the VM Name-label:

```
namelabel=`xe vm-param-get uuid=$vmuuid param-name=name-label`
```

This line then places each VM's MAC address from the `xe vif-list` command into a variable:

```
mac=`xe vif-list vm-name-label="$namelabel" params=MAC
device=$j | awk -F': ' '/^MAC/ {print $2}'`
```

The entire script is available in the blog post "bash-ing XenServer" on the Citrix site, and it's worth checking out as a great example to get you started:

```
http://blogs.citrix.com/2012/04/25/bash-ing-xenserver/
```

NOTE There are plenty of other ways you could script XenServer, but all will generally leverage native Linux shell techniques and tools, with the exception of the XenServer-specific command sets.

## Chapter 11

Additional Security Considerations for Virtual Infrastructure

This chapter will explore several different areas of virtualization, with some general security guidelines and considerations for each. The first area that will be covered is desktop virtualization. More and more organizations are investigating virtual desktop technologies as their existing workstations and laptops grow obsolete. There are a number of use cases that make sense for some organizations, and security concerns and challenges will vary from one to the next. The second area that we'll cover in this chapter is storage virtualization and the security concepts and controls that administrators need to be aware of within their storage environments. Finally, this chapter will delve into application virtualization, with specific security concerns and controls to evaluate.

In this chapter, you will learn about the following topics:

◆ Virtual Desktop Infrastructure (VDI) operations and security benefits and pitfalls

◆ VDI architecture, and using VDI for improved security

◆ Storage virtualization basics and security considerations

◆ Application virtualization fundamentals and security

VDI Overview

Virtual Desktop Infrastructure (VDI) is a type of virtualization that consists of virtualizing desktops into images that run on centralized hypervisor platforms. In many ways, VDI is similar to server virtualization because numerous VMs are being hosted on clusters of hypervisors, but there are many differences in how the images are created, managed, and in some cases, secured.

VDI desktops can be accessed in a number of ways. The most common access methods are standard Remote Desktop Protocol (RDP) services and specialized endpoint clients, which vary in format from both thick (traditional) to thin clients with a very small footprint. In most cases, some sort of brokering service or platform, which is essentially a connection manager, is involved with connecting clients to desktop images, and this adds complexity to your virtual infrastructure.

VDI Benefits and Drawbacks: Operations and Security

More organizations are considering the operational and security reasons for moving to VDI, which fall into three categories.

Operational improvements and cost savings   The major reason for moving to VDI is the opportunity to realize longer-term cost savings in hardware because end user hardware has a fairly short shelf life. Rather than continue to replace hardware for desktops and laptops that are very expensive, some companies feel that it makes more sense to deploy a centralized VDI environment that can be accessed by relatively low-cost terminals from companies like Wyse (now owned by Dell). However, there are a number of costs involved in a large-scale VDI rollout that may eclipse these savings if not carefully weighed.

Bring your own device (BYOD)   With BYOD, some organizations are allowing employees to bring their own laptops and other computing devices (like tablets and handhelds) to work on, with controlled connectivity to the corporate network. To protect data and systems, and maintain the organization's configuration and integrity standards, the actual work environment should be controlled by the company. VDI can help accomplish this because the operating system, applications, and data access can be controlled by central policies and security technologies within VDI images while a company-controlled client can be installed on the employee's device to permit access. One of the biggest growth categories in this area is the use of tablets like iPads. Workers can use a tablet with purpose-built client applications to access desktop images and other types of virtual machines.

Security   VDI can reduce the cost of compliance and security for desktops. VDI supports centralized policy control, ephemeral (short-term) desktop images, and granular and manageable change and configuration management tools and processes. In addition, fighting malware and responding to desktop-related incidents can be easier in a VDI environment because all of the infrastructure is centrally located and controlled and virtual machines can be easily deleted and created anew.

Along with these benefits are new challenges and considerations that arise.

Security Advantages and Challenges

There are both positive and negative aspects to this architecture model from a security perspective. Most of the features provide both advantages and challenges.

CENTRALIZATION

VDI involves a major shift from the traditional distributed desktop environment to a more centralized internal model in the datacenter. To many security and operations teams, the notion of desktops in the datacenter is a frightening one!

VDI offers an advantage here. One of the most notorious challenges IT operations and security teams have faced over the last decade is the proliferation of malware and lack of configuration and patch consistency across the desktop environment. With VDI, security and operations teams can define desktop policies and VDI templates and manage them in a central location. Given the evolution of advanced malware, targeted client-side attacks, and social engineering aimed at employees in the last several years, VDI may really help rein in some of these issues (although we'll likely never eliminate them altogether).

Loss of Data and Network Segmentation

With VDI it is more difficult to avoid intermingling data of multiple classification levels, and the need for proper data and network segmentation is greater than ever before.

Any virtualized environment introduces the potential for data classification and segregation challenges due to the highly dynamic nature of resource balancing technology like vMotion. VDI environments face the same challenges, and desktops will need to be assessed for data access and classification policies.

In all likelihood, however, segmentation can still be implemented and managed with virtual LANS (VLANs), existing network firewalls, and Application layer monitoring and filtering tools.

For VDI deployments, the focus should be on two things:

◆ The type of user that is accessing a desktop image. Users will need to be evaluated for resource consumption requirements and data access needs, which will largely dictate the types of desktop images provisioned for them as well as where the images run (from a separate cluster that caters to sensitive data access, perhaps).

◆ The types of disks being provisioned and the data retention needs of desktop images in use. The types of disks being provisioned will help determine how data classification and segmentation occur:

   ◆ Traditional persistent virtual disks will likely have sensitive data stored within them, which means the central virtualization-specific storage area will need to be carefully categorized and protected as well.

   ◆ In cases where the virtual desktop is entirely ephemeral, disappearing entirely when a user logs out, the user will need to store all data on a centralized storage drive mapped within the desktop image. Ephemeral images present a new risk type as well — logging, auditing, and forensics analysis of ephemeral images can prove much more challenging unless planned ahead of time (which isn't always practical).

Implementing physical network segmentation for VDI zones is also important whenever possible. Much like the network segmentation discussed in Chapter 3, "Designing Virtual Networks for Security," and Chapter 4, "Advanced Virtual Network Operations," virtual desktop segments should be separated based on various data classification types for production traffic, virtualization operations traffic, storage traffic, and management traffic (such as Active Directory and administrator access to servers and virtualization management, for example).

Access from Anywhere with Anything

With a VDI implementation, employees can potentially access a work desktop from anywhere, and with BYOD programs, employees use a variety of systems for work-related computing tasks. Access to the work environment (and its desktop images) can originate from any system that has a VDI client installed — systems at home, portable devices like iPads and other tablets, or even browsers on any system that has one! With a variety of systems accessing internal infrastructure, a real risk of sensitive data leaking out or being misused exists.

In theory, this risk is probably not greater than that traditional VPN access — or any sort of access based on a system other than internal computers inside the network. Fortunately, most VDI clients have some security *sandboxing* capabilities built in (covered later in this chapter, in

"Offline Images"), and these may help to prevent data from being copied or moved outside of the VDI image to a local system drive or printer.

LINKED CLONES

Some of the new capabilities VDI products afford can also raise new security questions, even while offering some amazing new capabilities. One example is linked clones, which is a feature in the VMware View VDI product. Linked clones allow VDI desktops to be deployed from a "parent" VM (really a template that acts as a master VM for the set). The parent VM spawns a "replica" when clients are deployed from it. This replica is what the desktops are linked to, leaving the parent image free for updates without affecting the "children." Later, the parent can be resynchronized and can push the updates out to the cloned VDI desktops. This can simplify configuration management enormously because patches and hardening controls can be implemented once!

However, there is a critical security risk with linked clones. If the parent VM is corrupted, compromised, or deleted, it will affect all the VM clones linked to it! As linked clones are created with the Desktop Composer tools running on vCenter server in vSphere, it is *imperative* to protect vCenter server more than ever, which we covered extensively in Chapter 5, "Virtualization Management and Client Security."

OFFLINE IMAGES

Another example of new VDI technology that can affect security decisions is VMware View offline images (similar capabilities are available with Citrix XenClient and other providers as well). Offline images are localized copies of the VDI desktop that are downloaded with the View client to an end user's system(s). Once on a local system, the image is subject to a variety of policies and security controls. The offline image is encrypted by default, protecting it from accidental exposure or theft. The offline image also has a life cycle policy applied to it: It will need to connect to a central connection broker at a set interval. If the offline image doesn't connect periodically, it may be locked to the user or even wiped completely. This helps prevent offline VMs from existing forever.

Another available function with VMware View is a sandboxing capability built on the VMware Assured Computing Environment (ACE) product. This allows the local VM image to be "locked" from reading or writing to the system where it resides and can also prevent printing, online browsing, and other functions that may lead to data loss or other exposure. ACE is no longer available as a stand-alone product, but its features have been integrated into View.

OPERATIONAL ISSUES

In addition to the security issues VDI presents, there are a number of purely operational concerns:

Bandwidth   When a large number of users need to access desktop images simultaneously, the amount of bandwidth consumed can be significant. For remote users accessing desktops, this can be even more troublesome because the amount of bandwidth allocated to inbound Internet connectivity may be limited.

Power   Much as with bandwidth, a large number of desktop images in use simultaneously could lead to major power spikes and an increase in overall consumption. Although many are tempted to compare VDI to traditional desktop power consumption, they aren't quite the same. For one, you now have both high-end hypervisor platforms *and* thin hardware clients that require power. In addition, the amount of power consumption for large-scale virtualization platforms sometimes outweighs the power draw from comparable numbers of desktops over time. Some good information from Intel can be found in the white paper *The Top 10 Myths about Virtual Desktop Infrastructure (VDI)* at `www.dabcc.com/downloadfile .aspx?id=1172`.

Politics   Most users in organizations like to feel that they have some control over the systems they use (even if this is not the case). When IT brings desktop control into the datacenter, and all desktops are centrally administered when needed, this may cause political friction in some organizations. I am often asked how to assuage this kind of issue, and unfortunately I have no good answer other than to communicate early and often about the VDI initiative and how it will affect users' control (real or perceived) over their desktop environments.

Complexity and skills   End-user desktop support skills are no longer nearly as important once VDI is implemented, especially skills that are focused on hardware. On the flip side, virtualization and datacenter operations skills become much more valuable and are harder to come by. Much of this is related to the growing complexity level associated with these technologies.

VDI Architecture Overview

In general, most VDI architectures contain several common components:

VDI clients   Clients can range from the simple, such as Remote Desktop Protocol (RDP) on Windows and the multiplatform Virtual Network Computing (VNC), to more complex and proprietary, such as VMware View Client, Citrix Receiver, and Remote Administration Tools for Hyper-V.

VDI security servers/gateways   The presence of a separate VDI security gateway or server will depend on the products you deploy as well as the type of architecture you deploy. When in place, these are used to manage secure connections (via SSL, for example) and user authorization actions. Most of the time, these servers will implement a variety of policies for desktop images based on user identities and locations.

VDI connection brokers   The connection broker is the most active element of a VDI implementation. It handles all connections to the backend virtualization platforms. Connection brokers manage any desktop image requests and control which desktops are allocated to users. Where the architecture employs a security server, the connection broker will communicate with this system to get its required policies to apply for desktop deployment. Connection brokers also manage the "shelf life" of each desktop. Some VMs may be static, where users can access a persistent VM desktop environment. Others may be ephemeral, where they are booted from a set image that simply maps a user's Active Directory profile to a shared storage drive for data retention, and then the image is destroyed after each use. This is determined in real time by the connection broker, which then allocates the appropriate image for the requesting user.

VDI hypervisors and storage   VDI architectures will employ a set of hypervisors running multiple desktop VMs, as well as a large-scale storage implementation that hosts the virtual desktop disk files in a myriad of formats. Most VDI implementations make heavy use of templates, so most VMs will be derived from one or more template files that are also stored on a SAN or NAS.

A sample VDI architecture that includes these elements is shown in Figure 11.1.

FIGURE 11.1
VDI architecture
components

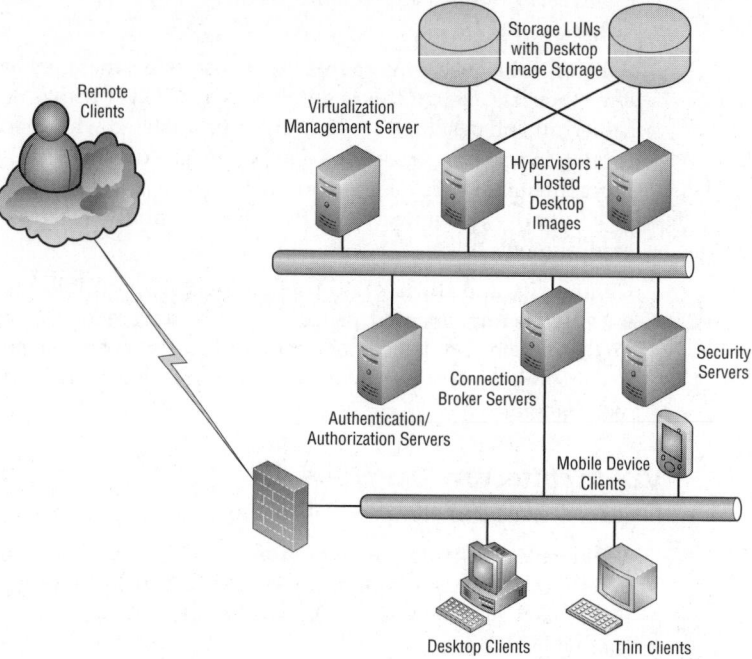

How should operations and security teams go about designing a proper VDI security architecture? The first stage of a secure VDI implementation is to decide which VDI products you will implement. Each has its own set of security and operations features that should be evaluated. Key criteria that will play into this decision include the existing virtualization platforms in house (as well as the knowledge to maintain them), the cost, and the scalability in various scenarios (for example, whether the VDI needs to cater to remote users or extranet users or only to in house employees).

There are two things to focus on at the initial planning and evaluation stage:

User-specific use cases You need to carefully consider different roles and use cases that the organization needs to fulfill before purchasing or implementing VDI. Some users may need highly specialized environments or hardware that VDI images don't support easily or at all. You should also evaluate the location from which the users will access desktops, which may make a difference in terms of performance tuning. Don't forget about data sensitivity and classification levels here! This will help you determine whether VDI makes sense at all, in some cases.

Product features Security features within the various products should be evaluated in the context of what use cases have been identified. For example, if the VDI must support many remote users, you might need a VDI platform that has more capable endpoint client security features.

At the next phase of VDI implementation, IT teams will need to determine any specific characteristics of the user desktops that will likely be needed. There are numerous operational choices to make here, ranging from operating systems to application software installed, and it's important to ensure that compatibility and performance requirements are developed.

For security teams, one of the most integral things to look at should be the VM desktop life cycle. As mentioned earlier, there are two major types of VDI desktops that can be deployed — persistent disk and ephemeral desktop — and most vendor solutions have their own variants:

Persistent disk   A persistent disk is a desktop image similar to a traditional desktop. The disk is available for and accessed by the user every time they log in.

Ephemeral desktop   Ephemeral desktops disappear every time a client logs out. They are provisioned on-the-fly when a user requests one, and the user's credentials are leveraged to map storage drives and other features into the desktop as needed.

Both kinds of desktop can exist simultaneously in a VDI deployment, of course, but they should be mapped to use cases. I suggest using ephemeral desktops for remote users connecting from untrusted locations on the Internet through a virtual private network (VPN) because this allows you to minimize the potential for persistent malware infections coming in from these users' systems. Another sound use case for ephemeral desktops is in kiosk scenarios like airport terminals or retail establishments, where the users of the system are likely unknown. Most internal VDI deployments should leverage persistent disks by default, unless certain storage types are scarce.

Next, security should validate whether existing security tools and controls will integrate with the VDI solution and how they'll work if so. During this phase, IT teams will want to include the following types of security solutions and options:

◆ Network and local access controls and authorization mechanisms

◆ Single Sign-On (SSO) and Identity Access Management (IAM) platforms

◆ Host-based security agents like antivirus and/or host-based intrusion detection systems

This is not a complete list by any means, but these will be the most immediate concerns related to traffic to and from the VDI environment, user authentication and authorization for access to desktop images, and security policy deployment.

Performance impacts in virtual desktop images related to local security tools also need to be evaluated. This point cannot be overstated; many of your existing security tools on desktops (antivirus in particular) will overwhelm a VDI environment if you do not plan and test appropriately. Newer tools like VMware vShield Endpoint and VM-aware tools from McAfee (MOVE) and Trend Micro may work better.

The last phase of VDI security architecture design is the implementation of security controls specific to the VDI environment. Likely the most pressing concern will be Network Access Control for traffic into and out of the VDI environment. To implement sound IP address and port-based controls in a number of places around the VDI environment, consider the following:

◆ Perimeter firewalls should control access from remote users into the VDI environment, although some (or most) of this may be handled by VPNs and reverse proxies.

◆ Physical firewalls should be enabled between VDI clusters of differing sensitivity and/or classification, although virtual firewalls may be useful in establishing various levels of internal segmentation as well.

◆ Firewalls should be in place and enabled between the VDI environment and the production assets that desktop images will access. I recommend maintaining rules between the connection broker and VDI images and between the connection broker and production subnets.

You'll also want to review and evaluate security controls related to VDI client behavior. Some of the security controls and policies you'll likely want to consider will be configured at the client level, and some will be configured and controlled at the VDI connection broker level or possibly even at the hypervisor/management levels. In general, most of the VDI products' client-focused security controls relate to client policies. Examples of these include remote sandbox controls related to data movement into and out of the client or desktop image and remote client/image termination when an employee is dismissed or has their system stolen. These kinds of features should be carefully evaluated and planned.

Leveraging VDI for Security

In many organizations, the user desktop environment has traditionally been like the Wild West; changes are constantly being made, applications are breaking, patching is difficult, and user permissions are often greater than needed. With the advent of VDI, operations teams can begin to regain control and maintain users' desktops in a more reasonable manner. Virtualization affords more control and central configuration management for desktop VMs, which can easily be cloned and turned into templates, and all VDI VMs can be deployed from these templates simply. In addition, by requiring that desktop user data reside on a centralized storage infrastructure, the risk of data loss or data theft, both accidental and intentional, goes down significantly.

Another security-specific scenario that many organizations are implementing or considering is the use of VDI for all remote access into the organization through VPNs and extranets. By forcing all remote users into a VDI image, all access to resources can be controlled and monitored, thus preventing direct connections from a remote client, potentially where the client's system does not meet policies or standards (a personal home system or tablet device, for example).

Many VPNs, extranet connectivity platforms, and proxies are now compatible with VDI in various levels of maturity.

Storage Virtualization

Storage virtualization is really a simple concept compared to some of the other virtualization types out there today. In fact, most organizations leveraging a large-scale storage area network (SAN) of any type are likely employing some level of storage virtualization, whether they realize it or not! In essence, storage virtualization is transparent abstraction of storage at the block level — in lay terms, that means that there's a layer of abstraction between the actual storage devices (disks) and the systems using the storage (servers, desktops).

Storage virtualization usually occurs at one of three levels:

Server level The first level is at the server, either virtual machines or hypervisors, or both. At this level, software is typically installed on a server that allows a virtual disk to appear either as a locally connected storage device or as a traditional remote storage type. This type of storage virtualization is often used for consolidating database server instances to specific virtual disks.

Storage network level   The second type of server virtualization occurs at the storage network level, within SAN switches (often called the SAN fabric). Within a storage switch, virtualization technology enables more heterogeneous storage access from any connected device, mapping virtual disks on the SAN to defined nodes and SAN address space or logical unit numbers (LUNs) representing a real or virtual SCSI target.

Storage device and platform level   The last major type of storage virtualization occurs on the storage devices and platforms themselves. Virtualization is defined within the storage controllers. This allows many virtualization operations to be performed, including taking snapshots, creating and deleting virtual disks, cloning disks, and others. In many cases, the virtualization capabilities within storage controllers also define cluster and other High-Availability arrangements. Modifying virtual disk capacity on-the-fly and creation of new RAID arrangements are also common tasks performed at this level.

Today, more and more storage virtualization features are being integrated into disk arrays. In fact, to offset costs and provide more flexible options for smaller and medium-size businesses, the logic associated with storage virtualization is increasingly being offered in the form of a virtual appliance that runs as a virtual machine on traditional hypervisor platforms. The following are common virtualized storage functions and features:

Virtual volume management: In essence, abstracting the creation and management of volumes allows physical disk structures to be dynamically allocated, whether on one physical platform or across multiple disk arrays. For example, a new VM that needs more space than is available on its mapped disk array could have additional space allocated from a different array on another physical device, all "behind the scenes" and managed by the storage virtualization controller or virtual appliance.

Snapshots: Snapshot creation and management is an integral element of storage virtualization and provides a great way for applications and systems to keep data backed up and available in the case of failure. Policies and rules governing the snapshot process for specified storage locations and connecting systems are defined within the storage virtualization platforms.

Replication: While storage replication is nothing new, and doesn't necessarily have anything to do with virtualization, it has traditionally been tied to one vendor or product. This has severely limited many organizations' storage strategies, especially between primary and secondary datacenters used for disaster recovery (DR), because any major shifts or upgrades in storage hardware and other technology could require a costly complete overhaul of both locations. With storage virtualization, replication can often be performed between storage platforms and systems from different vendors or at a minimum between different models from the same vendor.

Thin provisioning: In traditional SANs, admins would often have to overprovision the required (and planned) amount of space that a server might need to avoid running out of space at some point. With thin provisioning, or dynamic disk provisioning, the disk space on the SAN is only used as it's written to, which allows for significantly higher utilization rates and much more efficient storage use overall.

Storage federation: Some of the newer storage virtualization technologies offer storage federation capability. In essence, this is dynamic duplication of data between storage platforms in multiple locations, with automated mapping of the data in both locations to the systems and applications using the arrays where the data is located. In other words, VMs can be moved between datacenters with automatic remapping to a more local storage array, and array failure can lead to transparent remapping to the copy in the second datacenter with no need to reconfigure SAN access at the local host bus adapter (HBA) or other storage connector. Products that offer storage federation include EMC VPLEX and IBM SAN Volume Controller (SVC).

For smaller organizations without a dedicated central storage environment, new types of storage virtualization are becoming available from traditional virtualization vendors. One example is the VMware vSphere Storage Appliance (VSA), which can virtually "combine" disks from multiple hypervisor hosts into a datastore that VMs see as a central storage infrastructure like a traditional SAN.

What's all this got to do with security? In general, most of the security considerations around storage virtualization don't differ from those in the traditional storage realm. Here are some basic security guidelines for storage virtualization:

◆ Define data classification and data sensitivity domains that map to how the storage environment is laid out. This will allow you to consider the use of separate physical disks for very sensitive data types or the use of additional security controls where appropriate. Segment or zone the storage environment to allow only approved system and application access to these defined storage areas.

◆ Enable logging within the storage environment. In many cases, these logs will only be enabled within the vendor's specific implementation. Important events to monitor include management and configuration changes, sensitive data and/or LUN access, and availability and environment factors like low disk space or hardware failures.

◆ Restrict storage platform management access and interface access. In many ways, this recommendation boils down to proper network segmentation and segregation. When using virtual storage appliances, however, you'll need to plan for access to the hypervisors where the appliance is running, and to virtualization management components that the storage appliance integrates with. In addition, carefully define roles and privileges for accessing and managing the storage environment.

◆ Judiciously apply encryption and other data protection tools and techniques where appropriate. There are a number of encryption products that can be applied to the SAN or network-attached storage (NAS) appliances. New technologies allow for encryption of entire VMs, with strong policy and role-based controls for managing and accessing the VMs and the storage areas where they're located.

Besides the issues mentioned, all other security concerns around virtualized storage are the same as those for traditional storage. For Network File System (NFS) storage, the following are major security recommendations:

◆ Restrict the `/etc/exports` file to the root user on your NFS server(s). This prevents new storage mounts from being created or existing mounts from being manipulated.

◆ Limit IP addresses that can connect to the NFS system. This simple access control method can be reasonably effective in well-designed and carefully controlled networks.

◆ Use a dedicated storage network, leveraging physical and virtual network isolation and segmentation measures as discussed in Chapter 3 and Chapter 4.

For Fibre Channel networks, consider the following:

◆ Use port and zone World Wide Names (WWNs) for authentication instead of just node WWNs. A WWN is essentially the equivalent of a storage NIC MAC address. Using storage switch WWNs in addition to only the endpoint WWNs can help prevent spoofing and traffic hijacking attacks.

◆ Use hard zoning and/or port zoning for maximum zone security, including port locking on Fibre Channel switches if these features are available. This prevents spoofing and authentication attacks as well.

◆ Implement LUN masking properly. Logical unit numbers (LUNs) are identifiers on the storage infrastructure. Storage admins can "mask," or hide, specific LUNs if they don't need to be visible. Masking LUNs at the local adapter level is not a good idea, however, because an attacker with privileges could remove the mask and see storage they shouldn't. Instead, mask the LUNs at the storage switch or storage controller levels because these are much more difficult to compromise.

For iSCSI networks, consider these security controls:

◆ Always deploy iSCSI on a dedicated network, using isolation and segmentation techniques discussed in Chapter 3 and Chapter 4. If that's not possible, use virtual LANs (VLANs) for Layer 2 logical isolation.

◆ Enable the Challenge Handshake Authentication Protocol (CHAP) for mutual authentication between virtual systems and storage environments. While CHAP is not perfect as a security protocol, it is built into the iSCSI standard and is better than nothing!

◆ Implement vendor-specific security measures for any naming services in the iSCSI environment. This can prevent name resolution attacks and cache poisoning.

An excellent resource for storage security is the Storage Security Industry Forum (SNIA), which can be found at www.snia.org/forums/ssif.

Most other security recommendations related to storage virtualization concerns capacity planning and availability because overcommitment of the storage environment is a risk when using storage virtualization tools and techniques.

Application Virtualization

Application virtualization, as the name suggests, pertains to abstracting individual applications for use on remote systems. For example, a centrally hosted application virtualization environment could allow numerous clients to access spreadsheet and document editing apps from Microsoft Office or OpenOffice, email and calendar programs like Microsoft Outlook, or specialized applications written in house. These applications are run in their own "sandbox," isolated both from other applications and from the native operating system on the client side.

Most of the time, application virtualization deployments are focused on minimizing time and cost associated with installation, handling application conflicts, and simplifying application upgrades and changes. Maintaining proper licensing and controlling application access are also major drivers of application virtualization efforts.

Application virtualization involves a few key elements that warrant consideration from a security perspective:

Application servers: These are specialized hypervisors that serve up numerous sandboxed applications to clients that are connecting, in much the same way VDI images are managed and hosted by VDI-focused hypervisor deployments.

Management applications: Application virtualization products will rely on a management console where configuration and deployment controls are set up.

Clients: A variety of endpoint clients may be available for accessing and using virtualized application instances.

Protocols: Some vendors rely on specialized protocols to manage and display virtual application data to remote clients in conjunction with more standard network protocols.

The first thing to keep in mind is security at all levels of the application virtualization stack. Table 11.1 lists the types of security controls you should think about and where they go.

TABLE 11.1: Application virtualization layers and controls

VIRTUALIZATION LAYER	SECURITY CONTROL AREAS
Application client	Policies for authentication and local use, patching and upgrades to the client or browser (if Web based).
Network connections	Implementation of encryption using IPSec or SSL, proper cipher selection and connection establishment, Network Access Controls (router ACLs and firewall rules).
Custom protocols	Citrix, for example, uses its Independent Computing Architecture (ICA) protocol to facilitate data exchange between clients and XenApp servers. This protocol's encryption and integrity check features should be evaluated. Any vendor-specific protocols (such as Remote Desktop Protocol from Microsoft) should be evaluated for security options.
Application virtualization servers	Application virtualization hypervisors can run on a variety of platforms, some of which are Type I hypervisors (and may require much less security configuration), and others of which are traditional OS platforms that need a number of controls applied. Many of these systems support a variety of authentication and authorization types, ranging from smartcards to Kerberos and Active Directory, and these should be integrated and configured where appropriate. Windows Group Policy Objects (GPOs) and other policy controls should be put in place as well.
Applications	Any application security controls and configuration should be implemented as you would normally. Keeping applications patched and configured is actually much simpler because you need to do it only once!

The following are some additional general recommendations for deploying and managing application virtualization security:

◆ Lock down and secure the application hypervisor environment. Whether using Citrix XenApp, Microsoft App-V, or VMware vSphere, you'll need to follow the guidelines outlined in Chapter 2, "Securing Hypervisors."

◆ Design and enforce proper network segmentation. Each application server cluster should be situated in a zone appropriate to both the sensitivity of the data being accessed and the trust level of the users who are accessing the applications and data. This may necessitate the use of a secure gateway or proxy (sometimes implemented as a VPN gateway) in demilitarized zones (DMZs) for external users.

◆ Don't use default self-signed certificates from vendors. Because most communication channels with application virtualization solutions utilize some form of SSL, you should look into implementing your own certificates to prevent man-in-the-middle (MITM) attacks or breaches of trust when connecting to the environment.

Index

A

access controls, 100
ACE. *See* Assured Computing Environment
Active Directory, 78
Active Directory authentication
    ESXi, 46–47, 288
    firewall ports, 84–85
    PowerCLI, 288
    XenServer, 84–87
Add Network Wizard, 104
Address Resolution Protocol (ARP), 99, 146
Address Space Layout Randomization (ASLR),
    56–57
Admission Control, 270–271
Agobot, 6
AGULP model, 163
Amazon, 179, 183
AMD, 56
    processor virtualization capabilities, 8
anti-malware tools, adapting, 12–13
antivirus, 309
application data encryption, 184
application virtualization, 313–315
Applied Cryptography (Schneier), 184
App-V, 315
Arkeia Software, 255
ARP. *See* Address Resolution Protocol
Arvanitis, Nicholas, 180
ASLR. *See* Address Space Layout
    Randomization
Assured Computing Environment (ACE), 306
at, 78
auditing
    importance, 201–202
    logging options, 202–221
    Windows Audit Policy, 205
    XenServer, 220
Authorization Manager (AzMan), 63
"Automate the Hardening of Your Virtual
    Machine VMX Configurations" (Lam), 285
AVHD files, 195
AWS, 183
AzMan. *See* Authorization Manager

B

Background Intelligent Transfer Service
    (BITS), 170
backups. *See also* replication; snapshots
    encryption, 181
    ESXi settings, 29
    VCB, 164
baseline groups, 22–23
baseline profiles
    attaching, 25–26
    defining, 20–22
baselines, 202
BCP. *See* business continuity planning
BitLocker Drive Encryption (BDE), 57–58
BITS. *See* Background Intelligent Transfer Service
Black Hat conference, 8
Black Hat DC conference, 8
blade systems, 95
Blue Pill, 8
BMC Remedy IT Service Management Suite, 236
BMC Software, 236
bonded networks, 111
bootloaders, 77
botnets, 6
bots, 9
Brenton, Chris, 12
bring your own device (BYOD), 304, 305
business continuity planning (BCP), 253–254
    virtualization redundancy and fault
        tolerance, 256–270
BYOD. *See* bring your own device

C

CA. *See* certificate authority
CAM. *See* Content Addressable Memory
Catbird, 10
CBT. *See* Changed Block Tracking
Center for Internet Security (CIS), 152, 177
    Linux hardening guides, 76
    Windows Server 2008 Benchmark v.1.2.0, 53
CentOS, 72, 76, 120
certificate authority (CA), 27, 159, 170

certificate request (CSR), 159
certificates
    ESXi default, 27–28
    ESXi host verification, 29–30
    Hyper-V management, 54–55
    self-signed, 54, 158
Challenge Handshake Authentication Protocol
    (CHAP), 125–129, 313
change ecosystem
    IT infrastructure components, 232, 233
    major areas, 231–232
    visibility issues, 234
change management, 5
    component-control interrelations, 233
    downstream impacts, 229
    ecosystem, 231–234
    security, 230–231
    steps, 231
    virtualization impact, 234–235
    virtualization integration, 249–250
change management systems, 236
Changed Block Tracking (CBT), 255
CHAP. *See* Challenge Handshake Authentication
    Protocol
CIM. *See* Common Information Model
CIMV2, 68–69
CIS. *See* Center for Internet Security
CIS Windows 2008 benchmark, 234
Cisco, 100, 130, 256
Cisco Nexus 1000v, 100, 136
Cisco Nexus 7000, 256
Citrix. *See also* XenCenter
    hotfixes, 72
    virtual switches, 93, 98, 102, 148
    virtualization management platforms, 95
Citrix Receiver, 307
Citrix XenServer 6.0 Administrator's Guide, 200
Citrix XenServer vSwitch Controller Guide, 132
Citrix XenServer Workload Balancing 6.0
    Administrator's Guide, 270
"Clobbering the Cloud!" (Arvanitis, Slaviero, and
    Meer), 180
cloning, 237–249, 306
cloud VM reconnaissance, 179–180
Cloudburst, 9
clustering, 256–262
    host, 256
    Hyper-V, 259–260

    multicast, 141–142
    unicast, 141–142
    vSphere, 257–259
    XenServer, 261–262
CMDB. *See* configuration management database
code/file injection flaws, 178
Common Information Model (CIM), 48
Common Vulnerabilities and Exposures (CVE), 9
compliance, 202
configuration
    domains, 290
    drift, 229
    ESXi, 17–52, 286–290
    ESXi logging, 207–211
    Hyper-V, 52–72
    Hyper-V logging, 211–217
    hypervisor security, 15–17
    Microsoft management capabilities, 251
    NTP, 35–37, 59, 80, 287–289
    PowerCLI, 283–297
    PVLANs, 112, 113–115
    SNMP, 37–38, 59–60, 80
    SSH, 52, 88–89
    vCenter, 187
    vCenter Configuration Manager, 251
    vCenter Update Manager, 19
    vCLI, 285–286, 289–290, 293–294
    virtual switches security, 102–112
    VLAN, 112–117, 293–294
    VUM, 18–20
    XenServer, 72–91, 116–117
    XenServer logging, 219–221
configuration file security and monitoring, 16
    ESXi, 38–40
    Hyper-V, 60–63
    XenServer, 81
configuration management, 5, 229–234
    best practices, 235–237
    change ecosystem, 231–234
    cloning and templates, 237–249
    life cycle, 235
    snapshots, 238
    virtualization impact, 234–235
configuration management database (CMDB), 235
Configuresoft, 250–251
CONNECT role, 156
connection brokers, 307
Content Addressable Memory (CAM), 135

copy/paste operations, 188–189
Core IMPACT, 7
Core Security, 7
Create Cluster Wizard, 259–260
Create VM Template Wizard, 243
Create vSphere Distributed Switch Wizard, 106
Criscione, Claudio, 12, 179
CRM. *See* customer relationship management
cron, 78
cross-server private networks, 111
cryptographic hashing functions, 60
CSR. *See* certificate request
customer relationship management (CRM), 249
CVE. *See* Common Vulnerabilities and Exposures

D

daemon account, 41
dark fiber, 255
Data Execution Prevention (DEP), 56
data flow control, 255
Datagram SyslogAgent, 205
Datastore Browser, 295
datastore heartbeating, 272, 273
DB2, 156
db_owner role, 156
DCUI. *See* Direct Console User Interface
dcui account, 41
debug mode, 78
default settings, 16
    ESXi, 33–34
    ESXi key and certificates, 27–28
    Hyper-V, 56–59
    XenServer, 76–79
DefCon, 180
Defense Information Systems Agency (DISA), 152
Dell, 304
Dell EqualLogic, 255
demilitarized zones (DMZs), 10, 315
denial of service (DoS), 78, 178
DEP. *See* Data Execution Prevention
Deploy Template Wizard, 239–242
DER encoding, 159
Desktop Composer, 306
DHCP. *See* Dynamic Host Configuration Protocol
DHCP Guard, 125
Direct Console User Interface (DCUI), 40
    account for, 41

firewall configuration, 50
    Lockdown Mode, 289
    remote logging controls, 223
    restricting local root account, 43–44
directory traversal attack, 7–8
DISA. *See* Defense Information Systems Agency
disaster recovery (DR), 181, 253–254
    virtualization redundancy and fault
        tolerance, 256–270
    XenCenter scenario creation, 279–280
Disaster Recovery Wizard, 280
Distributed COM Users group, 68
Distributed Management Task Force (DMTF), 242
Distributed Power Management (DPM), 24, 265
Distributed Resource Scheduler (DRS), 160,
    262–266
distributed virtual switches (VDS/dvSwitch),
    105–107, 150, 237
    NetFlow, 139–140
    network monitoring, 137–140
    PowerCLI assessment, 292–293
    security policies, 123–124
    vDS, 113–115
DMTF. *See* Distributed Management Task Force
DMZs. *See* demilitarized zones
DNS. *See* Domain Name System
Dom0 virtual machine, 197
Domain Name System (DNS), 11, 46
domains, configuring, 290
DoS. *See* denial of service
double tagging, 112
downstream impacts, 229
DPM. *See* Distributed Power Management
DR. *See* disaster recovery
DR site, 254
DRS. *See* Distributed Resource Scheduler;
    Dynamic Resource Scheduler
DTP. *See* Dynamic Trunking Protocol
dvfilter API, 192
dvSwitch. *See* distributed virtual switches
Dynamic Host Configuration Protocol (DHCP),
    99
    monitoring, 100
dynamic memory migration, 94, 95
Dynamic Optimization, 275–276
dynamic patching, 21
Dynamic Resource Scheduler (DRS), 12
Dynamic Trunking Protocol (DTP), 129

E

EC2, 179
EMC, 250, 254–255
EMC VPLEX, 312
Enhanced vMotion Compatibility (EVC), 257, 258
EoMPLS. *See* Ethernet over MPLS
ephemeral desktops, 309
ERNW, 180
ESX, 6, 9
    command line, 27, 107, 108
    logging, 205–207
    network connection types, 104, 105
    network monitoring, 136–137
    NIC teaming, 133
    remote logging, 221–222
    Service Console, 107, 108
    syslog, 204
    VILurker attack, 153
    virtual switch security policies, 124
ESX Admins group, 46
ESX Console, 40
esxcfg-vmnic, 108
esxcfg-vswitch, 104, 107, 108, 113, 119
esxcli, 37, 125, 210–211
ESXi, 2, 9, 12
    Active Directory authentication, 46–47, 288
    baseline profiles, 20–21
    command line, 26–27, 107, 108, 113
    configuring, 17–52, 288–289
    Console, 107
    default key and certificate, 27–28
    default ports, 48
    default settings, 33–34
    domain configuration, 290
    firewall configuration, 48–51
    host certificate verification, 29–30
    IPSec, 31
    limiting local users, 41–43
    Lockdown Mode, 288–289
    log size and rotation, 209–210
    logging, 207–211
    network connection types, 104
    network monitoring, 136
    NIC teaming, 133
    NTP configuration, 35–37
    NTP sources, 287–288
    operational security, 34–38
    password policies, 45–46
    patching, 17–27
    persistent logging, 208–209
    PowerCLI configuration, 286–289
    remote logging, 222–223
    remote logging server configuration, 287
    restricting hypervisor console access, 47–52
    restricting local root account, 43–44
    secure communications, 158–160
    securing and monitoring configuration
        files, 38–40
    securing communications, 27–33
    securing local users and groups, 40–47
    settings backup, 29
    SNMP configuration, 37–38
    SSH access control, 52
    syslog-NG, 204
    time-out values, 30
    vCLI configuration, 289–290
    virtual disk manipulation attack, 180
    virtual switch security policies, 124
    vMotion support, 234–235
Ethernet over MPLS (EoMPLS), 256
EVC. *See* Enhanced vMotion Compatibility
Execute Disable (XD), 56
exploitation, 11
extlinux loader, 77

F

facilities, 203
failback, 135
failover
    notification, 135
    vSphere, 135
    XenServer, 145–146
Fast Clone, 247
fault tolerance (FT)
    high availability, 270–280
    Hyper-V, 274–277
    SCVMM, 274–277
    virtualization redundancy, 256–270
    vSphere, 270–274
    XenServer, 277–280
fault tolerance traffic, 48
FDE. *See* full disk encryption
Fibre Channel SAN, 125, 254, 313
filtering tools, 78–79

firewalls
  Active Directory authentication, 84–85
  DCUI, 50
  ESXi configuration, 48–51
  Hyper-V, 69–71
  physical, 10, 101
  trust zone separation, 100
  VDI environments, 309–310
  virtual, 10
  vSphere Client, 48–49
  XenServer, 89–91
Flick, Tony, 179
FQDN, 159
Frigger, Tobias, 301
FT. *See* fault tolerance
full disk encryption (FDE), 181
full virtualization, 98
fully virtualized security, 102

G

GHI. *See* Guest Host Interaction
Gibson Research Corporation, 56
global catalog debugging, 78
GnuPG, 40, 63
graphical user interface (GUI), 281
groups
  attaching, 25–26
  baseline, 22–23
  Distributed COM Users, 68
  `ESX Admins,` 46
  ESXi, 40–47
  Hyper-V, 63–68
  local, 40–47, 63–68, 81–83
  Microsoft Host, 275
  port, 103–112
  resource pools, 262–264
  SCVMM, 63, 172–175
  securing, 17
  vCenter, 163–167
  VUM, 22–23, 25–26
  XenCenter, 176
  XenServer, 81–83
guest, 1, 2
  anti-malware tool adaptation, 12–13
  stealing, 179
  virtual, 2
Guest Host Interaction (GHI), 193, 194

guest system, 2
GuestStealer, 179
GUI. *See* graphical user interface

H

HA. *See* high availability
hardware virtual machines (HVMs), 197
hashing tools, 40
HBA. *See* host bus adapter
HBR. *See* Host-Based Replication
heartbeat services, 270, 272
heartbeat SR, 278
help desk ticketing, 17
*Hey, You, Get Off of My Cloud: Exploring
  Information Leakage in Third-Party Compute
  Clouds* (Ristenpart, Tromer, Shacham, and
  Savage), 180
HGFS. *See* Host Guest File System
HIDS/HIPS. *See* host-based intrusion detection
  or prevention system
high availability (HA), 145, 253, 256
  Hyper-V, 274–277
  vSphere, 270–274
  XenServer, 277–280
Honeynet Project, 6
host, 1, 2
  anti-malware tool adaptation, 12–13
  certificate verification, 29–30
  clustering, 256
  monitoring, 270–271
  perimeter, 170–171
  reserves, 275
host bus adapter (HBA), 312
Host Guest File System (HGFS), 188–189
Host Welcome login page, 33–34
host-based intrusion detection or prevention
  system (HIDS/HIPS), 152, 309
Host-Based Replication (HBR), 48
host-based security agents, 309
hotfixes, 72–74
HP IT Change Management Suite, 236
HTTPS, 34
HVMs. *See* hardware virtual machines
HyperSafe, 9
Hyper-V, 9, 12, 102
  architecture, 52
  certificate management, 54–55

clustering, 259–260
configuring, 52–72
default rules, 70
default settings, 56–59
defining virtual switches and port
    groups, 109–110
event categories, 211–213
files, 195
firewall, 69–71
high availability and fault tolerance, 274–277
iSCSI CHAP, 128
load balancing, 141–142
local rules, 172
locking down, 195–197
log entry types, 205
logging, 211–217
network monitoring, 144–145
network operations, 141–144
network performance, 142–144
operational security, 59–60
operations, 66–68
patching, 53
port mirroring, 144–145
PowerShell scripting, 297–300
remote logging, 223–225
replication, 255
resource pools, 266–269
restricting hypervisor platform access, 68–72
roles, 64–68
secure communications, 170–171
securing and monitoring configurations
    files, 60–63
securing communications, 53–55
securing local users and groups, 63–68
TCP Chimney, 143–144
templates and snapshots, 242–246
traffic shaping, 142–144
virtual switch ports, 119–120
virtual switch security policies, 125
VLAN configuration, 115–116
Hyper-V 2012 Overview, 132
Hyper-V Manager, 68
    snapshots, 244–245
    virtual switches, 109–110
    VLAN configuration, 115–116
Hyper-V Virtual Machine Management
    Service, 54

hypervisors. *See also* virtual machine monitor;
    specific hypervisors
    architecture, 15
    communication channel, 7
    configuration and security, 15–17
    encryption, 181, 182–183
    locking down access, 17, 47–52, 68–72
    maintenance mode, 27
    network architecture considerations, 101
    NICs, 94
    privilege levels, 4
    templates, 237
    type I, 2, 4
    type II, 2–3, 4, 52
    VDI, 307–308
    virtual switches, 98
    VM escape threats, 6–9

I

IAM. *See* Identity Access Management
IBM, 8, 178, 312
ICMP. *See* Internet Control Message Protocol
iDefense, 7
Identity Access Management (IAM), 309
IDS. *See* intrusion detection system
IIS, 234
Image Management Service, 212
Immunity, Inc., 9
information leakage attacks, 178
Information Technology Infrastructure Library
    (ITIL), 230, 235
InGuardians, 7
inline devices, 132
instruction timing, 8
Integration Services, 212
Intel, 8, 56
IntelGuardians, 7
internal investigations, 202
Internet Control Message Protocol (ICMP), 78
Internet Printing Protocol (IPP), 89
intrusion detection sensors, 99, 137
intrusion detection system (IDS), 132
Invisible Things Labs, 8
IP address pools, 266, 267, 269
iPads, 304, 305
IPP. *See* Internet Printing Protocol
IPSec, 31–33

IPTables, 89–91
IPv6, 31–33
iSCSI, 94, 145, 182, 313
    securing connections, 125–129
ITIL. *See* Information Technology Infrastructure
    Library
*ITIL Glossary of Terms, Definitions and Acronyms
    V3*, 230

K

Kerberos, 59
kernel mode, 3
key loggers, 9
key management, 184–185
Kiwi Syslog, 225
Kortchinsky, Kostya, 9

L

L2TPv3. *See* Layer 2 Tunneling Protocol version 3
Lam, William, 283, 285
Layer 2 Tunneling Protocol version 3 (L2TPv3),
    256
Layer 2 VLAN segmentation, 93
LDAP stores, 78
Liguori, Anthony, 8
linked clones, 306
Linux hardening, 76
Linux Volume Manager (LVM), 197
Liston, Tom, 7
Live Migration, 53, 182
load balancing, 131
    Hyper-V, 141–142
    SCVMM 2012, 268–269
    vSphere, 133–135
    XenServer, 145–147, 270
local administrators, 168
local users
    ESXi, 40–47
    Hyper-V, 63–68
    limiting, 41–43
    password policies, 45–46
    restricting root, 43–44
    XenServer, 81–83
Lockdown Mode, 288–289
lockdown mode, 43, 44
log management platforms, 226
log rotation and conversion tools, 226

logging. *See also* syslog
    effective log management, 226–228
    ESX, 205–207, 221–222
    ESXi, 207–211, 222–223
    Hyper-V, 211–217, 223–225
    importance, 201–202
    management tools, 226
    monitoring, 40
    NIST recommendations, 227, 228
    options, 202–221
    remote, 221–226, 287
    replication, 256
    SCVMM, 171–172, 211–217, 223–224
    vCenter, 160–163, 211
    vCLI configuration, 289–290
    VMware VMs, 186, 189–190
    vSphere, 221–223
    XenCenter, 176, 218–221
    XenServer, 218–221, 225–226
logical unit numbers (LUNs), 311, 313
logrotate daemon, 207, 220
Lowe, Scott, 223, 238, 240
LUN masking, 313
LUNs. *See* logical unit numbers
LVM. *See* Linux Volume Manager

M

MAC. *See* Media Access Control
MAC address filtering, 100
MAC address pools, 266, 268, 269
MAC address spoofing, 142, 143
malware, 5–6
    bots, 6
    packer applications, 6
    VM template issues, 237
    VM-aware, 6
Managed Object Browser, 33–34, 295
management database
    SCVMM, 168–169
    vCenter, 155–157
Management Information Base (MIB), 38
management networks, 153–155
management NICs, 145
management platforms
    log, 226
    network architecture, 152–155
    security recommendations, 151–152

management traffic, 93, 95–97, 105
man-in-the-middle (MITM), 29, 75, 126, 153, 315
Mastering Microsoft Windows Server 2008 R2 (Minasi et al.), 53
Mastering VMware vSphere 5 (Lowe), 223, 238, 240
Matasano Security, 8
maximum tolerable outage (MTO), 254
maximum transmission unit (MTU), 111
McAfee MOVE Antivirus, 13, 309
md5sum, 40
Media Access Control (MAC), 12, 99
    binding, 146
    unicast clustering, 141–142
Meer, Haroon, 180
memory inspection, 8
Metasploit, 12, 153, 179
MIB. *See* Management Information Base
Microsoft, 12
    configuration management capabilities, 251
    locking down VMs, 195–197
    virtual switches, 93, 102
Microsoft Authorization Manager, 172
Microsoft Guide to Configuring Virtual Networks for Windows Server 2008 R2, 132
Microsoft Hardening Guides, 152
Microsoft Host Group allocation, 275
Microsoft Management Console (MMC), 54, 55
    Authorization Manager, 63
    remote access, 71
Microsoft Office, 313
Microsoft Server 2012, 152
Microsoft Systems Center. *See* Windows Server Update Services
Microsoft Windows Server 2012 Information, 132
Minasi, Mark, 53
mirror ports, 100, 132, 138–139, 144–145
MirrorView, 254
MITM. *See* man-in-the-middle
MMC. *See* Microsoft Management Console
monitoring capabilities, 99–100
monitoring ports, 132
Morehouse, Justin, 179
MPLS. *See* Multiprotocol Label Switching
MTO. *See* maximum tolerable outage
MTU. *See* maximum transmission unit
Multicast, 141
multicast clustering, 141–142
Multiprotocol Label Switching (MPLS), 255

N

NAC. *See* Network Access Control
NAS. *See* network-attached storage
National Institute of Standards and Technology (NIST)
    logging recommendations, 227, 228
    time services, 36
NetFlow, 139–140
Network Access Control (NAC), 100
Network Attached Storage (NAS), 125
Network File Copy (NFC), 48
Network File System (NFS), 41, 94, 125, 182, 312
network interface cards (NICs), 10
    bonding, 145–147
    failover detection, 135
    hypervisor, 94
    load balancing, 133
    management, 145
    physical, 94, 95–97, 129
    redundancy, 95–97
    teaming, 133–135
    virtual, 94, 212
network isolation, 99
Network Load Balancing (NLB), 135, 141–142, 269
Network Mapper (NMAP), 12
network monitoring
    ESX, 136–137
    ESXi, 136
    Hyper-V, 144–145
    SCVMM, 144
    sensors, 4
    strategies, 132
    vSphere, 136–140
    XenServer, 148–150
network performance, 131–132
    Hyper-V, 142–144
    vSphere, 135–136
    XenServer, 148
network pools, 266
network security devices, 94
network taps, 132
Network Time Protocol (NTP), 16, 34, 46
    ESXi configuration, 35–37
    Hyper-V configuration, 59
    PowerCLI configuration, 287–288
    vCLI configuration, 289
    XenServer configuration, 80

network-attached storage (NAS), 181, 312
networks
    architecture for virtualization management
        servers, 152–155
    components, 93–94
    design elements, 95–98
    management, 153–155
    physical, 93–94
    physical *vs.* virtual, 98–99
    segmentation, 112–117, 305
    virtual, 93–94
New VM Wizard, 247
Nexus 1000v, 100, 136
Nexus 7000, 256
NFC. *See* Network File Copy
NFS. *See* Network File System
nfsnobody account, 41
NICs. *See* network interface cards
NIST. *See* National Institute of Standards and
    Technology
NLB. *See* Network Load Balancing
NLB Manager, 141
NMAP. *See* Network Mapper
No Execute (NX), 56
Non-Uniform Memory Access (NUMA), 212
NTP. *See* Network Time Protocol
NUMA. *See* Non-Uniform Memory Access
NVRAM files, 186
NX. *See* No Execute

O

offline images, 306
Open Virtualization Format (OVF), 242, 248
Open vSwitch, 100, 125, 150, 237
OpenOffice, 313
OpenSSL, 27, 159
operating modes, 3
operating system (OS), 2
    encapsulation, 52
    ephemeral, 29
    securing underlying, 152
operational security, 16
    ESXi, 34–38
    Hyper-V, 59–60
    XenServer, 80
operational threats
    lack of visibility into environments, 4–5

separation of duties, 5
    VM sprawl, 4
operational trends, 202
operations traffic, 95–97
Oracle, 156
OS. *See* operating system
OSSEC Windows agent, 205
Ottenheimer, Davi, 179
Overlay Transport Virtualization (OTV), 256
OVF. *See* Open Virtualization Format

P

packer applications, 6
PAM. *See* pluggable authentication module
PAM files, 84
paravirtualization, 98, 197
"Passively Fingerprinting VMware Virtual
    Systems" (Brenton), 12
password policies, ESXi, 45–46
patching, 16
    centrally managed, 53
    command line, 26–27
    dynamic, 21
    ESXi, 17–27
    Hyper-V, 53
    vCenter storage, 294
    VUM configuration, 18–20
    XenServer, 72–74
Pate, Steve, 180
Payment Card Industry (PCI), 181
Payment Card Industry Data Security Standard
    (PCI DSS), 103, 181, 202
PCI. *See* Payment Card Industry
PCI DSS. *See* Payment Card Industry Data
    Security Standard
PCI DSS Virtualization Guidelines, 181, 182
peer-to-peer botnets, 6
pen testing
    cycle, 10–11
    scanning, 12
penetration testing tools, Core IMPACT, 7
perimeter hosts, 170–171
Perl, 281, 282, 289
persistent disks, 309
Phatbot, 6
PHD Virtual Backup and Replication, 255
physical firewalls, 10, 101

physical network security devices, 94
physical networks
    integrating with, 129–130
    virtual networks compared with, 93–94
    virtual networks *vs.*, 98–99
physical NICs, 94, 95–97, 129
physical switches, 93, 98
pivoting, 11
pluggable authentication module (PAM), 45, 84
port groups
    defining, 103–112
    Hyper-V, 109–110
    vSphere, 104–109
    XenServer, 110–112
ports, 98
    Active Directory authentication, 84–85
    ESXi defaults, 48
    Hyper-V defaults, 70
    limiting virtual network, 117–121
    mirroring, 100, 132, 138–139, 144–145
    monitoring, 132
    trunk, 129
    trust zone separation, 100
    XenCenter management server, 154–155
power optimization, 276–277
PowerCLI, 108
    Active Directory authentication, 288
    ESXi configuration, 286–289
    NTP sources, 287–288
    remote logging server configuration, 287
    scripting, 282–283
    vCenter configuration, 294–297
    virtual network configuration, 290–293
    VM configuration, 283–285
PowerShell, 53, 110, 196, 216, 295
    certificate management, 54
    Hyper-V scripting, 297–300
    interpreters, 282
    virtual environment assessment, 299–300
    virtual network information, 299
    virtual switch assessment, 299
    VM information, 298
PowerShell Management Library, 297
private VLANs (PVLANs)
    configuring, 112–115
    types, 114
privilege categories, 164–165
privilege levels, 3–4

production traffic, 95–97
promiscuous mode, 132, 136–137, 144, 148–149
protected mode, 3
PVLANs. *See* private VLANs
Python, 281, 282

Q

Quality of Service (QoS), 141, 145, 148, 255
Quest Software, 255
quiescing, 188

R

RARP. *See* Reverse Address Resolution Protocol
RBAC. *See* role-based access control
RDP. *See* Remote Desktop Protocol
real mode, 3
reconnaissance, 11
recovery point objective (RPO), 254
recovery time objective (RTO), 254
Red Hat Enterprise, 76
Reflex Security, 10
Remote Administration Tools for Hyper-V, 307
remote console sessions, 191
Remote Desktop Protocol (RDP), 54, 303, 307
Remote Desktop Services, 68
    securing, 71–72
Remote SPAN (RSPAN), 150
Renouf, Alan, 283
replication, 254–256
    HBR, 48
    logging, 256
    storage virtualization, 311
    Windows File Replication Service, 205
    XenCenter, 279–280
Replication Manager, 255
request for change (RFC), 236
resource pool templates, 167
resource pools, 256
    Hyper-V, 266–269
    vSphere, 262–266
    XenServer, 270
Reverse Address Resolution Protocol (RARP), 135
RFC. *See* request for change
Ristenpart, Thomas, 180
role-based access control (RBAC)
    Active Directory authentication, 85–87
    audit logs, 220

setting up, 87–88
subjects, 87
roles
    CONNECT, 156
    creation scenarios, 167–168
    db_owner, 156
    Hyper-V, 64–66
    inheritance, 166
    SCVMM, 172–175
    vCenter, 163–168
    XenCenter, 176
rolling pool upgrades, 72, 73
root account, 41
    restricting local, 43–44
rootkits, 8
Router Guard, 125
RPO. *See* recovery point objective
RSPAN. *See* Remote SPAN
RTO. *See* recovery time objective
Ruby, 281, 282
Rutkowska, Joanna, 8

S

Samsara, 8
SAN. *See* storage area network
SAN Copy, 255
SAN Volume Controller (SVC), 312
sandboxing, 305
SANS Internet Storm Center, 6, 12
SANSFIRE 2007, 7
Savage, Stefan, 180
scanning, 11, 12
SCCM. *See* System Center 2012 Configuration
    Manager
scheduled jobs, 78
Schneier, Bruce, 184
SCM/Pacifica, 8
screened subnets, 10
scripting
    importance, 281–282
    PowerCLI, 282–283
    PowerShell, 297–300
    shell, 282, 300–301
    types, 282
    XenServer, 282, 300–301
SCVMM. *See* System Center Virtual Machine
    Manager

SecurAble, 56
secure communications, 16
    ESXi, 27–33, 158–160
    Hyper-V, 53–55, 170–171
    SCVMM, 170–171
    vCenter, 158–160
    XenCenter, 175–176
    XenServer, 75–76
Secure Sockets Layer (SSL), 16, 99
    ESXi, 27
    Hyper-V, 72
    SCVMM, 170
    vCenter, 158–159
    XenCenter, 175
    XenServer, 75–76
Secure Technical Implementation Guides (STIGs),
    152
Securing the Virtual Environment (Ottenheimer
    and Wallace), 179
security information and event management
    (SIEM), 226
security policies, 100
    PowerCLI checking, 291–293
self-provisioning, 249
self-signed certificates, 54, 158
SELinux, 90
separation of duties, 5
Server Core, 53
Server Manager, 211
service accounts
    SCVMM, 169
    vCenter, 157–158
Service Console, 9, 41
    logs, 205–206
    security policies, 124
    virtual switches, 105, 106, 124
    VLAN configuration, 112
Service Location Protocol (SLP), 48
service principal name (SPN), 168
service-level agreements (SLA), 253
severity levels, 204
`sha1sum`, 40, 63, 77
Shacham, Hovav, 180
Shared Folders functionality, 7
shared storage and replication, 254–256
Shavlik, 17
shell scripting, 282, 300–301
ShmooCon, 179

SIEM. *See* security information and event
management
Simple Mail Transfer Protocol (SMTP), 11
Simple Network Management Protocol (SNMP),
16, 35
ESXi configuration, 37–38
Hyper-V configuration, 59–60
XenServer configuration, 80
Single Sign-On (SSO), 309
single user mode, 77
Site Recovery Manager (SRM), 255
Skoudis, Ed, 7
SLA. *See* service-level agreements
Slaviero, Marco, 180
SLP. *See* Service Location Protocol
SMM. *See* System Management Mode
SMRAM. *See* System Management Mode
memory
SMTP. *See* Simple Mail Transfer Protocol
SnapMirror Data Replication, 255
snapshots, 238
Hyper-V, 242–246
SCVMM, 245–246
storage virtualization, 311
vSphere, 242
XenServer, 247–249
Snare, 225
Snare Agent for Windows, 205
SNIA. *See* Storage Security Industry Forum
sniffers, 99, 132
SNMP. *See* Simple Network Management
Protocol
Snort, 132
social engineering, 6
Solarwinds, 225
SPAN. *See* Switched Port Analyzer
SPAN ports, 100
Spanning Tree Protocol (STP), 98, 129
specialized operations traffic, 95
Splunk, 225
Splunk Universal Forwarder, 205
SPN. *See* service principal name
spoofing, 126
SQL Server, 156, 168, 171
SRM. *See* Site Recovery Manager

SRs. *See* storage repositories
SSH, 40, 41, 50
ESXi access control, 52
XenServer configuration, 88–89
SSL. *See* Secure Sockets Layer
SSO. *See* Single Sign-On
Standard In (stdin), 7
Standard Out (stdout), 7
stdin. *See* Standard In
stdout. *See* Standard Out
stealing guests, 179
STIGs. *See* Secure Technical Implementation
Guides
storage area network (SAN), 313
encryption, 181
Fibre Channel, 125, 254, 313
replication, 254–255
securing connections, 125–129
storage federation, 312
storage network traffic, 95
storage repositories (SRs), 197
Storage Security Industry Forum (SNIA), 313
storage virtualization, 310–313
Storm worm, 6
STP. *See* Spanning Tree Protocol
subjects, 87
SVC. *See* SAN Volume Controller
switch spoofing, 112
Switched Port Analyzer (SPAN), 132, 138, 144, 148,
150, 234
switches. *See also* virtual switches; vSwitches
failover notification, 135
physical, 93, 98
ports, 98
VLAN support, 98
syslog, 160, 206, 210, 218
facility values, 203
header, 203
network options, 223
severity levels, 204
vSphere collector service, 223
syslog-NG, 204
sysprep, 240
system administrator workstations, 9
System Center 2012 Configuration Manager
(SCCM), 251

System Center Virtual Machine Manager
    (SCVMM), 68, 110, 152
    client security, 175
    cloning, 243
    clustering, 259–260
    high availability and fault tolerance features,
        274–277
    load balancing, 268–269
    logging, 171–172, 211–217
    management database, 168–169
    management server ports, 155
    network monitoring, 144
    NLB, 142
    privilege model, 172
    remote logging, 223–224
    resource pools, 266–269
    secure communications, 170–171
    securing local users and groups, 63
    service account, 169
    snapshots, 245–246
    templates, 243–244
    users, groups, and roles, 172–175
    Virtual Guest Services, 196
    virtual switch ports, 119–120
    VLAN configuration, 115–116
System Management Mode (SMM), 8
System Management Mode memory (SMRAM), 8

T

tablets, 305
tape backup and restore, 255
task definitions, 64
TCL, 282
TCP Chimney, 143–144
TCP Wrappers, 47, 88
TechNet, 152
templates, 237–249
    deploying VM from, 239–242
    Hyper-V, 242–246
    resource pool, 167
    types, 237
    vSphere, 238–242
    XenServer, 247–249
test labs, 236
Themida, 6

thin provisioning, 311
threats, 177–178
    malware-based, 5–6
    operational, 4–5
    platform vulnerabilities, 9
    VM escape, 6–9
time services, 36
time synchronization, 188
time-out values, 30
TLS. *See* Transport Layer Security
Tomcat, 12
*The Top 10 Myths about Virtual Desktop
    Infrastructure (VDI)*, 306
ToS. *See* Type of Service
TPM. *See* Trusted Platform Module
traffic analysis, 99
traffic capture and monitoring, 132
traffic filtering, 94
traffic monitoring, 94, 125
traffic shaping, 131–132
    Hyper-V, 142–144
    vSphere, 135–136
    XenServer, 148
traffic visibility, 99–100
Transport Layer Security (TLS), 16, 27, 99, 158
Trend Micro, 309
Tromer, Eran, 180
trunk ports, 129
trust zones
    physical separation, 100
    segregation, 10
Trusted Execution Technology (TXT), 8
Trusted Platform Module (TPM), 57, 59
TXT. *See* Trusted Execution Technology
TXT hack, 8
type I hypervisors, 2, 4
type II hypervisors, 2–3, 4, 52
Type of Service (ToS), 139

U

UMDS. *See* Update Manager Download Services
Unicast, 141
unicast clustering, 141–142
Unity, 194
Update Manager Download Services (UMDS), 19

user mode, 3
users. *See also* local users
  SCVMM, 172–175
  securing, 17
  vCenter, 163–167
  XenCenter, 176
  XenServer, 81–83

V

vApps, 24
VASTO. *See* Virtualization Assessment Toolkit
VCB. *See* VMware Consolidated Backup
VCDB database, 156
vCenter, 5, 95, 152
  Active Directory authentication, 46
  configuration changes, 187
  ESXi firewall configuration, 48–49
  host certificate verification, 29–30
  Inventory, 104, 105
  IPSec, 31–33
  Linked mode, 159
  logging, 160–163, 211
  logs, 206
  management database, 155–157
  management network, 272
  management server ports, 154
  network performance settings, 135–136
  NIC teaming, 133
  patches stored on, 294
  PowerCLI configuration, 294–297
  privilege categories, 164–165
  restricting local root account, 43–44
  role creation scenarios, 167–168
  secure communication, 158–160
  service account, 157–158
  SNMP configuration, 38
  Update Manager configuration, 19
  users, groups, and roles, 163–167
vCenter Configuration Manager, 251
vCenter Protect, 17
vCenter Server, 104, 108, 306
vCenter Server agents (vpxa), 160
vCenter Server Appliance, 156, 158
vCLI
  ESXi configuration, 289–290
  logging configuration, 289–290
  NTP configuration, 289

  remote logging controls, 223
  virtual network configuration, 293–294
  VM configuration, 285–286
VDI. *See* Virtual Desktop Infrastructure
VDS. *See* distributed virtual switches
vDS. *See* vNetwork Distributed Switch
Veeam, 255
VHD. *See* Virtual Hard Drive
VHDX files, 195
vicfg-ntp, 36
vicfg-snmp, 37
vicfg-vswitch, 104, 119
View VDI, 306
VIF. *See* virtual interface
VILurker, 12
VIPs. *See* virtual IPs
virtual appliances, 94, 248
Virtual Desktop Infrastructure (VDI), 303
  application virtualization, 313–315
  architecture, 307–310
  benefits and drawbacks, 304
  BYOD programs, 305
  centralization, 304
  clients, 307
  connection brokers, 307
  firewalls, 309–310
  hypervisors and storage, 307–308
  implementation, 309
  linked clones, 306
  loss of data issues, 305
  network segmentation issues, 305
  offline images, 306
  operational issues, 306–307
  planning and evaluation, 308
  remote access, 305–306
  security advantages and challenges, 304–306
  security leveraging, 310–315
  security servers/gateways, 307
  storage virtualization, 310–313
  VM desktop life cycle, 309
virtual disk manipulation, 180
virtual environments
  anti-malware tool adaptation, 12–13
  challenges for securing, 10
  lack of visibility, 4–5
  load balancing, 131
  PowerShell assessment, 299–300

threats to, 4–9
vulnerability testing challenges, 10–13
Virtual Fibre Channel, 212
virtual firewalls, 10
virtual guest, 2
Virtual Guest Services, 196
Virtual Hard Drive (VHD), 195, 197, 212
virtual interface (VIF), 149
virtual IPs (VIPs), 268
virtual LAN (VLAN), 95, 98, 100
    configuring, 112–117
    encapsulation, 139
    Hyper-V, 115–116
    iSCSI, 313
    Layer 2, 93
    management networks, 153–155
    network segmentation, 305
    physical network integration, 129
    private, 112–115
    RSPAN, 150
    switch support, 98
    trust zone separation, 100
    vCLI configuration, 293–294
    vSphere, 112–115
    XenServer, 111, 116–117, 150
virtual machine (VM), 2
    API access control, 192
    cloning and templates, 237–249
    cloud reconnaissance, 179–180
    deploying from template, 239–242
    encryption, 180–185
    PowerShell assessment, 298
    replication, 254–256
    snapshots, 238
    templates, 237
    threats and vulnerabilities, 177–178
    virtualization awareness, 98
Virtual Machine Communications Interface
    (VMCI), 191
virtual machine disk (VMDK), 12
    files for, 186
    security, 189
    templates, 238–239
virtual machine monitor (VMM), 2, 4, 15
Virtual Machine Queue (VMQ), 142
virtual machine security research, 178–185
virtual machine theft, 177–178

virtual machine traffic, 95
Virtual Network Computing (VNC), 176, 307
Virtual Network Manager, 109, 115
virtual network security devices, 94
virtual networks
    architecture considerations, 100–102
    design elements, 95–98
    limiting ports, 117–121
    operational challenges, 131–132
    physical networks compared with, 93–94
    physical networks *vs.*, 98–99
    physical NICs, 95–97
    PowerCLI configuration, 290–293
    PowerShell assessment, 299
    security considerations, 99–102
    security policy implementation, 122–125
    vCLI configuration, 293–294
virtual NICs, 94, 212
virtual private network (VPN), 309
Virtual Private VLAN Service (VPLS), 256
virtual server, 2
virtual sprawl, 118
Virtual Switch Manager, 109
Virtual Switch Tagging (VST), 129
virtual switches, 4, 10, 93–94, 98. *See also*
    distributed virtual switches; vSwitches
    configuration for security, 102–112
    defining separate, 103–112
    Hyper-V, 109–110, 119–120, 125
    hypervisors, 98
    isolating, 99
    Microsoft, 93, 102
    monitoring, 132
    physical network integration, 129–130
    physical NICs, 95
    port groups, 103–112
    PowerCLI assessment and configuration,
        290–291
    PowerShell assessment, 299
    Service Console, 105, 106, 124
    vSphere, 104–109, 118–119, 122–125, 237
    XenServer, 110–112, 120–121, 125, 148
virtual uplinks, 114
virtual volume management, 311
virtualization, 1
    change and configuration management
        impact, 234–235

change management integration, 249–250
clustering, 256–262
configuration management best practices, 235–237
PCI DSS supplement, 103
platform vulnerabilities, 9
redundancy and fault tolerance, 256–270
replication, 255
resource pools, 262–270
security adapting to, 9–13
shared storage and replication, 254–256
virtualization application traffic monitoring, 94
virtualization architecture, 1–4
Virtualization Assessment Toolkit (VASTO), 12, 153, 179
virtualization management platforms, 94–95
network architecture, 152–155
network connection isolation, 99
security recommendations, 151–152
VIX API, 192
VLAN. *See* virtual LAN
VLAN hopping attacks, 112
VM. *See* virtual machine
VM Drag-n-Sploit, 7
VM escape, 6–9
Blue Pill, 8
directory traversal attack, 7–8
HyperSafe, 9
TXT hack, 8
VM heartbeat service, 188, 270, 272
VM integration services, 196
VM monitoring, 272, 273
VM Self-Awareness, 192
VM sprawl, 4
vMA. *See* vSphere Management Appliance
VM-aware malware, 6
VMcat, 7
VMchat, 7
VMCI. *See* Virtual Machine Communications Interface
VMDK. *See* virtual machine disk
"VMDK Has Left the Building - Some Nasty Attacks Against VMware vSphere 5 Based Cloud Infrastructure" (ERNW), 180
VMftp, 7
VMkernel, 104, 105, 108
VMM. *See* virtual machine monitor

vMotion, 182, 234–235, 255, 257
VMQ. *See* Virtual Machine Queue
VMsafe API, 192
VMware, 2, 5, 9, 12
API access control, 192
configuration management capabilities, 250–251
device connectivity, 190–191
forums, 11
guest and host communications, 191–192
locking down VMs, 185–195
logging, 186, 189–190
recommended security settings, 193–195
remote console sessions, 191
shell scripting, 282
unexposed features, 193
virtual machine files, 185–187
virtual switches, 93, 98, 102
virtualization management platforms, 95
VMware Consolidated Backup (VCB), 164
VMware Distributed vSwitch Migration and Configuration Guide, 132
VMware Fusion, 189, 193
VMware GO, 17
VMware Tools, 188, 192, 193
VMware Update Manager (VUM), 12, 18
attaching baselines and groups, 25–26
baseline groups, 22–23
baseline profiles, 20–22, 25–26
configuring, 18–20
staging and remediation, 26
VMware View Client, 307
VMware View VDI, 306
VMware Virtual Infrastructure, 178
VMware Workstation, 2, 7, 186, 189, 193, 274
VMX file, 185, 190
VNC. *See* Virtual Network Computing
vNetwork Distributed Switch (vDS), 113–115
VPLEX, 312
VPLS. *See* Virtual Private VLAN Service
VPN. *See* virtual private network
VPN tunnels, 255
vPro chips, 8
vpxa. *See* vCenter Server agents
vpxuser account, 41
VSA. *See* vSphere Storage Appliance
vShield Endpoint, 13, 309

vSphere, 98, 197
    application virtualization, 315
    clustering, 257–259
    command line, 40, 108–109, 125
    defining virtual switches and port groups,
        104–109
    deploy VM from template, 239–242
    distributed virtual switches, 106–107, 237
    fault tolerance, 270–274
    high availability, 270–274
    iSCSI CHAP, 126–128
    limiting local users, 41–43
    load balancing, 133–135
    NetFlow, 139–140
    network monitoring strategies, 136–140
    network operations, 133–140
    network performance, 135–136
    remote logging, 221–223
    replication, 255
    resource pools, 262–266
    snapshots, 242
    SNMP configuration, 37
    syslog collector service, 223
    templates, 238–242
    traffic shaping, 135–136
    virtual switch ports, 118–119
    virtual switch security policies, 122–125
    VLAN configuration, 112–115
vSphere CLI, 281, 282
vSphere Client
    ESXi firewall configuration, 48–49
    logging, 211
    NIC teaming, 133–135
    plug-ins, 297
    virtual switch and port group defining,
        104–106
    virtual switch security policies, 123
    VLAN configuration, 113
vSphere Hardening Guide, 283
vSphere Management Appliance (vMA), 223, 289
vSphere Storage Appliance (VSA), 312
vSphere Web Access, 48
vSphere Web Client, 295
VST. *See* Virtual Switch Tagging
vSwitches, 93. *See also* virtual switches
    defining separate, 103–109
        IPv6, 31

    NIC teaming, 134
    PowerCLI assessment, 290–291
    private VLANs, 113–115
    promiscuous mode, 136–137
    security policy checking, 291–293
    traffic shaping, 135–136
    vCLI configuration, 293–294
    VLAN configuration, 112–113
    XenServer, 116–117
vulnerabilities, 177–178
vulnerability assessment cycle, 10–11
Vulnerability Research Team, 9
VUM. *See* VMware Update Manager

W

Wake-on-LAN (WOL), 48
Wallace, Matthew, 179
Web Access login page, 33–34
Websense Labs, 6
WHOIS records, 11
Windows Audit Policy, 205
Windows Event Collector Service, 223
Windows event log, 204–205
Windows Event Viewer, 171, 211–217, 223
Windows File Replication Service, 205
Windows Remote Management, 223
Windows Server 2003, 152
Windows Server 2008, 141, 142, 144, 152
    securing, 52–53
    Server Core mode, 53
Windows Server 2008 Security Guide, 53
Windows Server 2012, 103, 125
    iSCSI Initiator, 128
Windows Server Update Services (WSUS), 53
Windows Update agent, 53
Windows Vista, 8
WLB. *See* Workload Balancer
WMI Control, 68–69
Wojtczuk, Rafal, 8
WOL. *See* Wake-on-LAN
work recovery time (WRT), 254
Workload Balancer (WLB), 270
World Wide Names (WWNs), 313
WRT. *See* work recovery time
Wscript, 53
WSUS. *See* Windows Server Update Services

WWNs. *See* World Wide Names
Wyse, 304

X

XAPI, 78
XD. *See* Execute Disable
xe network-list, 121
xe pif-list, 121
xe vif-list, 120
xe vm-list, 120
Xen hypervisor, 8, 9
XenAPI service, 75
XenApp, 315
XenCenter, 95, 152
    Active Directory authentication, 85
    high availability and fault tolerance, 277–280
    logging, 176, 218–221
    management server ports, 154–155
    patching, 72–73
    replication and recovery scenarios, 279–280
    root password prompt, 89
    secure communications, 175–176
    setup, 175
    snapshots, 248
    templates, 247–248
    users, groups, and roles, 176
    VM modification, 198
XenCenter Audit Trail.log, 221
XenClient, 306
XenServer, 98
    Active Directory authentication, 84–87
    boot behavior, 77
    clustering, 261–262
    command line, 73–74
    configuring, 72–91
    console, 75
    debug mode, 78
    default settings, 76–79
    defining virtual switches and port groups, 110–112
    firewall configuration, 89–91
    high availability and fault tolerance, 277–280
    iSCSI CHAP, 128–129
    limiting services, 76–77
    load balancing, 145–147, 270
    locking down VMs, 197–200
    logging, 218–221
    management interfaces, 111–112
    network configuration, 78–79
    network monitoring, 148–150
    network operations, 145–150
    network performance, 148
    NTP configuration, 80
    operational security, 80
    PAM files, 84
    patching, 72–74
    platform access control, 88–91
    remote logging, 225–226
    replication, 255
    resource pools, 270
    role-based access control, 85–88
    secure communications, 75–76
    secure local users and groups, 81–83
    securing and monitoring configuration files, 81
    shell scripting, 282, 300–301
    single user mode, 77
    SNMP configuration, 80
    subjects, 87
    syslog, 204
    templates and snapshots, 247–249
    traffic shaping, 148
    update modes, 73
    virtual switch ports, 120–121
    virtual switch security policies, 125
    VLAN configuration, 111, 116–117, 150
XenServer Auditing Tools, 220
XenServer Resource Kit, 220
XenServer Tools, 198
Xenstored, 78, 221
X-Force, 178
XVA files, 248

Y

yum, 72

Z

Zdrnja, Bojan, 6